MUDDIED WATERS

A book in the series

Latin America Otherwise   Languages, Empires, Nations

Series editors:

Walter D. Mignolo, Duke University

Irene Silverblatt, Duke University

Sonia Salvidar-Hull, University of California

at Los Angeles

MUDDIED WATERS

Race,

Region, and

Local History in

Colombia,

1846–1948

■

Nancy P. Appelbaum

■

Duke University Press

Durham & London

2003

© 2003 Duke University Press   All rights reserved
Printed in the United States of America on acid-free paper ∞
Typeset in Trump Mediaeval by Keystone Typesetting, Inc.
Library of Congress Cataloging-in-Publication Data
appear on the last printed page of this book.

ABOUT THE SERIES

Latin America Otherwise: Languages, Empires, Nations is a critical series. It aims to explore the emergence and consequences of concepts used to define "Latin America" while at the same time exploring the broad interplay of political, economic, and cultural practices that have shaped Latin American worlds. Latin America, at the crossroads of competing imperial designs and local responses, has been construed as a geocultural and geopolitical entity since the nineteenth century. This series provides a starting point to redefine Latin America as a configuration of political, linguistic, cultural, and economic intersections that demands a continuous reappraisal of the role of the Americas in history, and of the ongoing process of globalization and the relocation of people and cultures that have characterized Latin America's experience. *Latin America Otherwise: Languages, Empires, Nations* is a forum that confronts established geocultural constructions, that rethinks area studies and disciplinary boundaries, that assesses convictions of the academy and of public policy, and that, correspondingly, demands that the practices through which we produce knowledge and understanding about and from Latin America be subject to rigorous and critical scrutiny.

Nancy P. Appelbaum's *Muddied Waters: Race, Region, and Local History in Colombia, 1846–1948* explores the intricacies of the words in the subtitle by examining meanings of race alongside Colombia's long processes of colonization. Her research, although based upon an examination of local history, has a more general import: It exposes the link between race and geography in the modern/colonial world, a link that has been theorized and developed toward complementary ends by the Peruvian sociologist Aníbal Quijano and by U.S. sociologist Immanuel Wallerstein. Appelbaum's account is a compelling one of the particularity of regionalism in Colombia. She sheds new light on one of the most troubled countries in the world today, while at the same time contributing to our understandings of how race has been spatially configured and constituted in Latin America.

For Amy and Hank
and in memory of Ruth

CONTENTS

ILLUSTRATIONS

ACKNOWLEDGMENTS

When I defended the dissertation upon which this book is based, I wrote twelve effusive pages of acknowledgments in which I thanked well over a hundred people. Since then, the list has only grown, while the space in which to acknowledge their contributions has shortened. The production of this book spanned a decade and involved institutions and individuals in both North America and Colombia. Their generous and thoughtful assistance, insights, and critiques influenced the questions I asked, the conclusions I drew, and the book that resulted. I take responsibility for any errors, while I share the credit for any contributions this research makes to our understandings of Colombia and of Latin American agrarian history and racial geography.

A Fulbright grant, supplemented by the Colombian Ministry of Education, first introduced me to Colombia in 1988. The Social Science Research Council and American Council of Learned Societies, Joint Committee on Latin America and the Caribbean, funded the bulk of this research from 1993 to 1995. The University of Wisconsin assisted with a Vilas Travel Grant and a Pre-Dissertation Field Grant. I also received a Dean's Research Semester Award from Harpur College, Binghamton University, State University of New York, for spring 2001. Carmen Ferradás, Director of the Latin American and Caribbean Area Studies Program, and Donald Quataert, Chair of the History Department, released me from teaching that semester and have consistently supported my research.

The maps were prepared by Onno Brouwer and the staff of the Cartography Lab of the University of Wisconsin, following my specifications. The photographs are my own except where otherwise noted. A significant portion of chapter 2 and some sections of chapter 1 appeared in briefer form in my article, "Whitening the Region: Caucano Mediation and 'Antioqueño Colonization' in Nineteenth-Century Colombia," cited in full in the bibliography.

For encouragement and inspiration, I thank my undergraduate advisors and first professional role models (known during my Vassar years as "the goddesses"): Leslie Offutt and Karen Stolley. I was very fortunate, moreover, to train in the dynamic and collaborative Latin American and Caribbean graduate history program at the University of Wisconsin–Madison. My mentors—Florencia Mallon, Francisco Scarano, and Steve Stern—pushed me conceptually to view the "whole forest" when I kept trying to hide among the coffee trees of Riosucio. I cannot thank them enough for their ongoing support. Among the many additional *madisonistas* who read and commented perceptively on parts of this research over the years, I am especially grateful to Blenda Femenias, Lillian Guerra, Joseph Hall, Roger Kittleson, Anne Macpherson, Patrick McNamara, Louise Pubols, René Reeves, and Karin Rosemblatt.

I also thank Binghamton colleagues and students, past and present, for insightful comments on my work, including Camila de Gamboa, Fa-ti Fan, Wilson Herrera, Francine Hirsch, Jean Quataert, Warren Rosenblum, Benita Roth, Linda Whang, and members of my graduate and undergraduate seminars. Several North American scholars of Colombia provided invaluable insights and corrections at various stages, especially Catherine LeGrand, Aims McGuinness, Mary Roldán, Frank Safford, and James Sanders. Parts of this research have been presented at conferences and seminars in the United States and Colombia; I thank participants and discussants, particularly Sarah Chambers, Catherine LeGrand, Charles Montgomery, Joanne Rappaport, and Barbara Weinstein.

I have been extremely fortunate to benefit from the expertise and guidance of Valerie Millholland, Miriam Angress, Leigh Anne Couch, and the staff at Duke University Press, as well as copyeditor Ruth Steinberg. The press's two anonymous readers, moreover, have improved the manuscript considerably with their informed critiques and suggestions.

Among the many people who housed, fed, and generally took care of me in Colombia during the 1990s, I particularly thank Beatriz Arango, Leonor Esguerra, Luisa Fernanda Giraldo, Ruth Morales, Hilda Ortiz and family,

Luz Helena Parra, Olga Inés Rendón, Dora de Rengifo, Magdalena Rengifo, Gabriela de Roldán and the late Alfonso Roldán, María Eugenia Torres, the extended family of Rosaura Trejos de Patiño, and Jaime Vallecilla. Consuelo Valdevieso of the Fulbright Commission also assisted me on many occasions.

Colombian scholars are asking innovative questions about regional identity that have greatly influenced my own approach to this project. Many Colombian and North American colleagues in Colombia generously shared ideas, contacts, manuscripts, and sources with me. I would especially like to acknowledge the assistance and insights of Víctor Alvarez, Beatriz Patiño, and their colleagues at the Universidad de Antioquia; Leah Carroll; Julio Castañeda; Luisa Fernanda Giraldo and her colleagues in the Facultad de Desarrollo Familiar of the Universidad de Caldas; Michael LaRosa; Christopher London; Otto Morales Benítez; María Teresa Pérez; Catalina Reyes and her colleagues at the Universidad Nacional–Sede Medellín; Mary Roldán; Joshua Rosenthal; Claudia Steiner; Albeiro Valencia Llano; Alonso Valencia Llano and his team at the Universidad del Valle; Jaime Vallecilla; and Víctor Zuluaga. The directors and staff of numerous historical archives and libraries went out of their way to assist me, especially at the Archivo General de la Nación, Archivo Central del Cauca, Archivo del Arcobispado de Popayán, Biblioteca Nacional, Fundación Antioqueña de Estudios Sociales, and the Hermeroteca de la Universidad de Antioquia.

In Riosucio and adjoining districts many people provided indispensable help in making contacts, finding documents, getting around, and negotiating local culture. Angela Gómez provided the interview transcripts upon which much of chapter 8 is based. Olga García Patiño assisted in the compilation of archival data on land transactions. I am also very grateful to Julián Bueno; Nidia Cañas; Consuelo Castaño; Conrado Cataño; Zulma Cataño; Gloria Lucía Cuellar; Carlos Cuesta; Ubaldo González; Marco Antonio Largo; Dora Inés Loaiza; Luisa Olaya; Olga Inés Rendón; Stela Trejos; César Valencia; Jorge Eliecer Zapata; the *alcaldes* and *notarios* of Riosucio, Supía, and Marmato; and the staff of several non-governmental organizations and government offices, including the Cooperative Cafetero; Dane; Incora; the Juzgado Civil del Circuito, Riosucio; the Oficina de Asuntos Indígenas; the Red de Mujeres de Riosucio; and the Registro de Instrumentos Públicos de Riosucio.

Various descendants of Antioqueño settlers and old Riosucio families shared their family and personal histories, including the poet/carpenter "Chepe," Luis Carlos Agudelo, Carlos Gil, Miguel Girardo Hernández, Girdardo Hoyos, Lucía Jaramillo Hoyos, Teresa Hoyos, Javier Naranjo, Francisco Navarro, Mariela Ramírez, "Tatines," Germán Trejos, and Rosaura Trejos, among others.

Indigenous leaders often received me with understandable skepticism, but eventually they took the risk of sharing their old files with this foreign stranger and recounting their versions of local history. I quickly overcame any illusions that I would uncover "smoking-gun" documents to help win their legal cases. But my findings will hopefully contribute to their efforts to understand and "recuperate" their history. In La Montaña, I thank Miguel Angel Largo, Euclides, José Julio Bañol, Miguel Antonio Morales, and Noé Motato; in San Lorenzo, I am grateful to Arahugo Gañán, Silvio Tapasco, Darío Marín, and Marta Rojas; in Cañamomo-Lomaprieta, I thank Gabriel Campeon, and the late Luis Angel Chaura, who was murdered by right-wing paramilitary gunmen on 24 November 2001; in Bonafont, I thank Medardo Largo; and in Guática, Señora Tunusco and Angel Batero. I also greatly appreciate the assistance, hospitality, and information provided by members of the Comunidad Negra of Guamal, especially Amanda Lucía Moreno and Aristóbulo Moreno.

As this book goes to press, the news from Colombia is especially grim. Peace negotiations between the Colombian government and the largest armed guerrilla groups have broken off. Political violence and economic crisis have endangered the lives, livelihoods, and loved ones of many of the people mentioned above. Riosucio, which was relatively calm in the mid-1990s, is once again in the thick of conflict. Local government officials have resigned in the face of death threats on the part of armed leftist guerillas, who kidnapped over fifty Riosucio residents in 2002. Meanwhile, a paramilitary group has carried out a series of assassinations of indigenous activists. One of the victims was María Fabiola Largo Cano, a former mayoral candidate and four-time governor of the indigenous community of La Montaña. She was gunned down on 9 April 2002 when two men on a motorcycle opened fire on an educational seminar in the indigenous community of Cañamomo-Lamoprieta. Hundreds of indígenas have fled their homes in La Montaña and Cañamomo-Lamoprieta. Concerns for my own safety, as well as that of my informants, have prevented me from carrying out a planned face-to-face dialogue with local inhabitants about the implications of my conclusions. I have given them my thesis, copies and transcripts of relevant documents, and essays in Spanish on some of my key findings. Until I can make the entirety of this work directly available in Spanish to my Colombian colleagues, friends, and informants, however, I can offer them little more than my admiration for their courage and my deepest gratitude.

Finally, my extended family and friends have contributed in both direct and indirect ways. My father's meticulous editing taught me as much about writing as did my many years of academic training. He, my mother, brother, aunts, uncles, cousins, and my late grandmother, as well as several other close friends, all provided unconditional love and support, even when I kept making extended visits to places to which they would have preferred I not travel.

I sat in the Plaza Bolivar, a grand square under a high, clear Andean sky. . . . I suppose it's the centre of the republic, a heart built of steak and emeralds and salt and gold and textiles and oil and cocaine. Most provincial capitals will have a space which duplicates this one. Each is a dreaming of the national capital, all towns are elements in a dreaming of national unity, and before Independence, the whole empire was a dreaming of Spain, the Plaza Major in Madrid, the King, and, of course, God. This was not uncommon in a Latin America haunted by interior and exterior distance and marked by the terror of social disintegration.
—Peter D. Osborne, 1993

Why am I enthusiastic for Riosucio? Simply because in a certain way it is the image of the Republic. It is the *municipio* that is born on the same day that the independent life of Colombia really begins. It is no small coincidence that the same year that Father José Bonifacio Bonafont launched the founding, would be the very day that Santander crossed over the Boyacá bridge and the Republic began to function on the ashes of the Spanish Government. The commemorative plaques . . . provide an image of what has been the germination of the Colombian state within the living innards of the province, the core of our nationality.
—Germán Arciniegas, 1988

INTRODUCTION

Riosucio:

Race, Colonization, Region,

and Community

RIOSUCIO

Most towns in the Colombian Coffee Region are laid out predictably on the Spanish-American model of a symmetrical grid emanating from a central square. Typically, an imposing church dominates a well-kept central plaza. The other three sides of the plaza are lined by brightly painted government buildings, businesses, and the balconied houses of leading citizens. Writer Peter Osborne, in a travel essay, juxtaposes the utopic symmetry of Colombia's urban grids with dystopic images of violence, isolation, and poverty. For Osborne, each town in Colombia "is dreaming of the national capital, all towns are elements in a dreaming of national unity." This yearning for unity is common, he suggests, "in a Latin America haunted by interior and exterior distance and marked by the terror of social disintegration."[1]

The town of Riosucio, however, has an unusual layout. Rather than the usual central plaza, there are two plazas of equal importance, an upper and a lower, each with its own equally imposing church. The town sits on the verdant eastern slopes of Colombia's western Andes at about 1,800 meters above sea level, surrounded by coffee groves and jagged rocky peaks. It is the seat (cabecera) of a township or district (municipio) of the same name that extends westward up to the mountain ridges and eastward down to the Cauca River. The outlying areas of the rural district are inhabited by poor country people (campesinos), the majority of whom refer to themselves as indigenous (indígenas). Riosucio's indigenous population and

Map 1. Colombia, ca. 1995

off-center layout make it an anomaly in the Coffee Region, a region known in Colombia for the whiteness of its inhabitants and the conservative orderliness of its picturesque towns. In recent decades, the district of Riosucio has had a heavy guerrilla presence and has suffered political and criminal violence, belying the region's image as an area of relative tranquility in this war-ravaged country.[2]

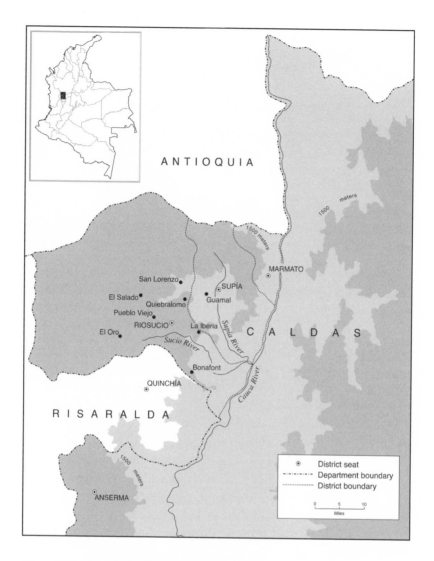

Map 2. Riosucio and Neighboring Districts, ca. 1995

This book views the history of the white, western Coffee Region from the perspective of mixed-race Riosucio. It is about how a town and a region came to be defined in racial terms and the implications of those definitions for the local inhabitants. As nineteenth-century Colombians explored, described, and colonized their interior, they mapped racial hierarchy onto an emerging national geography composed of distinct localities and regions. They elaborated a racialized discourse of regional differentiation

Figure 1. View of Riosucio from the West, 1994

that assigned greater morality and progress to certain regions—and to certain localities within regions—that they marked as "white." Meanwhile, those places defined as "black" and "Indian" were associated with disorder, backwardness, and danger.

When I first visited Riosucio in 1992, I called on the municipal officer in charge of cultural affairs, a folklorist named Julián Bueno, and asked him about the town's history. I was trying to learn about white-identified migrants from the neighboring region of Antioquia who had settled in and around Riosucio in the late nineteenth and early twentieth centuries. I had planned to study the conflicts that had occurred when Antioqueño pioneers encountered and displaced their racial "others"—local mestizos, blacks, and Indians. My own encounter with Bueno, however, displaced the focus of my research. In Bueno's dramatic recounting of local history, these "others" take center stage, as they do here in my book. Bueno insisted that in order to understand the history of Antioqueño migration, I first had to understand local history, especially the story of Riosucio's two plazas. He went on to tell me how the "plaza of the Indians" and the "plaza of the whites" had become one town and had forged a unified local "race," the *raza riosuceña,* which was later "invaded" by the *raza antioqueña.* I would hear and read versions of this local origin story time and again over the course of my research.

The tale, as Bueno and many other townspeople tell it, begins in the early nineteenth century, at the very end of the colonial era. Several groups of Indians lived in the area, which was richly endowed in gold. The biggest Indian community was La Montaña, which was ruled benevolently by a maverick republican priest, Father José Bonifacio Bonafont. Northwest of La Montaña was a Spanish settlement known as Quiebralomo, where African slaves worked the mines. Father Bonafont had enlisted the priest of Quiebralomo, one Father Bueno, to help him put an end to the acrimonious disputes between the two communities by uniting them as one. On 7 August 1819, Riosuceños say, the two priests founded the new town at a site that had long been known as "Río Sucio" (or "Dirty River"), after a muddy creek that runs down from the mountains above. The villagers of La Montaña and Quiebralomo carried their respective patron saints in processions from their village chapels to the new town, and the priests ordered their old chapels burned to the ground so that they would not return.

The founding date (which is not substantiated by historical documents) is highly significant. That same day in 1819, Simón Bolívar's pro-Independence forces won their first decisive battle over Spanish forces at the famous Battle of Boyacá, far away from Riosucio in Colombia's eastern cordillera. Colombians still celebrate August 7th as a national holiday. By claiming this patriotic date as its founders' day, Riosucio links its own history to that of the nation.

But the story does not end with Independence. The fragmented republic still had to become a nation, just as the dual town still had to become one. The Indians of La Montaña and the villagers of Quiebralomo still did not get along and refused to attend the same church. Each group maintained its own parish and its own plaza. The priest gave the higher, western plaza to the Quiebralomeños; the Indians received the lower, eastern plaza. A fence divided them. Yet, Julián Bueno told me with a smile, a new generation of young people began sneaking across the fence at night for sexual assignations, which often led to pregnancies and even marriage. The two "races" came together in sexual union as the fence came down. A new, or mixed-race (*mestizo*) community, formed. "Little-by-little," Bueno recounts in one of his writings, "emerged the racial element that was the true Riosuceño." By the 1840s, I was told, the president of the Republic had ordered the fence torn down because he was outraged to see his citizenry so divided.[3]

Figure 2. Upper Plaza of Riosucio, 1994

The significant founding date and the story about young lovers of different races coming together to form a town, has led some nationally prominent, liberal intellectuals to describe Riosucio as a microcosm of the mestizo nation. Riosucio, derided by other inhabitants of the Coffee Region as a regional anomaly, redeems itself as a national metaphor. As the Colombian intellectual Germán Arciniegas once wrote to one of Riosucio's most prominent sons: "Why am I so enthusiastic for Riosucio? Simply because in certain measure it is the image of the Republic. It is the district in which really began the independent life of Colombia."[4]

After the fence came down, the upper–lower dichotomy took on new meanings. In the mid–nineteenth century, inhabitants often told me, hardworking, fair-skinned "colonists" (colonos) from Antioquia settled in the highlands west of the cabecera. In the twentieth century, these highlanders moved down into the town itself and colonized the western, upper plaza, the "plaza of the whites." The lower plaza, meanwhile, remains the "plaza of the Indians." The partisan rift in Colombia between Liberals and Conservatives is also manifest in local geography. The upper plaza and the highlands above became a stronghold for the Conservative Party, while the slopes stretching eastward from the lower reaches of the town down to the Cauca River were dominated by Liberals. Cross-town and cross-party romances continued to blur political and social boundaries even after

Figure 3. Lower Plaza of Riosucio, 1994

partisan violence engulfed the countryside in the 1940s–1950s; such romances remain the subject of nostalgic anecdotes today.

This narrative about the melding of two races provides an example of how Colombians in one community, by referring to race, have made sense of their local, regional, and national history and geography. As this book will show, this narrative is not the only version of Riosucio's history, though it is the one favored by inhabitants in the cabecera. The construction of this narrative around a series of oppositions—upper versus lower, white versus Indian, Antioqueño settler versus local inhabitant, and Conservative versus Liberal—reflects townspeople's understanding of Colombian society as deeply and historically divided. Such a pessimistic view is not surprising in a country that has suffered repeated civil wars since its inception, has the oldest active left-wing guerrilla groups in the hemisphere (as well as right-wing paramilitary death squads and powerful criminal gangs), and in which the government has exercised tenuous control over the national territory. Anecdotes about young lovers overcoming racial and political divisions, about fences torn down and idealistic priests, however, also suggest a lingering optimism that such rifts may be overcome, that unity and peace might someday be achieved.[5]

Oral and written versions of local history provided one entry into my research about how Colombians worked out their identities "on the ground"

Figure 4. Church of San Sebastián, on the Upper Plaza, 1994

over time. While based in Riosucio from 1993 to 1995 and making trips to other towns and cities, I consulted a variety of sources, including local registries of land transactions, public notaries, local judicial archives, local newspapers, official gazettes, travel narratives, published books and articles by local and regional authors, administrative archives of municipalities and indigenous communities, regional administrative archives, ecclesiastical archives, and scattered documents that people pulled out of desks, boxes, file cabinets, coffee sacks, and paper bags. As texts, such sources provided many examples of the changing discourses of identity. The sources also provided insights into the daily workings of the colonization process by allowing me to trace transactions and relationships among indigenous leaders, politicians, land speculators, lawyers, priests, settlers, foreigners, and local and regional elites. These sources suffered from disrepair and loss. Key collections had been purposely destroyed during previous waves of political violence, and other archives had fallen to pieces due to neglect. I also faced the lexical challenge posed by my sources; words like "race" and "region" proved to have multiple and contradictory meanings that I found difficult to pin down.

In scholarly as well as popular accounts of the history of Riosucio and the Coffee Region, four terms, in particular, crop up repeatedly: *raza*, *colonización, región,* and *comunidad.* All four figure prominently in this book. Despite their frequent usage, their meanings vary according to his-

Figure 5. Church of La Candelaria, on the Lower Plaza, 1994

torical and social context. Translation into English renders them all the more problematic. They have been subject to slippage, misuse, and mistranslation even though, or perhaps because, their translation appears so transparently obvious. Because of the centrality of these key words in Colombian popular and scholarly discourse, and in my own analysis, I begin this book by historicizing them and considering the problems they present. The terms introduce the general themes that run through the remainder of the book. I start with one of the most historically significant, widely used, and slippery concepts in the Americas: Race.

RACE/*RAZA*

In 1907 a local official named Francisco Trejos sent a report on land conflicts in Riosucio to the new regional capital of Manizales. In it, he classified local inhabitants by *raza.* He referred to the local residents who traced their ancestry to the village of Quiebralomo as the *"raza quiebralomeña."* The Indians who occupied much of the adjacent rural hinterlands he called the *"raza indígena."* Finally, he called the settlers from Antioquia and their descendants the *"raza antioqueña."* To each of these groups, Trejos ascribed a specific "character," or set of inherent traits. Trejos wrote that the Quiebralomeños were given to music, art, and squandering their resources on festivities. The indigenous "race" was even worse: they were lazy, selfish, poor, and alcoholic, although the indígenas also monopolized the district's land and its mineral resources. The Antioqueños, on the other hand, were "known everywhere for [their] love of labor [and] enterprising nature."[6]

Trejos's report provides one example of how Latin Americans have long used race to justify transferring resources out of the hands of the poor and into the hands of the more commercially oriented. But the meanings associated with race have varied. Scholars today increasingly reject the term "race" as a scientific category. Yet even though the term is now considered a "social construction," scholars and census-takers alike still rely on the template, first developed in the eighteenth century by Enlightenment naturalists, which classifies major varieties of humankind according to physical characteristics and continental origin (Caucasian/white, Mongolian/East Asian, Ethiopian/black, American/Indian, and Malay/Southeast Asian). This classificatory scheme has coexisted historically, however, with other definitions of race. In nineteenth-century Colombia, as elsewhere in Europe and the Americas, race often referred, literally, to breed (as in a "race of cattle"), lineage, or kin-group. Races, moreover, were often identified with regions ("la raza antioqueña") and even with small towns and villages ("la raza quiebralomeña"), although nations could also be defined in terms of race (such as "la raza colombiana"). This implied that members of each "race" shared a common lineage, as well as common biological and cultural characteristics. Racial identity, then, has been as much about lineage, culture, and place of origin within the nation as about phenotype or continental origin.[7]

The word race, as used in Colombia, has thus been linked both to the nation as a whole and to human and spatial components within the nation. And, as Trejos's report suggests, different usages of the term have coincided and overlapped. There have also been some inhabitants of Colombia—that is, the indígenas—whose particular "race" seemed at times to place them off the map entirely. Classificatory schemes like Trejos's often described indígenas as a "race" apart—that is, one that was separate from the regions and localities that composed the nation. The very word, indigenous, adopted during the early republican period to replace the Spanish caste label *indio*, suggested a timeless presence on the land—a primordial claim that the indígenas themselves have cited time and again in their efforts to defend their landholdings. But the term has also been used against them, to exclude them from full membership in the modern citizenry. The indígenas of Riosucio have long spoken Spanish. But, as we will see in subsequent chapters, they have only partially integrated into the regional identities through which Antioqueños, Caucanos, and other "races" have claimed their regional affiliation and thus their national citizenship in this "country of regions." Indians have often remained off the map in terms of racial regionalization to a greater extent even than have blacks. For, as anthropologist Peter Wade's work on blackness and regionalism has demonstrated, "blackness" in Colombia has been, in part, a regional ascription.[8]

In order to study the multiple ways that race has been constructed, without reifying any single meaning, scholars such as Wade, Michael Banton, and others have adopted the term "racialization" to describe a process of marking and naturalizing human difference with reference to hierarchical categories. The racialization process, then, divides humanity into groups characterized by certain traits—which can be either biological or cultural—that are assumed to be inherited. In this book, I apply the racialization approach to Colombian history to explore how various identities—regional, national, local—became endowed with seemingly inherent characteristics. The geographical categories through which Colombians located themselves within the national community were racialized, and racial prejudices and inequalities were thus inscribed in the spatial ordering of the emerging nation-state.[9]

COLONIZATION/*COLONIZACION*

Historically, the spatial ordering of Colombia has not been static. Rural Colombians historically have been on the move, reshaping their geography as they went. Over the nineteenth and early-twentieth centuries, successive waves of migrating miners, farmers, and ranchers cleared and settled the forested slopes and valleys that lay between the scattered highland colonial towns. By far the most studied and celebrated of these migratory currents has been the *colonización antioqueña*, usually translated into English as the "Antioqueño colonization." Beginning in the late colonial era, and continuing throughout the twentieth century, the expanding population of what is now central and eastern Antioquia spilled over into neighboring areas, especially the department of Cauca. Antioqueño migrants expanded agricultural production and developed commercial networks throughout northwestern Colombia.[10]

These migrations contributed to the consolidation and expansion of the region of Antioquia and, in 1905, to the creation of a new administrative department, Caldas. The new department of Caldas initially consisted of territories carved out of the departments of Antioquia and neighboring Cauca. Riosucio, which had belonged to Cauca, was one of these. At the time that the department of Caldas was founded, coffee cultivation was spreading through Antioqueño villages on the volcanic, mid-range slopes (between about 1,000 and 2,000 meters above sea level) of the central and western Andean ranges. The new capital of Caldas, Manizales, had previously been part of Antioquia and was prospering as a hub in the coffee trade. The department of Caldas soon became synonymous with coffee. In 1957 it would split into three smaller coffee-growing departments. Colombians even today continue to refer to all three departments as one unified region, which they variously call the "Coffee Region" *(la región cafetera)*, the "Coffee Zone" *(la zona cafetera)*, the "Coffee Axis" *(el eje cafetero)*, the "Coffee Belt" *(el cinterón cafetero)*, or "Old Caldas" *(Viejo Caldas)*.[11]

Colombians generally describe this region as entirely populated by people of Antioqueño heritage; the history of Caldas is often presented as a "white legend," or, more literally, as a "rosy legend" *(leyenda rosa)* of "colonización." Colombians generally use this term to refer to the expansion of agricultural frontiers and the creation of settlements in previously uncultivated lands, and so, except for possible environmental consequences, the implications of the term are relatively benign. To translate the Spanish word colonización as merely "colonization," as geographer James Parsons and others have done, is somewhat misleading, because the strictly agricultural definition of colonization is no longer the most common one used in English. The word "settlement" more accurately encapsulates the domestication of a forested wilderness that was celebrated by Parsons and other proponents of the "white legend."[12]

Some popular and scholarly accounts present a "black legend" of Antioqueño colonization to challenge this "white legend." As Riosuceños point out, many of their ancestors occupied the area long before the Antioqueños. Cauca was not simply a "virgin" territory (as the "rosy" versions of the story tend to portray it) awaiting the civilizing impulse of the Antioqueño axe. Recent revisionist historians, moreover, have depicted a process of "colonization" in every sense of the word: the Antioqueño takeover of communities, local governments, commercial networks, and landholdings—what Julián Bueno of Riosucio referred to as an "invasion."[13]

This book argues that "colonization," in the common English sense of the word, provides a more accurate description of this process than the Spanish term "colonización," but I also attempt to avoid the "black legend" trap and do not conceptualize colonization as merely a top-down process of imposed submission. Studies of European colonialism in the Americas, Africa, and Asia have demonstrated that effective colonizing has historically involved the participation of the colonized, who have simultaneously resisted and adapted to colonization, thus shaping the different colonial systems that resulted. Just as the Black and White legends are each inadequate for describing the Spanish conquest, such legends are also too simplistic for understanding colonization in post-independence Colombia. Both the "bad" and "good" legends of the Antioqueño migration share a common flaw in that they tend to attribute agency almost exclusively to Antioqueños, thus reaffirming stereotypes that cast Antioqueños as inherently more energetic and innovative than other Colombians. Popular and scholarly accounts do not fully account for the active participation of other Colombians in transforming western Colombia. The importance of Caucanos in the "Antioqueño-ization" of northern Cauca has generally been overlooked. This book highlights the actions and goals of Cauca land speculators, politicians, and indigenous authorities, and thereby reconceptualizes the so-called Antioqueño colonization as a multilateral process of region formation.[14]

In facilitating Antioqueño settlement, Cauca's elite hoped to remake Cauca in the white image of Europe and the United States, or at least to remake it in the white-ish image of Antioquia. They sought to bring progress to Cauca by transforming its population—in other words, by colonizing it racially. By "progress," elite Latin Americans meant commercial prosperity and capitalist modernization, which they saw taking place in the nations of the North Atlantic, and even in Latin American countries, such as Argentina, that were attracting European immigration. In Cauca, however, demographic whitening through migration took place without a large-scale influx of Europeans. A handful of European migrants and investors did come to Colombia, but their actions as individual colonizers in this case were less important than the ideal of Europe (and, increasingly, the United States) as the paradigm of progress. Cauca lacked sufficient economic resources, accessibility, and infrastructure to lure and retain foreign immigrants, so it had to settle for Antioqueños as the next best thing. Members of the Cauca elite sought to augment their own black, indigenous, mestizo, and mulatto campesinos with migrants from

Antioquia, whom they perceived to be whiter, more industrious, and more inclined to participate in a commercial economy. Indigenous authorities and black Caucanos resisted certain aspects of this process, but they, too, seem to have associated whiteness with progress.[15]

The example of Antioqueño migration demonstrates that processes of colonization in the Americas did not end with the expulsion of European colonial powers. Scholars working within a variety of paradigms have argued that colonization in various forms continued after independence. In the 1960s and 1970s social scientists of the "dependency" school argued that "neo-colonialism" subordinated modern Latin American nations economically to the United States and Europe. *Dependistas* also identified internal structures, such as concentrated land ownership and the greater prosperity of certain regions over others, that they referred to as "internal colonialism." The state and the structure of the economy, they argued, served the interests of the export sector and maintained the peasantry and marginal provinces in poverty. This approach was revelational in exposing the impoverished underside of capitalist modernization—the "poverty of progress"—but dependency theory has also been rightly criticized by historians and other scholars for often subsuming historical contingency and human initiative to overriding, "top-down" economic structures and for simplifying the complex patterns of labor and land tenure that have characterized rural Latin America.[16]

Social historians of colonization "from the ground up" have shown how, in resisting and adapting, colonized peoples contributed to shaping the resulting social order. In western Colombia, this book argues, indigenous and black people took an active role in shaping regional transformations that gave rise to a new demographic and political geography. Through their participation in the patronage networks of political parties, as well as in various institutions created by the church and state, indigenous and black Colombians directly affected land tenure and government policy. In Riosucio, three indigenous communities negotiated with intermediaries and settlers, ceding a portion of their communal holdings yet maintaining most of their lands and institutions in the face of ongoing efforts to dismantle them.

Recent scholarship on "postcolonialism" and "coloniality" has incorporated certain insights of the dependency framework, especially regarding the extent to which capitalist modernization in former colonies implied the suppression of communal identities and ways of life that clashed with elite notions of progress. In theorizing the relationship between the grassroots community and the modern nation-state, however, such research sometimes places the nation-state in opposition to autochthonous local and ethnic identities that are implicitly or explicitly posited as the authentic identities of colonized rural peasantries. Rather than place the modern state in opposition to traditional communities, I look within the nation to the historical dynamics between region and locality to understand how each affected the other. My approach forms part of a growing body of ethnographic and historical scholarship on rural society that does not assume that local, racial, and even communal identities are necessarily more "authentic" than national identity. This scholarship also emphasizes the participation of "subalterns" in both resisting and creating nation-states.[17]

The cultural and linguistic emphasis of much recent scholarship on colonialism and postcolonial nation-state formation, moreover, has shown that colonial legacies are discursive and political as well as economic. Modern capitalist states reformed and sometimes radically revised the racial, gendered, geographical, and other social categories through which empires had previously classified and governed their subjects. "Technologies" of colonialism, such as cartography, census enumeration, and ethnography, provided tools for the consolidation of the modern state and the hierarchical orderings of populations and spaces within the nation. Colonized groups have paradoxically made use of these tools in redefining their own identities, even in those instances in which they have defined themselves in opposition to the state. Thus, post-independence colonization was not simply a continuation of earlier forms of colonialism. Postcolonial processes of colonization remapped social relationships onto new national geographies of power.[18]

REGION/*REGION*

Most Colombian historiography emphasizes the colonial-era origins of Colombia's regions. Drawing on the insights of recent scholarship on regionalism in Brazil, Europe, and other parts of the world, however, this book considers the emergence of regions as an integral part of the process of postcolonial nation formation in Latin America. I agree that the roots of regionalism run deep into the colonial past; local loyalties were paramount in the colonial period and independence wars. But the racialized discourse of regional differentiation and the full-blown regional identities that still affect Colombian life today took shape in the post-independence era.[19]

Colombia, like other Latin American countries, emerged from the independence wars of 1810–21 with a fragmented society, territory, and economy. In 1830, the sparsely populated young republic, then known as New Granada, nominally encompassed the disparate valleys and slopes of three Andean mountain ranges and two coasts, as well as part of the Isthmus of Panama. The mostly rural and small-town inhabitants were quite literally and physically separated by great "interior and exterior distance." Except for coastal ports, colonial New Granada's principal towns and cities had mainly sprung up among the high plains and temperate valleys of the Andes. The Andean population centers, each supplied by its respective agricultural hinterland, were separated from one another by mountains and lowlands. During the first struggles for independence from Spain, many of these towns and cities declared themselves to be republics; others were loyalist strongholds. They set themselves up as city-states and sometimes fought bitterly against their immediate neighbors. These local rivalries continued into the early national period. Jurisdictional boundaries between them remained vague.[20]

Beginning in the 1850s, Colombian politicians shaped the republic into a loose federation of "sovereign states," known colloquially as *países*, or countries, each with its own standing army, currency, postal service, and constitutional government. Communications and trade between states, and often within them, were tenuous at best. Colombia lacked cart roads; in many mountainous areas the steep, muddy trails were not even passable for mule trains. The federation suffered repeatedly from civil wars between Liberals and Conservatives that tended to take the form of conflicts between separate states. Federalism, as the following chapter will show, both reflected and contributed to the strengthening of regionalism in nineteenth-century Colombia.[21]

Also influential during this period were various efforts to map and describe the national territory. In the mid–nineteenth century, Colombian and foreign explorers enumerated, mapped, measured, and classified the national territory and its diverse inhabitants and climates. Some of the most important ethnographic and cartographic research was sponsored by the government over the course of the 1850s as part of a series of geographical expeditions under the auspices of the Chorographic Commission.

The commission's reports, maps, and illustrations constructed the new republic as a heterogeneous nation composed of various races tied to specific localities and regions that had "progressed" at different rates. The *costumbrista* fiction of the era, rich in ethnographic detail, further reinforced the image of Colombia as a country composed of distinct spaces and peoples.[22]

The elite writers who produced these texts tended to attribute the varying levels of economic progress and "civilization" obtained by the inhabitants of each locale to a combination of environmental conditions and inherited characteristics that presumably shaped racial stock. Manuel Ancízar, for example, traveled the Eastern Andes for the Chorographic Commission in 1850–51. He described the climate, customs, economic conditions, and apparent mixture of African, Indian, and European descent particular to each community. Based on these factors, he assessed their relative capacity for progressing. A decade later, José María Samper attributed New Granada's political instability to the coexistence of distinct "ethnographic zones." He described the civilized highlands as populated by whites, light-skinned mestizos, and the more easily assimilated Indians, whereas the tropical lowlands were inhabited by politically excitable blacks, zambos, and mulattos, along with barbaric Indians. Nineteenth-century writers like Ancízar and Samper were leading statesmen as well as intellectuals; they catalogued and interpreted Colombian history, geography, and ethnography as part of their project to build the Colombian nation.[23]

Colombian regionalism continued to fascinate twentieth-century scholars. The general consensus that region has been important historically, that regional loyalties often override national identity, and that Colombia is regionally divided has not, however, led to agreement among scholars as to how to define Colombia's regions or how to count them. The Antioquia physician Luis López de Mesa, writing in 1934, perceived the nation as composed of seven regions; the social scientist Virginia Gutiérrez de Pineda, thirty years later, described four. Both linked region to race and culture. López de Mesa referred to regional groups as "racial groups," while Gutiérrez de Pineda referred to "cultural complexes." Both López de Mesa and Gutiérrez echoed earlier writers, such as Ancízar and Samper, in describing each regional group as the product of a particular mix of what sociologist Orlando Fals Borda would later refer to as Colombia's "tri-ethnic" racial stock. They also considered the cultural and physiological adaptations that each group had made to its environmental niche.[24]

López de Mesa, like many Latin American intellectuals of his era, was influenced by a current of eugenics theory, according to which environment affected racial characteristics. These "neo-Lamarckians" believed that environmental adaptations were passed on from one generation to the next. For López de Mesa, environment and heredity together shaped Colombian character, culture, and phenotypes. In his analysis, those regional groups with the largest preponderance of European blood and dwelling in the country's temperate climates, such as the Antioqueños, were superior intellectually and physically to the blacker and more heavily Indian peoples of other regions.[25]

In the 1960s Gutiérrez de Pineda linked race and sexual behavior in drawing her own map of Colombia's regional cultures. She examined demographic patterns and ethnographic data, and she mapped patterns of male-female relationships, production, and household formation across the country. She noted, for example, a high frequency of Catholic marriage in Antioqueño-settled areas and, conversely, a high percentage of free unions and out-of-wedlock births in Afro-Colombian areas. Her innovative work was relatively free of her predecessors' explicitly sexist and racist judgments, and she placed what we now call gender at the center of her analysis. Yet, her widely cited study may actually have served to perpetuate the same stereotypes that had informed earlier writings on region.[26]

More recently, some researchers have interrogated the stereotypes themselves, examining how Colombia's regional identities have been constructed relationally and how racial stereotyping has played into that process. Particularly important for this book is the recent work of three scholars who analyze how Antioqueños have constructed their regional identity against an "other." Historian Mary Roldán, in her study of mid-twentieth-century political violence, locates the "other" on the periphery of the department of Antioquia. She argues that Antioquia's history and geography have been shaped by a "hierarchy of cultural difference." The old core of Antioquia, centered in and around the Aburrá Valley, has defined itself by "piety, Hispanic ('white'), legitimate birth, Catholic marriage, and capitalism." Antioqueños have tended to perceive their more recently incorporated periphery as "deviant" because of its heavily indigenous and black population. Anthropologist Claudia Steiner draws similar conclusions in her historical study of the administrative incorporation of one of these peripheral areas, the Caribbean zone around the Gulf of Urabá, into the department of Antioquia. Administrators from central Antioquia explicitly described Urabá inhabitants as racially inferior, and sought to transform the population's social customs, a goal the administrators referred to as *antioqueñización*.[27]

Peter Wade's influential study of race in contemporary Colombia juxtaposes the white–mestizo Andean core, epitomized by Antioquia, with a periphery constituted by the "Indian" Amazon basin and the black coastal regions. He argues that a "black/non-black" dichotomy prevails in Colombia, whereby the black regions constitute the principal "other" against which the non-black majority of mestizos and whites measure their superiority. Lowland frontier Indians, similarly, provide another version of this primitive "other." Indians and mestizos of the interior highlands, however, do not fit as comfortably into Wade's scheme. In focusing on the relationship between Antioquia and the peripheral coasts, he leaves largely unexplored the subtle interregional racial gradations that have historically pervaded the Andean interior of Colombia, as well as the nineteenth-century historical processes that shaped Colombia's contemporary regional map.[28]

Other historians and geographers of Latin America have struggled in their efforts to create a working model of the sub-national region as an abstract system and conceptual tool for historical analysis. I prefer to study regions as modern products of historical processes and as subjects for historical study, rather than, as historian Eric van Young conceptualizes them, as trans-historical "depersonalized abstractions." I prefer not to count or attempt to precisely map out Colombia's regions, or even to define and use "region" as an analytical tool in and of itself. Rather, this book examines region, like race, largely as a historically produced, discursive notion and meaningful collective identity.[29]

Expanding historically on Peter Wade's observation that in contemporary Colombia "region has become a powerful language of cultural and racial differentiation," I argue that Colombians' strong regional identities emerged in tandem with a national discourse of racial and regional differentiation that served to organize the emerging nation-state in space and to embed racial hierarchy on the mountainsides of Colombia. Underpinning this discourse of regional differentiation were assumptions about race (and, as we will see below, about gender as well). The discourse of regional differentiation associated certain regions with whiteness and thus with prosperity, sexual propriety, and progress, and other regions with blackness, Indianness, sexual impropriety, and backwardness.[30]

This book takes a constructivist approach to region, just as it does to race. Among the common-sense "truths" that we express in our cultural discourses, place is one of the more difficult to deconstruct, precisely because it appears to be a natural part of this Earth, and because our deepest and most cherished sense of who we are refers in part to where we come from. Recent historical geographers and other critical scholars of geography and power have argued for greater attention to the historical processes whereby power relations came to be embedded in territorial organization and perceptions of space—of how territorial space has been configured historically in a series of seemingly discrete and timeless, yet inherently unstable, overlapping, and contested places (regions, countries, homelands, neighborhoods, to name a few). Space, in this view, is a malleable social construct that manifests and reinforces power relations in society.[31]

Even the most hegemonic discourses and strongly felt collective identities, however, do not preclude agency or dissent. Widely accepted discourses—such as discourses of regionalism or patriotism, for example—can be used to make highly contradictory arguments and stake competing claims. Subsequent chapters will show how the racialized discourse of regionalism has provided a language that competing factions in Colombia have used in their debates over power and the distribution of resources in and among their local communities.[32]

COMMUNITY/COMUNIDAD

One way of describing Colombia's regions, to borrow a concept usually applied to nations, is as "imagined communities." Benedict Anderson defined the nation as "an imagined political community . . . imagined because the members of even the smallest nation will never know most of their fellow-members, meet them, or even hear of them, yet in the minds of each lives the image of their communion." Cynthia Applegate and Mary Roldán have both extended this notion of imagined community to apply it to regions within nations. Members of regional communities, even those who have never met, are bound by affective ties.[33]

Anderson used the "face-to-face" village community as a reference point for imagining the nation. As scholars have recently pointed out, however, "the apparently immediate experience of community is in fact inevitably constituted by a wider set of social and spatial relations." Anderson himself noted that even the "primordial villages of face-to-face contact" may "perhaps" be imagined as well, but he does not explore how such imagining might happen in such an intimate context. Moreover, his model does not fully consider the extent to which collective "imagining" has been imbued with struggles over power to lead and define the community. By focusing on local power struggles within Riosucio, as well as regional struggles involving Riosucio actors, this book provides examples of how community has been imagined at various levels of society—how people constructed and contested a series of nested communities.[34]

Like the other key words discussed above, "community" has various meanings. On the one hand, I use the word to refer to imagined collectivities. Colombian archival documents, on the other hand, yield more contextually and historically specific meanings for the term *comunidad*. In legal documents relating to land, "community" referred to groups of people, usually but not always linked by kin, who held property in common. The indígenas of Riosucio, from the nineteenth century and into the present, like other Andean peoples, have used "community" to refer to their landholding collectivities. For indigenous Colombians, comunidad is synonymous with *parcialidad*. Parcialidades were defined during the colonial period as intimate kin-groups. The colonial state recognized their landholdings, which it termed *resguardos*, and set up indigenous governing structures to administer them under the supervision of civil and ecclesiastic authorities. The resguardos were theoretically indivisible and unalienable, intended to provide the basis both for the community's subsistence as well as its tribute payments. Map 3 indicates the controversial boundaries claimed by Riosucio's three established indigenous resguardos.

Over the course of the twentieth century, by asserting their rights as members of indigenous comunidades, Riosucio's indígenas have challenged not only the regional mystique of whiteness, but also the mestizo identity put forth by Riosucio town intellectuals. Twentieth-century Riosucio officials and intellectuals have undermined the hegemonic myth of white Caldas by constructing their local communal history as the forging of a local (and national) mestizo race. Indigenous leaders in the outlying rural areas of the district have gone even further, by insisting that they are

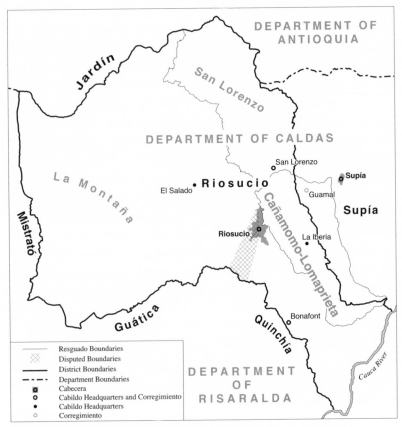

Map 3. Riosucio and the Indigenous Resguardos claimed by La Montaña,
San Lorenzo, and Cañamomo-Lomaprieta, ca. 1995

indigenous, rather than mestizo, and are thus entitled to specific rights
over much of the land and natural resources of the district. Like other
indigenous activists in Colombia and elsewhere in Latin America, they
now remember much of their nineteenth- and twentieth-century history
as a struggle to preserve communal lands and autonomy. Yet, historical
research in Riosucio shows that preserving the comunidad has historically meant, for indigenous leaders, active participation in the institutions of colonization.

Historical sources also reveal that, beyond the level of the landholding
comunidad, nineteenth- and early-twentieth-century indígenas and other
Colombians rarely if ever referred to the larger collectivities they constructed explicitly as "communities." Rather, the preferred metaphor was

an even more intimate social unit: the family. Colombians used familial metaphors to describe their own nation, regions, districts, towns, and even their landholding comunidades. Like any family, the imagined family involved affection but also hierarchy—a hierarchy structured by age and gender (and often by race and class as well, keeping in mind that the extended, patriarchal family in Latin America has often included servants, slaves, dependents, tenants, and illegitimate offspring). Family (like geography), and the gendered and generational relationships therein, is an intimate reality for most people that provides a way to explain other more abstract collectivities such as the region or the nation. The chapters that follow explore some of the ways that the discourse of regional differentiation was gendered as well as racialized. Assumptions about gender and race (categories that, like space, provide seemingly "natural" ways to organize difference) have shaped the imaginings of community at the local, regional, and national levels. The result has been continued inequality along race and gender lines at all levels of Colombian society and polity.[35]

In short, this book traces how one region, the Coffee Region, emerged in the early twentieth century out of the interstices of two nineteenth-century regions, Antioquia and Cauca. I examine how on-the-ground processes of colonization and partisan politics, along with elite efforts to map and categorize the national territory, shaped—and were also shaped by—a geography of racialized regions. The book argues that nineteenth-century Colombians developed a racialized discourse of regional differentiation that they used to classify the population and territory of their emerging nation. Then, in the early twentieth century, provincial intellectuals elaborated new theories about the regional components of the Colombian nation that built upon and further legitimated the racialized discourse of differentiation. Racialized definitions of local, regional, and national identity, however, proved to be exclusive and discriminatory and were contested at every level.

My narrative provides specificity and immediacy to this analysis by blending microhistory with regional and national history. I view the formation of the Coffee Region largely from the perspectives of the inhabitants of one district. On a local level, region formation was a process of postcolonial colonization that actively involved colonists, the colonized, and intermediaries. This book reconstructs the collaborative relationships as well as the tensions between these groups. In Riosucio, debates about collective identity were—and are—part of larger struggles and negotiations over natural resources and governance. Throughout Colombia and Latin America, such conflicts have been shaped by common-sense understandings of race and region that are themselves the products of history.

I chose the district of Riosucio as the site to explore these themes mainly because it experienced the intersection of two major historical processes that are usually studied separately in Colombia: the Antioqueño colonization and the privatization of communal indigenous landholdings. In the nineteenth century Riosucio formed part of a contested borderland that marked the frontier between Antioquia and Cauca. This mountainside district, moreover, provides a strategic vantage point from which to view a panorama of the transformations that occurred throughout post-independence Latin America: the consolidation of strong regional identities within the framework of emerging nation-states; the racial "whitening" of regions through migration, intermarriage, and myth-making; the conversion of indígenas into mestizos; the embedding of social hierarchies in national landscapes of racially differentiated spaces; the emergence of racialized discourses of modernization; the dismemberment of communal landholdings to promote commercial agriculture; and the ongoing tensions between homogeneous and heterogeneous definitions of the nation.

For the sake of brevity and coherence, I have chosen to concentrate on the district of Riosucio itself. The district is not studied in isolation; surrounding villages and other historical actors appear in the text when their histories affect and converge with that of Riosucio. But the book traces in depth only those communities that historically have been located within Riosucio's own administrative jurisdiction. My archival research focused on the indígenas, mestizos, and whites who have made up the bulk of Riosucio's inhabitants. I allude only sparingly in the chapters that follow to the black villages located outside of Riosucio's boundaries in the neighboring districts of Supía and Marmato; their stories still remain to be told.

Chronologically, this study focuses mainly on a century of Colombian history in which overt political and social conflict was channeled into partisan conflicts between the Liberal and Conservative parties, and factions thereof. The book is framed by two momentous political developments in Colombian national history. It begins in the late 1840s, just as the two main political blocs in Colombia took the names "Conservative" and "Liberal." Locally, Riosucio was officially unified as a single parish district in 1846, at about the same time that families from Antioquia were starting to settle there. The study concludes with the outbreak of the last great Liberal–Conservative conflict in 1948. La Violencia, as this mid-twentieth-century undeclared civil war is known, wreaked tremendous violence on the Coffee Region and on rural Colombia more generally, and marked the transition to a much more violent, late-twentieth-century series of conflicts, involving a broader array of ideologies and actors— conflicts that continue in the present.[36]

The book is divided into three parts. The first two parts follow a conventional periodization for the political history of Colombia. Part 1 covers the period from the mid-1840s through the mid-1880s, when the republic was violently contested by Conservatives and Liberals, with the result that the republic was split into a federation. The Liberals dominated the weak federal government, while the Conservatives consolidated their control over certain states. Part 2 covers the political era from 1886 to 1930, known in Colombia as the "Conservative hegemony." Historians have also referred to this period as the "white republic" because of the elite's emphasis on Colombia's Hispanic heritage. The centralist 1886 constitution replaced the semi-autonomous "sovereign states" of the federal period with departments. The new department of Caldas, which corresponded to the booming Coffee Region, was the economic, political, and cultural showplace of the Conservative white republic. Part 3 transcends the periodization of the first two parts to explore the interplay of collective memories and identities in the town of Riosucio and the indigenous community of San Lorenzo.

More specifically, the three chapters in Part 1 focus on aspects of regional and local history in the mid–nineteenth century. Chapter 1 uses nineteenth-century published texts to show how the discourse of regional differentiation attributed certain racial and sexual stereotypes to the western Colombian regions of Antioquia and Cauca. Conservative Antioquia was a fair "beauty" in contrast to the dark, Liberal "beast" of Cauca. The chapter also outlines the political and social processes that gave rise to these images. Chapter 2 uses local and regional archival and published sources to show how Caucanos fostered Antioqueño migration into northern Cauca. Indigenous communities lost part of their land as a result. Chapter 3 uses the same sources to discuss the participation of the indigenous communities themselves in the colonization process, focusing on the patron-client relationships through which indigenous authorities participated ambiguously in the larger political community of Riosucio. Colonization took place through partisan networks, and the result was a local geography defined not only in racial terms but also in partisan political terms. Some communities developed lasting identities as Liberal, and others as Conservative.

Part 2 shows how Riosucio's inhabitants experienced their incorporation into the white Coffee Region and the Conservative "white republic." Chapter 4 examines the Regeneration movement itself on a national and local level, including a discussion of the Regeneration's protective legislation toward indigenous communities, aimed at civilizing them and incorporating them into the republic in a subordinated status. The Regeneration, and the Conservative government to which it gave rise, placed indigenous and black communities under white Conservative tutelage. Nonetheless, the judicial documents and land registries examined in chapter 5 reveal that Riosucio's indígenas, rather than allow themselves to be "civilized" out of existence, used the Regeneration-era legislation, as well as partisan networks, to protect their landholdings from the encroachment of settlers, incurring high costs along the way. Chapter 6 traces the creation of Caldas and the emergence of the Coffee Region and shows how racialized regionalism provided a common language for political debate among rival elites. Commercial and political leaders in the new departmental capital constituted themselves in their publications as a regional elite, the leaders of a homogeneous regional race. Riosucio intellectuals, meanwhile, expressed dissent in their own local newspapers and private correspondence; they argued that Riosucio constituted a "race" apart.

Part 3 explores how local communities imagined themselves in contradictory ways during the twentieth century through narrating, or "remembering," the past. Chapter 7 returns to the story told in the first pages of this introduction, to show how intellectuals in the town center of Riosucio elaborated a narrative of local history that challenged the hegemonic myth of white Caldas. Chapter 8 studies one indigenous community, San Lorenzo, over the long term, from the late-nineteenth century until it was officially dismantled in the 1940s, and expresses how indigenous inhabitants experienced locally the historical transformations traced in the previous chapters. The chapter concludes with a discussion of how San Lorenzo's indigenous identity has been reconstructed and remembered over the last two decades.

The concluding chapter reflects upon the implications of viewing Colombian national geography as historically constructed and racialized. The "country of regions," I argue, was a spatial manifestation of a view of modernity that associated national progress with racial whitening and homogeneity. The racialization of progress, manifested in regionalism, has directly affected the lives of contemporary Colombians, including the black and indigenous inhabitants of the Coffee Region. Nonetheless, in Riosucio today, collective memories of "Indianness" challenge both the hegemonic regional myth of white progressive Caldas and the local ideal of mestizo Riosucio. On a national level, indigenous Colombians have been at the forefront of efforts to disarticulate progress and the modern nation from whiteness and *mestizaje*; they define Colombia as neither a white republic nor a mestizo melting pot, but rather as a racially plural nation.

PART 1

COUNTRY OF REGIONS,
1846–1886

CHAPTER ONE

Beauty and the Beast:
Antioquia and Cauca

"As far as family life is concerned, the Caucano must be seen as the polar opposite of the Antioqueño."—Friedrich von Schenck, 1880

Mid-nineteenth-century Riosucio was located on a frontier between two emerging and increasingly antagonistic regional states: Antioquia and Cauca. The sprawling state of Cauca, to which Riosucio officially belonged, extended to the southwest all the way to Ecuador and along the west coast up to Panamá, nominally including the Amazon basin as well (see map 4). Bordering Riosucio district to the north was the state of Antioquia, a smaller and (at that time) landlocked state. As Cristina Rojas de Ferro observes in an insightful essay on violence and national identity, "in nineteenth-century Colombia, political parties, regional identification, and racial distinctions all became relations of antagonism." And yet, paradoxically, the emergence of bitter regional and other divisions occurred in tandem with the process of nation-state formation. As historian Fabio Zambrano has noted, in Colombian history "the emergence of a national identity happens simultaneously with the appearance of regional identity."[1]

Geographically, early New Granada had been composed of a confusing array of overlapping and constantly changing local provinces, cantons, and parochial districts. A series of new constitutions and laws from 1821 to 1853 repeatedly redrew the national map, fragmenting it into ever-smaller entities. A key moment in the process whereby the fragmented early republic emerged as a "country of regions" was the decade of the

Map 4. United States of Colombia, 1863–1886. Adapted by permission from James William Park, *Rafael Nuñez and the Politics of Colombian Regionalism, 1863–1886* (Baton Rouge: Louisiana State University Press, 1985).

1850s, when the federal system was created at the same time that the Chorographic Commission explored and mapped the national territory. The national legislature imposed order on geographical chaos by consolidating the country's three dozen provinces into nine large "sovereign states." These states would prove relatively stable, even though they were often in conflict. The process of consolidating the nation-state was thus also a process of dividing it. Federalism reflected and reinforced emerging regional identities and animosities, even though the state boundaries did not everywhere coincide with the blurry and unstable borders of emerging regional identities.[2]

This chapter focuses on the prose and politics of region formation in nineteenth-century western Colombia. The first section draws on published descriptions of Antioquia and Cauca, from the 1850s onward, in order to show how nineteenth-century Colombian intellectuals defined regions in racial terms. This prose characterized Antioquia and its inhabitants as prosperous, orderly, peaceful, and moral (the Beauty), while portraying Cauca as impoverished by dissolution, laziness, racial inferiority, violence, and social divisions (the Beast). The racialized discourse of regional differentiation emphasized stark differences between regions and attributed these differences to the inherent characteristics of each regional "race." Recent scholarship, however, points to a more complex set of historical factors that differentiated Cauca and Antioquia. The second part of this chapter draws on this research to discuss nineteenth-century power struggles and alliances that shaped regional identities and gave rise to regional stereotypes. Scholarship suggests that the elite of Antioquia proved relatively successful in allying with rural poor and middling sectors. Antioqueños consolidated a strong collective regional identity—a raza—that integrated key aspects and symbols of popular rural culture. Cauca, on the other hand, was rent by highly visible social, racial, and partisan divisions. The varying extent to which popular sectors overtly resisted, or integrated into, elite regional projects was key. Regional identities at their strongest, as in the case of Antioquia, served to bind members of distinct social class and gender in an imagined community by casting outsiders as the "other." Cauca, we will see below, provided just such an "other" against which Antioqueños unified, and against which Antioqueños measured the superiority of their own race.

NINETEENTH-CENTURY DESCRIPTIONS
OF ANTIOQUIA AND CAUCA

The publications of the Chorographic Commission and other texts from the mid–nineteenth century construed Colombia as a heterogeneous nation composed of distinct races inhabiting diverse environmental niches. The authors of these texts assigned certain levels of morality and progress to each climate: blacks and the most "savage" Indians subsisted lazily in the unhealthy tropical lowlands of the coasts and interior valleys. The coldest and highest reaches of the highlands in eastern, central, and southern Colombia were portrayed as the domain of partially "civilized" Indian villagers whose lives were as desolate as their windswept landscape. The climate considered healthiest for whites and most conducive to national progress was to be found in the mid-range altitudes of the highlands, where temperatures approximated a European spring or fall. The challenge facing New Granada was how to achieve progress, given the relative backwardness and diversity of most of the population, the mutual isolation of Colombia's scattered towns and villages, and the lack of infrastructure. Every geographical report and travel memoir from the nineteenth century contained painful descriptions of Colombia's notoriously steep and muddy mountain trails, which elite and foreign travelers plied on foot, on mules, and even on the backs of indigenous human carriers.[3]

In 1852 several exhausted members of the Chorographic Commission crossed paths in the town of Santa Fé de Antioquia with Manuel Pombo, a Liberal politician and "man of letters" originally from Popayán, who was making his way from Medellín back to his home in Bogotá. In Pombo's picturesque account of this trip, he described Antioqueños as rough-hewn and obstinate, but also progressive and respectable. He likened them to *yanquis*, echoing a similar observation by the Swedish immigrant "Carlos" de Greiff. De Greiff had noted that Antioqueños displayed qualities similar to those for which North American Yankees were already famous: "the industriousness that distinguishes them. A rare intelligence . . . the natural propensity for material improvements and for the march of progress; self-love and the most noble egoism; the spirit of independence that stimulates them to obtain for their families as much as for themselves, a property all their own."[4]

Pombo's and de Greiff's descriptions of Yankee-like Antioqueños had antecedents. As early as the 1820s, European Carl August Gosselman had visited a highland Antioquia village and described the light skin and rosy cheeks of some local inhabitants as indicative of their health and beauty, which he attributed to the fresh mountain climate and "lack of mixing with the blood of blacks." He also noted that Antioqueños were famous for their honesty in trade. Clearly, a set of stereotypes regarding Antioquia was emerging by this time. But this early-nineteenth-century regional imagery was not entirely cohesive. Unlike later travelers, Gosselman also emphasized racial and social diversity within what was then the province of Antioquia.[5]

Over the nineteenth century, published descriptions increasingly homogenized Antioqueños and de-emphasized their diversity. The Chorographic Commission noted in 1854 that the inhabitants shared "identical characters, inclinations, and customs, different in all from those of the other Provinces we have visited." Rather than emphasize the differences among Antioqueños from different towns and altitudes, as Gosselman had, writers increasingly referred to "the (male) Antioqueño" as a single "type" (*tipo*). Such nineteenth-century descriptions of the essential Antioqueño varied in detail and emphasis, but they displayed certain consistencies. Some writers emphasized Antioqueño asceticism and austerity, while others noted the Antioqueño man's propensity for drinking and gambling. In seeking to define Antioqueños racially, some observers emphasized their white appearance, while others noted the early mix of Spanish settlers with indigenous peoples that resulted in a relatively fair-skinned, whitened mestizo, less visibly Indian than the inhabitants of the high altiplanos around Bogotá or southern Cauca, and less visibly black than the inhabitants of the lowlands. The accounts generally lauded the Antioqueños' commercial acumen, but some writers—including some Antioqueño writers—also criticized them as greedy and obsessed with financial gain over all other considerations. The characterizations of Antioqueños as mercantile misers and successful financiers were tied to a myth that the Antioqueños descended from Jewish converts. (Frank Safford, however, has shown that the Jewish myth grew out of rivalries between the elite of Antioquia and that of the national capital of Bogotá.)[6]

Virtually all of these writers—Antioqueños and outsiders alike—agreed that "the Antioqueño" was devoutly Catholic (even if descended from converts), hardworking, and commercially oriented. Observers also emphasized the central role that patriarchal "family life" played in ordering Antioqueño society and in differentiating Antioquia from surrounding regions. De Greiff and Pombo described Antioqueños using the terms "morality" and "customs." Pombo, for example, quoted an Antioqueño writer regarding how "the morality of their customs is due also to the passion for family life and to how popular marriage is among them."[7]

In the national context, the Antioqueño was emerging as one regional and racial type among many. José María Samper compared the "white Antioqueño" to the "primitive" Indian of Pasto in southern Cauca, the "stupid" Indian of the eastern cordillera, the "turbulent" mulatto of the coast, and the "aristocratic" creole of Bogotá, along with other "races" or "types" that "coexisted" in New Granada. The Antioqueño was handsome and industrious, shaped by his environment and his Jewish and Spanish blood. Samper and other mid-nineteenth-century writers thus constructed the nation as heterogeneous while constructing each of the nation's regional and racial components as internally homogeneous. Each type was marked off from his neighbors by a set of essential characteristics that characterized his "race" and located him in a specific place on the national map.[8]

Pombo's travel narrative, likewise, constructed a dichotomy between practical Antioquia highlanders, on the one hand, and passionate lowlanders of the Cauca and Magdalena River valleys, on the other. His contrasting vignettes of customs pertaining to each region were typical of nineteenth-century writing and illustrated the salience of notions of race, sexuality, and gender in the delineation of Colombian regional identities. For example, Pombo described the harmonious home of his Antioqueño friends Alejo and Ana María. Their children were smart and adventurous, "*Antioqueños de pura raza.*" Ana María was "efficient . . . methodical; better informed than her husband about his own transactions. . . . She has given her husband eight children, all male, all healthy, all taught by her to read, pray, do their chores, and behave well." Pombo's description of Ana María included many elements of what is still a common stereotype of Antioquia womanhood. The stereotypical *madre antioqueña* is fertile, maternal, obedient, and virtuous, yet, at the same time, intellectually and morally equal (if not superior) to her husband.[9]

Pombo's memoir juxtaposed idyllic and orderly Antioqueño family life with images of unbridled and violent sexuality among black inhabitants of the steamy lowlands of the Magdalena and Cauca River valleys. A seductive dance in Cauca between a mulatto woman and black man was interrupted when "another black broke the circle that surrounded the dancers and, agile as a tiger, reached the mulatta in one leap and stuck a knife through her heart." In this scene, Pombo portrayed Afro-Colombians as everything that the Antioqueños were not: overtly sensual, uncontrolled, and dangerous. The Afro-Caucanos were described almost exclusively in terms of their unbridled physicality and sensuality, as if they acted only on the basis of spontaneous animalistic urges rather than out of the self-regulating foresight that Pombo and other writers associated with Antioqueños.[10]

Elite intellectuals at mid-century often attributed racial and cultural differences to climate and topography. Geographers Agustín Codazzi and Felipe Pérez of the Chorographic Commission bemoaned the nudity, lack of love for work, and lack of ambition for material comforts that they perceived among blacks and Indians in the low-lying zones of the Cauca Valley and the Pacific Coast. Codazzi, Pérez, Pombo, Ancízar, and other such writers portrayed the environment as determining the behavior and morality, and even the physical characteristics, of inhabitants. In their writings, topography took on moral qualities, whereby the cool highlands—*la tierra fría*—demanded a rugged lifestyle and imparted a healthy, rosy glow to its inhabitants. These highlands were contrasted with the torrid, steamy, and unhealthy lowlands—*la tierra caliente*. The geographers viewed low-lying areas such as the Cauca Valley, the Magdalena Valley, and the Pacific Coast as unhealthy, not only because of endemic diseases, but also because the lowlands were, ironically, too verdant and too fertile; the lowlands provided too easy a life, conducive to laziness. That peasants could subsist on the fruits of their own labors, in their own plots, was inimical to elite visions of progress linked to commercial production, markets, material commodities, and wage labor.[11]

The use of racial and gendered imagery to delineate regional identities continued over the course of the nineteenth and twentieth centuries. Several accounts by northern European travelers in the 1880s explicitly linked race, family, climate, and social order in defining *lo Antioqueño*. While other Colombians sometimes described Antioqueños as crass and avaricious, reflecting an ambivalence provoked by regional rivalries, foreign visitors generally professed admiration. Perhaps these late-nineteenth-century Europeans found in the regional "Yankees" a reflection of themselves and their own aspirations. Friedrich von Schenck and his contemporaries portrayed Antioqueños, more than any other Colombians, as approximating late-nineteenth-century Western ideals of moral and physical soundness and entrepreneurialism.[12]

Von Schenck contrasted the "weak mulattos and spent inhabitants of the lowlands" with the "tall and athletic" Antioqueños, including "their pretty women, with their healthy coloring." "Tall" Antioqueño men were implicitly more virile than their "spent" lowland counterparts; Antioquia women made attractive wives and healthy child bearers. Antioqueños, moreover, did not share the moral corruption of other regions. He went on to attribute the orderliness he perceived to Antioquia's family life: "This healthy family life influences the number of crimes and robberies, which in Antioquia must be significantly lower than in the rest of the states." He noted that "family life is exemplary. . . . Voluntarily the numerous children accept the authority of the father." Men and women reputedly married young, while still in their teens, and free unions were thought to be scarce. In family life, Antioquia and Cauca were "polar opposites." For von Schenck, the only part of Cauca for which there was any hope was the more conservative mountainous northeastern section—the part that included Riosucio and was attracting migrants from Antioquia.[13]

In many accounts, Cauca appeared as the foil for Antioqueño regionalism. Yet, these texts did not generally portray Cauca as a whole. Rather, they focused on the low-lying Cauca Valley and to some extent on the Pacific coastal mining area known as the Chocó, both of which had significant Afro-Colombian populations. An important foil for Antioqueño racial identity, the exotic "others" against which Antioqueños were defined, by themselves and by outside observers, were (and continue to be) non-white Colombians, especially blacks. As we will see below, over the course of the nineteenth century, Antioqueños increasingly referred to Caucanos in general as "blacks." By painting Cauca black, the Antioqueños and their admirers were, in effect, painting themselves white.[14]

The treatises and travel accounts also contrasted Antioqueños with Indians. Writers such as the influential German geographer Alfred Hettner compared the Antioqueños' industriousness and progressive nature with Indians' perceived laziness and backwardness. Hettner saw Antioqueño migrants as responsible for waking up the sleepy frontier "Indian towns" of Cauca (including Riosucio) and saving them from stagnation. He described the Indian resguardo of Quinchía, for example, as a backward place, a "dead-end alley," the only hope for which was the increasing presence of Antioqueños.[15]

One aspect of the racial/regional dichotomy that cast Cauca against Antioquia (and also worked to differentiate areas within Antioquia) was a division between lowland mining zones and highland agricultural zones. Writers described Afro-Colombian mining communities, such as the Cauca town of Marmato, as exotic and tumultuous. They portrayed rampant illegitimacy, blurred gender roles (e.g., black women miners dressed and worked like men), and frontier anarchy. Von Schenck even compared Marmato to the gold-rush frontier towns of the United States. Towns settled by agriculturalists were generally described in much more laudatory terms as stable, moral communities in which the church was always the first public building, the parish priest played a decisive role in local affairs, families were well-ordered, and illegitimacy was low.[16]

Regionalist discourse in Colombia was oppositional. To define Antioqueños as a race—and thus to define Antioquia as a region—implied defining them as something that other Colombians were not, and comparing them, whether favorably or unfavorably, with other groups. Antioqueños were white to the extent that the former slaves of Cauca and the Coast were black; they were progressive to the extent that Indians were backward; prosperous to the extent that other Colombians were poor. The elite of Medellín were often described as entrepreneurial, self-made men who were perhaps crass but more vital than the patrician aristocrats of Popayán or the cultured bureaucrats of Bogotá. By placing the Antioqueños in a basically favorable light as progressive and energetic (their supposed "vulgarity" and "avarice" notwithstanding), such discourse justified their ascendant economic position in Colombia.

The above discussion has focused almost exclusively on explicit discourse as revealed in published sources by elite Colombians and foreigners who saw Colombia filtered through their own prejudices. Despite their inherent biases, these writings do provide evidence that by the early nineteenth century, Antioqueños and other inhabitants of New Granada—of all social classes, literate and otherwise—had begun to develop collective identities that were transcending the parochial limits of each village or town. The use of such words as *maicero*, to denote Antioqueño, as early as the 1820s reflects the importance of consumption patterns (such as eating maize products) and other shared cultural practices that accompanied migration and the expansion of commercial networks. The literate minority of the mid-to-late nineteenth century did not imagine regional communities out of thin air. Through the literati writings they described and preserved various cultural practices as the defining characteristics of each region. The flirtatious dances of some dark-skinned Caucanos and the orderly homes of some rosy-cheeked Antioqueños became social facts—*costumbres,* in nineteenth-century parlance—that defined and differentiated the regions that made up Colombia. Moreover, these writers ascribed a hierarchy to the regional components of the nation by constructing certain regions as racially and morally superior. And they based these constructions on their observations of cultural practices as interpreted in light of their own nineteenth-century assumptions about sexuality, climate, gender, and race.[17]

Writings by Colombians and foreigners coalesced to form a relatively cohesive discourse of Colombian regional variation. Later-nineteenth-century Colombian intellectuals debated over the particulars (e.g., were Antioqueños of Jewish descent or not? were the men of Antioquia avaricious misers or exemplary entrepreneurs?), but they shared a common assumption that each regional raza had its own authentic essence. These opinions influenced the interpretations of foreign visitors, who quoted and paraphrased their Colombian informants. In turn, the foreign travelers' accounts were translated into Spanish, and ultimately proved to be of more lasting influence among Colombians, in terms of helping them define Colombia, than among the foreign audiences for which they were originally intended.

The accounts of literate elites and foreigners provide only faint and distorted echoes of the voices of the illiterate majority of nineteenth-century Colombians. Both Antioquia and Cauca were far more varied and internally complex than the published versions of the discourse of regional differentiation would suggest. The remaining sections of this chapter consider some of these complexities. I draw upon recent scholarly studies about economic, social, and political history to re-tread the same treacherous economic, social, and political terrain that the nineteenth-century travelers charted, as they trudged through the mountains and valleys of western Colombia, on their own feet and on the backs of mules and human carriers.

ECONOMY AND SOCIETY

Colombia's mountainous topography and lack of infrastructure has long been blamed for the country's relatively slow economic development as well as marked regionalism. And yet, one of the nineteenth-century states most notorious for its physical isolation—Antioquia—also boasted the country's most prosperous mercantile economy, as well as its most consistent links to the capitalist world-system. The Antioqueños' privileged access to gold helped them attain economic predominance, but the much larger and much poorer state of Cauca also boasted great gold deposits. Cauca also had the advantage of more abundant lands suitable for large-scale tropical agriculture, access to the Pacific Ocean, and one of Colombia's main waterways, the Cauca River. Cauca (including the gold-rich Pacific Coast) had produced and exported most of the gold in colonial New Granada. By the end of the eighteenth century, however, Antioquia was reportedly producing around 40 percent of Colombian gold and, by the 1830s, over half. In addition, the gold produced in the important Cauca border districts of Marmato, Riosucio, and Supía was processed in Antioquia and traded via Medellín.[18]

Why Antioquia expanded economically while Cauca declined was not, then, merely a question of physical geography. Antioquia history is one of the most studied topics in Colombian historical scholarship, and theories abound to explain its exceptionalism. Antioqueños today answer the question much as their forbears did a century ago: the raza antioqueña is more enterprising and hardworking than its lazier neighbors. Mid–twentieth century social scientists reinforced this belief with scholarly terminology, citing Antioquia's entrepreneurial culture. Demography and family structure have often been cited as well. Antioquia's population density was much greater than that of Cauca; productive land was less readily available for cultivation, forcing inhabitants to seek other alternatives for surviving and investing.[19]

Without attempting to resolve this question entirely, it is worth citing a few economic and social factors that affected the historical development of these two neighboring states. The social structures of southwestern Colombia, on the one hand, and of most Antioquia towns, on the other, emerged somewhat differently during the colonial period, even though both Cauca and Antioquia boasted elites who had consolidated their fortunes in gold and had invested in land, agriculture, and livestock. Antioqueños are famous for defying the conventional stereotype of Latin American elites as unenterprising, hereditary *latifundistas*. The colonial and early republican elite invested in land, commerce, livestock, agriculture, and mining, and proved willing to break up and redistribute landholdings in order to foster agriculture. They then invested their capital throughout Colombia and led the export-oriented coffee boom at the end of the nineteenth century. Historical scholarship, however, has shown that Antioquia's colonial society was not as mobile or free of racial prejudice as some regionalist intellectuals have argued. As elsewhere, an oligarchy emerged in the principal towns by the late colonial period and went to great pains to defend its identity as Spanish or white, to monopolize town *cabildos*, and to conserve economic resources and political power through strategic marital alliances and relationships of *compadrazgo*. Still, some enterprising plebeians of mixed background managed to break into elite circles.[20]

Slavery, important in Antioquia during the seventeenth century, declined considerably there by the mid–eighteenth century. The cost of bringing slaves in through the mountains was high, and Antioquia lacked a large plantation sector in which to employ them. The mining economy increasingly relied on wage workers, and especially on semi-autonomous *mazamorreros* who panned for gold in rivers and streams. Scholars have suggested that many, if not a majority, of mazamorreros were poor women and men of visibly Afro-Colombian, indigenous, and mestizo features who could not easily claim whiteness. People of mixed heritage were in part responsible for settling and expanding Antioquia's frontier. Scholars suggest that blacks and mulattos were often considered suspect or vagrant and suffered disproportionately from the constricted agricultural opportunities in the densely settled core of Antioquia. They reportedly migrated to the less populous zones of the Antioqueño frontiers and northern Cauca. Their expulsion from Antioquia's core areas may have served to reinforce the "bleaching" of Antioquia's population over the course of the nineteenth century.[21]

Cauca was more geographically extensive as well as explicitly diverse in its racial composition. Given the multiplicity of local and ethnic identities found in Cauca, it is questionable whether one should refer to the whole of Cauca as a coherent region, as something more meaningful to most of its inhabitants than a mere administrative entity. The heart of actual Cauca identity in the nineteenth century was a relatively populous zone that included the old colonial capital of Popayán and the surrounding highlands in the south, along with the fertile plain of the middle Cauca River valley (now the departments of Cauca and Valle, respectively). In contrast to Antioquia, slavery remained important into the nineteenth century. When the Liberal central government in Bogotá abolished slavery in 1851, Conservative Cauca slave owners went to war in part to defend the institution.[22]

The highlands around Popayán more closely approximated the classic image of Latin American society as made up of large estates existing symbiotically (though tensely) with neighboring indigenous communities. Popayán and the leading towns of the Cauca Valley were dominated by elite families which, while having profited from mining, also invested in land and prized themselves on Spanish lineage and learning. Still, the feudal semblance of the Cauca economy has been exaggerated and may have been more a product of economic depression than a cause. Research by economic historians reveals that the nineteenth-century elite diversified from sugar cane, mining, and livestock, into tobacco, quinine bark, and frontier colonization, while they also experimented with various coercive and semi-coercive labor systems as slavery fell apart. Economically troubled estates in the Cauca Valley were sold off in small parcels, facilitating a proliferation of small holdings.[23]

The economic leaders of mid-nineteenth-century Cauca lacked neither entrepreneurial skills nor profit motives. They desperately sought a stable export. But they were bitterly divided politically, and they faced an almost insurmountable obstacle: overt popular resistance. What most clearly differentiated Cauca from Antioquia in the nineteenth century was widespread class and racial confrontation expressed through violent partisan political conflict. The myth of master–slave fraternity and equality, which was propagated in Antioquia, was unsustainable in most of Cauca; memories of the brutalities of slavery, as well as of violent reprisals on the part of slaves and former slaves, were too fresh on both sides. The War of the Supremes (1839–41) had pitted slave owners in Cauca against a popular coalition consisting of slaves, Indians, and landless whites allied with General José María Obando, who brought many of his followers into the Liberal camp. In the 1848–51 Cauca Valley uprisings, Liberal bands terrorized Conservative landowners who had usurped and enclosed the city's common lands. These multiracial rioters also sacked slave plantations.[24]

Cauca did not lack enterprising capitalists or adventurous settlers who founded new communities and expanded the agricultural frontier. Caucanos, like Antioqueños, sought progress. But Cauca suffered more sustained and violent intra-elite and interclass conflict and could not consolidate a strong export economy around gold or agriculture. The reasons for its failure were not simply topography or the society's racial makeup, nor even a lack of enterprise culture. Rather, the differences that observers perceived and emphasized between Cauca and Antioquia had a lot to do with the configurations of popular protest and partisan politics in each state.[25]

PARTISAN POLITICS IN THE FEDERAL ERA

Liberals, Conservatives, and the Vanishing State

The end of the War of the Supremes in 1842 left the country of New Granada divided into two loosely aligned political camps, the *ministeriales* and the *progresistas*. The division partly reflected an earlier rivalry between the followers of Simón Bolívar and those of Francisco de Paula Santander. In 1849, the former group assumed the name Conservatives.

Their opponents called themselves Liberals. Each party largely consisted of a loose coalition of regional strongmen (*caudillos*) who would occasionally switch sides. Most notably, Tomás Cipriano de Mosquera, an Independence hero from the southern regional capital of Popayán (and president of the Republic during the 1840s), left the Conservative camp in the 1850s. He and his followers eventually joined the Liberals. Both political parties drew support from poor people. The Conservatives, for their part, gained the allegiance of the majority of the clergy, who in turn drew in many of their Catholic parishioners from among townspeople and peasantry, including some Indian and even black communities. In general, Conservative discourse tended to emphasize the maintenance of order, while the Liberals advocated doing away with all remnants of Spanish colonialism. Both generally favored a liberal economic model. Across the country the most consistent issue that divided the Liberals from the Conservatives was, as in most of Latin America, the role of the Catholic church in society and governance.[26]

New Granada (like several other Latin American countries) went through a period of radical Liberal reforms at mid-century. In 1850, Congress instructed the provincial assemblies to divide up protected indigenous resguardos. In 1851, the government abolished slavery, which had already been eroded by earlier free-birth legislation. The 1853 Constitution decreed universal male suffrage, the separation of church and state, and full freedom of worship. Taxes and tariffs were reduced. David Bushnell suggests that "the state itself seemed intent on withering away." Colombian Liberals split during this period between Obando's faction, known pejoratively as the "Draconians" by its rivals because of its military leadership, and a more intellectually led faction known as the *gólgotas,* or Radicals. The era of the López and Obando governments was particularly heady for the popular sectors of Liberalism in Bogotá, the Cauca Valley, and elsewhere. The Liberals organized local Democratic Societies. In the Cauca Valley, Democratic Societies led the popular uprisings against Conservative landowners.[27]

During the 1850s (which Bushnell refers to as the decade of "creeping federalization"), several former provincial entities became semiautonomous "sovereign states." The sovereign state of Antioquia was founded in 1856, the sovereign state of Cauca in 1857. Decentralization culminated with the constitutional assembly of 1863, which produced the radically federalist Rionegro Constitution and renamed the country the United States of Colombia. Each of the nine states attained almost complete autonomy over its internal political and economic affairs, including the right to determine its own policies regarding suffrage, currency, mining rights, landholdings, crime, and vagrancy.[28]

Explanations for the turn toward federalism emphasize the weakness of the central state as well as the relative weakness and factionalism of the country's political and economic elite. Laissez-faire ideals notwithstanding, Colombia's commercial and political leaders lacked stable export products. The elite was severely divided along regional as well as partisan lines; no single faction was economically or politically strong enough to impose its will on the rest of the country for long. After 1867, Radical Liberals dominated the central government, while Conservatives consolidated regional strongholds. Meanwhile, Mosquera led a faction of Liberals that dominated Cauca and allied with Liberals in the Atlantic Coast region.[29]

Conservative Hegemony in Antioquia

Antioquia was not always a Conservative stronghold. Recent scholarship has shown how the "Conservativization" of Antioquia was a spatial as well as historical process. Local elites from various Liberal- and Conservative-dominated towns competed for regional domination. While their Conservative counterparts in Cauca went to war in 1851, the Conservatives of Antioquia also took up arms, but not to preserve slavery, which they declared abolished. Rather, they fought to unify Antioquia, which had been divided by the Liberal national government into three provinces. Antioquia Liberals had benefited from this division, which bolstered their control over their local strongholds. The Conservatives were vindicated in 1855–56 when the national Conservative administration unified Antioquia and then created the sovereign state of Antioquia with Conservative-leaning Medellín as its state capital.[30]

As Antioquia took shape, the locus of regional political power was shifting, hand-in-hand with that of commercial predominance. Medellín became the region's indisputable commercial and political center. Meanwhile, the Liberal elites of the important colonial centers of Rionegro and Santa Fe de Antioquia were increasingly marginalized politically. The national division between Radicals and Draconians had weakened the Liberal Party further and favored a homogenization of Antioquia's political image. Both the political identification of Antioquia as a largely Conservative region, and the spatial configuration of Antioquia as an administrative entity dominated by Medellín, thus resulted from struggles for regional hegemony between locally based elites allied with local popular sectors and with politicians in Bogotá.

According to eminent Colombian historian Marco Palacios, no single political party or bloc has ever been fully hegemonic in a Gramscian sense on a national level in Colombia. Yet there were specific historical moments at which what Florencia Mallon calls a "hegemonic balance" was arguably attained on a regional level. Palacios and other historians point to the example of Conservative Antioquia as one example of hegemony. In 1864 Conservative Pedro J. Berrío took over the state government. Over the next decade, the Antioquia government maintained a tense modus vivendi with the federal government, conditioned upon the non-interference of each administration in the other's affairs. Berrío and his allies focused their attentions internally. They "consummated" (in the words of scholars María Teresa Uribe de Hincapié and Clara Inés García) their control over Antioquia through the imposition of a series of surveillance and control mechanisms, such as Conservative-controlled local election boards, a strict vagrancy code, Catholic schools for girls and boys, and popular Catholic lay associations. By allying themselves with the church, channeling popular religious sentiment, and ascribing high moral value to physical labor, commerce, and the legally constituted family, Conservative leaders utilized the precepts of Catholicism and popular morality to benefit their political and economic interests. Local officials controlled the state militia and determined who was subject to forced war taxes, municipal work detail, and militia duty. Such strong-arm tactics doubtlessly served to delegitimize the ruling party in the eyes of some members of the opposition. But Conservative politicians were effective in securing support, or at least acquiescence, through familial, financial, and affinitive relationships, patronage, and alliances with the clergy.[31]

The Berrío administration crystallized the image of Antioquia as socially peaceful and cohesive. Berrío's Antioquia was an imagined family, with Berrío as the respected patriarch. Berrío may have been a loving patriarch, but he was also an authoritarian one. Antioquia still had a considerable Liberal presence and class disparity, so the twin goals of social cohesion and political conservatization were somewhat contradictory. The Conservative state resolved these contradictions by initiating repressive measures against those who would not or could not conform.

Antioquia's particularly strict vagrancy laws directly and indirectly stimulated frontier migration. Entrepreneurs reportedly used penal settlements and forcibly indentured "vagrants" to promote agriculture and colonize the state's uncultivated peripheries. People charged with vagrancy and other crimes, moreover, escaped forced labor by fleeing across the state border, prompting Cauca officials and journalists to complain of the influx of Antioqueño criminals.[32]

Liberalism and Class Struggle in Cauca

Meanwhile, Liberals in Popayán and the Cauca Valley gained the upper hand. Conservatives had wielded considerable power in Cauca in the 1850s, but in the 1860s Mosquera joined the Liberals and his faction came to dominate the state's fractious politics. Liberals achieved this dominance in part by mobilizing Caucanos of indigenous and African descent. As a Liberal leader, Mosquera proved adept at allying with popular groups, including some indigenous communities, whose support he rewarded by recognizing their land claims. Mosquera wielded the fearsome image of Cauca's "black rabble" to his own advantage in order to intimidate opposing armies. In the war of 1876–77, black and mulatto Caucanos participated in sacking the city of Cali and once again traumatized the elites of the Cauca Valley.[33]

Despite considerable popular support for Mosquera's faction, however, Liberals in Cauca were never able to match the relative stability enjoyed by Antioquia's Conservative entrepreneurial politicians. In addition to the severe long-term economic crisis and extreme social divisions in Cauca, Liberals suffered from their own internal political divisions. Radicals accused Mosquera of militarism and demagoguery; the Mosqueristas retorted that the Radicals were "oligarchs" who monopolized political power through electoral fraud.[34]

The civil wars of the nineteenth century constituted key historical moments in the consolidation and racialization of oppositional regional identities. Mosquera's Liberal armies became known in Antioquia as the "blacks of Cauca." These "hordes" terrified Antioqueño settlements along the Cauca border, particularly during the civil war of 1876–77, which resulted in a Liberal victory over Antioquia's Conservative forces and ended a decade and a half of Conservative autonomy in that state. The villages and towns of the border suffered the humiliation of military occupation by the disparaged and feared Cauca soldiers. The Conservative inhabitants of Antioquia towns referred to all of the Liberal soldiers and administrators from Cauca—regardless of their complexions—as *los negros del Cauca*.[35]

CONCLUSIONS

In Antioquia, and to some extent in Cauca, elites promoted regional identity and interregional animosity. In doing so, they advanced their own political, military, and economic goals. Cauca Liberals forged pacts with poor Caucanos, but Cauca remained divided by race, class, partisan factionalism, and geographic dispersal. Antioquia elites were far more successful in fostering a sense of ethnic and political homogeneity that served to obfuscate disparities and may have also served to silence other discourses of Liberal political allegiance or of black or Indian racial identity. Antioqueños stressed regional homogeneity by emphasizing the racial, political, and moral difference of Caucanos. Observers who traveled to western Colombia from Bogotá or from foreign countries repeated and expanded upon the discourse of the regional elites, exaggerating in their publications both the internal homogeneity of each state as well as the social and racial gulfs that separated the states from each other, thus reifying a national geography that construed Colombia as a country made up of morally and racially differentiated regions. A series of binary oppositions (white vs. black or Indian; moral vs. immoral; mercantile vs. patrician; mountain vs. valley; peace vs. violence; order vs. anarchy; virtuous women vs. lascivious women; hardworking men vs. lazy men) became social realities, in the sense that foreign writers, regionalist intellectuals and politicians, academics, and the public more generally increasingly used them to define Antioquia and Cauca.

In concluding this chapter it is important to point out that, while regional identities, particularly in the case of Antioquia, have been solidified in the discourse of regional elites, regional stereotypes were not merely elite inventions. As is particularly clear in the case of Cauca, the images that came to characterize *el caucano* as black, lazy, and bellicose and *la caucana* as sexually uninhibited resulted from nonconformity and overt resistance on the part of plebeian men and women. Even while forging political alliances with certain sectors of the Liberal Party, Cauca's black, Indian, and mixed-race inhabitants did not conform to elite efforts to control them culturally and economically; they repeatedly asserted their own cultural practices and economic demands. For this reason, regional elites, along with visitors from other regions and nations, came to fear and caricature Caucanos.

Nineteenth-century Antioquia also suffered considerable class conflict, particularly around the opening and settlement of frontier areas, where long-running disputes raged over land. Harsh vagrancy measures reflected elite determination to control, isolate, and expel dissenters. Despite these conflicts, Antioquia elites were apparently far more successful in propagating a myth of racial and social harmony and integration. Of course, we have only fragmentary access to nineteenth-century popular consciousness, so its not possible to say just how deeply the poor of Antioquia internalized the regional mystique. Nonetheless, the relative political coherence and internal stability of Antioquia for several decades suggests that the civil, religious, military, and educational mechanisms of control and surveillance were effective.

Palacios notes that the Antioquia elite embraced rather than disdained many aspects of popular culture. Patrician whites of Cauca explicitly denigrated the racial and cultural characteristics of the plebeian majority— even while courting their military electoral support. The Antioquia elite, meanwhile, embraced popular images, such as the barefoot *arriero* (mule-driver), the *colono* (agricultural settler or squatter), the farm wife, and the mazamorrero. Elite writers—some of whom were of humble origins themselves—lauded the working folk as heroic pioneers, the cornerstones of an industrious and prosperous regional society. Swollen bare feet, corn and beans, straw hats, leather shoulder bags, and axes were markers of poverty, reflecting lives of painful physical labor. Yet, rather than symbols of shame, these aspects of daily life were converted into symbols of regional pride, accessible to virtually everyone, regardless of social class. Thus, von Schenck reported that when the elite merchants of Medellín and their families left the city for the mountains, they changed out of their fashionable European clothes into peasant clothing. On the road, these elite women and men were visibly distinguished from humbler folk mainly by their shoes.[36]

EPILOGUE

In the European tale of Beauty and the Beast, Beauty kisses the Beast and makes him beautiful. In the case of Antioquia and Cauca, the reverse seems to have taken place; both are now plagued by monstrous violence. By the late twentieth century, Medellín and Cali (the major hub of the Cauca Valley, now the capital of the department of Valle), became booming regional commercial and manufacturing centers (Popayán, meanwhile, was an economic backwater). Yet, at the same time, Cali joined Medellín in becoming a center for the international trade in illicit drugs. During the 1980s, rival drug-trafficking "cartels" based in each city waged a violent war—complete with bombs, drive-by shootings, and massacres—for dominance of the cocaine trade. The drug traffickers, particularly in Antioquia, joined other landowners and the military in arming paramilitary forces to protect themselves and their landholdings from left-wing guerrillas and to massacre the civilian Colombian left. As a result, both Antioquia and the Cauca Valley suffer from internal warfare, class conflict, astronomical homicide rates, and atrocious human rights violations.[37]

Nineteenth-century travelers and social commentators would not have been surprised at the Cauca Valley's twentieth-century violence, which they might have seen as the logical outcome of what they described as racial animosity, familial disorder, and political anarchy. But how did Medellín deteriorate from a model of civil peace and social order to an international byword for criminality and violence? Antioqueños commonly cite a breakdown in the patriarchal family values of "our grandparents" (*nuestros abuelos*) as the cause of Antioquia's role reversal. But much of the recent research cited in this chapter suggests that the revered abuelos themselves may have sowed the seeds of today's violence in Antioquia. Violence was integral not only to "disorderly" Cauca society, but also to "orderly" Antioquia.

As in the stereotypical Antioquia household, Antioquia's leading abuelos were highly successful in imagining their regional society as a family, in which legitimate patriarchs used a mix of coercion and affection to control and discipline subordinate family members. In Cauca, on the other hand, the subordinates often refused to recognize the authority of their ostensible patriarchs, while the fathers of this imaginary family ultimately refused to embrace blacks and Indians as their legitimate relatives (much less as their fraternal equals) and thus gave up their opportunity of forging a lasting pact. Socially and culturally, white patricians in Cali, Buga, and Popayán disdained the black, Indian, and mixed-race majority, even while opportunistically courting their political support.

For the Cauca elite, the primary racial and social "other" was within, whereas the Antioquia elites managed, over the course of the nineteenth century, to absorb, win over, repress, whiten, and expel much of their internal "other," and to cast Cauca as an external threat against which Antioqueños of all classes could unify. In other words, the Cauca elite was not so successful as its Antioquia counterpart in tapping into popular regional culture to create a positive regional image and a strong cross-class regional identity.

CHAPTER TWO

"Accompanied by Progress":

Cauca Intermediaries and

Antioqueño Migration

Both the "black legend" and "white legend" of Antioqueño colonization attribute initiative to Antioqueño migrants, portraying other Colombians—when they are mentioned at all—as either obstacles to progress or unfortunate victims of the Antioqueño invasion. Most of the scholarly and popular literature on the Antioqueño migrations into Cauca, both traditional and revisionist, reinforces the stereotype laid out in the previous chapter: that Antioqueños were inherently more enterprising than Caucanos. Many commercially minded nineteenth-century Caucanos, however, actively promoted Antioqueño settlement. These Caucanos framed their diverse arguments in favor of Antioqueños within the discourse of regional and racial differentiation. They associated Antioqueños with civilization and progress while denigrating the rural poor of their own state as backward. They sought to bring progress to Cauca by replacing blacks and Indians with more desirable settlers. The indígenas in and around Riosucio were a particular source of irritation, because the indigenous resguardos "monopolized" fertile lands and rich mineral deposits.

Cauca intermediaries encouraged Antioqueño settlement at a time when statesmen throughout Latin America were trying to increase their populations by encouraging European immigration. Latin American elites often showed a marked preference for European workers over those from other continents and over their own popular classes of African and indigenous origin. The Colombian elite was no exception. Nineteenth-century Colombian politicians sought unsuccessfully to populate the wilderness and "augment the white race" through foreign immigration. Historians have recognized and discussed the international dynamics of racial whitening for countries that did attract Europeans, but the interregional dynamics of whitening and migration have received little attention. The case of Antioqueño colonization demonstrates that efforts to enlarge and whiten the population also occurred in regions that lacked the necessary infrastructure and capital to facilitate large-scale foreign immigration. When European immigration proved unattainable, some regional elites identified their own neighbors as potential "immigrants."[1]

This chapter shows how local leaders and regional elites in Cauca— epitomized by the lawyer-*cum*-politician-*cum*-land speculator Ramón Elias Palau—undertook to transform a section of northern Cauca by bringing in Antioqueños. The chapter briefly discusses how Palau and others like him assisted Antioqueño settlements in Cauca on the eastern side of the Cauca River. We then follow Palau as he moved his operations to Riosucio and adjacent districts on the western side of the river. During the federal era, these districts—which included Marmato, Supía, Quinchía, Guática, Arrayanal (now Mistrató), and Anserma, as well as Riosucio— were known collectively as Cauca's "northern districts." The chapter also describes the Antioqueño enclaves that emerged within these districts and the local elites who prospered from the partial privatization of indigenous lands. The following chapter examines the roles of Riosucio's indigenous authorities in the Antioqueño colonization.

The story of the northern districts is an important one to tell, because it does not conform even superficially to the "classic" model of pioneer settlers clearing unsettled forests. Perhaps because they do not conform, these districts tend to get short shrift in the migration narrative. The Antioqueño migration into Riosucio and surrounding districts is one of the lesser known and least-told episodes of the colonization epic. In these districts intersected two historical transformations that are usually studied separately: Antioqueño migration and the dismemberment of indigenous resguardos.[2]

SETTLERS AND "LAND ENTREPRENEURS"

The Antioqueño migration into northern Cauca formed part of a larger migratory trend that dated back to the colonial period. During the eighteenth and early nineteenth centuries, Antioqueños founded new towns to the south and southwest of their older towns in and near the Aburra Valley. Investors and groups of settlers then moved farther south along the central cordillera and founded a series of highland towns during the first half of the nineteenth century. As available land was occupied, settlers pushed southward into the forested slopes along the ill-defined Antioquia–Cauca border. In 1848 a group of Antioqueños founded Manizales high on a central Andean mountain ridge overlooking Cauca in what was then the southern tip of Antioquia. Other Antioqueños crossed the Cauca River southwest of Medellín and founded communities in the western cordillera, including Andes, Támesis, and Jardín. These Antioquia towns developed important economic ties with the Cauca mining enclaves in Riosucio, Marmato, and Supía, which lay just to their south, and provided some of the first Antioqueño migrants to settle in Riosucio. Beginning in the late 1840s Antioqueños moved into northeastern Cauca and settled in the mountains on the eastern and western sides of the Cauca River on public unclaimed lands and on lands claimed by indigenous communities or heirs of colonial-era mining concessionaires. But Antioqueños did not carry on this process alone. To mediate with prior claimants and to gain official recognition of their settlements from the Cauca government, migrants needed the assistance of intermediaries— educated Caucanos with legal expertise and political connections, such as Ramón Palau.[3]

Palau epitomized what his contemporaries referred to pejoratively as *negociantes de tierras* (land traffickers) or *especuladores* (speculators), and what historian Catherine LeGrand refers to as "land entrepreneurs"; he used political connections to gain access to land, and he profited from promoting settlement. His long political and legal career is worth examining in detail because he was a leading promoter of Antioqueño migration throughout northeastern Cauca, especially Riosucio. Born in the Cauca Valley and active in Popayán politics, his life followed the Antioqueño migration in reverse. He got his start as an advocate of Antioqueño settlement during the late 1850s as a young lawyer and follower of Mosquera. He helped new settlements in northeastern Cauca gain legal recognition and land grants, and wrote glowingly to Mosquera of the prosperity brought by the migrants. In middle age he migrated to the town of Riosucio on the border with Antioquia, where he labored to dismember indigenous landholdings and settle Antioqueños therein. A decade later he moved on to Medellín, the capital of Antioquia, where he lived out his final years.[4]

The early history of the new settlements in Cauca underscores the importance of Cauca intermediaries such as Palau in the colonization process. The first permanent Antioqueño settlement in Cauca was Santa Rosa, founded in 1843 on public lands in the central cordillera on a narrow strip of Cauca territory on the eastern side (*banda oriental*) of the Cauca River. In 1863 Cauca officials and migrants from Santa Rosa and Antioquia founded another town named Pereira, in honor of the Cauca family that had donated land for the settlement. Pereira swelled with Antioqueño migrants during the 1870s.[5]

The founding of Pereira provides an example of the active participation of Palau and other land entrepreneurs in the Antioqueño settlement of Cauca. Francisco Pereira Martínez, a Cauca lawyer with political ties to the Cauca state government, made an advantageous purchase of public lands with the express intent of founding a town. His heirs were important Liberal politicians and businessmen who actively promoted Antioqueño migration. His son Guillermo Pereira Gamba, who made the initial land donation to the migrants, obtained government concessions in the 1860s to build mule trails connecting Antioqueño settlements. When Pereira Gamba balked at pressure from the residents of Pereira to cede additional lands for their cultivation, they turned to Palau. Palau used his legal skills and political connections to help new settlements obtain land. Most notably, he convinced the state legislature in 1869 to pass a law to grant a total of 12,000 hectares of public lands to several new villages. He wrote letters on behalf of Santa Rosa and Pereira settlers and helped the Pereira settlement win a land concession from the Cauca legislature in 1871. Palau benefited economically by mediating such deals; cash-poor communities typically paid their lawyers in land.[6]

Lawmakers in Popayán also proved amenable to Antioqueño settlement. In 1855 the legislature awarded special privileges to Antioqueño homesteaders in various new villages in Cauca. Palau lobbied with considerable success for laws benefiting specific communities such as Pereira and Santa Rosa, and he also helped obtain legislation that would favor Antioqueño settlement more generally. An 1873 law allowed contractors to recruit settler families and individual laborers from outside the state. The law's racial bias was evident in its prohibition of recruiting "Chinese and individuals of the Malaysian race." In 1883 some legislators proposed setting aside public lands to attract European immigrants. A legislative committee report contrasted Cauca's lack of dynamism and progress with the advancement of nations such as Argentina, the United States, and

Chile, due mainly, the report argued, to European immigration. As a last resort, Cauca would accept "some hardworking families from the States of Antioquia, Tolima, Santander, or Boyacá" (all of which were noted in other nineteenth-century sources as boasting significant white populations). Though ultimately voted down, this proposal reflects the extent to which some lawmakers considered white migration from neighboring states to be the next best thing to European immigration.[7]

Once he had helped dot the central cordillera on the eastern side of the Cauca River with new settlements, Ramón Palau turned his focus toward the mining enclaves and indigenous communities of Riosucio and surrounding districts on the other side of the river, on the slopes of the western cordillera. In and around Riosucio, allies and relatives of Palau were already sponsoring Antioqueño migration onto Indian lands.

THE NORTHERN DISTRICTS

To reach Riosucio and the surrounding municipal districts from the settled heart of the central Cauca Valley, nineteenth-century travelers would walk—or rather, trudge, climb, grapple, ford, and wade—north for three or more days on a steep trail. During the rainy season, the path dissolved into mud and was blocked by swollen rivers. Finally, the exhausted traveler would stumble out of the forest and encounter a series of towns and villages perched on the eastern slopes of the western cordillera. The larger towns boasted parish churches and plazas, surrounded by thatch-roof houses painted white and bright colors. White, mulatto, and mestizo townspeople lived alongside some European technicians who had come to work in the mines. The outlying rural population, scattered in hamlets and small farms, largely consisted of poor inhabitants who mostly identified as indigenous, though many might also have been described as mestizo; some were considered mulattos or blacks, especially in the mining areas. By the nineteenth century, they almost all spoke Spanish. Administratively, these parish districts were nominally subject to the cabecera town of Toro, located down in the Cauca Valley. Federal-era Cauca politicians referred to this area as the "northern districts."[8]

Of the northern districts, the recently incorporated Riosucio boasted the largest population (4,104 according to the 1851 national census). Riosucio's two plazas sat on a sloping ledge under the towering peak still known by its indigenous name, Ingrumá. To the east, a half-day's hike down the slopes of the western cordillera through pastures, farm plots, and forests sat the warm, colonial-era town of Supía (see map 2). Supía and Riosucio districts together encompassed three indigenous landholding communities (see map 3), each with its own resguardo: La Montaña (in Riosucio district), San Lorenzo (part of Riosucio until 1866, when it was annexed to Supía; in the twentieth century it became part of Riosucio once again), and Supía-Cañamomo (which straddles both Supía and Riosucio and is now known as Cañamomo-Lomaprieta). Riosucio district also included the colonial gold mining village of Quiebralomo.[9]

To the west of Riosucio was Arrayanal (now the district of Mistrató), inhabited by Chamí indígenas. Unlike the other indigenous communities of the northern districts, the Chamí spoke (and still speak) their Chamí-Embera language. South of Riosucio district, along the trail from Toro, were the colonial-era *pueblos indios* of Quinchía and Guática, each with their own governing cabildo and resguardo lands. The town of Anserma, further to the south on a high mountain ridge, had been a bustling mining hub during the colonial era but declined during the independence wars. Anserma parish district contained two additional indigenous landholding communities: Tabuyo and Tachiguí.[10]

The northern districts, especially Supía and Marmato, were also known for their black populations, though by the time of final emancipation in 1851 only a few hundred inhabitants were still enslaved. In Supía, on the border with the district of Riosucio and within the boundaries of the Supía-Cañamomo resguardo, were the Guamal gold mines, which the Moreno de la Cruz family had worked with a slave gang. The descendants of those slaves formed the community of Guamal. To the northeast of Supía were the gold veins of the *cerro de Marmato*. The national government had sold part of the Marmato mines to English investors after independence to pay war debts. The Marmato enclave attracted British and German immigrants, some of whom remained for their whole lives, had sexual relationships with mineworkers, married into the local town elites, and invested in landholdings and mines in the northern districts. The British company and local concessionaires worked the mines of Marmato mountain during the late colonial period and the early republic with gangs of slave women and men. Once freed, these former slaves and their descendants became paid laborers. They lived in small villages, including the village of Marmato itself, perched precariously atop the gold mines on the hollow and eroding slopes of the cerro.[11]

Local authorities had complained since colonial times that the Indians were insolent, litigated excessively over their landholdings, drank excessively, did not respect authorities, and underutilized their extensive natural resources. The mayor (*alcalde*) of Quiebralomo complained in 1805 that "the Supías and Lorenzos have the only lands . . . occupied only here and there with plantings of cane for their drunken binges." The Indians of Supía-Cañamomo responded that they did not monopolize the lands, that they rented their lands freely to outsiders, and that "the white *vecinos*, what they want is to take over our lands, depriving us of the legitimate and ancient possession that we have in them." The discourse of Indian laziness, drunkenness, and waste would prove remarkably resilient. Vecinos would repeatedly hurl similar accusations against the rural Indians (as they still do today). Town notables thought these lands should go to more deserving settlers.[12]

By the late 1850s the racialized discourse of regional differentiation was evident in local documents. Local authorities started identifying Antioqueños explicitly as the deserving settlers who should replace the Indians. When an assembly met in 1857 to draft a constitution for the new autonomous state of Cauca, residents of the northern districts sent petitions requesting, among other concessions, that indigenous resguardos be divided into individual properties. According to the Riosucio petition, if the indigenous resguardos were privatized, then "our neighbors, the Antioqueños, essentially hardworking, vigorous, and active, oppressed in their country by the excess population and scarcity of free lands to cultivate, would come rapidly to our soil to enjoy the many advantages provided by a virgin and fertile land." The petitioners characterized lands long utilized by indigenous communities as "virgin," reflecting assumptions that subsistence-level swidden agriculture practiced by indigenous communities was not "work." Dismissing the Indians as lazy, and indigenous land claims as illegitimate, the same petition went on to ask rhetorically: "Would it not be more in accord with justice, reason, and economic principles, that these terrains without legitimate or known owner be given to industrious and laboring classes, rather than allow them to be the doubtful patrimony of those who have an aversion to work?"[13]

In addition to economic imperatives, the petitioners had partisan reasons for promoting Antioqueño settlement. The list of Riosucio petitioners was headed by Ramón Palau's brother Miguel Antonio and the parish priest Manuel Velasco. Miguel Antonio Palau was an avid Conservative, as was his father-in-law Santiago Silva. Father Velasco, like parish priests throughout Colombia at that time, allied himself with the Conservative Party. During the mid–nineteenth century, various political bands struggled for control over the northern districts. The town of Toro itself was dominated by Radical Liberals. The Conservative notables of Riosucio, the Radicals of Toro, and Liberals and Conservatives in Supía and Marmato, all fought each other to dominate local governments. Most blacks in the area, as in the rest of Cauca, were Liberals. As the next chapter will show, politicians of various factions sought indigenous electoral (and, during wartime, military) support. These politicians also strengthened their electoral (and military) bases by bringing in migrants who shared their partisan affiliations.

The affinity that certain local leaders felt toward Antioqueños extended to the Conservative government of that state. In 1860, in the midst of a civil war between Cauca and Antioquia, a Conservative "Committee of Citizens"—including Silva, Palau, and Velasco, among others—assembled in Riosucio's upper plaza to proclaim their independence from the state government of Cauca. Cauca, under Mosquera, had rebelled against the Conservative national government. The Riosuceños declared their loyalty to Antioquia. The Liberal forces under Mosquera, however, won. In 1864 Miguel Antonio Palau led another local uprising and again attempted unsuccessfully to secede. Riosucio was known as a Conservative stronghold in subsequent civil wars, although Riosuceños participated on both sides.[14]

By this time, some Antioqueño settlers were already crossing the state border into indigenous resguardos in the western cordillera. The first documentary evidence that Antioqueño families had settled in Riosucio district with the intent to form a permanent community dates from 1850. In 1854 the provincial legislature legally recognized the Antioqueño settlement of Oraida, "in the spot known as La Montaña de Oro, in the district of Riosucio." This law made no mention of the fact that Oraida (also known as El Oro) was founded on lands claimed by the parcialidad of La Montaña.[15]

Antioqueños began settling in La Montaña around the same time that the Riosucio parish district was officially unified and incorporated at Father Velasco's request. Velasco, originally the priest of Quiebralomo and of the non-Indian, upper-plaza parish in Riosucio, had been a driving force behind the unification of the upper and lower parishes into one district under his religious jurisdiction. The death in 1845 of his rival, Father José Bonifacio Bonafont, the parish priest of La Montaña and the lower plaza, had cleared the last obstacle to the parish's unification in 1846. Velasco had long defended the land claims of the Quiebralomeños to La Montaña's land. Along with Santiago Silva, he now promoted Conservative Antioqueño settlement on resguardo lands.[16]

Ramón Palau commented to Mosquera in 1859 that Silva, who was Miguel Antonio Palau's father-in-law, "managed everything" in Riosucio and Supía. In 1865 the cabildo of La Montaña hired Silva to represent them in land transactions. Silva was one of a series of local political bosses and lawyers who used their legal knowledge and access to high political circles to "help" indígenas lose their resguardo lands. He held important municipal posts, such as secretary of the Circuit Court. He assisted settlers in attaining plots within the resguardo of La Montaña and obtained land for himself in the resguardos of Quinchía and Supía-Cañamomo. He built relationships with the settlers on the one hand and the indígenas on the other. The patterns he initiated would be repeated, by both Liberals and Conservatives, throughout the surrounding districts. The alliances that such men formed with indigenous leaders and settlers would have a lasting impact on the demographic and political geography of the zone.[17]

In the early 1870s Palau found that Riosucio provided fertile terrain for cultivating his frustrated political ambitions. Having lost an election for the legislature in 1871, he then discovered the key to both electoral success and personal enrichment in Riosucio. Following the lead of his relatives, Palau started working with the indigenous cabildos. Palau signed separate contracts in 1872 with the authorities of two neighboring communities, Supía-Cañamomo and Quinchía, to help them obtain the official colonial titles to their resguardos, which had been lost. In 1880 he cemented his ties to Riosucio by marrying one of his associates in a local mining venture: Purificación Ortiz, heir to various mining shares and indigenous land rights that her father, retired colonel Felipe Ortiz, had accumulated since the 1850s.[18]

Soon after signing the contracts with the indigenous cabildos, Palau was elected to the state legislature in Popayán, where he sponsored legislation to partition the very resguardos he had been contracted to protect. The indígenas of Quinchía then complained that he had tricked them. They claimed to have paid him with an estate that included a salt mine as well as some other properties, in place of his honorarium of two hundred pesos. They maintained that they had paid him to "take our resguardo documents to the legislature for their approval," but were horrified when "he returned them along with the law of partition [*repartimiento*], and he sold the salt mine to señor Santiago Silva, for more than a thousand pesos." Palau was cheating his own legal clients. He and his commercially minded allies on both sides of the partisan divide had apparently concluded that the indígenas were useful as clients for their legal services and for providing votes, but at the same time posed an obstacle to Antioqueño settlement, mining, and commercial agriculture. During the 1870s, in addition to supporting laws that promoted migration, Palau led a legislative assault on the indígenas' landholdings.[19]

PRIVATIZATION OF INDIGENOUS LANDHOLDINGS

In order to rid the new republic of colonial vestiges, Colombian independence leaders had mandated the partition of the resguardos as early as 1821. In 1832 a national constitutional convention again abolished tribute and called for privatization of the resguardos, leading to the rapid dissolution of indigenous communities in the eastern highlands around Bogotá. Then, in 1850, Radical reform legislation assigned to each province the task of regulating and partitioning its own indigenous resguardos.[20]

In southern and central Cauca, some mid-nineteenth-century landowners (both Liberal and Conservative), sought to disband the resguardos, while others preferred to control and protect indígenas within the framework of colonial-era institutions. To protect their interests, indigenous communities pressured and reached out to politicians such as Mosquera, who needed indigenous electoral and military support. The state legislature enacted Law 90 of 1859, which prohibited individual indígenas from selling portions of their resguardos. In addition, the law reinforced the authority of the indigenous communal governing body—the cabildo—that had been created by the crown and subsequently modified by the Republican government. Each "small cabildo," elected for a term of one year and headed by its Governor, would maintain its census and land titles and distribute usufruct rights among the members. Each cabildo could rent forests and unoccupied land to outsiders in order to pay its administrative costs.[21]

Nonetheless, the Cauca legislature was far from united in its opinions toward the resguardos. Investors in real estate and mines advocated partitioning resguardos into private plots, particularly in areas such as the northern districts that might attract Antioqueño settlement. During the 1870s, Ramón Palau and some like-minded legislators—including fellow Riosucio-based investors Rudecindo Ospina, José Hernández, and Carlos Gärtner—renewed their efforts to gain legal access to communal lands and mines. In 1873 Palau made a long statement in the Cauca legislature in favor of a proposal to partition the resguardos of Supía district. He argued that partition was legally imperative and would serve the indígenas' own best interest; restrictions on indigenous property were colonial holdovers that only denied the indígenas the full rights and benefits of citizenship. By "property rights" he meant less the right to hold on to property than the right to dispose of it at will. He also noted that Supía district's mineral wealth would attract the industrious "sons of Antioquia" who would establish family homesteads and private mining establishments.[22]

The bill was amended to extend to all of the resguardos within the state of Cauca. The resulting legislation, Law 44 of 17 October 1873, declared that all indigenous lands were subject to partition. Law 44 mandated the creation of a *padrón*, or census, of each community. Each cabildo would pay for two surveyors, who would then proceed to partition its resguardo. The law also provided that in the interim, until such a partition could be implemented, the individual indígenas (male and female) would enjoy the same property rights as any shareholders in any corporation. This provision would have considerable impact in the northern districts. Members could sell their birthrights as "shares" (*acciones*) or "rights" (*derechos*) even before their individual plots were titled, and regardless of whether or not their communities ever went ahead with a formal partition. In other words, their membership in indigenous communities—and thus their legal identity as indígenas—was going up for sale. The result of these laws was a feeding frenzy, as local vecinos and new arrivals from Antioquia and southern Cauca both jostled each other and collaborated to gain access to a feast of indigenous lands and mineral resources.[23]

The combined effects of legislative assault, mediation by Antioqueño and Caucano land entrepreneurs, and settlement by local vecinos and Antioqueño migrants, caused the biggest indigenous communities of the northern districts, including La Montaña, Quinchía, and Supía-Cañamomo, to lose over a third of their landholdings. The indígenas of Guática ultimately would be cornered into the lower part of their resguardo. Meanwhile, two of the smaller indigenous communities, Tabuyo and Tachiguí, would disappear by the end of the century.[24]

The buying and selling of resguardo lands and official membership opened the way for permanent Antioqueño settlement. By the end of the nineteenth century, a settlement pattern was evident. Antioqueños settled first in the cold highlands, in enclaves linked internally and to each other through familial relationships and common communal origins in Antioqueño towns. Familial and commercial links between the highland settlements were often stronger than links to the cabecera towns of the Cauca districts. Antioqueño settlers and storekeepers were also increasingly present in some district cabeceras, especially in towns along main transportation routes. In the 1870s, for example, Antioqueños took over the depopulated colonial-era town of Anserma.[25]

Law 44 of 1873 gave rise to a local real estate market where virtually none had existed before. For the years 1860–73, no land sales specifically involving Indian lands were recorded in the local office responsible for registering such documents. For 1857–60, before the passage of Cauca Law 90, only 10 such transactions were recorded. From 1857 to 1873 there were only 204 legal documents recorded of any kind, for all of the northern districts, including not just land sales but wills, contracts, powers of attorney, and so forth. Real estate transactions of all sorts accelerated with the passage of Law 44. In 1874–75, Supía district alone registered 147 real estate transactions, of which 27 referred specifically to indigenous resguardo holdings (one of which was in San Lorenzo, the rest in Supía-Cañamomo).[26]

Recent scholarship on Latin America has revised the assumption that indigenous peasants were overwhelmingly dispossessed by the privatization of communal landholdings in the nineteenth century. Scholars of Mexico, El Salvador, and the Colombian eastern Andes have shown that indigenous communities did not universally oppose land privatization and that at least some sectors of the indigenous population favored privatization and benefited by buying their neighbors' lands. Other scholars, most notably Jeffrey Gould, have continued to emphasize the tragic effects of late-nineteenth-century dismantling of communal landholdings, especially in areas that produced coffee and other export crops. Nineteenth-century Riosucio was neither as traumatic as the Nicaraguan cases analyzed by Gould nor as rosy as the examples described by the revisionists. The two local communities that registered the most sales in the 1870s–1880s were La Montaña and Supía-Cañamomo, and almost all of the people who bought land from individual indígenas, or who obtained land in payment for services from the cabildos, were outsiders.[27]

The parcialidad of La Montaña immediately felt the impact of Law 44 of 1873. The cabildo finally yielded to historic pressures from Quiebralo-meños for land. By December 1874 the parcialidad, represented by admin-istrator Santiago Silva, agreed to cede more than a quarter of its resguardo to the vecinos of Quiebralomo. Law 44 also allowed Conservative settlers of El Oro in La Montaña to gain official recognition of their landholdings. La Montaña's resguardo stretched upward and westward from Riosucio town (see map 3). Antioquia bordered it to the north and the Chamí indig-enous resguardo to the west. Most of the resguardo territory was tierra fría, at an altitude of over 2,000 meters. For outsiders, it must have seemed there for the taking, because the indigenous population tended to concen-trate in the eastern and lower sections of the resguardo most suitable for their principal subsistence crops. For more than twenty years, highland settlers had bought and sold their "improvements"—including plantings, fences, houses, and other structures.[28]

Present-day residents of the tierra fría recall that their ancestors cleared and obtained "large expanses" of land; archival documents suggest that, indeed, the settlers did not do too badly. During 1875 and 1876, Antio-queño surveyor Manuel Maria Hoyos measured off the "improvements" of various squatters in the highlands of La Montaña. The squatters, who were mostly Antioqueños, apparently paid all or part of the cost of mea-suring their plots. According to a booklet of yellowed receipts still pre-served in the archive of the Montaña cabildo, Hoyos measured off twenty-six plots, ranging in size from less than 1 hectare to 143.5 hectares (with a mean average of about 40). Some of the individuals mentioned had more than one piece of land. For example, José María Villa had just over 30 hectares in a spot known as Rioarriba del Oro and another 30 in Cambía. Higinio Aguirre had two separate plots in El Oro, totaling just over 56 hectares.[29]

Unfortunately (and rather suspiciously), the official title registry books for Riosucio district during the crucial years of 1874–75 are missing from the Registry of Public Instruments, where the titles are kept, so the exact mechanism whereby ownership of some of these lands was transferred from indígenas to Antioqueños remains unclear, but later transactions provide evidence that the settlers had bought land from the indigenous cabildo or its representatives. For example, on 28 May 1876 José María Villa registered a title to a 30-hectare plot in Río Arriba del Oro which he had originally bought from Santiago Silva, administrator of La Montaña, for forty pesos. The plot corresponded to one of the plots that José María Hoyos had measured on his behalf four days previously. Most of the land sold in La Montaña from 1876 to 1885 consisted of plots sold off by the cabildo *administrador,* who could be an indigenous or non-indigenous employee or agent of the cabildo. Santiago Silva was the first administrator and was followed in that office by members of the community: Nicolás Largo and Marco Evangelio Gaspar.[30]

Relatively few of the individuals who appeared as buyers in the Riosucio registry were known to be indígenas. An exception was Vicente Largo, who, in company with Ramón Palau and four other investors, purchased a piece of land near the El Salado coal mine from administrator Nicolás Largo (possibly, but not necessarily, a close relative of Vicente) in 1880. The partnership apparently dated from 1877, when Ramón Palau, Purificación Ortiz, and a prominent Riosuceño named Francisco Bueno had formed a partnership with several indígenas to mine the coal of El Salado. Palau claimed mineral rights as the mine's "discoverer"— although its existence had been recorded for more than a decade—and presumably buffered his claims with the land rights that his indigenous partners had in the community. Vicente Largo lent his credentials to other partnerships as well. In 1876 he had appeared as a partner in a landowning group that included Santiago Silva. The following year, Largo joined Palau in a nearby salt extraction venture at El Salado.[31]

Partnerships with indígenas constituted one example of the mechanisms whereby outsiders gained access to resguardo mines and lands. El Salado partner Vicente Largo had presided over the cabildo in 1865 and had signed the original retainer agreement with Santiago Silva. The example of Largo suggests a phenomenon that was also true for Supía-Cañamomo: well-placed cabildo officials could benefit from the partition of their communal lands through political and financial alliances with prominent vecinos. Nonetheless, the gains made by a few indigenous leaders were small in comparison to those of the outsiders.

LAND TRANSACTIONS IN SUPIA-CANAMOMO

Law 44 affected the resguardo of Supía-Cañamomo with particular intensity. After all, Ramón Palau and his cohort had sponsored the law with the specific intent of gaining access to this community's resources. Its fertile slopes stretched invitingly from Riosucio eastward and downward into Supía district, encompassing part of the Supía River valley, and reaching almost to the Cauca (see maps 2 and 3). The resguardo contained salt-water springs as well as gold and other minerals. Even before coffee, its varied warm and mid-range altitudes were highly suitable for crops that could be marketed domestically, such as maize, sugar cane, tobacco, cacao, plantains, and beans. Several private estates, gold mines, amalgamation plants, and saltworks already sat within the resguardo boundaries. The mining enterprises required a forest reserve to provide wood for their furnaces. Some hacendados and miners traced their property claims back to the colonial period, as did the black community of Guamal, which was also situated within the boundaries claimed by the indigenous cabildo. Non-Indian Caucanos, including many locally born vecinos from Supía and Quiebralomo, made inroads into the lower-lying lands and mineral resources of the indigenous resguardos, especially in Supía-Cañamomo. Initially, the colonization of these warmer altitudes was mainly a local enterprise. Antioqueños generally preferred the highlands until the 1880s and 1890s when, with the advent of coffee, the mid-range slopes became increasingly attractive.

The commodification of indigenous land shares was most pronounced in Supía-Cañamomo, where intermarriage and mestizaje had already blurred ethnic boundaries to a greater extent than in neighboring parcialidades (see chapter 3). In 1874 communal censuses, or *padrones*, were drawn up with the intent of fixing fuzzy communal boundaries. Identifying and enumerating the population facilitated dividing up the resguardo. If an individual had one parent who was considered to be of indigenous or even part-indigenous descent, then the individual had the right by "one line" to a "half share" in the resguardo. An adult member with two indigenous parents ("two lines") had a right to a full share. Cabildo authorities drew up the padrón for Supía-Cañamomo under the supervision of the Jefe Municipal of Toro, who in 1874 was the ubiquitous Ramón Palau.[32]

The census proved controversial and subject to manipulation. In the final months of 1874, 160 people, almost evenly divided between men and women, successfully took advantage of a clause in Law 44 allowing people to contest their exclusion from the communal padrón. Then they signed over a portion of the rights they had won on appeal to the legal representative who had secured those rights for them. On 8 October 1874, for example, twelve men and sixteen women signed one-third of their land rights over to Eustaquio Tascón, "by virtue of the services and efforts that the latter has proffered them in sustaining their claim to be recognized as participants in the Resguardo of the parcialidad of Supía and Cañamomo, by the rest of the enrolled comuneros." Four days later, Juan Gregorio Trejo, administrator of the same resguardo, signed another document recognizing thirty-two more members, all of whom turned one-third of their derechos over to Tascón. Similar documents ensued, whereby groups of individuals gained access to the communal lands and then handed over a third of their rights to their legal representatives, including, among others, Tascón, León Hernández, Erasmo Trejo, and even Juan Gregorio Trejo himself—the ostensible agent of the cabildo.[33]

It is doubtful that all the appellants sincerely considered themselves indígenas. A few of those who yielded a third of their land rights had last names historically associated with the Supía-Cañamomo parcialidad, such as Aricapa, Tapazco, Guapacha, and Chaurra. Others had last names common among the indígenas of La Montaña, including Largo and Morales. Most, however, had Spanish surnames common among natives of the mixed-race community of Quiebralomo or the heavily black mining enclaves of Marmato and Guamal: Guevara, Quebrada, Betancurt, Ortiz, Moreno, and Castro. They were generally native to the zone; none appear to have been Antioqueños. In some cases, entire families were listed together. The majority may have been people who lived and farmed within the resguardo over several generations, and thus felt they had some justifiable claim. One group of fourteen petitioners, however, consisted of thirteen residents of Quinchía and only one of Supía. To some extent, the cabildo officials themselves must have been complicit in the deals, although it is not clear if the decision-making power lay with the Jefe Municipal, the indigenous cabildo, or the courts. One of the people who sued for inclusion was Marcelino Betancurt, who was likely the brother of the indigenous governor at that time, Feliciano Betancurt. The cabildo's own hired representative, Juan Gregorio Trejo, also benefited from this scam.[34]

Trejo was from a Riosucio family with roots in the colonial mining settlement of Quiebralomo. He did not claim indigenous ancestry himself, but he did claim membership in the community of Supía-Cañamomo by virtue of his deceased indigenous wife. On 8 October 1874, Trejo signed an agreement on behalf of the parcialidad with the district authorities of Supía, Marmato, and several private citizens with land claims in the resguardo, including Santiago Silva. Trejo, as the administrator of the resguardo, agreed to sell 150 hectares to private miners, the proceeds from which were to pay "the lawyer who secured for the indígenas the property of the Resguardos," that is, Ramón Palau. Additional resguardo lands were designated for the districts of Supía and Marmato, and a school. The parties agreed to respect preexisting rental agreements whereby the foreign mining company in Marmato had access to wood for its furnaces, and to recognize the validity of various property claims within the boundaries of the resguardo—including several gold mines near Marmato and the black community of Guamal, among others. Attached to the Registry copy of the document was a page filled with the names of indígenas, male and female, who ostensibly affirmed, mostly by proxy, that Trejo was their representative and that the accord was legitimate.[35]

A flood of land sales ensued, as Trejo sold off additional portions of the resguardo. The district governments adjudicated and sold some of the lands awarded to them. Poor squatters who had long resided in the resguardo were finally able to legalize their possessions. In 1876 Trejo and Supía district authorities agreed that locally born residents squatting on lands assigned to either the resguardos or the districts would receive up to one hectare of land for free. The authorities also provided for the growing population of Antioqueño settlers. Settlers who had resided within the resguardo for ten years received automatic title to a half-hectare; those with fewer years received less. As in La Montaña, almost no indígenas appeared as buyers of resguardo lands.[36]

Political enemies of Ramón Palau criticized the dismantling of the resguardo. As a result, the state government in Popayán temporarily suspended the repartimiento of Supía-Cañamomo in 1874. Resident Ricardo Sanz wrote to the president of the state of Cauca in November 1874 that Palau was illegally continuing with the repartimiento and was manipulating his clients:

> Because of the personal interest that this functionary has as representative and lawyer for the supposed indígenas, he made them pay his fees by selling various lots of land, the most important and valuable, which, without proceeding with an assessment, survey, and map, were passed into the power of the buyers and he still expects that they will sell more rights to pay the surveyor, in addition to a considerable lot which, in order to gain one more convert, he has offered to cede to the alcalde of this District.[37]

In criticizing Palau, however, Sanz did not affirm indigenous land rights. Rather, he expressed skepticism toward the whole idea of the so-called resguardos and the "supposed" indígenas. The president of Cauca responded to Sanz's complaints by reiterating the moratorium, but the legislature reversed this decision the following September by passing a law that verified the resguardo land transactions in the northern districts.[38]

Tensions among townspeople over the distribution of indigenous lands were evident. That same month, just before the new law was passed, a plot to overthrow the local government and assassinate people who had taken active part in dividing up the resguardos was unrecovered. Alleged conspirator Bonifacio Zabala was reported to have said "that the best method was to resolve with bullets the tricks of Dr. Ramón Palau, and in a town riot all those bosses will leave here." Surprisingly, none of the alleged conspirators included indígenas, and the official investigation made no note of indigenous support for the proposed rebellion. An alleged conspirator had told one of the witnesses that "Supía is against the division of the lands, and we have the support of Quiebralomo." Why would the townspeople of Quiebralomo and Supía have opposed the repartimientos from which they themselves could benefit materially?[39]

The answer had to do with partisan political factionalism. Palau's flouting of state government mandates provided an opportunity that his political enemies tried to exploit in order to bring him down. Among the conspirators were Radical Liberals from Supía, who apparently sought to ally with Conservatives from Quiebralomo to oust their common local rivals, the Mosquerista Liberals led by Palau. The accords whereby Quiebralomo received land from La Montaña may have represented in part an effort by Palau and his Conservative relatives (Miguel Antonio Palau and Santiago Silva) in Riosucio district to ameliorate opposition sentiment and to forestall a full-blown rebellion. The controversy, moreover, seems to have hinged more on the question of dividing the spoils of the partition than on preserving indigenous landholding. Bonifacio Zabala, one of the plotters, was soon named to the post of *procurador* of Supía, in charge of the disposition of indigenous lands by the local government. In that office, he was able to assure that he and his own family members attained lands. Local bosses apparently resolved the crisis by buying off the opposition (as Sanz alluded to above). Complaints by Sanz and by the indigenous communities themselves did have an effect, however. The legislature responded by passing Law 41 of 1879 "on protection of indigenas," which began by stating that "from almost everywhere in the State come demands for a measure that will assure the indigenous class the few lands or resguardos to which this disinherited race has at last been reduced, and which would prohibit and avoid further plundering in these places of asylum."[40]

The 1879 law rescinded Law 44 of 1873 and prohibited individual indígenas from selling their portions of undivided resguardos. But, citing the 1863 federal Rionegro Constitution's guarantee of private property, the new law did not prohibit breaking up the resguardos. Rather, the law mandated that the partition of the resguardos among individual indígenas should continue, which it did in many areas, though neither Supía-Cañamomo nor La Montaña was ever fully privatized. In any case, the local land market in both Supía-Cañamomo and La Montaña had already moved from the initial stage of alienation from the indigenous communities to a stage in which privatized shares and lands were traded as commodities between non-indígenas. By the end of the 1870s, most of the sellers of land were neither indígenas nor their legal representatives.

In 1880, moreover, Juan Gregorio Trejo began titling specific plots of land to shareholders in the resguardo—to those who claimed membership through inheritance and those who had obtained shares through purchase or as payment for services. In Supía-Cañamomo a one-line half-share generally corresponded to about 5–8 hectares, but there were exceptions. For example, María Escolástica Morales, a "full," or "two-line," indígena (and single mother who acted on her own behalf, as she had no husband to represent her) received 80 hectares from Trejo in 1880. María de Jesús Román, on the other hand, was assigned only 15 hectares (her husband, Crisanto Gañan, received the title to this land from Juan Gregorio Trejo on her behalf in 1883). Clearly, the apportioning of titles was subject to manipulation, and, moreover, the community was internally differentiated economically. Even before the partitioning process began in the 1870s, access to land was not uniform. Although all adult women and men theoretically enjoyed equal rights to resguardo lands, access actually depended on a variety of factors, including gender.[41]

Men could take advantage of their legal status as the administrator of their wives' and female dependents' properties to accumulate shares in the resguardo. For example, in November 1880, Bibiano Romero, who was listed in the 1874 census as a one-line member, received from Trejo three lots of land totaling 105 hectares in three parts of the resguardo. Romero claimed that the first lot of 40 hectares corresponded to him in his capacity as member enlisted in the padrón. He claimed the second lot of 40 hectares as the representative of his cousin María Eulalia Guapacha, and the third lot as the husband of María del Rosario Moreno. Both Moreno and Guapacha were among those who had sued in 1874 to be included as members in the community.[42]

In neither Supía-Cañamomo nor La Montaña were the indigenous inhabitants themselves the primary beneficiaries of the privatization process. The people who profited most from the partition of Supía-Cañamomo were those who were able to obtain—either through purchase or in payment for services rendered—multiple plots, ranging in size from 4 to 174 hectares per transaction. Some individuals and mining partnerships amassed holdings that totaled hundreds of hectares. Buyers included people originally from Cauca, Antioquia, and Europe. In La Montaña, however, many of the first outsiders to gain title to the indigenous lands were farmer-settlers on middle-sized plots, while in Supía-Cañamomo the first to come in were miners and speculators, who later would subdivide and sell off parts of their holdings to locally born and Antioqueño agriculturalists. The partial dismemberment of the indigenous resguardos in the 1870s and 1880s gave rise to a mining boom, provided the resources for Cauca intermediaries to consolidate their position as a local elite, and facilitated increased Antioqueño migration into the northern districts.[43]

MINING BOOM

The 1870s–1880s brought a resurgence of the local mining industry. Since the colonial era, many outsiders had been drawn to the Riosucio area for gold, as the name of Riosucio's first Antioqueño settlement, El Oro, reflects. Gold in rivers, veins, and pre-Columbian burial plots drew poor treasure hunters and placer miners as well as more prosperous investors. The mining zone of Anserma-Supía-Riosucio-Marmato constituted one of three principal mining areas in nineteenth-century Cauca. Historian Alonso Valencia Llano has compiled a list of ninety titles to mines that the government of Cauca awarded to individuals from 1871 to 1890. Fifty-one, including mines of silver and coal as well as gold, were in the northern districts. This area produced just under half (46 percent) of all of the gold officially recorded for Cauca in 1887–90.[44]

Mining partnerships in and around Riosucio followed a pattern similar to those of Antioquia, as described by economic historian Roger Brew. A mine, including surrounding properties and machinery, would be divided into twenty-four shares, which would be divided among a smaller number of people. Smaller mines were worked physically by original claimants and perhaps some family members. Larger mining enterprises, such as those in Marmato and Quiebralomo, employed workers drawn principally from the local mixed-race and Afro-Colombian populations.[45]

The mining industry of the Riosucio area was relatively prosperous compared to most of late-nineteenth-century Cauca. The local mining economy was linked closely to Antioquia; local gold was exported through Medellín. British miners in Marmato had access to foreign capital and could presumably remain somewhat immune from Cauca's destructive partisan warfare. The British enclave, moreover, formed an integral part of the local economy of the northern districts. In the late nineteenth century, wealthy Supía resident Bartolomé Cháves ran a mining operation adjoining that of the Western Andes Company on Marmato mountain. The Western Andes Company employed managers from leading local families. Foreign-born employees and their native-born counterparts in turn expanded the gold industry by staking their own claims and obtaining titles to mines and forest lots (for fuel) in Marmato, Riosucio, and Supía. Gold mining thus served as an impetus for privatization, real estate speculation, Antioqueño settlement, and commerce, and provided an economic base for the local elite.[46]

LOCAL ELITE

Many inhabitants of Riosucio and surrounding towns, both Liberal and Conservative, prospered modestly from the economic and social changes of the 1870s and 1880s, and a few became wealthy. The local elite was rejuvenated by the real estate and mining boom. Old-time mining families forged political and marital alliances with newly arrived land entrepreneurs and foreign technicians. They consolidated their economic position by working for indigenous cabildos, buying and selling resguardo lands, investing in small mining operations, extending credit, and producing food for local markets. They used political posts to take advantage of the new opportunities offered by the privatization of resguardo lands. Often bitterly divided over politics, they nonetheless formed marital and business relationships that bridged the partisan divide. Thus they consolidated their status as a political, social, and economic elite at the local level.

Bartolomé Chávez was the most successful locally born resident and is still remembered as the richest man in Supía. He also provides an example of someone who profited from the privatization of indigenous lands. Born in Riosucio, he inherited some lands and mines in Quiebralomo. As an adult, he divided his time between Supía and his mines in Marmato. He owned shares in several banks in Medellín and Popayán. He maintained bank accounts in London, where he bought merchandise and equipment. In cash-starved Supía and Riosucio, where there were no banks at all before the 1880s, he provided credit to his neighbors. Significantly, Chávez obtained most of his local landholdings and mines during the heady decades of the 1870s and 1880s. In partnership with his three sisters, he amassed considerable holdings within the boundaries of the Supía-Cañamomo resguardo.[47]

Among the Riosucio clans who also prospered were the interrelated de la Cuesta, Cock, and Gärtner families. Jorge Enrique Federico Gärtner had immigrated from Hanover to Marmato and married a local woman, María Columna Cataño. One of their sons, university-educated lawyer and Liberal politician Carlos Eugenio Gärtner Cataño, married Evangelina de la Cuesta. Her paternal grandfather was a Spanish immigrant and her father was a prosperous late-nineteenth-century local mining investor, Vicente de la Cuesta. Evangelina's mother also came from lineages founded by nineteenth-century immigrants; the mother's last names were Cock and Bayer. The Cock Bayers and the Gärtners were among the few Riosucio families to enjoy regional and national prominence in the late nineteenth and twentieth centuries. Julián Cock Bayer would become governor of Antioquia in the 1890s, and Jorge Gärtner de la Cuesta would become governor of the Department of Caldas in the 1930s.[48]

Over generations, the local elite tended to forget that their patrimonial haciendas were once held by the indigenous communities. Governor Gärtner recalled, in his memoirs, that he spent much of his turn-of-the-century childhood in the family's hacienda of Palermo near El Oro. He claimed that his forbears had created Palermo through purchases "of bits of very small spaces . . . and the rest in adjudications of public lands" to which they later added adjoining farms purchased from their neighbors. The Gärtner family's collective memory of a slow and methodical accretion of small private and public plots obviated indigenous claims to these lands. Documents in the Registry of Public Instruments tell a different story: Palermo and other such landholdings were carved in substantial chunks out of lands belonging to the indígenas of La Montaña.[49]

Local fortunes were mostly modest in comparison to those of Latin America's grand mining centers and plantation regions. One might expect, given the large indigenous population, that the local elite would become something of a rural gentry, separated from the common rural folk by tremendous gulfs of race and class. Instead, they followed a pattern akin to their neighbors in Antioquia. They mixed their landholding, mining, and mercantile enterprises, and dressed and lived much in the same style as their poorer neighbors. As much as they disdained blacks and indígenas in their writings, local elites presented themselves as close to the people. They actively promoted the immigration of poor Antioqueños and developed relationships with members of the indigenous, black, and mixed-race communities that facilitated their access to indigenous lands.

Even the most successful families indulged in few luxuries. Accouterments of wealth and status might include shops, a network of debtors, a few gold jewels, shoes, and a couple of farms and mining claims. They built town houses with tile (rather than thatch) roofs and intricate woodwork in the distinctive colorful style for which the Antioqueño colonization would become famous. They made donations to local parish churches and chapels, they maintained private burial spots, but some of them reportedly still walked barefoot to their country haciendas. They taught their male children to participate in and supervise daily farm labor before sending them off to Medellín, Popayán, or Bogotá for the education that would most clearly distinguish them from their poorer neighbors and allow them to run local governments and courts. Lines between the wealthiest families and the middling sectors—including muleteers, shopkeepers, the more substantial farmer-settlers, and teachers—were somewhat fluid. But significant cultural and class divisions did separate upper and middling townspeople of the northern districts from the poor rural masses, most of whom were illiterate and still referred to colloquially as *indios, mulatos,* and *negros.*[50]

Some of the land entrepreneurs who speculated in real estate and mediated the process of Antioqueño settlement were themselves Antioqueños. Rudecindo Ospina, for example, a Liberal crony of Ramón Palau, served in various public offices in the early 1880s and bought shares in gold and salt mines in Marmato, Supía, Antioquia, and other regions of Colombia. He and his wife Leonarda Botero owned a house in Riosucio, as well as farms that by the 1890s were growing coffee. During the 1870s the Ospina Botero daughters married into families of miners and land entrepreneurs,

including the Palaus. Foreigners, Antioqueños, and Caucanos from farther south were thus absorbed into the local elite through marriages and
business partnerships.[51]

In the highlands of the northern districts, intermediaries such as Silva
and Ospina helped farmers from Antioquia create their own enclaves. The
following section of this chapter describes the way of life that migrants
and descendants re-created in their new highland settlements. In so doing,
the migrants preserved a sense of their own difference from the local
inhabitants of Cauca.

ANTIOQUENO SETTLEMENTS

Juana María Hurtado, a resident of El Oro, died while visiting Guática in
1883. She left a husband, Francisco Ramírez, and two grown children. Most
likely, Francisco and Juana María had migrated as a young couple from
Antioquia to live with or near his family. Or perhaps she came alone, be-
trothed to an already-established settler. Antioqueño kinship and residential practices in El Oro today, and apparently then as well, have tended
toward patrilocality; young married women commonly move in with their
husbands' families or move to their husbands' communities. Hurtado's
relatives in Guática included her daughter Filomena and son-in-law, the
land entrepreneur Tomás Medina. Hurtado's ties to Guática were examples of the familial connections that linked Antioqueño settlements together. Regional historian Alfredo Cardona Tobón writes that "Oraida was
the base for the Antioqueño occupation of the cordillera. . . . Oraida was a
way-station. From there, the paisas invaded the indigenous resguardos of
Guática, Arrayanal, Tachiguí, and dispersed through the hills."[52]

Hurtado left a farm in El Oro and some livestock. She also left 16.8
pesos—about enough to buy another small plot of land or a share in an
indigenous community. Her possessions reflect some common patterns
among middling nineteenth-century settlers in these districts. The capital of a relatively successful settler family would include lands obtained
through inheritance, squatting, or transactions; livestock; and land "improvements" such as houses and crops. Their houses, like those of the
other campesinos in rural Riosucio, had mud walls and thatched roofs,
with separate kitchen shacks. Poles and beams were made from a bamboo-
like plant, *guadua*. The family might also own one or two pieces of gold
jewelry, some wooden furniture, and rudimentary farm tools. Settlers in

the lower altitudes, like their locally born neighbors, also owned copper pots, used for boiling sugarcane to make rough alcohol.[53]

Local marital registries, notarial documents, and family lore reveal that settlers came from all over Antioquia, including some from the area around Medellín. Although documents are too incomplete to permit reliable quantitative analysis, it appears that the majority came from the southern districts near or on the Cauca border. The settlers in El Oro and the highlands came primarily from communities that were founded in southwestern Antioquia in the nineteenth century, especially Jardín (which is adjacent to El Oro).[54]

As noted in the previous chapter, Antioqueño agricultural communities were known for their stable families and legitimately married couples. Tierra fría communities such as El Oro were no exception. They acquired middle-sized landholdings suitable for family-based production specializing in livestock and dairy products. Patriarchs consolidated their properties and ensured their families' modest prosperity by keeping their daughters relatively secluded and marrying them off young to relatives and neighbors. They incorporated the wives of their sons into their households until the young couples could set up their own farms. Antioqueños were famous for marrying early; girls reportedly wed in their early teens. Patriarchal controls over children's labor power, sexuality, and reproductive potential helped to maintain ethnic boundaries. In the tierra fría, parents were particularly successful in enforcing endogamous marital patterns and thus avoiding intermixing with indígenas. They preserved a sense of their own difference from, and superiority over, "the indios below." Today, Oreños and other denizens of the tierra fría are still renowned for their endogamy and their light skin, which is popularly associated with beauty.[55]

CONTROVERSY AND THE END OF THE PALAU ERA

While the settlers formed their communities up in the highlands, some of the Caucanos and Antioqueños who had promoted Antioqueño settlement were mired in controversy down in the cabeceras. Ramón Palau, Rudescindo Ospina, Eustaquio Tascón, and their cohort continued to occupy top municipal posts and exercise considerable influence over local political and economic affairs in the northern districts into the mid-1880s. Palau, in particular, attracted controversy. In 1884, Conservative opponents of Palau founded the first known local newspaper, *El Iris*, which accused him of conspiring with Eustaquio Tascón to obtain lands from the indigenous cabildo of Supía-Cañamomo on behalf of an Antioqueño. The editors, apparently wary of being accused of voicing anti-Antioqueño sentiment, were careful to defend the migrants as "hardworking and honest by innate virtue." *El Iris* blamed not Antioqueños but rather "Caucano malefactors" for nefarious land dealings.[56]

The letter sparked a flurry of antagonistic correspondence. Palau responded by claiming to be a champion of private property who had defended the property rights of both settlers and indígenas. In a letter to *El Iris*, he lashed out at his adversaries—including other speculators and administrators of indigenous resguardos—as the real enemies of the indígenas:

> From the Legislature I pledged to guard the property of the Antioqueño and Caucano improvers [*mejoradores*] in the Resguardos . . . combating for this reason the existing prejudices against the Antioqueños. . . . If I contradict and will litigate . . . certain territorial properties, as the attorney of the indígenas, they are those bought at shabby price.[57]

The editors responded by accusing Palau of monopolizing land for himself and a small group of indígenas who did not sufficiently cultivate the land: "Here one does not tread an acre of land that does not belong to the Indígenas . . . or better said, to Dr. Palau. From whom can I obtain 20, 30, 100 or more hectares? . . . From Dr. Palau who is the attorney of the Indígenas."[58]

Palau and his rivals competed to portray themselves as the true defenders of indigenous territorial rights, private property, and Antioqueño migration, without acknowledging any potential conflict between these roles. *El Iris* also defended Antioqueño migration: "The impulse given by the immigrations is incalculable; with them come commerce, mining, agriculture, arts and sciences. They come accompanied by every class of progress." Despite their disputes, local literate elite members of all competing political factions agreed that Antioqueños were the bearers of progress and that Antioqueño migration was the best hope for the economic future of the northern districts and the state of Cauca more generally.[59]

Within a year of this debate, the Conservatives would come into office locally on the coattails of the national political coalition known as the

Regeneration. With the end of the Liberal-dominated Federal period in the 1880s, Ramón Palau retired from Riosucio politics and land speculation. He left the state of Cauca to practice law in Antioquia. He died just outside of Medellín in 1914.[60]

CONCLUSIONS

Over the course of his long and contentious public life, Ramón Palau took active part in several of Colombia's major nineteenth-century social, economic, and political experiences: partisan political and military campaigns, *caudillismo*, speculation in lands and mines, migration, the founding of new settlements, and the dismemberment of indigenous resguardos. Born in the Cauca Valley, he worked his way north and ended up in Antioquia. Along the way, he crossed paths with Antioqueños who were heading south and seeking their fortunes in Cauca. Palau was partially responsible for the policies that helped them acquire land. He envisioned a regional transformation whereby Antioqueños would bring progress to Cauca.

This chapter has used aspects of his story, and those of his allies and rivals, to tell a larger tale: that of the amorphous process whereby northern Cauca was incorporated into "greater Antioquia." The Cauca intermediaries helped create the demographic and economic conditions that favored the subsequent emergence of the Coffee Region at the end of the century. Most accounts (both celebratory and critically revisionist) refer to this process as the colonization carried out by Antioqueños. This chapter has touched on the lives of such migrants and has reconstructed the patterns that their settlement followed, but unlike most accounts that focus mainly on Antioqueños, I highlight the actions of people such as Palau in order to make the point that the so-called Antioqueño colonization was not exclusively an Antioqueño initiative, but a Caucano initiative as well. Caucanos as well as Antioqueños shared a racialized discourse of regional differentiation whereby they associated progress with Antioqueños and backwardness with blacks and Indians. Caucanos as well as Antioqueños participated in the colonization of indigenous resguardos. Regional authorities and investors were joined in this effort by local notables, including priests, politicians, lawyers, miners, and real estate speculators of both Liberal and Conservative persuasion. Whatever their own political ideologies and economic interests, Cauca promoters of

Antioqueño settlement were united in their aspirations for civilization and progress, which they associated with private property, wage labor, commerce, and European descent.[61]

In an effort to entice Antioqueños and to wrest control of natural resources from Cauca's own rural peasantry, Cauca legislators gave land grants to settlers. In the 1870s, moreover, Cauca legislators led by Palau attempted to partition the indigenous resguardos once and for all. As this chapter has shown, they were somewhat successful. The emergence of enclaves of Antioqueños, the partial commodification of land rights, the disappearance of some resguardos, the "refounding" of Anserma, and the resurgence of the local mining industry were among their triumphs. In the 1890s the coffee boom on the temperate middle slopes would attract more settlers and link local agricultural production with international markets.

This chapter has begun the task of overturning conventional narratives of the "Antioqueño colonization" by highlighting the agency of Cauca actors. But the chapter still tells only part of the colonization story. Colonization was not simply a one-sided process. Some of the evidence cited above—the manipulated census rolls, the mining partnerships, the seemingly contradictory actions of indigenous authorities—suggests that indígenas played ambiguous but important roles in both defending and dismembering their own landholdings. This chapter has only provided the broad outlines of the regional transformation. The following chapter delves into the actions of the indígenas themselves.

CHAPTER THREE

"By Consent of the Indígenas":
Riosucio's Indigenous
Communities

One morning in early 1995, on a street in the town of Riosucio, I encountered the governor and secretary of the indigenous cabildo of La Montaña on their way to the office of the district alcalde. They were carrying new maps and copies of colonial-era documents to support their claims that more than half of the district of Riosucio, including part of the town center itself, belonged to them. Their meeting that day with district authorities was just one stage of drawn-out negotiations with district and regional authorities over the legal existence and boundaries of their resguardos. The indígenas argue that they are carrying on the same struggles for land that their ancestors carried on in the colonial period and throughout the nineteenth and twentieth centuries (see map 3).

Yet these struggles have not been entirely consistent. Leaders of the indigenous community of La Montaña joined their Riosucio neighbors in petitioning the 1857 constituent assembly for the dissolution and breakup of indigenous resguardos. In 1865 the cabildo of La Montaña hired a local lawyer and promoter of Antioqueño settlement, Santiago Silva, to "seek the repeal of the law for protection of the indígenas, in order to distribute the lands of the district of La Montaña." Such documents seem at first glance to support the arguments made by some revisionist historians and nineteenth-century politicians that most indígenas desired the privatization of their landholdings. And yet, for every document in which indígenas appeared to favor privatization, other documents showed indigenous leaders forcefully defending the integrity of their resguardos.

Such contradictory evidence has lent itself to such different conclusions as: heroic indigenous leaders defended their lands at all costs; forward-minded indígenas welcomed the opportunity to convert their communal lands to private properties; ignorant indios were manipulated by unscrupulous individuals; or avaricious indigenous authorities sold out the interests of the majority. Yet, none of these generalizations quite encompasses the complexities of local indigenous resistance to and participation in the privatization of indigenous resguardos and the "Antioqueño-ization" of Riosucio.[1]

The partition of resguardos, while never fully completed in Riosucio, facilitated the alienation of communal resources and contributed over the long term to the impoverishment of these communities, even as a relatively prosperous region emerged around them. Yet, the scattered archival evidence available does not support a characterization of the indígenas as only subjugated victims any more than it supports an interpretation of them as constant resisters. Santiago Silva, Ramón Palau, and their cohort were successful in gaining access to resguardo resources in part because of their relationships with indígenas. Indígenas themselves took part, albeit ambiguously, in their own colonization and the transformation of northern Cauca into a new region.

Historians of indigenous peasants have increasingly concluded that resistance and accommodation are not diametrically opposed. Colonial historian Steve Stern describes the long-range processes whereby indigenous peoples of Latin America resisted the depredations of Spanish colonialism while at the same time adapting to the colonial order, as "resistant adaptation." Historically, people have often participated in their own colonization while at the same time they have limited its detrimental effects. Indigenous peoples adopted colonizing institutions (such as censuses, courts, churches, cabildos, and land reserves) as their own, modified them according to their own needs, and used them to guarantee their collective survival. Such tactics implied internal fissures, reverses, and substantial losses to the communities of Riosucio.[2]

Colonization, resistance, and adaptation were not exclusively about land and mining rights. Also at stake were access to, and control over, religious institutions and local governments. Colonization involved the formation of political networks through which colonizers often gained access to land in exchange for political favors. This chapter, therefore, is not only about struggles over land; it is also about the factionalization and alliance-building that linked indigenous community members with specific patrons and political parties.

This chapter focuses mainly on the indigenous community for which the most documentation is available for the federal period, La Montaña, while also discussing related processes in adjoining parcialidades, especially Supía-Cañamomo. (The rather distinct case of San Lorenzo is discussed in the last chapter of the book.) The chapter reaches back into the colonial and early republican periods to explain the larger history of these indigenous communities. Then it goes on to examine the demographic and cultural conditions of the indigenous communities in the crucial decade of the 1870s, as portrayed in communal censuses. The chapter then traces indígenas' efforts to preserve their resguardos during the 1870s and 1880s, as well as their participation in local politics. The tension between defending their communal interests and participating in larger political communities explains the apparent paradox of simultaneous resistance and collaboration.

BACKGROUND: FROM RIO SUCIO TO RIOSUCIO

As noted in the introduction to this book, twentieth-century town intellectuals elaborated local historical narratives that identified Riosucio district as one unified community. They described the founding of Riosucio town and district as the melding of divided racial groups into an undivided whole. Indígenas, however, remembered the founding of Riosucio differently; for them, the forced unification of Riosucio signaled a loss of communal autonomy.

Prior to the conquest, interrelated confederated groups (remembered as the Pirsas, Sopías, Ansermas, and Escopeteras, to name a few) occupied what are now Riosucio and its neighboring districts, where they mined for salt and gold. With the arrival of Spaniards in the 1540s, the population was decimated. By the seventeenth century, the colonial state had set up villages for surviving indígenas under the tutelage of Spanish priests and trustees (encomenderos) and governed internally by Indian cabildos headed by hereditary caciques. Each Indian village possessed a communal resguardo.[3]

By the late eighteenth century, Indians, especially in La Montaña, were defending their resguardos from encroachment by inhabitants of the Quiebralomo mining settlement, which lacked land for agriculture. Civil and ecclesiastical officials sought to give Quiebralomeños access to res-guardo land. Most of their efforts centered around the temperate and natu-rally irrigated spot known as Río Sucio, which La Montaña claimed as part of its landholding. Repeated efforts were made to force the Indians to share Río Sucio with the Quiebralomeños or to cede it to Quiebralomo altogether. Various administrators tried to relocate La Montaña's main village to Río Sucio and found a town there dominated by Quiebralo-meños. Meanwhile, Quiebralomeños and Indians were setting up houses, pasturing animals, and congregating at Río Sucio with or without official approval.[4]

A compromise of sorts fulfilled the Quiebralomeños' longstanding as-pirations to settle on lands claimed by La Montaña. Sometime during the second decade of the nineteenth century, two separate parishes were erected side-by-side at Río Sucio, the Parish of San Sebastián on the upper, western side, and the Parish of Nuestra Señora de la Candelaria on the lower, eastern side. This forced relocation set the stage for modern con-flicts over control of land, local governments, and churches. During the twentieth century, those townspeople in Riosucio who did not identify with any of the indigenous parcialidades commemorated the unification of Riosucio as a founding moment in their own communal history. The primary community for them, which they still tend to regard with great affection and allegiance, has been Riosucio. For the indígenas of the par-cialidades, however, Riosucio was superimposed upon their own preexist-ing indigenous comunidades. The indígenas had to negotiate two overlap-ping structures of communal governance and affiliation: their indigenous landholding communities and the larger municipal community in which they were also expected to play a role—albeit a subordinate one.[5]

Another factor that affected land tenure was the protective legislation passed by the state of Cauca. Cauca Law 90 of 1859 codified the "small cabildo," headed by an elected governor (who replaced the hereditary ca-cique after independence). Communal officers were to be "named" by their own people for one-year terms. The law defined the cabildo as "eco-nomic"; it was responsible for administering communal lands and fi-nances, maintaining records, hiring legal representatives, and leasing communal lands to outsiders. In addition to administering the commu-nity's lands, the cabildo also retained its colonial function as a regulator and arbitrator of indigenous society. The indigenous governor, and an-other cabildo officer known as the alcalde indígena, could punish minor crimes with up to one day of confinement. The governor and his agents were also expected to enforce civic obligations mandated by the state; they were to ensure that indígenas appeared to perform manual labor and military service when called upon.[6]

Republican laws had replaced the colonial caste label "Indian" with the presumably less pejorative "indigenous." But legislation such as Cauca Law 90 did not explicitly define the meaning of "indigenous," except to note that rights to communal lands were hereditary. The resguardos were reserved for "indígenas or their descendants." Membership in indigenous communities was not determined by visible physical or cultural characteristics but rather by descent from tribute-paying indios of the colonial period. The law was ambiguous about whether these descendants were actually considered indígenas themselves, or merely descendants who inherited certain economic and legal rights but were otherwise indistinct from other Colombians. The fact that the indigenous governors legally retained some portion of the enforcement and social responsibilities of the colonial caciques suggests, however, that the notion of indígena hinged on more than just hereditary land rights. The state classified the indigenous population as a special and disadvantaged group needing particular protections and restrictions in order to guarantee its survival. Their disadvantaged status was reflected in the clause that defined indígenas as "deserving poor" (pobres de solemnidad). As such, they were exempted from paying certain taxes.

Law 90 also made the cabildos responsible for maintaining communal censuses, or padrones, some of which have been preserved in communal, local, and regional archives. Part of an 1871 census from La Montaña, along with 1874 censuses of the neighboring parcialidades of Supía-Cañamomo and San Lorenzo, yield some rough demographic figures and thus provide a partial portrait of indigenous communities at the beginning of the land frenzy of the 1870s.[7]

COMMUNAL SELF-PORTRAITS

Each census was a portrait of a community as the census-takers thought it should be portrayed, so their accuracy is questionable at best. The censuses were taken by local indigenous authorities, constituted in census committees (juntas de empadronamiento). Local government officials, such as the jefe municipal (who in 1874 was none other than Ramón

Palau), also played a part in supervising and legally verifying the census information. So, in addition to reflecting indigenous perspectives of their own communities, the census documents were mediated by non-Indian officials to an extent that is difficult to gauge. The San Lorenzo padrón, for example, bore what appears to be Palau's own flowery signature. Both the Supía-Cañamomo and San Lorenzo censuses include a few extra names at the end, appended by order of Palau. As noted in the previous chapter, the Supía-Cañamomo census was greatly amended later on with the addition of hundreds of additional individuals.

The censuses were supposed to count only members of the indigenous parcialidad descended from tribute-paying indios of the colony. The figures encompassed men, women, and children, some of whom claimed indigenous descent through only one parent. The law mandated that the extent of one's land right was determined by whether a community member was defined as fully or only half indigenous. As reflected by the obvious manipulation of the census rolls in Supía-Cañamomo, the label "indígena" should not be taken at face value. To identify as indigenous in 1874 brought specific material advantages in terms of land rights.[8]

According to these padrones, the membership of La Montaña totaled 1,443 in 1871. San Lorenzo counted 393 in 1874, and Supía-Cañamomo 336 (not counting the people who subsequently petitioned to be added). Of the three documents, only the padrón of La Montaña provided information on age and occupation. Occupations reflected an agricultural society with a gendered division of labor. Out of the first 241 individuals listed, all of the men over the age of fifteen, except for one agricultural "servant"— probably a farmhand, perhaps a relative—were listed as agriculturalists. Two single women in the sample were listed as agriculturalists, and one elderly woman was listed without an occupation. Otherwise, all the women over sixteen were listed as housewives (administradoras de casa). The strictly gendered division of labor, however, whether in Antioqueño settlements or indigenous communities, was perhaps an ideal more than a reality. The census listed only primary occupations. Women's additional work in agriculture, marketing, and placer mining was thus obscured.[9]

Some differences in the makeup of the communities become apparent when we look even more closely at the reported structures of these families. Supía-Cañamomo had a higher percentage of female-headed households (including households headed by widows and single mothers): 30 percent (27 households) compared to 18.5 percent in San Lorenzo. Supía-

Cañamomo also had more mothers who gave birth out of wedlock than did either La Montaña or San Lorenzo. The local leaders who recorded the censuses, as well as the individual heads of household who answered their questions, created these records within a Catholic society, whereby families were ideally supposed to consist of married couples and their progeny. One should not assume that every couple reported as "married" had in fact received the sacraments of the church.[10]

The apparent disparity regarding legitimacy and single motherhood appears related to the starkest difference separating Supía-Cañamomo from San Lorenzo: that of lineage. In the San Lorenzo census of 1874, specifically drawn up for the purpose of allotting land rights, 95.2 percent of the individuals—including adults and children—were listed with two indigenous parents, and were thus entitled to full shares of the resguardo. The Supía-Cañamomo census, which was drawn up for the same purpose, listed only 9.8 percent of the inhabitants as fully indigenous—and this was before Supía-Cañamomo's census rolls were expanded, which undoubtedly diluted the indigenous percentage even further. Of those listed in the Supía-Cañamomo census, 70 percent were admittedly of mixed heritage, and 13.1 percent were described explicitly as non-Indians who were included in the rolls by virtue of marriage. In San Lorenzo, only 4.1 percent were listed as mestizos, and less than 1 percent were non-Indians. By the 1870s, the degree of explicit mestizaje in Supía-Cañamomo already was overwhelming, whereas San Lorenzo still portrayed itself as a pueblo indio. The census for La Montaña did not contain this information, but it was probably somewhere in the middle. La Montaña to this day has maintained a reputation as less mestizo than Supía-Cañamomo but more so than San Lorenzo.[11]

Non-indígenas had settled in the resguardos—especially Supía-Cañamomo, where intermarriage and mestizaje were most common. Antioqueños were also moving into the resguardos, although most of them apparently eschewed intermarriage with indígenas and blacks, at least initially. While Antioqueño settlement in La Montaña had begun over two decades before these censuses were taken, the early settlers there did not marry their indigenous neighbors to the same extent that the local vecinos in the resguardo of Supía-Cañamomo did. The highland Antioqueños remained aloof and continued to identify with their separate regional heritage. The indígenas of La Montaña and especially San Lorenzo tended to identify as indigenous and to marry other indígenas, while most members of Supía-Cañamomo had long since mixed with their neighbors.

Notably (as discussed in chapter 8), the most endogamous and Indian-identified of the three communities, San Lorenzo, experienced the fewest sales of portions of its resguardo and the least encroachment of settlers in the 1870s–1880s, whereas the more exogamous, Supía-Cañamomo, experienced the most.

The combined official population reported for the Riosucio and Supía districts in the 1870–71 national census was 8,689 (5,689 and 3,000, respectively). Only a minority of the population was enrolled in indigenous communities that owned most of the land. Since the colonial era, the non-Indians had sought access to the resguardo lands. Many were residents of the towns, but many were also residing within the resguardos and exploiting plots and mines to which they might have had longstanding customary rights.[12]

In short, both Riosucio and Supía districts encompassed indigenous resguardos and urban centers, as well as populations of rural campesinos of ambiguous racial identity who farmed small plots to which they might have had customary claim. Supía-Cañamomo and La Montaña faced increasing pressure on their resources from landless and land-poor vecinos and migrants, as well as from investors who sought to make profits from mining or speculating in agricultural land and from migrants. The permeability and fluidity of Supía-Cañamomo's racial boundaries, moreover, allowed inhabitants to gain access to its lands through census-roll manipulation and intermarriage, while La Montaña and especially San Lorenzo were largely free of such manipulation and saw much less intermarriage. In all of these communities, indigenous authorities faced the growing pressure on their lands and communal institutions with a combination of resistance and adaptation. They formed alliances with local politicians and participated in struggles over religious institutions and local governments.

LA MONTANA AND THE STRUGGLE FOR RIOSUCIO

In February 1863 Liberal General Tomás Cipriano de Mosquera and his political allies and adversaries assembled in Rionegro, Antioquia, to hash out a new constitution that would embody liberal ideals of laissez-faire economics and federalist politics. During the same month, the parcialidad of La Montaña (referring to itself as the "Parcialidad de Riosucio") headed by its governor, Indalecio Bañol, sent a petition to Mosquera asking him to preserve the protective legislation embodied in Law 90 of October 1859.

The indígenas had heard that "certain señores" of their district were plotting to divide up the indigenous resguardos. They defended the protective legislation passionately, noting that Mosquera himself had signed it into law as the chief executive of Cauca in 1859. Without it, they argued, many indígenas would sell their lands. Outsiders would settle in the resguardo and have a pernicious influence, given that "a bad neighbor is the most notorious Contagion for the ruin and desolation of all the Generations." The result would be poverty for the indígenas, who would be forced to leave and go begging. The letter also insisted that "no one of this parcialidad desires such a partition [repartimiento]. . . . We do not find a just and legal motive that other individuals not being indígenas, lacking any right to make a claim, are the most interested in obtaining the said partition." This sentence was far from gratuitous, given the claims of nineteenth-century politicians that indígenas actually wanted their resguardos to be divided up and privately titled.[13]

The indígenas also petitioned the Bishop of Popayán. In this petition, they recounted the story of their church of Nuestra Señora de la Candelaria, situated on the lower of the two plazas of Riosucio. Their misfortunes began with the death of their "meritorious" priest and protector, Father José Bonifacio Bonafont. The church over which he had presided subsequently fell in a storm. They began to rebuild, with considerable sacrifice in order to meet the costs, but the tiles they had ordered for the roof were faulty, and the civil war of 1860 had disrupted construction. The structure fell apart, and they asked for permission to build another church. In addition to this chronicle of recent woes, moreover, the petitioners recounted their longer-range history. They claimed that an earlier bishop, on a visit in 1846, had designated the lower church of La Candelaria to be the parish church of Riosucio. They also cited the earlier visit of colonial administrator Lesmes de Espinosa y Saravia, who they claimed had ordered "that No indígena, should sell, Rent, or Alienate any part whatsoever of the resguardo, that they all should live united and Separated in Their pueblo with their Church and Priest, Apart from the whites, pardos, and mulattos." They argued that they should not therefore live together with the Quiebralomeños. Rather, the cabildo sought permission to abandon the plaza and to move back up to Pueblo Viejo. Separating from Quiebralomo, they claimed, would guarantee their felicity, as mandated by colonial and republican authorities.[14]

This petition underscores the importance of the church building itself as the central organizing symbol and focal point of a community and of the priest as a communal authority. The symbolic and religious importance of the church was reinforced by its practical importance: administrative divisions equated electoral districts with parish districts; priests were traditionally involved in economic and political affairs that dated to the colonial period; the church was the social and cultural center of the community; and community members worked church lands to supply the church as well as to help meet their own subsistence needs. Questions as to who administrated the parish, what were its boundaries, and who controlled the church building and lands were of paramount importance for local inhabitants. Even after the parish was officially unified, the affiliates of the lower Candelaria church repeatedly faced off against the upper plaza over whether the congregations should be amalgamated or kept separate, which church would predominate, which plaza would host the weekly market, who would be the patron saint, and how funds would be allocated.[15]

These 1863 petitions eloquently defended communal autonomy and land rights. Yet during the 1850s and 1860s, indigenous cabildo members from La Montaña were also making political alliances with Santiago Silva and signing letters that called for the dissolution of the resguardos. Leaders from La Montaña had signed the 1857 vecinos' petition cited in the previous chapter that sought the dissolution of the resguardos, denigrated the indígenas as lazy, and favored bringing in hardworking Antioqueño settlers. Some indígenas also signed an accord in 1858 (subsequently nullified by the Cauca state government) whereby the parcialidad signed over to the non-indigenous residents of Riosucio one-third of their resguardo lands. This paradox reflected a tension between two competing notions of community rather than a contradiction between "resistance" and "accommodation." On the one hand, the indígenas of La Montaña clearly were concerned with preserving their "comunidad indígena," as they had been for over a century. But they were increasingly drawn into another kind of emerging community. Although the indígenas would not have used the word "comunidad"—which referred to a common landholding shared among a group of comuneros—to describe Riosucio, it was beginning to emerge as what we might refer to as an imagined community—a jurisdictionally defined place that provided a common identity and sense of membership that linked otherwise diverse inhabitants. In order to promote their own collective and individual interests, indígenas increasingly had to cast themselves as players in this new political arena.[16]

These tensions are best illustrated by comparing the 1863 petition to the bishop with another petition to the same office, written four years later and signed by the indígenas of La Montaña in collaboration with non-indigenous vecinos who identified with the plaza of La Candelaria. By 1867, disputes over rebuilding the churches had intensified. At issue was the allocation of funds and materials collected by the whole town. Lorenzo Villa, a miner and land buyer, had stepped in and offered to pay part of the cost of rebuilding San Sebastián. According to the Candelaria partisans, Villa and the new curate—Antioqueño priest José Joaquín Hoyos—concentrated all of the parish resources on San Sebastián alone. Hoyos and Villa complained in separate letters to the bishop that the Candelaria people were stealing their materials and violently obstructing the construction of San Sebastián.[17]

The partisans of La Candelaria described themselves in 1867 as "the economic Cabildo of the parcialidad of indígenas of the district and the private vecinos who subscribe affection and are natives of the Plaza of the Candelaria." The plaza and church of Nuestra Señora de la Candelaria were no longer the exclusive province of the indígenas, but now encompassed a sector of townspeople who did not all identify themselves with La Montaña. Unlike in the earlier letter of 1863, moreover, the indígenas did not ask to separate from Riosucio and withdraw to Pueblo Viejo. Rather, they had formed a coalition with allies in the town to ask that materials and funds be divided fairly and that their church, along with that of San Sebastián, be rebuilt. The longstanding rivalry between Quiebralomo and La Montaña was giving way in part to a rivalry expressed in terms of the upper plaza versus the lower plaza; San Sebastián versus the Virgin of the Candelaria. This rivalry was increasingly conceptualized as a fight between two halves of one collectivity, Riosucio, for control over that collectivity.

The petitioners from La Candelaria were very clear, however, that this intracommunity rivalry originated historically in an intercommunity struggle between two rival peoples defined in the colonial legal order as separate castes or races. As in the 1863 petition to the bishop, they cited history. The 1867 petitioners argued that the land was historically theirs in the first place: "Is it not certain that the congregation of San Sebastián today treads on our soil by consent of the indígenas owners of these resguardos?" Even as they became invested in the community of Riosucio, the indígenas were not conceding, at least not in this letter, their longstanding territorial claims. By signing this letter, even the non-Indian residents of La Candelaria were validating these claims.

The fact that the indígenas had not always been so consistent in defending their resguardos appears inexplicable unless we take into consideration that the indígenas of La Montaña were not necessarily concerned exclusively with land. The local context of the 1857 petition that called for the privatization of the resguardos was one of struggle between the towns of Toro, Riosucio, and Supía for predominance and cabecera status within the larger administrative province of Toro. The 1857 petitioners also sought that the circuit court remain in Riosucio, to which it had recently been moved from Supía. The whole document reads as an assertion of civic pride. It portrayed Riosucio as a new, progressive, and vibrant town that would rejuvenate the decaying older mining villages around it.[18]

Historians have presumed that indígenas were easily manipulated as a result of their ignorance and illiteracy. Indígenas themselves repeatedly emphasized their own ignorance. No doubt they were often duped or pressured into signing documents that did not reflect their best interests. And yet, perhaps the indígenas of La Montaña were more astute than one might assume. By signing this letter, they were joining other local notables in making a public statement on behalf of Riosucio. In so doing, they were asserting themselves as Riosucio notables with a stake in the future of the district as a whole. In effect, they were making a bid for power and importance that went beyond the exclusive concerns of preserving the resguardo. Perhaps they were not successful in this early bid for power, which might explain in part why they retreated temporarily to a separatist position in 1863. That was the last documented instance that the indígenas of La Montaña tried to separate from Riosucio.

Another factor that helps explain their inconsistency was internal factionalism. The two apparent factions in La Montaña were seemingly embodied by Indalecio Bañol and Vicente Largo. Their names appear repeatedly in mid-nineteenth-century documents. Indalecio Bañol was governor of La Montaña in 1863 when the indígenas petitioned Mosquera and the bishop for their segregation from Riosucio. Bañol had also been one of the four indígenas who had sought to defend the land from encroachment by Antioqueño settlers in El Oro in 1855. He also signed the 1857 petition discussed above, but Vicente Largo, not Bañol, served as governor at that time. Largo also governed in 1865, when he led the cabildo in signing an agreement with Santiago Silva to overturn Law 90. Largo again led the cabildo in 1867, when the indígenas joined the vecinos of La Candelaria in petitioning the bishop for funds for that church. Indalecio Bañol turned up as governor later, in 1882. He was seeking documents that would prove La Montaña's claims to the area known as "Pirsas" (now Bonafont), which the parcialidad had purchased during the eighteenth century because of overcrowding in the lower areas of the La Montaña resguardo. Most significantly, Indalecio Bañol did not figure as a member of the cabildo under Vicente Largo in any of these documents, nor did Largo show up as a member of Bañol's cabildo. In other words, Indalecio Bañol was the community's leader and designated representative precisely at those moments when the community most explicitly sought to conserve the integrity of its resguardos. He apparently was more opposed to privatization than was Vicente Largo, who forged alliances with political patrons such as Santiago Silva that ultimately facilitated the alienation of resguardo lands. The fact that they did not serve simultaneously on the cabildo reinforces the supposition that Largo and Bañol each led a different tendency within the parcialidad.[19]

Largo's and Bañol's somewhat different life circumstances might help to explain their distinct approaches. Vicente Largo was said to be fifty-four years old in 1871 and he was married to Francisca Gaspar. They lived in a rural section of the resguardo with three grown children. Everyone in the family was listed in the census as an agriculturalist except one daughter who kept house. Indalecio Bañol was more than a decade younger. He married Tomasa Largo (Largo was the most common last name in La Montaña), and they had four children ranging in age from five to thirteen. The family resided in the town of Riosucio itself and seems to have enjoyed a slightly higher socioeconomic status and educational level than that of the more rural Largo–Gaspar family. Bañol was also an agriculturalist, but his wife and daughters were able to withdraw their labor from the field and occupy themselves in domestic tasks, while the oldest son was in school. Perhaps Bañol's relative youthfulness and urbanity facilitated his taking a more independent stance vis-à-vis the local bosses and their clientelist networks.[20]

As noted in the previous chapter, Vicente Largo was one of a few indígenas who benefited from the real estate boom, at least in the short term, by amassing somewhat larger landholdings than those of his neighbors and forming mining partnerships with outsiders. Vicente Largo apparently obtained a sizable amount of land; in 1888 he personally sold fifty-nine hectares of uncultivated terrain to an Antioqueño, Juan María Mejía, for fifty-three pesos and twenty centavos, which was very cheap (the same month, Antioqueño Waldo Hoyos paid Inocencio Arcila ninety-four pesos for eighteen hectares in El Oro). However much Vicente Largo may ultimately have been cheated in such transactions, he seems to have participated in the real estate boom much more actively than did Indalecio Bañol, who did not register personal purchases of resguardo lands.[21]

Vicente Largo and his allies associated with Silva and subsequently with Palau. Members of his faction thus gained access to some of the offerings (if only table scraps) of the real estate feast, as well as some positions of political importance within the larger Riosucio community. Sometime around 1880 another member of that alliance, Nicolás Largo, the former administrator of La Montaña's resguardo, served as alcalde of Riosucio parish district, apparently under the patronage of the then municipal chief of Toro, Ramón Palau. Largo's administration ended in a violent incident, the details of which remain hazy. Apparently, Largo shot at several people in Riosucio and was accused of killing at least one of them, a child. Palau evidently shielded Nicolás Largo from the town's wrath. Palau's collusion with the alcalde, in combination with other factors, apparently provoked an armed uprising, and Palau and Largo were briefly forced to flee.[22]

The causes of the uprising of 1880 remain murky. In addition to Nicolás Largo's excesses, partisan politics and intercommunal rivalries also played a part. Before examining the uprising, however, it is worth considering the partisan political rivalries that divided the northern districts.

INDIGENOUS PARTICIPATION IN PARTISAN POLITICS

Land entrepreneurs such as Santiago Silva and Ramón Palau were also politicians who sought the indígenas' votes. They could not overtly cheat and brutalize their entire constituency; they needed to cultivate supporters within the communities. They needed allies to facilitate their access to resources and provide electoral and military support. In order to gain such support, the politicians had to offer something in return. The indígenas needed patrons, or intermediaries, to facilitate their access to the courts and to the regional authorities. Through the asymmetrical patron–client alliances that resulted, indígenas participated in partisan politics.[23]

In the parcialidad of Supía-Cañamomo, as we have seen above, Ramón Palau and his pro-Mosquera Liberal faction encountered circumstances that facilitated recruitment of clients. The population of Supía-

Cañamomo had long been an amalgam of blacks, indígenas, and people of mixed background. The padrón of 1874 suggested that even most of those who claimed to have inherited land rights to the resguardo claimed to be of only partial indigenous descent. The cabildo of Supía-Cañamomo, suffering poverty, with communal ties weakened by mestizaje and a long history of land loss, was vulnerable to manipulation by Palau and his cohort.

Some Supía-Cañamomo leaders did try to defend the integrity of their resguardos on their own. In June 1871 indigenous governor Julián Batero and his cabildo sent a poignant petition to the municipal chief of Toro. The cabildo claimed to be "representing itself without an Attorney for having no way to Appoint one because this Ancient Pueblo Is very poor." The letter complained that the proliferation of gold-processing plants was depleting the community's natural resources. The English mining company in neighboring Marmato was contaminating their water supply. In some parts of the resguardo, the petition stated, the "poor" indígenas had been deprived of all the land suitable for agriculture. They protested that speculators were staking mining claims within the resguardo and then selling the mines and improvements while letting animals overrun the indígenas' crops.[24]

While the letter attests to these indígenas' efforts to defend their resguardo, it also reflects the limitations of their own self-advocacy. They complained that they lacked access to important legal documents and asked for a copy of their colonial title. They asked for copies of the mining code as well as the laws governing indigenous resguardos, complaining that the district mayor ignored them: "We lack the laws that Guarantee the Economic Governments of the parcialidades of the Parochial Districts. In this Pueblo of Supía, The alcalde acts like he doesn't know anything about the future nor about the past nor the present we have asked in the district for the Laws 90, 67, 22 and the mining Code of the Government of the State and they answered that they did not know anything about them."[25]

This quote indicates one reason why indigenous leaders turned to outsiders of questionable motives to represent them. Petitions written by indigenous leaders who lacked such patronage did not go far. The municipal chief in Toro merely remitted the 1871 Supía-Cañamomo petition to the alcalde of Supía, who filed it away in his archive (where it still sits today). Without an attorney, the indigenous leaders found themselves with little access to legal information and political influence. Little wonder, then, that the cabildo of Supía-Cañamomo, headed by a new governor, signed a contract with Ramón Palau in 1872 to help obtain its land titles. In fact, the 1871 petition suggests that the cabildo already had established, or was seeking to establish, a relationship with Palau. In an accompanying cover letter, the indigenous governor asked the recipient to give his regards to Palau.[26]

In contrast to portrayals of the indígenas as merely ignorant pawns of educated lawyers, the 1871 petition suggests that the indígenas, a very few of whom were literate themselves, took part of the initiative in hiring legal representatives and establishing relationships with political patrons. Like the Antioqueño settlers of Santa Rosa and Pereira, discussed in the previous chapter, the cabildos turned to intermediaries such as Palau when other options were limited. When they retained Palau, the indígenas were already in the process of seeking out their land titles and demanding access to legal information. They placed great importance on colonial-era documents and republican codes that, they believed, would validate their claims. They were well aware of the configuration of political power that blocked their access to such resources. Palau's regional prominence and influence in high circles of Liberal Cauca politics gave him the clout and access that they themselves sorely lacked.[27]

The results of this alliance have been indicated in the previous chapter. Ramón Palau obtained legislation that allowed him to initiate the division of the resguardos to favor him and his cohort. Once they gained influence over the cabildo, lawyers-cum-speculators manipulated the census rolls in order to add more than a hundred people who yielded part of their newly won land rights to the lawyers. In addition, the cabildo also paid the lawyers in land shares, the location of which the recipients were often able to choose. Thus, the cabildo ceded many of the choicest portions of its resguardo. Each newly recognized member gained his or her share in the resguardo through a relationship with a local land entrepreneur, a pact that involved not only transferring material resources but also forging political ties. Moreover, every cabildo member who gained a particularly large share indebted himself and his family to men such as Ramón Palau. Thus, partition went hand-in-hand with partisan political recruitment. The partial privatization of the resguardo of Supía-Cañamomo was accompanied by the "Liberalization" of Supía-Cañamomo and the district of Supía. Supía (which in the 1860s had sought annexation to Conservative Antioquia) became a bulwark for Mosquerista Liberalism during the 1870s and has remained a heavily Liberal district ever since.

In La Montaña, a parallel process took place whereby many, possibly the majority, of the inhabitants were recruited to the Conservative side. In La Montaña, the process of partisan politicization was not as rapid or complete. There, alliances followed a partisan political trajectory characterized by twists and turns. Throughout the nineteenth century, indigenous leaders from La Montaña were found in both camps, and many took up arms and even sacrificed their lives as soldiers in Liberal and Conservative armies during the civil wars. Conservatives such as Silva, his son-in-law Miguel Antonio Palau, and Father Velasco apparently forged ties with some indígenas as early as the 1850s, creating a Conservative base, which they augmented with Conservative settlers from Antioquia. Velasco and Silva also led vecinos of the former parish of Quiebralomo, who dominated Riosucio town and district politics, into the Conservative camp. But a Liberal minority remained active within Riosucio town and district, apparently based (as would remain the case in the twentieth century) in Riosucio's lower half: the lower plaza, La Candelaria, as well as the hamlets and villages that lay just to the east of and below Riosucio town in the resguardo of Supía-Cañamomo. Lurking silently behind the documentary disputes for church funding in 1867 was, possibly, a "hidden transcript" of partisan political division. Perhaps the lower-plaza Liberals kept quiet about their politics so as not to provoke the Conservative bishop of Popayán into ruling on behalf of their adversaries. (They need not have bothered; he ruled in favor of the upper plaza/Quiebralomo faction in any case.)[28]

Despite the continued presence of Conservatives, by the 1870s Liberals controlled most of local politics in the northern districts through their manipulation of local electoral boards and their affiliation with the Liberal politicians who ran the state at the regional level. Ramón Palau headed the clique that increasingly dominated Supía politics by the 1870s. Palau built his electoral base in Supía in order to fight against the Radicals of Toro. The factional division among Liberals was partially related to a geographical conflict between Toro and the northern districts, from which the latter emerged victorious. By 1878, the cabecera shifted permanently to the north. The town of Toro itself was marginalized, while Riosucio, Anserma, and Supía competed to be named cabecera of the administrative entity that was still officially called the Municipalidad of Toro.[29]

In the mid-1870s, meanwhile, a new Liberal faction emerged on the national scene, headed by the *costeño* Rafael Nuñez and known as the *independientes*. The Independents gained the support of many Mosquera Liberals, many Conservatives, and some Radicals as well, leading to Nuñez's presidential victory in 1880 and the period known as the Regeneration. In the 1876–77 civil war the Conservatives in Cauca and elsewhere sought unsuccessfully to exploit the Liberal split between Independents and Radicals. Conservative Antioqueños in league with Conservative Caucanos invaded northern Cauca, reaching as far as the Cauca Valley, where they lost a hard-fought and protracted battle at Los Chancos. The northern districts sent hundreds of men as combatants to Los Chancos, incurring losses on both sides.[30]

How individuals such as Vicente and Nicolás Largo and Indalecio Bañol fit into this picture is not altogether clear. The Largos most likely began as Conservatives in the 1850s, in alliance with Silva and Miguel Antonio Palau. (It is tempting to envision Indalecio Bañol as an idealistic, hothead young Liberal, perhaps a childhood protégé of the republican Father Bonafont, who refused to collaborate with Velasco or any vecinos, but such clear divisions between "accommodationist" and "resistant" Indians, or between ideological liberals and conservatives, have rarely if ever been so clear.) Until 1857 Mosquera and his loyal follower Ramón Palau, brother of Miguel Antonio, were Conservatives as well. Some La Montaña leaders apparently followed Mosquera and company into the Liberal camp during the war of 1860–61; others may have been Liberals all along. La Montaña became known as a Conservative bastion by the early twentieth century.

Indígenas such as the Largos and Bañol were actors in a highly conflictive political arena that involved the popular classes as well as local elites. The decade of the 1870s was one of constant strife in and around Riosucio. As noted in chapter 2, controversies over indigenous lands and resources were heating up at the same time that a conspiracy plot against Palau was reported in 1875. The civil war of 1876–77 involved much of the male population. Moreover, scattered letters from officials and residents of that period complained of growing waves of unspecified violent crimes, roving armed bands, murders, threatened uprisings, and political corruption. In 1878 the treasurer of the municipality of Toro, Vicente de la Cuesta, publicly accused Palau of embezzling municipal funds.[31]

Rural Colombians in some regions experienced much of the late nineteenth century as one long civil war (as they would also experience the late twentieth century, but that is another, and even more tragic, story).

When soldiers returned from battle, local officials of the winning side would collect arms, at least from their enemies. But it was not difficult to conceal a rifle and a few rounds of ammunition in an isolated homestead or a hard-to-reach village, and everyone had machetes. In border areas such as the northern districts, situated on the frontier of hostile states and contested by all of the major political factions, conflict was an ever-present possibility. Rumors of impending invasions and uprisings constantly circulated. The blatant manipulation of municipal elections (and presumably the manipulation of indigenous cabildo elections, especially in Supía-Cañamomo), along with the obvious inequities and schemes involved in the division of the resguardos, all combined to increase the climate of insecurity. According to Marco Palacios, elections throughout Colombia involved mass mobilization and intimidation: "The people voted in groups who arrived at the polls shouting *vivas* and *abajos;* the insult, the threat, and the fight with machetes and knives was part of the routine." The mining and real estate booms, moreover, raised the economic stakes; people were no longer just fighting to gain control over a small local government treasury but also to gain access to mineral wealth and land. The uprising of 1880, whereby the indígenas took up arms and temporarily succeeded in ousting Municipal Chief Ramón Palau, took place against this backdrop of strife.[32]

Throughout western Colombia, tensions ran particularly high following the 1876–77 civil war. In the recent agricultural settlements of southern Antioquia, proud Conservatives chafed with resentment to see their town plazas occupied by Mosquera's "black" legions. In Riosucio, as elsewhere in Cauca, prominent Conservatives had been subject to forced loans and property confiscation during the 1876–77 war. Priests had fled. After the war, the Liberals split. By 1879, Cauca was engulfed in an internal armed conflict as the Independents and Radicals fought for power. Indígenas and other inhabitants of Riosucio and Supía took active part in this conflict and reportedly retained their arms afterwards.[33]

During the strife-torn decades of the 1870s and 1880s, a racialized partisan geography (which remains to some degree in effect today) was emerging in the northern districts. Reflecting trends in other areas of Cauca, the higher, western areas tended to be dominated by Conservatives, and the lower, warmer areas became known as Liberal. The Antioqueño enclaves in the highlands of Anserma, La Montaña, and Guática were heavily Conservative, as was Quiebralomo. Liberals predominated in the lower reaches of the town of Riosucio and in the black and mestizo villages just to the east in the Supía-Cañamomo resguardo, down toward the valley floor of the Supía River, and in the town of Supía. San Lorenzo was contested by various political factions. The Quinchía indígenas, possibly the Guática indígenas, and most but not all of the black descendants of slaves in Marmato and Supía, tended to identify as Liberals. Liberalism and Conservatism were woven into the fabric of local communal identities. Identifying with a place increasingly implied identifying with a specific political party or faction. Nonetheless, flux and contestation were evident. Some indígenas in La Montaña were still Liberals at the end of the 1870s. When the indígenas of La Montaña rose against Ramón Palau in 1880, Palau blamed the uprising on "oligarchs" who had recruited indigenous support.[34]

UPRISING OF 1880

In June 1880 a group of indígenas and vecinos armed with 110 rifles and 29 bayonets took over the town of Riosucio and succeeded in running Palau, then jefe municipal of Toro, out of town. On 31 July, Cipriano Botero, a state government official, arrived in Riosucio to reestablish order. His public report blamed Palau's "abuses" for the uprising, arguing that the rebels were not traitors, but rather true patriots who merely sought a more just administration. He declared that the armed rebels were "only indígenas," and that the uprising had been peaceful, causing neither destruction of property nor bloodshed. Botero concluded that the indígenas had not rebelled against the state but rather had justifiably expelled a corrupt clique of local officials. He even took it upon himself to name a new municipal chief from among the non-Indian leaders of the rebels; he selected Ulpiano Quintero. The state government, however, was dominated by Independents and ultimately chose to accept Palau's version of the events and reinstate him as municipal chief.[35]

Botero claimed that the rebel forces were made up entirely of indígenas and that the rest of the population had not taken part. But Ulpiano Quintero clearly played a leading role, as did several radical Liberal leaders. On 2 July, Quintero, calling himself the "Military and Civil Chief" of the municipality of Toro, had sent a communiqué to the state government, reporting that Palau had been expelled and order restored, and that Quintero and his men awaited orders from the state government. He accused

Palau and his cohort of murder and embezzlement. Quintero also made an eloquent plea for a more honest government: "With great scorn the government has seen this Municipio worthy of a better fate . . . who will give it an honorable and truly patriotic government, who will come to it [not] only to fatten their pocket, who will not scorn the education of the people . . . who will not violate the rights of the people, who will give guarantees to property." Palau had allegedly "taken the property of others" and sheltered Riosucio's murderous mayor along with another official who embezzled municipal funds. In short, Quintero's letter was primarily an indictment of avaricious and corrupt outsiders who had come to the northern districts to enrich themselves at the cost of the native-born residents, both indigenous and otherwise. The letter was signed by a number of men described as his officers, with non-indigenous vecinos identified as filling the higher posts, followed by captains and lieutenants with surnames from La Montaña, and then a list of signatures, mainly of indígenas from La Montaña. His band was patterned after the rebel armies of the large-scale civil wars, headed by a "Military and Civil Chief" followed by ranked officers in descending order. Although indígenas comprised a majority of the rebels, they were assigned subordinate roles.[36]

Upon his return, Palau dismissed the indígenas as mere pawns. He preferred to blame the revolt on Radicals and a Conservative Guatemalan "adventurer," Felipe Morant. Palau claimed that the indígenas were repentant and "very angry at having been tricked." He focused repression on the non-indigenous Radicals and Conservatives he considered to be the ringleaders. Unlike Palau, however, the rebel captains in their own published statement attributed the initiative for the revolt to the indígenas—perhaps in order to de-emphasize their own roles. They claimed to have merely taken part in "the local movement that the indígenas of this district initiated against the Palau dictatorship."[37]

The documents surrounding the 1880 rebellion, taken together, suggest that the revolt was largely the work of a coalition of Radical Liberals and indígenas from La Montaña. The rebels' statements did not mention specifically the issue of dividing the resguardo, but focused instead on questions of political administration and corruption, with only vague references to property rights. This omission, of course, does not preclude the likelihood that the indígenas followed a "hidden script" of their own and were fighting for their communal landholdings. No documents authored by indígenas have surfaced that might explain their own reasons for taking up arms. The documents produced by Palau, Botero, and Quintero each characterized the indígenas' motives in such a way as to serve the author's own interests and glossed over the indígenas' concerns.

CONCLUSIONS

We glean from such "public transcripts of the powerful" that the indígenas of La Montaña had risen up not simply to defend their own indigenous community, but also to defend a new and broader imagined community—the district of Riosucio—from avaricious and violent outsiders, as well as from collaborators within their own community. For indigenous leaders who signed petitions to the civil and ecclesiastical authorities in the 1850s and 1860s, and participated in the 1880 revolt, Riosucio was not simply a mestizo community to which they were adversaries. Rather, it was their community as well, one which they defended with arms.[38]

The 1880 revolt and its denouement, however, also revealed the limitations faced by indígenas who attempted to take an active leadership role in the emerging community of Riosucio. Men like Nicolás Largo, who aspired to high administrative posts, did so only with the patronage of regional politicians, and as such were dismissed as pawns by their patrons' adversaries and may even have been regarded as turncoats within the parcialidad. Those who took up arms, on the other hand, did so within the confines of reigning hierarchies. The indígenas who participated in the so-called "indigenous uprising" were assigned subordinate roles in the insurgent hierarchy. Their lower rank might have protected them from subsequent reprisals, but it also served to nullify whatever initiative they had taken in the revolt, and made it easier for Palau and other politicians to ignore any demands the indígenas might have put forth.

Political parties constituted "imagined communities" of a sort as well. Scholars have noted that nineteenth-century political parties both divided the nation and integrated it, in the sense of tying people together across spatial boundaries. Parties and factions thereof increasingly provided an arena for political action on the part of indígenas, as for other citizens. The 1880 uprising was a partisan affair. In addition to defending their imagined community of Riosucio, the indigenous rebels were defending their political terrain from a Liberal clique based in Supía that was attempting to establish control over Riosucio and the rest of the northern districts. Patron–client relationships with local politicians provided the avenue through which indígenas gained access to such arenas.

Partisan political alliances and parochial communal affiliations took precedence over any notion of solidarity among distinct indigenous communities. The 1880 revolt did not involve great numbers of indígenas from Supía-Cañamomo, the community from which Palau and other local elites extracted the greatest wealth. While the indígenas of La Montaña revolted against Palau, the cabildo of Supía-Cañamomo continued to sign legal retainer agreements with him. Indígenas appeared to align themselves according to local configurations of partisanship and patron–client alliances of power. Although some individuals from San Lorenzo and Supía-Cañamomo may have participated in the uprising, no evidence suggests solidarity among the distinct indigenous communities.

Leading scholars of indigenous ethnicity argue that ethnic identity is a product of political struggle. People gain a sense of themselves as pertaining to a larger "Indian" identity when they engage in political movements that transcend parochial boundaries. In nineteenth-century Riosucio, such transcendent notions of a collective extracommunal Indian ethnicity were not in evidence. To be an indígena in the nineteenth century primarily meant membership through inheritance in a specific community, a definition reinforced by legislation that declared indigenous identity to cease once such communities were dissolved and the (male) members fully incorporated into the national citizenry of independent property owners.[39]

Obviously, cultural practices, language, location, economic class, and phenotype often shaped people's understanding of what it meant to be "Indian" or "indigenous," especially in an endogamous community such as San Lorenzo (see chapter 8). In many areas of nineteenth-century Colombia, indigenous communities did affiliate with larger linguistic/cultural groups (such as the Paeces and the Guambianos in the highlands east of Popayán). Even in Riosucio, some familial ties still linked indígenas of La Montaña with some of their neighboring communities, and some indígenas claimed or obtained land rights in more than one resguardo. But the indigenous communities of the northern districts also had a long history of fighting against each other over communal boundaries and resources. Intercommunal litigation and violence dated back to the colonial era, when colonial authorities structured each Indian pueblo as a separate unit with its own internal governing structure, tribute requirements, and land reserve. As Spanish-speakers, they were no longer linked by language. Not until the advent of national and international indigenous rights movements of the late twentieth century would the indigenous communities of Riosucio identify and ally with each other across communal boundaries. Even then, solidarity would occasionally be undercut by intercommunal rivalries.

The colonization of the indigenous communities of Riosucio took place through the expansion of partisan political networks. Indígenas participated actively in partisan politics, though in subordinate roles. The land petitions, the real estate boom, and the influx of Antioqueños in the northern districts were accompanied and facilitated by partisan politicization. Through patron–client relationships, indigenous communities were increasingly tied into specific political factions and parties. Such relationships resulted in a new political geography whereby towns and villages were identified politically as well as racially.

Until the ethnic rights movement of the late twentieth century, the indígenas of Riosucio and Supía did not describe themselves as part of a larger ethnic community that transcended parochial boundaries. Rather, they participated in regional and national political struggles primarily as residents of specific villages, municipal districts, and through political parties. They took up arms and voted as Liberals or Conservatives to defend their factions rather than an "Indian cause." The indígenas negotiated and fought—through litigation, petitions, and armed rebellion—on behalf of a series of collectivities—their parcialidad, their district, and their partisan political faction—rather than on behalf of any transcendent ethnic identity.

To some degree, these tactics were successful; despite internal divisions, poverty, and loss of lands, as chapter 5 will show, the three indigenous cabildos of Riosucio functioned into the twentieth century and retained part of their resguardos. But during the crucial decades of the 1870s and 1880s, despite the fact that the indígenas were armed with weapons and (in the case of men) with votes, and despite their often eloquent petitions in defense of their historical rights and the integrity of their land grants, they participated ambivalently in the politicized process of colonization, out of which the "white" Coffee Region would soon emerge.

PART 2

THE WHITE REPUBLIC,
1886–1930

CHAPTER FOUR

Regenerating Riosucio:
Regeneration and the Transition
to Conservative Rule

In January 1885 the municipal council in Riosucio, now headed by Miguel
Antonio Palau, echoed the language of politicians in Bogotá when it proclaimed that the nation was undergoing a "fundamental political and social regeneration." A coalition of Conservatives and Independent Liberals
was attempting an "administrative regeneration" to unify and modernize
Colombia. They called themselves the National Party in an attempt to
overcome Liberal–Conservative animosities. La Regeneración, however,
did not succeed in overcoming regional divisions or partisan discord. The
Regeneration marked a transition from the federal era, during which Liberals predominated in government, to an era of centralized Conservative
Party rule that lasted until 1930. The Regeneration and the ensuing Conservative era left Colombia more divided along party, class, regional, and
racial lines than ever before.[1]

Historian Jorge Orlando Melo has referred to the centralized Conservative state created by the Regeneration as "the white Republic" (la República de los blancos) because the Regeneration's ideologues lauded Colombia's Spanish heritage. They sought to foster national unity on the
basis of a shared Spanish culture and Catholicism. Unity, however, did
not imply equality. They tried to create a Catholic nation-state governed
peacefully by an enlightened elite with limited popular participation.
Moreover, I argue in this chapter, the Regeneration reorganized the Colombian polity, legal codes, and administrative geography in such a way as
to institutionalize racial hierarchy.[2]

This chapter examines the Regeneration and the transition to Conservative rule on both a national and local level. Riosucio's experience demonstrates some of the causes of the Regeneration, as well as some of its contradictory effects. The Regeneration had significant appeal in turbulent small towns like Riosucio, where political leaders sought to impose order after decades of political strife and popular mobilization. The case of Riosucio illustrates the tensions embodied in the restructured nation-state, thus indicating some of the reasons that the Regeneration's goals were never fully realized.

"REGENERATION OR CATASTROPHE!"

In 1878 Rafael Nuñez, head of Colombia's Independent Liberal faction, made a speech in which he uttered his famous slogan: "Fundamental administrative regeneration or catastrophe!" Two years later, in 1880, Nuñez won the presidency with Conservative support. Nuñez and his allies used the word "regeneration" to signal an end to elitism and corruption on the part of the Liberal "oligarchy" and an end to regional and partisan hostilities. More than a mere "administrative" reform, they sought for the nation to be reborn.[3]

Conservatives soon gained the upper hand in the Regeneration coalition, especially with the defeat of a Liberal uprising in the Civil War of 1885. Weakened by the defection of many Liberal leaders from the Independent camp, Nuñez depended heavily on Conservative support to quell the rebellion. During the war, Nuñez and his Conservative allies formed the National Party. Nuñez served as Colombia's president in 1880–82 and again in 1884–94. He had gained the support of many Cauca Liberals, such as Ramón Palau in Riosucio, and Conservatives such as Ramón's brother Miguel Antonio. Nuñez, though originally a Liberal, shepherded the changes from federalism to centralism, from Liberal rule to Conservative rule, and toward a greater role for the church in formulating and carrying out state policies. Conservative scholar Miguel Antonio Caro, another architect of the Regeneration, took over the government upon Nuñez's death in 1894. Liberals would not regain the presidency until a Conservative split in 1930.[4]

Once the Radicals were defeated on the battlefield, Nuñez voided the Liberal 1863 Rionegro Constitution and convened a constitutional council. Caro, the Conservative future president, was the principal author of the 1886 Constitution. The Constitution reduced the previous sovereign states to the status of departments, with governors appointed by the president of the Republic. Local executives were in turn appointed by the governors, thus ensuring an executive monopoly by the party in power. The president was given a longer administrative term and greater executive control over Congress, and governors retained veto powers over ordinances passed by elected municipal councils. Moreover, the Constitution reinstated income and property qualifications for male voters, although all adult men were to vote for municipal councils and departmental assemblies.[5]

Some of the most controversial policies of the Regeneration involved state intervention in the economy to protect national industries and to centralize the monetary system. For example, Nuñez replaced the banknotes that circulated separately in various regions of the country with a unified currency, and in 1895 the Caro government imposed an export tax on coffee. Such actions angered regional banking and export sectors, especially in Antioquia.[6]

Regarding the relationship between church and state, historian Miguel Angel Urrego argues that the Regeneration leaders conceived society "as a great space for worship where the virtuous Catholic was to replace the citizen bearer of rights and obligations, and to this end they designed mechanisms that assured the supremacy of the church in society." Unlike the secular Constitution of 1863, which derived its authority from the "people" and from the regional states that represented them, the 1886 Constitution began: "In the name of God, supreme source of all authority." The government went on to sign an accord with the Vatican in 1887 that provided compensation for church properties confiscated in 1861. This agreement also confirmed the church's legal status and its autonomy from civil authority. The church gained control over marriage and civil registries, as well as considerable power over public education.[7]

Catholicism, in schools, public rituals, and lay organizations, was supposed to provide a set of common rituals, a common culture to bind the country together. As had already occurred in Antioquia, Catholic lay organizations expanded, incorporating politically marginal social sectors (for example, workers, women, children) into organized Catholic civil society in subordinate positions. As during the colonial era, the lines between church and state blurred. The Catholic church was entrusted with functions previously reserved for the state as well as expanded social functions. In addition to education and regulating morality, the church was put in charge of Colombia's frontiers, where it received responsibility for "civilizing" Colombia's "savage" Indians.

"CIVILIZING" THE "SAVAGES": LAW 89 AND DECREE 74

The Regeneration signaled a break with liberal ideals of male equality. The 1886 Constitution, in laying out property restrictions for certain elections, reflected the Regenerators' assumption that the right to participate fully in the political life of the nation was contingent upon economic status, and the right to participate fully in the economic life of the nation was contingent on the level of "savagery" versus "civilization." (Both rights were also contingent upon gender, as women could not vote and their rights to enter into contracts or manage their own property were circumscribed.) Savages were presumed to be inferior to civilized Colombians and required special protection as well as monitoring. Savages were thus, in some ways, more like colonial subjects than republican citizens. The Regeneration thus institutionalized a racial hierarchy—coded as a hierarchy of relative civilization—along with class and gender hierarchies. The full political and civil rights and prerogatives of the "white republic" were reserved for a select group of "civilized," economically secure, presumably autonomous male citizens.[8]

The Regeneration's major national legislation regarding the indígenas was Law 89 of 1890, "by which should be governed the savages over the course of their reduction to civilized life," according to which "savagery" was a transitory condition. All indigenous communities were to be "reduced," or absorbed into the national society, economy, and legal system over a fifty-year period. The title and language of the law echoed the colonial-era *reducciones* of Indians. Law 89 divided the indígenas into two main categories: "savages" in need of civilizing and indigenous communities "already reduced to civilized life." According to this law, both groups stood outside the mainstream of Colombian society and were exempted from certain aspects of the legal code as it applied to other Colombians. The law exempted the most savage Indians from Colombian laws, including the penal code, and placed them under the authority and care of missionaries. Such Indians were thought to be nomadic and unproductive; they needed evangelization and protection.[9]

The bulk of the law, however, was more concerned with those highland indígenas who were already "reduced" into sedentary communities. Like the Cauca elite of the 1850s, supporters of the new protective legislation—including several leading Cauca politicians—voiced fears of the social forces that would be unleashed if masses of indígenas were to rapidly lose their lands and swell the ranks of the urban poor. These indígenas were implicitly not fully assimilated, and thus required special protection and regulation. The text of the law was not clear as to what cultural or physical attributes might separate these admittedly more "civilized" communities from the rest of the Colombian population, other than their obvious condition as communal landholders. Law 89 focused mainly on the landholdings, which were to be administered by the indigenous cabildo. The cabildo also had certain authority over the members of the community and was supposed to correct "minor faults against morality" as well as represent the community in court.[10]

For the purpose of transactions involving resguardos, Law 89 explicitly categorized indígenas as under-age minors who were not allowed to enter into binding contracts without authorization from their guardians. In this case, the "guardians" were the courts and the district prosecutors (fiscales). Labeling indígenas as minors exempted them from various provisions of constitutional law. The indígenas' status was thus analogous to that of colonial subjects, and also to that of married women, who were likewise prohibited by law from disposing of their own property without their husbands' or the court's permission. The Regeneration thus deprived indigenous men of full membership in the community of Colombian men and denied the adult personhood of all grown indígenas, male and female.

While partially converting male indígenas into colonial subjects, legal children, or non-men, the law did provide a framework whereby indigenous communities could take action to reclaim whatever lands they could prove had been taken from them through fraudulent or unlawful means, protect their resguardos from further dismemberment, and maintain their own governing institutions. The law ordered cabildos to legalize their land titles and to assemble sworn affidavits in those cases in which colonial documents had been lost. As had been the case previously in Cauca, all indigenous cabildos were to be elected within the community and were to be confirmed by municipal officials. Cabildos were to govern for one-year terms beginning on 1 January, and they were charged with maintaining censuses and fairly allotting farm lands among families and single adults. Indigenous cabildos wielded a limited authority over the moral affairs of their community and could impose brief jail sentences. Individual indígenas were prohibited from selling or renting out their own usufruct plots until the ultimate partition of the resguardos fifty years hence.

Law 89 embodied two potentially contradictory approaches to the indigenous question, identified by Frank Safford as running through Colombian history since the colonial period: integration, on the one hand, or special status and protection, on the other. Like nineteenth-century integrationist legislation in various Colombia states, Law 89 provided for the eventual dissolution of indigenous communal lands and resguardos. Like Cauca's rather exceptional protective legislation of 1859, however, Law 89 of 1890 protected the indigenous resguardos and recognized the indigenous cabildos. Law 89 partly embodied Cauca's tradition of protective legislation and projected this tradition onto the nation as a whole.[11]

The governor of Cauca in 1898 issued Decree 74 to implement Law 89. Decree 74 offered a definition of an indigenous parcialidad per se: "Understood as parcialidad a community of indígenas, linked by ties of beliefs, language, customs, etc. that possesses a more or less extensive portion of land uninterrupted by lands of private property." This definition hinged on communal landholding, but it also mentioned, albeit vaguely, cultural aspects of identity. Notable by its absence, however, was any reference to descent from tributaries as the basis of indigenous identity, as earlier nineteenth-century laws and legal customs had maintained. Even with the new emphasis on culture over descent, however, the communal land was legally the basis of the indigenous community. The decree stated that, following the eventual partition of the indigenous parcialidad after a period of fifty years, "the indígenas of the extinguished parcialidad will pass into the condition of ordinary citizens or proprietors." This clause embodied the Regeneration portrayal of indígenas as not-quite-citizens and the Regenerators' goal of transforming them (or at least the men) into full citizens and independent economic actors.[12]

On an individual basis, the legal definition of a person as indigenous still hinged entirely on his or her membership in the landholding community. Decree 74 elaborated mechanisms whereby an individual indígena could lose his or her legal status by forgoing communal membership. A cabildo was mandated to expel a member who was absent for over three years. Some of the grounds for expulsion clearly discriminated by sex. Thus, a male indígena who married a non-indígena or an indígena from another community would retain his rights and obligations within his native community and his children "would follow the condition of the father." When a woman married outside of the community, however, she would lose her "condition as such"—her legal membership in the indigenous community.[13]

The law thus enforced distinct norms for men and women. It regulated women's marital choices, and by extension their sexuality and reproductive power, to a greater degree than for men. Such blatant discrimination reflected the subordinate legal status of all Colombian women, whereby married men controlled their wives' property. By excluding women who married outside the community, along with their husbands, the law was no doubt intended to prevent communal land rights from falling into the hands of non-members. Some of the more tightly knit indigenous communities, exemplified by San Lorenzo, already enforced female endogamy. Other communities, in Riosucio district and elsewhere, complained to Cauca authorities that they were losing their lands because indigenous women were marrying outsiders. Women's subordinate status within the communities was further reflected in the distribution of land and political power. Cabildos were to distribute plots to families, rather than individual adults, placing control largely in the hands of men. The community was set up legally as an aggregate of nuclear families, each represented in communal affairs by a *padre de familia*.[14]

Decree 74 was largely protective, but it also directed those communities which had not already done so to turn over a portion of their resguardos to local districts for residential settlements. Law 89 and Decree 74 thus ratified the land transfers whereby communities such as Supía-Cañamomo, Quinchía, Guática, and La Montaña had previously been forced to turn over large portions of their resguardos to adjacent towns.

The protective policy toward indígenas, along with church–state relations more generally, distinguished Colombia from most other Latin American countries, where liberals had emerged victorious by the end of the nineteenth century. Much has been written in recent years about state-formation in nineteenth-century Latin America, mostly focusing on the shaping of Latin American liberalism, as if the modern state was an exclusively liberal project. Liberal Latin American governments, which were also predicated on racist assumptions about Indian backwardness, renewed their efforts to dissolve and repress indigenous communities, while the Colombian government chose instead to protect them. The conservative approach begs further study and comparison across national boundaries. In its indigenous, religious, and economic policies, the Regeneration model for achieving national order harkened back to the colonial state. The "white republic" was, however, also influenced by classic economic liberalism and positivism, particularly as regards the need for social peace, foreign investment, and export agriculture in order to achieve economic progress.[15]

CULTIVATING THE REGENERATION: THE COFFEE ECONOMY

In the late nineteenth century, Latin American national economies expanded on the basis of commodity exports. Colombian coffee production integrated campesino cultivators into the international market economy. The expansion of commercial agriculture accelerated the settlement of the interior forested slopes that had divided Colombia's major population centers, thus stimulating the growth of towns, infrastructure, and production for domestic consumption, while decimating much of the remaining forest.[16]

By the 1890s, the proliferation of coffee was transforming Colombia's political and cultural, as well as physical, landscape. Commercial coffee production for export had commenced in Colombia in the 1860s. Coffee became the country's leading agricultural export by the 1870s, at which time production was still centered on estates in the eastern Andes. Entrepreneurs in Medellín and Manizales started investing in coffee production, and by the 1890s the epicenter of coffee production had shifted from the eastern Andes to the north-central and western Andes, the zone of Antioqueño settlement. Coffee expanded on large Antioqueño estates and, increasingly, spread onto the small plots of new settlers and other inhabitants, who interspersed coffee with their food crops. While small farmers carried out much of the production, credit and marketing were controlled by merchants, larger growers, and export houses. By 1896, coffee accounted for around 70 percent of the value of Colombia's total exports. That year, however, global overproduction led prices to decline, leading to an economic crisis. The decline in coffee prices, combined with the coffee export tax, increased discontent among political factions opposed to the Regeneration.

The hierarchical social edifice that the Regeneration tried to build was not as solid as its architects might have hoped. Partisan rivalries, disputes over fiscal policy, economic fluctuations, and regional interests caused cracks in the facade of unity among the national elite. Meanwhile, in districts such as Riosucio, growing Conservative exclusivity only served to further embitter local conflicts. By the turn of the century, such fissures at all levels were threatening the regenerated state's foundations. The Regeneration edifice was shaken to its core by a civil war of unprecedented national scope and violence: the Thousand Days War.

THE THOUSAND DAYS WAR

The civil war of 1899–1902 is etched on collective memories; older people in Riosucio still recount stories of their grandparents' involvement in the war. Thus, like earlier conflicts, the Thousand Days War marked a key moment in the consolidation of partisan identities and hatreds. The war also closed a century characterized by political instability, without heralding lasting peace. On the contrary, the war, which outstripped the previous nineteenth-century civil wars in length, breadth, and loss of human life, marked the opening of a much more violent twentieth century. The conflict began as a classic nineteenth-century war for control over the state, pitting partisan armies against each other on the battlefield; it ended as an irregular guerrilla struggle, more characteristic of the violent conflicts that would plague Colombia in the second half of the twentieth century.

The elite political machinations and divisions that led to the war have been studied and debated in considerable depth elsewhere and thus do not require a detailed description here. By the early 1890s, Liberals were increasingly discontent with their exclusion from power and the authoritarian restrictions, such as press censorship, enacted by the government. Moreover, regional elites in both parties were concerned about losing their autonomy in the face of administrative and fiscal centralization. In the early 1890s Antioquia Conservatives led a faction that broke with the National–Conservative Regeneration. They claimed for themselves the mantle of "true" Conservatism by calling themselves the "Historical Conservatives" (históricos). Some Liberals, especially in the eastern Liberal stronghold of Santander, began calling for war, hoping to take advantage of the split in the Conservative Party and controversies over such policies as the coffee export tax. The "war Liberals" also received encouragement from Liberal administrations in Central America. Liberals in neighboring Venezuela and Ecuador, meanwhile, undertook successful uprisings of their own, which encouraged the war Liberals to act.[17]

With the outbreak of civil war in Colombia, however, the anticipated alliance between Liberals and Históricos never materialized. The country split once again along Liberal/Conservative lines. Confrontations between the partisan armies culminated in the prolonged and bloody battle at Palo Negro in 1900. Liberals, rather than conceding defeat, then carried on guerrilla warfare against the Conservative army. The conflict took on a dynamic of spiraling local vendettas of attack and revenge, sowing bitter seeds that would come to fruition in La Violencia of the 1940s and 1950s. Liberal leaders finally surrendered in 1902. Charles Bergquist suggests that, in addition to fatigue and justified fears of increased U.S. intervention (within a year, Colombia would lose Panamá), elite leaders on both sides decided to negotiate out of their fears of the popular forces that the war had unleashed.[18]

The Conservative regime that resulted from the Regeneration and the Thousand Days War signaled a shift in the regional balance of power within the nation. Ironically, Antioquia Conservatives, who had been among the most reluctant to support the centralized state, would find their Catholic hierarchical model projected upon the nation as a whole. No longer relegated politically to their regional stronghold, and prospering from trade and investments in coffee and bananas, Antioqueño businessmen became national leaders in politics and industry. Economic policies would favor the growth of an industrial sector in Medellín. Politicians in Cauca, on the other hand, had initially supported the Regeneration only to be closed out as the Conservatives consolidated control. The extensive department of Cauca was dismembered piece by piece starting in 1905.[19]

Historians refer to the Conservative era that the Regeneration ushered in as an era of unique social peace, the "New Age of Peace and Coffee." As in Berrío's Antioquia, however, peace was acquired at great cost, in that it was based on a hierarchical vision of society and an expanded, increasingly repressive national security force. At a local level, in Riosucio and towns across the country, the Regeneration had been ushered in by townspeople clamoring for progress, but its authoritarian elements only served in the long run to embitter factional disputes.[20]

REGENERATING RIOSUCIO

For the townspeople and campesinos of Riosucio, the federal era was a period of armed uprisings, constant rounds of corrupt elections spread out throughout the year, and transferals of natural resources from the indigenous communities into private hands. Even many people who had profited from the real estate and mining booms tired of the scandals that they blamed on the politician and speculator Ramón Palau and his circle. His enemies characterized him and his allies as populist demagogues who had mobilized dangerous forces. The editors of *El Iris* demanded an end to "intolerance, the result of the preaching of absolute democracy, causing the masses to go off of their natural track, [which] has launched them on misdirected paths." The newspaper was referring to the Afro-Colombian population of the mining enclave of Marmato district. The editorial went on to complain about murders, robberies, fights, and the lack of safeguards for private property. The poor needed "high ideas of morality based on example." They needed, in other words, to be put back in their place, guided firmly but honestly by an honorable patriarch. The editors also went after the indígenas, whom they characterized as unwilling to till the soil. Hardworking Antioqueño migrants were needed.[21]

One local official reported: "Now all the men who live from the industries to which they are consecrated desire only order so as to continue under its protection, expanding their capital through restorative labor." In this context, "order" implied control. Evidently, the elite realized that its control over indigenous peasants and black mineworkers was tenuous at best. Many local notables considered that the masses had taken a too-active part in civil wars, electoral politics, uprisings, and crime, which Conservatives blamed on "absolute democracy." Little wonder, then, that these local leaders, including initially many Liberals, embraced the Regeneration. In particular, the Regeneration appealed to Conservatives, who had been excluded from local office and whose religious institutions had been attacked. Enthusiasm ran so high that Supía's richest miner, Conservative Bartolomé Chávez, baptized one of his mines in Marmato "La Regeneración."[22]

By the late 1890s, here as elsewhere, the Conservatives took over. One way that regional and local Conservatives in Riosucio, and in Cauca more generally, imposed greater control was through administrative redistricting. The Cauca government grouped municipal districts into provinces, each with its own prefect. The prefects were nominated locally and then officially appointed by the governor of the department. The old entity of Toro, which had once subjected Riosucio district and the other northern districts to the nominal control of the distant Radical Liberal town of Toro, was abolished. (The town of Riosucio had already been the official cabecera since 1882.) The town of Toro and its neighboring villages in the Cauca Valley were separated off into another province. The northern districts officially became the province of Marmato, known colloquially as the province of Riosucio. This province was comprised of the districts of Riosucio, Marmato, Supía, and Anserma.[23]

Regeneration redistricting, moreover, blatantly favored Conservatives over Liberals, and whites over other racial groups. The town of Riosucio was favored to become the provincial seat, not only because of its relative size and temperate climate in comparison with neighboring towns, but also because of its history of Conservative politics. Supía and Marmato were notoriously Liberal. Marmato, in particular, had a reputation for Liberal black rabble. Partisan redistricting thus provided a mechanism for spatially constructing the "white republic." Correspondence from the era suggests that at least some officials intentionally placed "white people" (gente blanca) in positions of authority over indígenas and blacks. National–Conservative leaders in Riosucio set up a new municipal district to the south of Riosucio district, which they named Nazareth. The cabecera, Pueblo Nuevo, was located on a rise along the principal trail running south from Riosucio and was dominated by Antioqueño migrants, explicitly referred to by local officials as "white." The government forcibly grouped the indigenous parcialidades of Guática, Arrayanal, and Quinchía into Nazareth district under the control of Conservative Antioqueño settlers in Pueblo Nuevo, over the protests of the Guática indígenas. The racial overtones of partisan redistricting were also explicit in other areas of Cauca, particularly in the heavily indigenous far south (today the department of Nariño, which borders on Ecuador). There, an education inspector recommended suppressing districts that were indigenous or Liberal and submitting them to Conservative cabeceras populated by "white people." Thus, the new districts "will form respectable entities, capable of taking care of themselves." Respectability and self-sufficiency, for this official, were clearly white prerogatives. Redistricting also reified the discursive highland-over-lowland dichotomy, favoring upland cabeceras such as Riosucio and Pueblo Nuevo.[24]

Bureaucratic reports proliferated as the Regeneration increased the reach of the state into local affairs. Each provincial prefect, along with school inspectors, road-builders, and other officials, sent detailed public reports to the departmental government; these were often published in the official gazette. The reports employed the rhetoric of the Regeneration, which in the words of one report would "establish the practical Republic, promoting everywhere labor and industry, which are the only means by which to make our Patria great, strong, and happy." The prefect in 1892 described the town and district of Riosucio as "progressive" and hardworking, with a healthy climate. He insisted that public order and peace had been restored; the police punished crimes with appropriate severity. He noted that Riosucio's two churches each presided over a plaza with its own public fountain. Griseldino Carvajal, a visiting road engineer who traveled through the province in 1894, noted, however, that only the upper church of San Sebastián had been completed and crowned with a lovely bell tower, while the lower church was still unfinished, thus implying that the upper church was still favored by local officials. Carvajal reported that the town center included many gaily colored, two-story houses with tiled roofs. "Commerce Street" (la calle del comercio) was paved and linked the upper and lower plazas. In short, local officials and inspectors promoted the town's entrepreneurial spirit, piety, and economic progress, characterizing Riosucio as embodying Regeneration ideals.[25]

The officials were centrally concerned with the economy. They listed dozens of working gold mines in Marmato and Quiebralomo, as well as a coal mine and several saltworks. In the 1880s, estate owners in low-lying areas introduced imported breeds of cattle and new pasture grasses to meet rising demands for beef. They bought cattle in Antioquia markets and fattened it to feed the mines. By the 1890s, Antioqueño settlers and their descendants in the western highlands of Riosucio district were becoming Riosucio's premier dairy farmers. Officials still complained, however, that indigenous "monopolies" over land prevented livestock production from expanding.[26]

In addition to cattle, local officials promoted the province's potential for commercial agriculture. Its varied altitudes and climates, they noted, made it suitable for a wide variety of crops. Local cultivators had long grown cacao, beans, maize, plantains, and fruits for consumption and local markets. Inhabitants of the lower slopes and valleys cultivated sugar cane, which they made into brown-sugar loaves and liquor. Coffee, noticeably absent in all earlier reports, made its first local appearance in the 1890s.[27]

The bureaucrats compared the province's great potential with its lamentable poverty. They argued that the indigenous communities stymied prosperity. The resguardos were "a true Great Wall" (una verdadera mu-

ralla china) that enclosed the town centers and "asphyxiated" commerce. Riosucio and the surrounding districts constituted a "vast colonial fiefdom belonging to seven indigenous Parcialidades and three private Communities, that . . . maintain private property in perpetual annihilation." According to these reports, the indígenas and other comuneros refused to allow more productive people (read: Antioqueños) to settle on their lands. Carvajal wrote that "no measure is more fitting than that of increasing the mass of Caucano inhabitants . . . with the hard working Antioqueño element." He argued that the indígenas were sufficiently "civilized" to protect their own rights and dispose of their own lands, and therefore should not be subject to the special privileges and rights afforded by Law 89 of 1890: "Even the dialect has disappeared and now they have more than the necessary malice to be citizens like everyone, who know their duties and know how to defend their rights. . . . They have no traces of their primitive race."[28]

The writers also complained about the "communities of private citizens" (*comunidades de particulares*), apparently referring to the community of Quiebralomo (in Riosucio district) and the small group of descendants of slaves in Guamal (Supía district), as well as a common landholding that was formed in the village of Bonafont (Riosucio district) among campesinos who were no longer inscribed in any official resguardo. Such landholding communities, Prefect Velasco complained, "are groups of worse condition than the Parcialidades, because they have a greater degree of malice."[29]

By emphasizing such "malice," the writers argued that the indígenas and other comuneros were not semi-savage innocents who deserved special protection. As Jeffrey Gould has pointed out for nineteenth-century Nicaragua, Indians as such were denied historical agency. They were either characterized as passive victims, or, whenever they attempted to act in their own defense, their protagonism was cited as proof that they were not authentically indigenous after all; elites considered indigenous communities a "farcical ruse to hold on to territory better suited to elite needs."[30]

Local officials and elites, who otherwise supported many Regeneration initiatives, and who couched their reports in Regeneration rhetoric, strongly objected to Law 89 of 1890 and Decree 74 of 1898. These laws did not accord with their own analyses of local economic and social conditions. Regarding the indígenas of Marmato province, the officials considered only the Chamí Indians of Arrayanal, to the southwest, to be "savage" Indians, in need of special protection and regulation. Riosucio's local indigenous population was seen as sufficiently competent ("malicious") to conform to Colombian law more generally; the indígenas should in all fairness be treated as Colombian citizens, not as children or wards of the state. Thus, the local writers couched their arguments in favor of partitioning indigenous landholdings both as defenses of indígenas' rights and duties as citizens and as critiques of indigenous land monopolies. Prefect Gutiérrez, in particular, portrayed himself as speaking on the indígenas' behalf by arguing that the indígenas really wanted their lands to be divided so as to increase value and encourage industry. These officials lauded the goals of the Regeneration, but they also pinpointed some of its contradictions. The protective impulses of the white republic toward its ostensibly inferior components collided with the economic goals of regenerating commercial production on private property.[31]

The local case of Riosucio also illustrates the extent to which the Regeneration had the unintended effect of embittering partisan political rivalries. During the nineteenth century, Riosuceños had gone to war in the name of political factions and ideologies. Yet, at least until the war of 1876–77, a certain fluidity and mutual tolerance was noticeable in the partisan political identities of individuals and families (such as the various Palau brothers, each affiliated with a different faction), who would follow local and regional caudillos from one camp into another. The increasingly violent and traumatic wars of the last quarter of the nineteenth century, especially the Thousand Days War, served to harden these political identities, as families passed on memories of their enemies' abuses from generation to generation. For example, Liberal politician Jorge Gärtner de la Cuesta later recounted that in 1884 the local parish priest had refused to afford the sacrament of marriage to his parents, Carlos Gärtner and Evangelina de la Cuesta. To marry, they had to secure the intervention of the Papal Nuncio on their behalf. In 1886 this same Conservative priest forced Carlos Gärtner to exhume the remains of his own father and remove them from the Catholic cemetery. The Gärtners subsequently created a cemetery just across the road, on their own property, which they called the "free cemetery." Such bitter disputes over religious practice fueled support for armed rebellion.[32]

Jorge Gärtner de la Cuesta, who was born in 1890, later remembered his early childhood as an era marked by political persecution. His memories were marked indelibly by the harassment of his family. During the Thousand Days War, his father Carlos was imprisoned after having been betrayed to the authorities by one of his own estate workers, a man from the Antioqueño settlement of El Oro. Later, during the upheaval of La Violencia, the Gärtner family, like so many others who owned property in areas controlled by their political rivals, sold their highland estate. Documents cited in the next chapter show that Carlos Gärtner and his brother Jorge were not completely excluded from local office during the late nineteenth and early twentieth centuries; in actuality, they continued to wield considerable authority on a local level. Nonetheless, memories of persecution and resistance were firmly etched in young Jorge Gärtner de la Cuesta's memory. For the Gärtner family, like other prominent and less-prominent dissident families of towns such as Riosucio, the Regeneration was remembered for ushering in a twentieth century initially characterized not by harmony and unity, but rather by repression, violence, and a deeply internalized Liberal identity forged in resistance to a Conservative state.[33]

CONCLUSIONS

The Regeneration emerged in part as a reaction against popular mobilization. It replaced an egalitarian ideal of a Colombian federation composed of equal and autonomous regional states—themselves made up of equal (male) citizens—with a blueprint for a centralized and hierarchically structured state and society. Regeneration efforts to guarantee unity and hierarchy included, among other policies: territorial redistricting, indirect elections, suffrage restrictions, resguardo protection, police codes, expanded Catholic schooling for boys and girls, and consecration of the nation to the Sacred Heart. The Regenerators wanted to situate each and every Colombian in his or her place according to class, familial, political, racial, and gender hierarchies. In the regenerated state and civil society, whites ideally would govern blacks and Indians—as well as govern the racially amorphous urban plebe and rural poor. Men would govern women; fathers would rule over their legitimately constituted and church-sanctioned families. Conservatives would rule over Liberals, the central capital over peripheral regions, white towns over black and Indian villages, respectable civilized people over savages, and the "healthy" highlands over the lowlands. This spatial and political hierarchy was influenced by racial assumptions embedded in the nineteenth-century discourse of regional differentiation.

The Regeneration's hierarchical vision of the Colombian nation did not foresee that prominent Liberal families would open their own cemeteries, consolidate their own political bases, and otherwise continue to resist the impositions of the Conservative state. The attempt at national unification served to aggravate already existing partisan disputes, harden political affiliations into personal identities, and further encourage regionalist chauvinism, particularly on the part of Antioqueños, Costeños, and other regional elites who resented the centralization of the state. The authoritarian and exclusionary tendencies of the "Conservative hegemony" only served to accentuate and solidify oppositions of region and partisan political identity. As the next chapter shows, moreover, Regeneration efforts to protect and control indígenas through special legislation inadvertently heightened their political and legal activism. Riosucio embodied some of the central contradictions of the Regeneration, contradictions that the indigenous population found ways to exploit.

CHAPTER FIVE

Regenerating Conflict:
Riosucio's Indígenas in the
White Republic

In the district of Riosucio, as elsewhere, the Regeneration goals of unity, order, and commercial prosperity were never fully realized. As the previous chapter showed, divisions between Liberals and Conservatives became increasingly bitter and violent at the end of the nineteenth century. The Regeneration's indigenous policy also had some unintended and contradictory consequences. Law 89 of 1890, intended to protect indigenous resguardos for fifty years, did not afford them complete protection during that period, in part because the legislation coincided with a boom in agricultural production for domestic and international markets. The suitability of the intermediate slopes for coffee made Riosucio's indigenous resguardos increasingly attractive to Antioqueño migrants. Legislation provided only partial protection in the face of increased economic pressures. Despite the new restrictions on sales of resguardo lands, colonization continued. The alienation of indigenous resources and the colonization and whitening of Riosucio and surrounding districts continued even during the fifty-year period in which indigenous resources were legally protected.

While the legislation did not in and of itself stop the loss of communal lands, it did however provide a tool that some communities were able to use to protect themselves from complete disintegration. The effects of Law 89 were uneven and depended on the particular array of pressures that each community faced and the actions that each community took. Some communities made use of the law to maintain their landholdings and institutions permanently. Although Law 89 mandated the gradual assimilation of the indígenas and the eventual dissolution of their resguardos, some resguardos were never dissolved. Paradoxically, late-twentieth-century indigenous activists would cite this legislation in their efforts to strengthen distinct identities and to forge movements that united indígenas across communal boundaries on a regional and national level.

THE LIMITS OF LEGAL PROTECTION

In Riosucio, local investors and officials did not succeed in abrogating Law 89 of 1890, but they did find ways to stretch the limits of, and circumvent, the law in their efforts to take advantage of the boom in coffee and the growing domestic demand for agricultural and animal products. The 1890s brought increased land pressures. At the lowest altitudes of Riosucio and surrounding districts, peasant producers and larger plantation owners cultivated sugarcane. New coffee groves graced the intermediate slopes of the western cordillera. Intermediate-level terrain between about 500 and 2,000 meters, where most of the area's indígenas had their subsistence plots and villages, was highly coveted for commercial agrilcurial production. Ranchers at all altitudes planted improved strains of pasture grass to fatten their cattle and meet growing local and regional demand for beef and dairy products. Meanwhile, mining continued. Investors and settlers disputed and parceled up the remaining public lands outside of the resguardos, resulting in the emergence of several new towns south of Riosucio. Settlers and local inhabitants also founded the village of Bonafont in the southeastern corner of Riosucio district. Bonafont had been settled over the previous century by indígenas from the neighboring resguardos of Quinchía and Montaña, who were joined in the early twentieth century by Antioqueños.

Antioqueño migration into the high western tierra fría of the La Montaña resguardo continued, despite legal prohibitions against selling resguardo lands. Indigenous authorities continued to resist and adapt to the ongoing colonization of their territories. For example, they cooperated in the founding of at least one new Antioqueño settlement, known as El Rosario, high in the western cordillera, bordered to the north by the department of Antioquia and to the west by territory claimed and traversed by the Chamí Indians of Arrayanal (now the district of Mistrató). Land entrepreneur Rafael Tascón bought up resguardo shares from individual indígenas in 1898, and in 1899 he petitioned the cabildo to have the far northwestern corner of the resguardo allotted to him. The document that approved Tascón's land allocations referred to Tascón as a "shareholder in the lands of the parcialidad, by purchase that he has made of rights from legally recognized indígenas."[1]

The notarized document by which the cabildo approved Tascón's land allotment stated that Tascón was "promoting the Establishment of the settlement of El Rosario, situated in the portion of terrain that he occupies, with which the value of the terrains of the resguardo in general have increased thus benefiting the interests of the Parcialidad." This land was an area that La Montaña had often disputed with the Chamí. Some Montaña leaders may have felt that the emergence of a "progressive" settlement in this wilderness would help "civilize" their own community and assist them in establishing control over their own frontier. The increasing value of their lands did not, however, benefit the parcialidad in the long run. El Rosario attracted dozens of Antioqueño families, who bought shares from Tascón as well as from individual indígenas. Thus, the land, contrary to the protective clauses of Regeneration legislation, passed into the control of outsiders.[2]

El Rosario initially flourished. By one account, the area had 1,000 inhabitants by 1905 and had attained the status of subdistrict (corregimiento). It was located along a proposed major transportation route between Chocó and Riosucio through Chamí territory. Families came from the neighboring Antioquia town of Jardín, cleared forests, and set cattle to graze on the formerly wooded slopes. Moreover, El Rosario was very much a cultural product of the Catholic Regeneration; it was something of a missionary colony. According to Regional historian Alfredo Cardona Tobón, Father Marco Antonio Tobón arrived there from Antioquia in 1903. Father Tobón founded a vocational boarding school designed, in his own words, "to Christianize the Indians of Chamí." He intended that his school, the Workshops of San José, would "provide civilization to more than 3,000 errant savages." The institution's mission was to instruct "orphaned and abandoned children . . . to form honorable and profoundly Catholic artisans" and to help sustain the church with its profits.[3]

Father Tobón's brief memoir about El Rosario did not mention that in tending to the Chamí "savages" his friends had carved their domain out of lands obtained from the indígenas of La Montaña. Rather, he told a classic tale of frontier settlement, in which pious, hard-working pioneers cleared a "solitary wilderness" in order to erect an orderly plaza and a chapel. The "savage" Chamí, however, did not take kindly to such efforts to "civilize" them; Cardona Tobón tells us that one group actually attacked and terrorized the settlers. Father Tobón's brother Germán, the local police inspector in 1905, reportedly responded violently with a "hard hand." The settlement itself also was plagued by internal conflicts, although whether these squabbles erupted over land, gold, partisan politics (El Rosario attracted both Liberals and Conservatives), or a combination thereof, is not clear. Father Tobón was forced to leave, along with his brother Germán, under a cloud of sexual scandal. El Rosario remained physically isolated from Riosucio, and its population declined. "Legend has it that Father Tobón cursed the pueblo and condemned it to become a weedy swamp. . . . Now there is no trace of the plaza, nor the chapel nor the streets . . . it is a swampy field of stubble."[4]

El Rosario's ephemeral existence illustrates some trends of the period. The settlement epitomized the Catholic utopian aspects of Regeneration discourse. Indianness was equated with "savagery," which could be overcome through a process of evangelization and education. Civil and ecclesiastic authorities sought to incorporate savage Indians into the white republic as humble laborers. El Rosario, moreover, formed part of a larger wave of migration that continued to wash over northern Cauca, incorporating Riosucio ever more into greater Antioquia, facilitated by Cauca intermediaries such as Rafael Tascón and indigenous authorities. In emphasizing the hardy pioneering of Antioqueño settlers, Father Tobón's account was like many nostalgic tales of Antioqueño migration. The fact that Tascón and his neighbors in El Rosario were able to buy resguardo shares, moreover, illustrates that Law 89 was limited in how much protection it afforded the resguardos.

The limits of Law 89 are also evident in auction notices published in Riosucio's local press during the first decades of the twentieth century. In the Riosucio newspaper La Opinión (founded in 1911), at least thirty-eight notices of court-supervised "voluntary sales" (i.e., not the result of a foreclosure or court order) of resguardo shares on the part of indígenas (individuals or families) appeared between 1911 and 1918, mostly referring to the Quinchía resguardo. Clearly, despite legislative initiatives to protect the integrity of indigenous resguardos, a slow leakage—or in some areas a hemorrhage—of indigenous resources continued. And these notices, of course, represented only one specific legal channel for the transfer of resources in addition to other methods that outsiders commonly used to obtain access to indigenous lands, such as intermarriage, rental agreements, squatting, expanding property boundaries, staking mining claims, and letting cattle run loose.[5]

Decayed documents, exhumed in recent years by court employees from a dank and partially flooded back room of Riosucio's Circuit Court, detail the legal proceedings that led to such sales. I encountered documents from thirty-seven cases between 1902 and 1920 in which individuals, married couples, or families sought judicial permission to sell inherited one- and two-line shares in indigenous resguardos. (There undoubtedly were more cases that have since disappeared. The auction notices cited above show that there must have been at least thirty-eight successful petitions for such sales between 1911 and 1918 alone, not counting those that were denied or published elsewhere.) Most of the petitions (thirty-one) corresponded to Quinchía.[6]

The court-approved sales of individual shares constituted one example of how officials mediated the transfer of resources from indigenous communities to other vecinos, and especially to Antioqueño migrants. In most cases, the Circuit Court judge—an office occupied by various local notables, ranging from Liberal Carlos Gärtner to Conservative Guillermo Santacoloma—approved the sales without hesitation. The local municipal official responsible for safeguarding the indígenas' interests under the law usually voiced no objections. Certain local lawyers and paralegal tinterillos specialized in representing the indígenas and brokering such deals. Purchasers were of Antioqueño and local origin.[7]

For these sales to go through, more than just the collusion of non-indigenous officials was needed; cooperation from the indigenous cabildos was essential. In several cases, including petitions for sales that were submitted by people in San Lorenzo, the petition for judicial permission failed precisely because the cabildo filed a brief in which it actively opposed the sale. When a cabildo used the provisions of Law 89 to its advantage and took an active stance against such sales, it could sometimes prevent them. In the 1870s–1880s, San Lorenzo had lost fewer of its lands than the surrounding communities. After 1890, the San Lorenzo cabildo (for reasons explained in chapter 8) proved more aggressive than any of the neighboring resguardos in making use of the new legislation to preserve the integrity of its resguardo lands. In at least two cases, the San Lorenzo cabildo argued that sales of resguardo lands were prohibited under Law 89 and, moreover, that the individual petitioner in question was not a recognized "participant in the resguardo." In one case, the cabildo argued that the petitioner and his wife had been absent for three years and had thus forfeited all rights.[8]

Notwithstanding common assumptions about Indian vulnerability, when indigenous authorities—such as the cabildo of San Lorenzo—assertively sought the enforcement of the protective laws of the Regeneration, they were sometimes able to safeguard their own interests. Despite the assumptions of the more sympathetic officials that the indígenas were too naive to take care of themselves, the archival record suggests that the actions of the indigenous cabildos were decisive in determining the extent to which they conserved their resguardos. What is perhaps even more remarkable than the continued sale of indigenous lands under Law 89 in Quinchía is the fact that the resguardos of La Montaña and San Lorenzo registered few such auction notices between 1900 and 1920.[9]

Clearly, Law 89 of 1890 and Decree 74 of 1898 did not in and of themselves protect the indigenous resguardos. Local officials and institutions, including those charged with protecting the interests of the indígenas, could not always be counted upon to enforce the protective clauses. The Regenerators had passed protective legislation because they assumed the indígenas could not take care of themselves. But the extent to which these laws could actually work to benefit the indígenas ultimately depended on the actions of the indígenas themselves.

The Regeneration—contrary to the stated intentions of its architects, who wished to promote social harmony while fortifying social hierarchy—ushered in a period of intensified indigenous agitation over land. As the next section will show, during the same period that the Quinchía cabildo let its members sell off its resguardo in bits and pieces, other cabildos (and even the Quinchía cabildo itself, in a few instances) were making active efforts to defend their lands and even to regain lands usurped by large private landowners. Such resistance, however, could prove costly.

THE HIGH COSTS OF RESISTANCE

Provincial administrator Francisco Trejos complained in 1906 about the "intense nightmare of the Comunidades and Parcialidades of Indígenas," which "stagnated progress," threatened private property, and, worst of all, flooded his office with litigation. His office, which was the first instance for legal disputes, was overwhelmed with lawsuits on the part of indigenous communities. He accused them of filing frivolous suits, for which he blamed Law 89 of 1890. He also blamed administrators and legal hacks, whom he accused of fomenting conflicts in order that they themselves might speculate on Indian lands.[10]

Unfortunately, the mayors' archives of Riosucio, where these cases would have initially been filed, have largely disintegrated to an unrecognizable state. Fortunately, the archives of the local Circuit Court—the next step up the judicial ladder—still contain cases from the turn of the century, which provide glimpses into some of these disputes. Such documents suggest that Trejos was right when he said that some indigenous and mixed-race communities in and around the district of Riosucio were utilizing the legal tools provided by Law 89 and the Colombian justice system. He was also justified in his complaint that other individuals of questionable motivation were involved. In contrast to his assertions that Indians had free access to the courts, however, the documents show that the costs of litigation to the parcialidades were far from negligible.

Despite the high costs of such disputes, indigenous communities persevered. In doing so, they involved themselves ever more deeply in complex relationships with outsiders and they sacrificed portions of their resguardos. But they managed to preserve their communal institutions and the larger part of their resguardos. Some local indigenous authorities, encouraged by the legislative initiatives and frustrated by the growing influx of Antioqueño migrants as of the 1890s, protested vociferously to regional and national authorities, initiated lawsuits under the provisions of Law 89 and Decree 74, and enlisted more powerful intermediaries to protest and litigate on their behalf. Various suits and related correspondence involving the indígenas of La Montaña during the 1890s, however, illustrate the difficulties they faced when they took an active stand in defense of their territory, and the ambiguity of even their victories.

Justiano Pescador, governor of La Montaña in the 1890s, complained—in a letter drafted by a professional, possibly the parcialidad's legal representative at that time, Miguel Vargas—of the predations of both locals and Antioqueño migrants. He proposed physically fencing or walling off a large part of the resguardo to stop "the great, arbitrary, and notable usurpation that individuals from here and especially various natives of the neighboring Department of Antioquia are effecting in the terrains of our Resguardo, without legitimate property title, taking possession arbitrarily of various portions of it." Such a wall was, of course, unfeasible, as the author was no doubt fully aware, but the image was a powerful one, invoking the specter of hordes of outsiders from which the resguardo had to be protected.[11]

Two years later, Pescador and attorney Miguel Vargas sought judicial permission to sell off a section of the resguardo lands to pay legal fees and related debts. But the local fiscal, the official legally responsible for safeguarding the indigenous communities' interests, objected to the sale. He argued that the debts were the responsibility of individuals who, in representation of the cabildo, had received payment and kept it for themselves or squandered it, and that this amount was enough to pay off the other debts. He expressed concern that the parcialidad was selling off its resources. The fiscal and the judge apparently agreed that the cabildo was being manipulated by lawyers and land speculators, that the indigenous authorities were incompetent, and that the community was being cheated out of its land. After forcing Vargas to submit and amend the paperwork four times, the judge denied permission for the sale.[12]

Fiscales, judges, legal representatives (apoderados), and even indigenous authorities themselves played ambiguous roles, at times defending the integrity of the resguardos, and at other times encouraging or allowing the alienation of indigenous lands. Cabildo member Isaias Largo protested in 1899 that it was useless to "file complaints before the authorities of the place, because all of the cases that have been opened have been relegated to oblivion, doubtlessly because of the negligence of the apoderados, and as all of us Indians are very poor, we cannot attend to the frequent expenditures that they demand."[13]

In one 1905 dispute over land between an Antioqueño and several Montaña indígenas, the Circuit Court in Riosucio actually interpreted Law 89 in such a way as to discount the very indígenas it was intended to protect. The Antioqueño, Luis Ospina, had obtained shares in the community by purchase from indígenas and others. He then claimed that these shares gave him rights to possess lands that an indigenous family, also with the surname Pescador, had been farming. The judge concluded that the Pescador family did not legally own their land, but rather had use of it by virtue of their membership in the community. Therefore, the Pescadores could not fence off the land or otherwise prevent Ospina from evicting them.

This legal argument was overturned by a higher court in Manizales, but local authorities continued to find ways to prevent the Pescadores from retaking possession of the land, for example, by charging them for the improvements that Ospina had made. The paper trail ended without clarifying if the Pescador family ever regained their plot.[14]

This case is illustrative of some of the contradictions embodied in Regeneration policy toward indígenas. On the one hand, the law treated indígenas as "minors of age" and not-quite-citizens, which some local officials interpreted as limiting indígenas' access to the courts. The court in Manizales affirmed that the legislation could provide a tool for indígenas to defend their rights. But this tool had two blades; it cut both for the indigenous communities and against them. The costs of wielding this tool were high; indígenas had to slice away at their property and cede a portion of it in order to maintain the whole. The case of the Pescadores versus Ospina also shows how land sales could serve to intensify internal conflicts within each parcialidad. In selling off some lands to pay for the defense of the whole resguardo, or in allowing individuals to sell their plots, cabildos came into conflict with individual indígenas who had competing claims to those same lands. Finally, this case illustrates the extent to which local elites were able to wield their political and economic power to blunt the sharpness of Law 89. The same individuals who invested in lands and mines also controlled the local courts.

THE CASES OF MAPURA AND EL PENOL

One type of dispute involved private land grants surrounding colonial-era concessions of mineral rights to subsoil resources and saltwater springs. The colonial government had granted rights to several families in saltwater springs located within indigenous resguardos. Each concessionaire also received a "globe" of land surrounding the saltworks, generally delimited in very vague terms that, during the nineteenth century, would become the subject of controversy. One example of such a controversy was a long-running dispute during the 1880s and 1890s between the indígenas of Quinchía and the Soto Fernández family from Cartago regarding lands around the salt spring of Mápura, located within the Quinchía resguardo. The legal dispute centered around differing interpretations of the wording of the original land grant, the extension of which was "a league of land around" (una legua de tierra en contorno), radiating out from the saltworks. The indígenas' lawyer, Carlos Gärtner (who as judge would later rule against the Pescadores in the case cited above) did not dispute the Soto Fernández's claim to own the saltworks, despite its location within the Quinchía resguardo, because he said his clients did not want to impede "progress." He simply claimed that the original globe was to have a diameter of one league, whereas the Soto Fernández family's lawyer, Marco Tulio Palau, interpreted the colonial grant to mean a radius of one league (a diameter of two).[15]

Another long-running dispute over a similar land and mineral concession, and involving some of the same people, was that of El Peñol, a hacienda and saltworks located within the boundaries of the Supía-Cañamomo resguardo. Archival documents from this litigation provide details on a dispute between a local elite family and an indigenous community. It is one of the few cases that also provides us with a partial interior view of political disputes within a local indigenous community. During the course of this litigation, bitter controversies emerged within the parcialidad regarding who had the right to represent the community.

As previous chapters have shown, Supía-Cañamomo was an amorphous entity that ambiguously encompassed hundreds of Indians, mestizos, settlers, and descendants of slaves. The inhabitants were spread out in various hamlets and small farms and they had intermixed and intermarried for generations. More than the inhabitants of La Montaña, San Lorenzo, and the other neighboring indigenous communities, the Supía-Cañamomo residents often seemed to lack a consistent collective identity as indígenas. The sprawling resguardo, which reaches from the lower edge of the town of Riosucio to the Cauca River, did not have a central village or an organizational scheme of halves or quadrants, as did San Lorenzo and La Montaña. It was punctuated with privately held haciendas, mines, settler small holdings, and the autonomous black comunidad of Guamal, which professed no allegiance to the cabildo. According to the disputed 1874 communal census, the vast majority of those who claimed membership in the community either considered themselves or were considered by census takers to be of mixed descent.

Previous chapters showed that this permeable community provided ample opportunities for local politicians, investors, and settlers to gain membership and access to communal resources through various means: intermarriage, manipulating census rolls, buying individual plots, and charging high fees for legal and surveying services. Yet, like their more cohesive and better-organized neighbors, some indigenous leaders of Supía-Cañamomo did take note of Law 89 and attempted to use it to reclaim and redefine their community. Law 89, in this sense, seems to have become a rallying point for communal unity and collective self-definition. As the Peñol case shows, however, achieving any degree of collective unity in defense of the land could prove difficult.

The national government sold the hacienda and saltworks of El Peñol in 1874 to Rudecindo Ospina, a local politician of Antioqueño origin and one of the biggest investors in real estate in the northern districts. Eventually, El Peñol ended up in the possession of Avelina de la Roche. In 1891 she sought to have the exact boundaries of her property legally delineated; she cited incursions by indígenas into the forested reserve that provided fuel for her saltworks. The indígenas, acting through their legal representative Marco Tulio Palau (who had been representing the Soto Fernández family in the similar legal case against the Quinchía indígenas and who now was on the opposite side), formally objected. Indigenous families had planted sugarcane and plantains. Palau said his clients did not dispute the private ownership of the Peñol salt mine itself, even though it formed an integral part of the resguardo, because the indígenas did "not in any manner oppose the development of industry" (an argument similar to that of his opponent in the Mápura case). But his clients objected to de la Roche's attempt to claim more land than the twenty-five hectares included in Ospina's original purchase. Palau presented the colonial documents that the indígenas considered to be their land titles. He called several local notables to testify on the indígenas' behalf, including his own client in the Mápura case, Manuel Fernández de Soto. Several actors from the Mápura dispute reappeared in the Peñol case, but they were playing different roles. Carlos Gärtner, the Indians' lawyer in the Mápura case, represented the landowner. Clearly, the contradictory roles played by the lawyers—as defenders of the Indians or of the private property owners—depended more on their particular alliances with specific comunidades and individuals than on any deep-seated convictions they might have held about preserving indigenous landholdings.[16]

Circuit Court Judge Guillermo Santacoloma ruled against the indígenas of Supía-Cañamomo in August 1893. Palau, in an action approved by indigenous governor Eusebio María Tapasco, accepted the ruling and forwent a judicial appeal. De la Roche proceeded to evict the indígenas who were cultivating the lands in question. The indigenous cabildo's capitulation, however, provoked a split in the parcialidad. On 25 August, a group from the parcialidad, headed by José Tapasco and Pedro S. Cataño, submitted a petition to the court in which they claimed that they represented a new cabildo, elected in February of that year. Palau and the previous governor, they claimed, were not authorized to represent the community or to forfeit the community's right to an appeal. The judge, however, refused to recognize the new cabildo. Palau, for his part, attributed the cabildo's campaign to the machinations of one of his political rivals, Celio Díaz, who had also been active in organizing the comuneros of Quiebralomo to maintain their own lands intact. Palau argued that Díaz was ineffective in trying to build a political base in Quiebralomo and was now trying to control the indigenous community. Indeed, Díaz was involved to some degree. In March 1893 the men listed in the petition, claiming to represent themselves and their wives, had contracted Celio Díaz to pursue their case in the Superior Court.

The dissident cabildo followed up its first angry letter with additional accusations. It accused Palau of selling out the community he claimed to represent. Specifically, it claimed that he had received 200 pesos in gold from Gärtner and de la Roche as a payoff. Gärtner claimed that the payment was simply a settlement to reimburse the community for any legal expenses incurred in the course of the litigation. Nonetheless, the dissident governor, Pedro Cataño, pursued the case to the Superior Tribunal of Cauca, where he demanded that Palau be prosecuted for misrepresenting his clients. The dissidents also complained that the provincial prefect had placed Cataño and his allies in jail for three days, releasing them on bond only under the condition that they not return to the areas in dispute. In another letter, dated 1 October, the indígenas launched accusations against a variety of local officials, including the former indigenous governor, characterizing him as an "instrument" of Tulio Palau, whom they accused of "speculative machinations." They accused the former indigenous governor, Eusebio Tapasco, of selling off portions of their resguardo, portraying him as a pawn of local officials.

In another letter, the dissidents emphasized the unjust actions of local authorities by making brief historical allusions to the Indians' primordial rights: "In other times the Parcialidades were supported and protected, and today they are attacked and despoiled, without attention to reasons, nor to laws, nor to rights, by the force that despoils us of that which we were left by the first champions who discovered and governed our continent for the first time." They sarcastically compared colonial administrators favorably to Republican officials: "And if the Señor Fiscal . . . does not favor us, without a doubt we will be left with nowhere to turn except to the Viceroy so that he might delineate a new resguardo for us in another place, but where will this Viceroy be found?" Thus, these indigenous intellectuals described themselves as an oppressed community. Their ironic reference to the colonial-era viceroy suggests their sense that their rights antedated the republic, and that colonial authorities had provided better protection than those currently in office.[17]

These letters were apparently more than the ranting of a few marginalized and disgruntled activists. The letter of 1 October bore the names of almost two hundred women and men and filled four pages. Most of these people, including all of the women, were signed for by proxy, ostensibly because of their complete illiteracy. If these names actually reflected the support of the individuals named, then the dissident cabildo had succeeded in mounting a collective communal challenge to the clique that collaborated with Palau. In addition, this petition represented one of the first local public documents regarding any sort of legal or political dispute in which women's names appeared. Although incorporated as subordinates within the social and political order of the Regeneration, women—even indigenous women—were increasingly taking explicit part in disputes that affected their communities and their livelihoods during the 1890s.

The Peñol case provides a window into the internal politics of an indigenous community. The view is tantalizing, but the viewer is frustrated because the window remains half shut, and as yet we have no documentation to pry it open much further. To what extent the upstart cabildo was able to consolidate the power it obtained on the basis of communal frustrations remains unclear, and we do not know the extent to which it ultimately allied politically with Celio Díaz, or what kinds of compromises such an alliance entailed. It is not clear if the Peñol case became a catalyst around which the amorphous, heavily mestizo community of Supía-Cañamomo crystallized a clear oppositional identity as an indigenous community.

Disputes over the agricultural lands adjacent to El Peñol would continue for decades and recur in the 1970s. The indígenas would continue to face the problem that the outcome of local court cases was too often determined not by the legal merits of the case but rather by the dynamics of political collusion and rivalries among local officials and landowners. In 1909 two local former Liberal military heroes from the Thousand Days War, Ramón "El Negro" Marín and Emiliano García, wrote to the national Liberal leader Rafael Uribe Uribe regarding the plight of these indígenas whose votes the Liberal party counted upon. Marín and García noted that the Indians had lost land through machinations and illegal sales to local elite families, including the Cocks and Zabalas, as well as the Tascón–de la Roche family discussed above. The letter mentioned lands included in the Peñol court case as well as in other, similar disputes to argue that local officials colluded to deny justice to them: "The Indians of Cañamomo do not have anyone here to whom they can turn: the principal lawyers, who are the Señores Gärtner, are on the side of Señor Zacarías M. Cock; the Municipal and Circuit judges, who are also Gärtner, belong to the family of Doctor Zacarías, and this employee is who should defend the poor indígenas; Dr. Rafael A. Tascón—who was Prefect until just yesterday . . . is the seller of the Saltworks and lands of El Peñol." The writers concluded with a historical reference comparing twentieth-century depredations with the infamous barbarity of the colonial conquest: "Here they stopped hunting Indians only to notify them of the plundering of their properties."[18]

The Peñol case, like the Pescadores case and many others, reveals some of the mechanisms whereby local landowners and miners managed to blunt the impact of national legislation intended to defend the integrity of the indigenous resguardos. Local investors in lands and mines not only controlled the local courts and government, they also monopolized the legal expertise needed to take such cases to higher authorities. Thus, they were able to establish themselves as legal and political intermediaries between the indigenous communities and the regional and national state. They even promoted indigenous lawsuits against their peers. They may have used some of these lawsuits to settle political scores, while at other times they seem to have colluded with their seeming adversaries to make sure that the lawyers on both sides profited, along with the private landowners, at the indígenas' expense. But they had to be careful; if they abused their clients, their support could evaporate and the indígenas could turn to rival intermediaries. This competition for clients and votes gave the indígenas some leverage and room for maneuvering, but not much. The most astute lawyers and politicians made sure that their clients received some benefits and managed to use their apoderado roles as stepping stones to a political career by building electoral bases among their clientele.[19]

CONCLUSIONS

This chapter has considered some of the contradictions that emerged in the implementation of Regeneration-era legislation intended to protect indigenous communities over a fifty-year period while gradually integrating their inhabitants into the market economy and the common citizenry. As the previous chapter showed, Law 89 of 1890 and Decree 74 of 1898 were predicated on the notion that indígenas were helpless and best treated as minors, subjects, or wards of the state, until they—or at least the men among them—could reach maturity through a process of "civilization" and attain the civil and economic prerogatives of adult male citizens. The law assumed that, in the meantime, the indígenas needed the state to intervene on their behalf.

In Riosucio, however, the local representatives of the state—the courts and municipal officers—proved uneven at best in enforcing the protective legislation. The state at a local level was not the best safeguard of the indígenas' interests, for the simple reason that it was controlled by people who felt that the indigenous legislation went directly against their own interests. Local authorities smoothed the contradiction that emerged between the national paternalist impulses, on the one hand, and the agricultural and demographic boom, on the other, by doing what they could, legally and extralegally, to circumvent Law 89.

The extent to which the Regeneration legislation did work to preserve indigenous landholdings and institutions, then, should not be credited to the representatives of the state—not even to those occasional sympathetic officials who voiced dismay at the continued bleeding of the indigenous resguardos. Rather, the extent to which Law 89 could protect the resguardos was determined by the actions of individual indígenas and especially of indigenous cabildos. Those cabildos, such as San Lorenzo, that most actively opposed sales by individual indígenas were better able to preserve the integrity of their resguardos. Nonetheless, such activism had its costs, which was one of the problems with Law 89 and Decree 74. Although these measures allowed them to avoid some minor court costs, cabildos paid legal fees to unscrupulous representatives. Indígenas often engaged in costly litigation just to gain permission to alienate land with which to pay the costs of previous litigation. Individual governors and cabildo members often worked diligently in defense of their resguardos and even assumed some of the costs themselves. But they—like their lawyers—sometimes sought personal material rewards for their labors or mismanaged communal funds, which resulted in even more problems and losses for the parcialidades. (Chapter 8 will show how San Lorenzo was, for a time, able to avoid this costly trap.)

Law 89 was important for indígenas throughout Cauca and the rest of Colombia as well. Between 1910 and 1920 the southwestern corner of Colombia was rocked by an uprising known as La Quintinada, started by a Páez Indian named Manuel Quintín Lame in the highlands of Cauca near Popayán. At the height of his movement, Lame managed to unite several distinct language groups spread across dozens of separate resguardos. Thus, unlike the struggles described above, Lame's movement was characterized by links of intercommunal ethnic solidarity. He rallied followers from several ethnolinguistic groups around a shared set of demands—including compliance with Law 89—and a shared notion of indigenousness that marked them off as a race with their own historical and genealogical origins.[20]

I found no documents from early-twentieth-century Riosucio that suggested any awareness of, much less identification with, the *lamistas* of southern Colombia. Nor did I find any evidence that the indígenas of Riosucio's various parcialidades identified closely with each other across communal resguardo boundaries. Such pan-communal notions of indigenous solidarity would have to wait until the late twentieth century. And yet, Riosucio's more mundane legal struggles did share a common characteristic with the better known, more confrontational Quintinada, as well as with later movements: an emphasis on preserving the integrity of the resguardos and the authority of the cabildos, institutions that were created during the colonial period and reinforced legally by Law 90 of 1859 and Law 89 of 1890. The defense and enforcement of Law 89 came to be of central importance, not only for the legal disputes in Riosucio, but also for much more radical and confrontational indigenous movements such as the Quintinada. Lame was originally aligned with the Conservative Party and his Indian utopia was shaped by the legal context of the Regeneration. Rather than re-create indigenous society from scratch or according to completely alternative models, Lame, like the methodical indigenous cabildos of Riosucio, sought to ensure that the state would live up to what he understood to be its duty: protecting indigenous land rights by enforcing Law 89.

Anthropologist Joanne Rappaport has found that the Cumbal indígenas of southern Colombia have incorporated Law 89 into their oral historical narrative. One informant recounts how Christopher Columbus and the first Spanish conquistadors arrived on the shore and brought three sheets of paper with Law 89 of 1890 inscribed therein. She also found that indígenas commonly conflated Law 89 with the document that they considered their land title. She argues that Law 89 was believed by the Cumbales "to demarcate indigenous autonomy by virtue of its historicity, not its juridical force." Building on research by Myriam Jimeno and Adolfo Triana, Rappaport also suggests that indígenas "fetishized" the law. In other words, they ascribed mystical powers to it and perceived it as guaranteeing and defining far more rights than it actually did. While Law 89 afforded indígenas only transitory rights to occupy their land communally, indígenas interpreted it to guarantee their permanent land rights. The indígenas in and around Riosucio did not seem to fetishize the law in the sense of investing it with greater powers. They basically used Law 89 of 1890 much in the same way that, a generation earlier, they had used the protective Cauca legislation of 1859. Each of these laws provided both legal evidence and historical evidence that, along with the oft-cited 1627 *visita* of colonial official Lesmes de Espinoza y Saravia, justified their permanent land rights.[21]

Even after the legal, fifty-year transition period ended in the 1940s, and despite a series of twentieth-century laws that modified some of its clauses, Law 89 would provide the legal framework for national indigenous policy until the 1991 Constitution replaced Law 89 with permanent guarantees of indigenous communal landholdings and autonomy. Law 89 would also provide a focal point for nationwide indigenous rights movements in the late twentieth century. They would demand, among other things, the continued enforcement of its protective clauses. Several generations of indígenas throughout Colombia would hold their cabildo elections and govern their parcialidades according to the precepts of this law. They would use it, time and time again, to demand that these institutions be respected. As they had since the colonial period, indígenas worked within and defended the very laws and political institutions that the colonial and republican state had created to facilitate colonization.

Law 89 was a product of Regeneration efforts to shelter, control, and gradually integrate vulnerable indigenous "minors" into the life of the nation in a subordinate social position. What the Regenerator patriarchs did not foresee was that these "children" would use this very law to assert themselves ever more forcefully in political and legal arenas. Nor did they foresee that indígenas in southern Cauca, Riosucio, and throughout Colombia would ultimately develop a pan-communal ethnic identity as an indigenous "race" that refused to be "reduced" into subordination and, moreover, often refused to give up its land.

CHAPTER SIX

Riosucio on the Margins
of the
"Model Department"

The Caldense is well aware, without a doubt, of his Antioqueño origin, but, with an almost childlike enthusiasm, he boasts of being a new race and endeavors, in every class of affairs, to eclipse his older brothers.—Walter Röthlisberger, 1929

In Caldas there is no departmental unity because it is chemically impossible.—*La Unión* (Riosucio), 1932

"Hallelujah!" rang out a newspaper headline in the city of Manizales on 15 April 1905. The editors were celebrating the designation of their growing mountaintop city as the capital of the new department of Caldas. Antioqueños had founded Manizales about fifty years earlier in what was then southern Antioquia, along the border with Cauca. Manizales had become an important Conservative military outpost. The founders had prospered from gold mining, commerce, and real estate. Overlooking the slopes of Colombia's central Andes, Manizales was well situated to capitalize on the coffee boom and was beginning to industrialize. The new coffee-growing department of Caldas would be the economic and political centerpiece of the Conservative republic.[1]

The political and commercial leaders of Manizales portrayed themselves as leading examples of the raza antioqueña, which they described as "the most generous, most patriotic, and driven race of our country." Caldas was, in their words, a "homogeneous" department, a true "ethnographic region." They would go on to use such scientific-sounding terms to justify the annexation of additional territory, in particular the booming

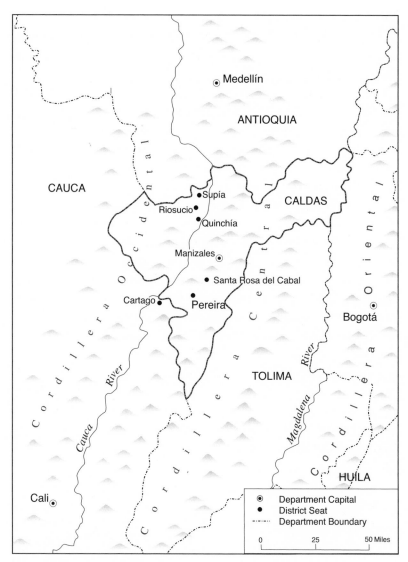

Map 5. Department of Caldas, ca. 1915

Quindío Valley to the south. By emphasizing the racial, cultural, and
economic unity of Caldas, they defined a region that corresponded to their
administrative boundaries and their growing commercial empire. They
drew upon gendered familial metaphors and nostalgic images of Antioqueño regional chauvinism at the same time that they adopted scientific
terminology drawn from the social sciences, medicine, and eugenics.

Their vision of regional homogeneity obscured the social conflict that characterized frontier colonization. Moreover, the Manizaleños' portrayal of Caldas as a homogeneous region pointedly ignored the indigenous and black identities of people in and around the district of Riosucio.[2]

This chapter demonstrates how the turn-of-the-century Manizales elite combined the established Colombian discourse of regional differentiation, replete with family metaphors and assumptions about proper gender and racial hierarchy, with scientific terminology in order to justify their own control over the new administrative entity of Caldas. The chapter traces the creation of Caldas as an administrative department during the first decade of the twentieth century and the simultaneous emergence of Caldas as a cultural, economic, and "racial" region. The chapter concludes with the objections of local leaders in Riosucio, who resented their subordination to Manizales. Riosuceños elaborated an alternative communal identity that challenged the hegemonic pretensions of the Manizaleños. But at the same time that the Riosucio intellectuals challenged the discourse of regional unity, they accepted some of the central precepts of regional discourse, namely the use of scientific-sounding jargon and the equation of "race" with "region." While the Manizaleños celebrated the ascendance of their Antioqueño–Caldense race, moreover, some Riosucio intellectuals began to define themselves as racially distinct. In doing so, these Riosucio townspeople began to embrace, however ambiguously, some aspects of their district's rural indigenous and black heritage that they had previously disparaged.

CREATING A DEPARTMENT TO CONSOLIDATE A NATION

The national government created new departments with the explicit intent of blurring old regional borders in order to unify the nation and strengthen the state. President Rafael Reyes dissolved the National Congress and assumed dictatorial powers in 1905. Reyes's program included reforming the monetary system, building roads and railroads, incorporating Liberals into his cabinet, improving river transport, and breaking up the large regional geographical entities that had long divided the country. Fresh in Colombian memories were the recently ended Thousand Days War and the loss of Panamá; additional secessions seemed possible. That same year, Reyes' new national assembly created two new departments, including Caldas. By dictating new territorial subdivisions and demonstrating the malleability of internal borders, the national state would manifest its overarching sovereignty. A legislative committee report stated that departments did not constitute sovereign territories with fixed boundaries and therefore could be reshaped in order to destroy "the old antagonisms that have long impeded Colombians from looking at each other as true siblings, children of the mother Colombia." The new subdivisions would help to construct the nation as an imagined community, or rather, as it was commonly described, a national family.[3]

The Reyes administration carved Caldas out of territories belonging to Antioquia (including Manizales) and Cauca (including Riosucio and Pereira). In 1907 Caldas also received some territory from the department of Tolima to the southeast, along the Magdalena River. Reyes continued to divide and rearrange the national territory in response to the demands of local political interests. In 1908 a local plebiscite in the Quindío favored annexation to Caldas. Following Reyes's downfall in 1909, many of his smaller new departments were eliminated. But Caldas, which met certain new requirements in terms of population and revenues, survived and even grew. In 1913 a frontier area known as Pueblo Rico, lying to the west of Riosucio, was also annexed to Caldas.[4]

With the aforementioned territorial additions to Caldas, the entrepreneurial elite of Manizales expanded its commercial horizons. Pueblo Rico was still a semi-open frontier, in the sense that it contained much land not titled to private owners. It was inhabited by Chamí indígenas and increasing numbers of new settlers. In obtaining the Quindío, moreover, Caldas got Colombia's premier zone for growing coffee—an internal agricultural frontier that was experiencing a frantic land grab and population boom. The eastern portion of Caldas, acquired from Tolima, provided access to the Magdalena River, Colombia's principal navigable waterway, which fed into the Atlantic.

The creation of Caldas was mainly the result of administrative maneuvering by the national government rather than a response to a groundswell of public opinion. Even so, there were local historical antecedents dating from the nineteenth century. Since the late nineteenth century, Manizales had employed the gendered familial metaphors of the discourse of regional differentiation to fit their own desires for political autonomy. During the late 1880s, several leading citizens of Manizales initiated a press campaign for a new department. Referring to new settlements in the departments of Cauca and Tolima, their newspaper exhorted: "Flesh of their flesh and bone of their bones. How can they deny their origin! . . . Loving Mother, Manizales, open your arms to the Antioqueño families dispersed in other neighboring places where they have gone as emigrants from their own home." Antioqueños, wherever they lived—even those residing outside of Antioquia proper—were biologically linked; Manizales was their "mother."[5]

In August 1904 the municipal council of Manizales passed a resolution in favor of creating the department of Córdoba, named after an Antio-queño independence hero, out of territories segregated from Cauca and Antioquia. Invoking a typical familial metaphor, a newspaper editorial argued that neither Cauca nor Antioquia would object to "the separation of their younger brother." But some Cauca politicians did object to the name Córdoba. The national government chose the name Caldas instead, after José Francisco de Caldas, a Popayán native and martyr to the inde-pendence struggle who was also a pioneering geographer. By whatever name, Manizaleños enthusiastically embraced their new domain. For the civic leaders of Manizales, the inclusion of the Cauca provinces in their new department was a de facto recognition of northern Cauca's integra-tion into *Antioquia la grande*. They, the "pure-breed Antioqueños" (*anti-oqueños de pura cepa*), "the children of the mountain" (*los hijos de la montaña*), had ostensibly built this region and now claimed it as their own.[6]

IMAGINING REGION, RACE, AND FAMILY

In the pages of their local press, Manizaleños heralded the creation of the new department and justified their own preeminence within it by empha-sizing its racial unity and superiority. In imagining their own new re-gional community, they freely conflated nineteenth-century notions of locally and regionally based races with the international scientific dis-course of genetically differentiated continental races. The Manizales writers described the inhabitants of Caldas as a single group unified bio-logically and culturally. They used high-sounding scientific terminology, along with familiar categories of regional and local identity that for their readers would be recognized as experiential truths. They drew on interna-tional scientific racial discourse that reinforced the assumption of white superiority. Thus, they gave their arguments an aura of scientific accuracy and, at the same time, folk authenticity. In addition, when they talked about their "race," they also brought in notions about gender and kinship.

They employed gendered metaphors and archetypes to imagine their region. In the early twentieth century, Caldas came to be known as one of Colombia's whitest departments. At the same time, Caldas promoted an image of itself as modern and efficiently administered, Colombia's so-called "model department."[7]

An observer would later recall Antioqueño migrant workers of the late nineteenth century: "I managed to witness, in my infancy, the opening of the haciendas. It was still the epoch of the migrations of laborers from Abejorral, Sonsón, and Aguadas. All of them white, tall, and strapping. They brought neither disease nor vice of any kind." Caldenses tended to view (and like most Colombians, generally still continue to view) whiteness as attractive and desirable. Whiteness was associated with external beauty and health, as well as with intrinsic qualities such as morality. In this quote, whiteness was intertwined with other positive physical attributes of masculinity, as well as with physical and moral cleanliness.[8]

Historian Aline Helg perceptively locates Colombia "between Argentina and Mexico" in terms of its racial ideology, with the white and the mestizo competing as the national ideal. Caldas is no exception. In addition to the picturesque portrayals of white migrants, some early-twentieth-century texts referred to Quindío migrants as mestizos: "The majority of the new inhabitants that are arriving are young bachelors, robust mestizos. . . . They find pretty girls, blood of their blood and flesh of their flesh, with whom they may unite their fortunes from an early age, as is the use and custom of the race." Such descriptions suggest that the settlers may have been seen as white, mestizo, or whitish mestizos in appearance—as long as they were neither Indian nor black. Their intrinsic and overriding "racial" identity was Antioqueño. As Antioqueños, rather than as whites or mestizos per se, they ostensibly shared the same fair "flesh" and the same "blood" and "customs."[9]

These passages linked gendered traits with regional race. Female and male members of the favored race exhibited certain attributes and behaviors considered to be positive and appropriate to their respective sexes. The men were "strapping," "robust," and without vice; the "girls" were "pretty." They married at an early age. In other words, the young migrants were appropriately gendered, fertile, and prone to reproduce. Thus, they were well-suited to domesticating and populating a wild and virgin frontier. According to a newspaper editorial, the famous "fecundity of our women" would fill the remaining "empty" spaces of Caldas.[10]

Early-twentieth-century Manizaleños faced the challenge of consolidating and justifying their control over conflictive agricultural frontier zones, in which families and groups of migrants were clearing the mountain slopes. Much of the land upon which migrants squatted was claimed by distant landowners, sparking long-running and frequently violent legal disputes. Even when they owned their land outright, smaller farmers could lose their properties to the local merchants who supplied credit and purchased their crops. Settlers and investors battled with indigenous communities and with each other for access to land. Compounding these agrarian struggles, moreover, were partisan and ethnic conflicts, as well as rivalries between neighboring districts.[11]

Carved out of territory obtained from three longstanding regional powers, Caldas sprawled over two major mountain ranges and various river valleys, linked together only by treacherous paths and a few telegraph lines. Yet the Manizales elite argued that the creation of their department, while appearing to run counter to the natural dictates of geology, made sense scientifically from an "ethnographic" perspective:

> The ethnographic region is not the same as the hydrographic region. If the Antioqueños . . . have colonized vast regions in other Departments of Colombia, they have lost neither their character nor their customs nor the mode of being of their race, and wherever they establish themselves they remain as Antioqueño as in Medellín or Manizales; it seems that what they have done as they have spread to other areas is not to stop being Antioqueños but, on the contrary, to enlarge Antioquia, dilate its limits, expand its territory, and exalt its name.[12]

This passage combined an ostensibly scientific analysis of the bonds tying society together with a regional Antioqueño discourse analogous to North American "manifest destiny." Antioqueño identity not only denoted place of birth, but was becoming a more fluid and portable ethnic identity, defined, in part, by "customs," "character," and "mode of being." Notable also were the two uses of the word "region." On the one hand, "region" referred to a cultural entity; on the other, it meant a physical entity defined by geological phenomena.

Newspaper writers in Manizales went on to use a similar mix of social scientific terminology and regional and national sentiment in their bid to obtain the Quindío Valley for Caldas:

> If politically this region has not belonged to Antioquia because it has been subject to the Cauca authorities . . . ethnographically it be-

longs to us with the most saintly of rights, which is that of race, and with the most respected in every civilized nation, which is that of property. . . . It is natural and just that peoples desire to be ruled and governed by peoples of their same blood, who have their same customs . . . rather than by men of other origin.[13]

They thus conflated notions we might think of as referring to culture—"ethnography" and customs—with the biological notion of "blood." "Race," meanwhile, was so primordial as to constitute the most "saintly of rights." Likewise, the writer brought up the notion of private property as the basis of civilized nations. The same editorial continued: "Manizales is the obligatory center of all commercial transactions in the whole region . . . and even far beyond the limits of this department, almost all the landowners of the great estates in the region of Quindío are Manizaleño and have their businesses concentrated in this plaza." The word "region," as used here, thus had economic implications. The writer referred to the Quindío itself as a region, but he also referred to the "whole region" over which his cohort, the commercial elite of Manizales, held sway. The Manizaleños' property interests in the Quindío, in addition to their racial "rights," justified the annexation of the Quindío to their domain. The leaders of Manizales were explicit in linking their own economic interests and political aspirations with their discursive construction of race and region.[14]

Writers also used familial metaphors to help make sense of a Caldense regional identity that was both separate from, and related to, the older departments from which it sprang. In 1905 Manizaleños needed to define a separate regional identity to coincide with their new administrative borders. At the same time, it was in their interests to emphasize the Antioquia origins of the new entity and thus to assure their own dominance over, and right to, the territories carved out of Cauca. They asserted their own autonomy, without severing their Antioquia ties altogether, by using family images. Caldas writers tended to refer to their new department as either the younger sibling or the progeny of Cauca and Antioquia. By describing Cauca and Antioquia as parents or older siblings from whom a child naturally would have to separate, they emphasized that these old behemoths, particularly Cauca, now had no hold on them. They naturalized the creation of their administrative department by equating it with biological processes of parturition and maturation. They fashioned their familial metaphors in such a way to foster a continued allegiance to

Figure 6. Sofronio López G. of Supía. He is carrying a leather carriel shoulder bag and wearing a sombrero aguadeño and canvas alpargatas. Studio portrait, Medellín, 1913. Photographer: Benjamín de la Calle. Courtesy of the Centro de Memoria Visual, Fundación Antioqueña de Estudios Sociales, Medellín, and the Biblioteca Pública Piloto, Medellín.

Antioquia, often referring to themselves as *hijos de la Montaña* (which could either imply that they had a sibling relationship with their fellow Antioqueño *hijos*, or that the Caldenses were the progeny of mother Antioquia, also known colloquially as La Montaña). By metaphorically creating a genealogical and filial relationship with their "mother" Antioquia, while distancing themselves from Cauca, such writers associated

Figure 7. *Horizontes,* by Francisco Antonio Cano, 1913. Bolsa de Valores, Medellín.

themselves with what they viewed as Antioquia's positive attributes: its perceived whiteness, ordered families, modernity, prosperity, Conservative politics, and devout Catholicism. They distanced themselves from the legacy of Cauca, which they associated with blacks, Indians, disordered families, and Liberalism.[15]

Along with gendered metaphors, Caldas intellectuals used gendered archetypes metonymically to describe the content of their culture. Such archetypes, which consisted of idealized and standardized versions of common figures in popular culture, such as the mule-driver/merchant (arriero) and the farmer-settler (colono), were reproduced and idealized in popular periodicals, published fiction, editorials, photographs, and paintings. One recurring image was that of the wandering male *paisa* (he could be a colono, arriero, or mazamorrero) who plied the region with his familiar accouterments, including canvas *alpargata* sandals (or bare feet), a straw hat made in the Antioqueño–Caldense town of Aguadas, a *carriel* bag (see figure 6), and a light cotton *ponchito* folded over one shoulder. This male archetype (later made famous in the advertising campaigns of the Colombian Coffee Growers Federation) was generally portrayed as the principal protagonist of the epic Antioqueño colonization and the coffee boom.

Regionalist discourse cast the male-headed settler family as the fundamental unit of regional society. The idealized migrant family was epitomized in a well-known painting by Antioquia artist Francisco Antonio Cano entitled *Horizontes* (1913; see figure 7). The painting portrayed a young, fair-skinned colono family sitting on a bluff, surrounded by gently sloping mountains. As one commentator rather nostalgically observed: "The capital that they invested in the adventure is inventoried in the painting *Horizontes* by Cano: an axe, a bundle with seeds and other tools, the wife, and the progeny; confidence in God, confidence in himself, and confidence in the wife." In the painting, the young couple and child are likened to the Holy Family, with the woman dressed in blue and white like the Virgin Mary, with a baby on her lap. The man sports a mustache, a common marker of white paisa masculinity even today, and a straw hat. He is located at the very center of the painting, reflecting his centrality as the male protagonist of the epic narrative of colonization. The gazes of the wife and even of the child are guided by his outstretched arm; they follow his finger (which evokes Michelangelo's *Creation of Adam* in the Sistine Chapel) pointing toward a distant horizon. A traveling bundle lies behind them. They are clearly in the process of staking out a piece of this local version of paradise in which to establish a home and farm. They are poor, yet—in Antioqueño slang—*echados pa' adelante* (forward-moving, upwardly mobile). The landscape is wide open, majestic, and full of promise.[16]

The salience of images of the rustic-but-respectable pioneer family reflected the growing importance of small- and medium-scale agriculture, in which the farm family was the principal unit of production and consumption. Much has been written about the peasant family unit in coffee and other agricultural production. The small holdings and tenancies were highly efficient in terms of cost and productivity precisely because the labor of women and children was unpaid, and because many of these workers' basic wants, including healthcare and education, went unmet. Heads of household, usually male, organized the lives, reproductive potential, and labor power of their dependents in order to maximize their productive capabilities and minimize consumption. As agricultural frontiers were occupied throughout Caldas, family-based farming units proliferated. In addition to producing food crops for familial consumption and local and regional markets, these small farmers and tenants became Colombia's most important export producers. The coffee they grew, interspersed with plantains and beans, linked them and their nation to the capitalist world economy.[17]

Coffee was the economic and symbolic nexus around which Caldas as a region emerged and was consolidated. At the same time that they were writing newspaper editorials about their "ethnographic" region, Manizales entrepreneurs were also tying Caldas together economically, with Manizales at its hub. They built an infrastructure organized increasingly around the cultivation, transport, marketing, processing, and export of coffee. Coffee, as both symbol and commodity, defined Caldas's regional image at home and abroad. Even today, long after Caldas splintered into smaller administrative entities, the entire area is still referred to as the Coffee Region.[18]

In the early twentieth century, Caldas became Colombia's principal coffee producer. According to a story repeated throughout the coffee zone, village priests, who themselves often invested personally in land and commerce, would instruct their parishioners in the confession booth to plant a specific number of coffee trees as penance for their sins. Given that coffee trees take several years to mature and begin to produce, the initial labor may well have seemed like penance to rural parishioners, who would later find that their sins had monetary reward.[19]

One of the first priorities of the new departmental government was to build a transportation infrastructure. The transportation system was still inadequate for exporting coffee, much less for sustained capitalist development; the mountain trails were barely suitable even for pack animals. The entrepreneurs and politicians of Manizales tried to develop transportation links that would facilitate trade while sustaining Manizales's preeminence as a regional hub. Their most audacious project was an aerial cargo cable way, completed in 1922 by a British company. The cable extended seventy-two kilometers, from Manizales to Mariquita, near the navigable Magdalena River. The regional economy was thus configured in such a way as to favor Manizales and the core coffee-producing districts, much to the irritation of inhabitants of mining districts. Mining elites in towns such as Riosucio considered their economic interests threatened by regional centralization. Moreover, serious disruptions in the local mining economy of the Riosucio–Supía–Marmato area coincided with the creation of the department of Caldas and served to fuel separatist sentiments in Riosucio.[20]

In the new department of Caldas, mining was second to commercial agriculture in economic importance. Mining of gold and other minerals was centered principally in areas previously belonging to Cauca, particularly in Riosucio and the neighboring districts of Marmato, Supía, and, to a lesser extent, Anserma. Manizaleños invested in mining, but their priorities were agricultural. Whereas coffee was associated with settled, well-ordered, yeoman agricultural families, mining was generally associated with communities descended from slaves. A town such as Marmato, perched precariously on a hollowed-out mountain—and socially, culturally, and economically organized around mining—was increasingly seen as a marginal anomaly. Marmato was made all the more alien in the eyes of Antioqueños by its largely black population and its disordered appearance. Unlike an Antioqueño farming settlement, it had no central square and was not laid out on a clear grid.[21]

Manizales-based entrepreneurs generally did not have great personal stakes in the mining industry of Marmato province. An important part of the mining sector, namely the principal mines and refineries of Marmato mountain, were in the hands of foreign companies. The gold produced in the Marmato–Supía–Riosucio zone tended to move directly out of Caldas through Medellín rather than through Manizales. Virtually at the same time that the department of Caldas was founded, moreover, the Marmato mining center became embroiled in a fierce international legal dispute that would drag on through the 1930s and contribute to its decline.[22]

During the 1890s, an Antioquia firm known as the Ospina Brothers (the children of former president Mariano Ospina Rodríguez) invested in Marmato mines and refineries and disputed the claims of a British company, the Western Andes Mining Company, to several important mines on and near Marmato Mountain. In 1905, in the months following the founding of the department of Caldas, the Reyes government abrogated all agreements with the Western Andes Mining Company and declared that several key mines, including most of Marmato Mountain, belonged to the nation. Troops evicted the English company representatives as well as miners, shopkeepers, and residents of Marmato. Violence and disputes over boundaries and sales of contraband continued for several years. A local Liberal war hero, General Ramón ("El Negro") Marín, protested vigorously to national officials on the part of poor black Marmato residents. Among the angry voices of protest and dissent were those of investors from Riosucio and Supía who were infuriated by the sudden loss of their mines and businesses. The Riosucio newspaper, *La Opinión,* complained of mistreatment of "honorable" citizens. The fact that the departmental government in Manizales officially backed up the decisions of the national administration only served to intensify local resentment.[23]

Over the course of the twentieth century, memories of these events would linger. New British investors would partially modernize the mines and refineries of Marmato, and gold exports from Caldas increased after 1909. But the Caldas mining industry never really took off and production began to decline in the late 1920s. Marmato mountain, in particular, was crippled by continued legal disputes that culminated in a protracted and total work stoppage (from 1926 to 1931). By 1940, the state had assumed control of the Marmato mines. Moreover, changes in the international gold market and the discoveries of much larger gold mines in other parts of the world hurt older, less productive mines. During the 1940s, Quiebralomo's mines closed down.[24]

Thus, the Reyes era bequeathed a different legacy to Riosucio than to Manizales. For Manizales, 1905 was the beginning of what one intellectual would refer to as the "half century of gold." He was referring to a "golden era" of coffee, of course, not to gold mining. Manizaleños celebrated the founding of *Caldas cafetero* as the vindication of their destiny to lead Colombia's newest, most progressive region. The businessmen of Manizales looked forward to a rosy economic future based on their dominance over the cultivation and trade of Colombia's leading export commodity, along with other cash crops and livestock, in a new and modern era of export-oriented commercial agriculture. They constituted a dominant regional class in which few surnames from the Riosucio–Supía area would be represented.[25]

For many Riosucio townspeople, on the other hand, 1905–1906 signaled a traumatic rupture, a humiliating subordination to Manizales and the beginning of their long decline. The future looked uncertain at best. Riosuceños would invest in coffee but, unlike elites in the booming cities of Armenia and Pereira, they never fully competed with Manizales. They did not have the wherewithal to modernize their mining operations, industrialize their local economy, or set up coffee-processing plants. They had not overcome indigenous resistance to the privatization of the resguardos; the indígenas still claimed much of the district's agricultural land. The mining entrepreneurs now had to contend with what they considered unfavorable national and departmental mining policies and the arrogance of the new *capitalinos* in Manizales. They faced litigation and resistance to privatization on the part of the indigenous cabildos. Thus, it is not surprising that while the Manizaleños wrote glowingly about the future, some Riosuceños began to write nostalgically about their own past, and in so doing differentiated themselves from the new regional elite and its discourse of regional unity.[26]

IMAGINING RIOSUCIO

The creation of Caldas sparked local debates over Riosucio's racial and regional identity. Some Riosuceños expressed opposition to the new department, while others felt compelled to declare their loyalty to Caldas in the official press. Such differences of opinion were related in part to political factionalism within the dominant Conservative Party. Thus, for example, Riosuceño Francisco J. Bueno, in a pro-Caldas letter to the national government in 1905, dismissed the simmering anti-departmental sentiment in his town as the mutterings of discontented Históricos, a reference to the faction of Conservatives who had opposed the Regeneration and who later joined the Republican Union Party led by Carlos E. Restrepo.[27]

In Riosucio, various local newspapers came and went during this period, each reflecting the views of a different political faction. One of the more durable local papers was *La Opinión* (1911–18), published in support of Restrepo and his Republican Union, which had split off from the Conservatives. When Restrepo became president in 1910, his cabinet included a wealthy local mining investor and Liberal, Tomás Eastman, of Supía. Like Restrepo, *La Opinión* criticized the Reyes' dictatorship. *La Opinión*, moreover, became the principal forum in Riosucio for separatist, anti-Caldas sentiment. Meanwhile, *La Opinión*'s local rivals, *El Conservador* and *El Deber*, published by mainstream Conservatives, generally supported Caldas. Separatist sentiment was not, however, merely an echo of national partisan political quarrels. It outlasted both the Republican Party and *La Opinión*, and was taken up by new writers and politicians during the 1920s and beyond.[28]

While expressing their opposition to the department of Caldas, the contributors to *La Opinión* and other like-minded intellectuals shared with their counterparts in Manizales a common understanding of natural order. They all portrayed society as a natural organism, bound by what they referred to as common "ethnographic" customs. The existence of regions as predetermined entities was thus naturalized and reified. Regions were racially and culturally "homogeneous." Only by respecting the natural boundaries of regions could a harmonious relationship between society and government exist.

This discourse set the terms and limits of the debate. Fighting upon the same discursive field, two clearly differentiated opposing camps emerged. Proponents of Caldas unity, including the Manizales elite as well as some provincial intellectuals from Riosucio and elsewhere, argued that the "ethnographic" conditions for such harmony did obtain in all of Caldas. They argued that the entire department was settled by a single race and thus constituted an organic region. The Riosucio opposition, however, argued that such conditions did not obtain, that in fact Caldas was not homogeneous but rather racially and culturally heterogeneous. Therefore, the creation of a unified department was not justified. In other words: the dissident Riosuceños argued that Caldas was not really a region.

In 1905–1907, the departmental official register in Manizales published letters by residents and local officials of Riosucio in which they defended their loyalty to the departmental government and distanced themselves from various separatist petitions that were circulating. Municipal officials felt pressure to confirm publicly their support of the new territorial division, inasmuch as General Reyes reportedly had threatened to imprison officials who did not comply. Riosucio's parish priest and other men from Riosucio and Anserma wrote public letters to the president, using familiar terminology to state that "economically, ethnographically, and topographically, this region has had and has a life independent of Cauca, and only politically has been part of it."[29]

La Opinión, on the other hand, cited the "traditions, features, etc." of the towns in the province of Marmato to argue that most inhabitants favored separation from Caldas and reintegration into "glorious Cauca." The provinces that had belonged to Cauca, they argued, were different from Manizales, "as the former are fully Caucano, and the latter is constituted by Antioqueño immigrants." The Antioqueños, the editorial continued, had taken advantage of Cauca laws hospitable to immigration and settlement by outsiders. On the pages of *La Opinión* and in their own correspondence, Riosuceños extolled an earlier Cauca past, upon which they based a distinct identity. They were not Antioqueño–Caldenses, they argued. They were a different race.[30]

In 1909 Riosucio journalist and self-styled socialist Eliseo Vinasco wrote to his *compadre*, Carlos E. Restrepo, that the unity of the department of Caldas was endangered by local resentments of the arrogance and fiscal centralism of Manizales. Vinasco described "customs" and "castes" as the determining factors of government stability and social harmony. He also used a medical metaphor:

> The Dept. of Manizales [is] composed of heterogeneous elements, in itself the germ of its dissolution, or at least the *bacillus* that has to infect and destroy its organism. Every caste has its uses, customs, traditions, and even its virtues which to it are particular, and therefore its ordinances . . . so that from the contentment and harmony between the governors and the governed will surge the true felicity of the peoples.[31]

Vinasco, despite his socialism, made references to "harmony" and "castes" that resonated with the hierarchical national society and state envisioned by the Colombian Regeneration of the 1880s–1890s and by Conservatives more generally. Like other intellectuals of the early twentieth century, Vinasco also used scientific terminology to lend authority to his arguments. Rather then a healthy organism, Caldas was weakened by its own internal heterogeneity.

Defining themselves as racially and regionally distinct from Antioquia was problematic, however, because they were heavily influenced by the discourse of regional differentiation that associated Antioqueños with progress. Riosuceños often still felt the need to separate out the modern and backward racial elements in local society. Thus, for example, the provincial alcalde, Francisco Trejos, reported in 1907 that "the progress of Riosucio and Quinchía is bogged down, thanks to those parcialidades." He lambasted the indígenas for impeding progress. Finally, Trejos, who was also one of the local officials who had felt compelled to publicly state his loyalty to the department of Caldas, spoke very highly of the Antioqueño race, which, he noted, was well known for its love of work, entrepreneurial talents, and reliability.[32]

Trejos's comments notwithstanding, the local commercial and political leaders of Riosucio were finding that Manizaleños conflated them with the more "backward" elements of their local society. The Riosuceños noted, to their horror, that when the Manizaleños peered down toward the western districts from their high mountaintop city, they saw not dynamic entrepreneurs, but rather . . . *indios*. The Riosuceños were becoming known as the "Indians of Caldas," as they still are sometimes called today. Thus, *El Conservador* indignantly repudiated an editorial published in a

Manizales newspaper whereby a Manizaleño had described the province of Marmato as composed of "'thatch-roofed and miserable villages such as Supía, Guamal, Riosucio, and Quinchía . . . the former two populated by black miners who recently . . . had worn the shackle of the slave, and the two latter by savage Indians alien to civilization and progress.'"[33]

Such attacks against the Riosuceños' dignity could be met with various rhetorical tactics. One was to do as Trejos, and many officials before him, had done: affirm the growing importance of Antioqueño migration and actively promote it. Another response was to paint Riosucio as even whiter than Antioquia. For example, *La Opinión* traced Riosuceños' genealogical roots back to Spain. *La Opinión* also emphasized the contributions made by immigrants from northern Europe. Meanwhile, the Riosucio municipal council also made several efforts to change the "ugly" name of "Muddyriver" to something more elegant and peninsular. In 1910 they petitioned the departmental legislature unsuccessfully to change the town's name to Sevilla. They tried again in 1915. This time, they proposed the name Iberia. Finally, in 1916, they petitioned for and received a name change to Hispania, which they chose in honor of Spain, their *madre patria*. Thus, in accordance with Hispanodolatry of the Conservative white republic, they emphasized their Spanish heritage. The new name lasted only a few years; by the 1920s, the town had reverted to its customary nomenclature.[34]

A third tactic was simply to react to racist slights with a certain sense of humor and even ironic pride. Some Riosuceños began to appropriate the negative stereotypes to make fun of themselves and of their haughty critics. They laughed about their Indian heritage, but at the same time they began to defend it. They referred to themselves as the descendants of the valiant, sixteenth-century Pirsas, who reportedly fought against the Spanish conquerors. One anonymous contributor to *La Opinión* in 1919, referring to himself jokingly as a rustic indio, wrote that "it is no secret to us that a small number of Manizaleños dislike us Caucanos who live in these mountains. . . . Don't think . . . that it offends us to remember our descent from indígenas: with pride we carry blood of the aborigines."[35]

Separatist sentiment in Riosucio would outlive *La Opinión* and the Republican Union and would continue during the 1920s. One of the strongest separatist voices would be that of Nestor Bueno Cock, a local political leader during that period and editor of the Conservative newspaper *El Minuto*. He used economic rather than "ethnographic" arguments. Ac-

cording to Bueno Cock, unhappiness reigned due to excessive centralization, corruption, and infrastructural neglect. As president of the municipal council of Riosucio in 1927, he proposed that Riosucio and other
former Cauca districts should secede from Caldas and join the department
of Valle. He cited various complaints, including the unequal allocation of
departmental revenues. He sought a railroad link, and most importantly,
he complained of the suspension of work on the road that would connect
Riosucio and surrounding districts to the main highway.[36]

Throughout the first several decades of the century, inhabitants of the
western municipios fretted that their taxes were being directed toward
Manizales and the center of Caldas, while their towns remained in a state
of "abandon." They also complained of lack of funds for hospitals and
schools, but their principal concern was economic infrastructure. The
merchants, miners, and commercial farmers of Riosucio sought to integrate themselves more fully into national and global markets. Actual
roads were finally being built across the Colombian highlands; long-
isolated small towns and cities scrambled to get connected. Highways,
railroads, and aerial cables all were symbols of progress and modernity as
well as conduits of economic integration.[37]

One aspect of growing separatist sentiment was an increasingly visible
ambivalence about Antioqueño migration into the area, and even outright
resentment. Riosuceños were starting to distinguish themselves from the
Antioqueño areas of Caldas just at the time that Riosucio, and even more
so the surrounding towns and countryside, were becoming increasingly
populated by Antioqueño migrants. Jorge Gärtner de la Cuesta lamented
the takeover of Riosucio by Antioqueños. In his memoirs he nostalgically
recalled his turn-of-the-century childhood in Riosucio:

> In the final decade of the century the habits . . . of old Cauca predomi-
> nated. Almost the totality of inhabitants were born in the municipio,
> except for a few families from Cartago, Buga and Popayán. . . . This
> situation was being modified slowly by the entrance of the Antio-
> queño element, not without violent and frequent shocks, until, by
> the middle of the second decade of the twentieth century, the uses
> and practices of the neighboring Department predominated in all
> aspects.[38]

Gärtner de la Cuesta, like many of his era, expressed ambivalent feelings
toward the Antioqueño migration that his father's generation had pro-

moted. He and his cohort credited the Antioqueños for bringing progress, but he also portrayed them as vulgar and mercantile. These traits, however necessary in the modern world, contrasted with the gentility of (presumably middle- and upper-class) Caucanos.[39]

CONCLUSIONS

The debates that swirled around the creation of Caldas may seem arcane today, particularly given that Riosucio never succeeded in breaking off from Caldas, even when other, more prosperous areas did. Yet these debates were more than just spats between local political cliques, and they were about more than just local or regional pride. On the pages of local presses and in their personal and political correspondence, elite leaders of competing localities and factions fought to establish hegemony. For a local elite, such as that of Manizales, to become regionally hegemonic, it had to define the region it sought to represent and govern. The Manizales elite, in efforts to consolidate their predominant place in Caldas, used the press as a forum for imagining the regional community, for creating a regional discourse. The commercial and political leaders of Manizales defined Caldas as a region and defined themselves as the race naturally suited to govern it. In other words, their hegemony implied defining and organizing space and society through discourse in such a way as to favor their own economic interests.[40]

Pierre Bourdieu describes regionalism as "performative discourse" that serves to naturalize a given social division and legitimate the authority of those who govern it. The aspiring regional elite in Manizales justified Caldas by constructing the department as a racial region and recounting its history in the glowing terms of the rosy legend of Antioqueño migration. Political and commercial leaders performed the region when they wrote about themselves and their forefathers as protagonists in the epic tale of the settlement and founding of Caldas. Like their counterparts in Medellín, they also performed their regionalism by donning clothing associated with the pioneer settlers, building their rural haciendas in the distinctive, colorful regional style that made use of local building materials and techniques, and eating local foods that they enshrined as emblematic of regional culture.[41]

Of course, the turn-of-the-century elites did not speak of "hegemony" or "performative discourse." They had their own jargon and their own metaphors. Even so, the debates were not as abstract as their (or my) terminology would suggest. Despite their own use of familial and medical metaphor and high-flown social-science terminology, the writers cited in this chapter were discussing concrete and immediate concerns. They were arguing over the very nature of the regional economic transformation and who would benefit from it. Debates over administrative borders and political representation were also arguments about mining legislation, fiscal policy, infrastructural improvements, and control over the lucrative coffee trade. The formation of Caldas was thus a power-laden and conflictive process of imagining a new regional community.

All of these debates took place on a common discursive field that equated regional unity and racial identity. Thus, the various passages cited above provide a window into turn-of-the-century attitudes about race. Colombians used "race" to refer to place of origin. Their spatially oriented notions of race freely conflated lineage, biology, climate, and culture. They continued to use the familiar familial and genealogical metaphors of nineteenth-century discourse about regional and local races to advance their respective causes. But they were also influenced by international discourses about phenotypically and genetically defined human races and the racial superiority of European whites over other races. In their efforts to be modern and progressive, writers in both Riosucio and Manizales appropriated the latest scientific terminology. The first two decades or so of the twentieth century thus may be seen as a moment of discursive transition, a time when the international scientific discourse of eugenics was increasingly disseminated and conflated with familiar notions of localized racial identity. The assumptions of racial science were incorporated into, and served to strengthen, the racialized discourse of regional differentiation.

The term "region" increasingly supplanted the former países, provinces, and sovereign states that people had talked about in the nineteenth century. Both the pro-Caldas and the separatist writers assumed the existence of regions as real entities. They agreed upon the importance and concrete reality of economic and "ethnographic" regions, but disagreed about where to draw the boundaries between regions. The leaders of Manizales emphasized their identity as the offspring of Antioquia. And they claimed that their region coincided with the new departmental borders of Caldas. The separatists in Riosucio, on the other hand, disavowed Caldas as a region. They also disavowed Antioquia's historic influence in their district. Rather, they emphasized their distinct origins in Cauca.

By so doing, however, the Riosuceños placed themselves in a bind. They wanted to be known as "progressive," but Cauca was generally known as backward, heterogeneous, and disorderly. In explicit contrast to white Antioquia, Cauca was notorious for its black and Indian "hordes." Moreover, Riosucio district had a largely indigenous population and the town itself had been founded by Indians and people of mixed Spanish, indigenous, and African descent. Neighboring districts still had distinct black communities as well. Riosucio town intellectuals, in attempting to portray themselves as distinct from Manizales and as non-Antioqueño, had to incorporate these long-disparaged rural elements into their imagined community—their local raza—as reflected in their writings on the pages of *La Opinión* and elsewhere.

As the next chapter illustrates, this process of imagining a local community implied imagining a collective past. In the pages of the very same periodical, *La Opinión*, Riosucio intellectuals remembered Riosucio. They wrote its history, a history that predated the Antioqueño influx and reached back to the colonial period. This narrative to some extent incorporated the Indians themselves as subordinate actors while reflecting the narrators' ambivalence about their own heritage.

PART 3

REMEMBERING RACE, REGION, AND COMMUNITY

CHAPTER SEVEN

Remembering Riosucio:

Imagining a Mestizo

Community

PROLOGUE: RIOSUCIO, 7 AUGUST 1994

On 7 August Colombia celebrates the 1819 Battle of Boyacá, a turning point in the independence struggle in which Bolívar's forces won a key victory. For Riosuceños, the date is particularly significant, because they trace the founding of their town to that very day in 1819. Every year, while the rest of Colombia displays the formal pageantry of a national patriotic holiday, Riosucio enjoys a local celebration of its own: townspeople celebrate both the founding of nation and the creation of their town.

In 1994 townspeople turned out to watch the annual parade of school-children dressed in school uniforms and costumes intended to reflect Riosucio's culture and history. Groups of young girls in flowered skirts carried hand-woven baskets to represent the indigenous communities. One little boy was dressed as the Devil, the symbol of Riosucio's January festival. He walked arm-in-arm with two boys in clerical garb representing the town's founding *padres*, Father Bonafont and Father Bueno. In their usual humorous fashion, Riosucio townspeople cheerfully celebrated their own identity and their own past, even in the face of ominous events. In the surrounding mountains, guerrilla insurgents had just carried out an eighteen-day military offensive, meant to show a new president that they were a force to be reckoned with. In Bogotá, President Ernesto Samper took office that very day, inaugurating what would prove to be an especially weak and scandal-plagued administration.

One event that week, as much as the change of administration or the guerrilla offensive, upset the consciousness of the town intelligentsia. On Thursday evening, 4 August, Cali-based journalist Alvaro Gärtner Posada, a member of one of Riosucio's leading families, gave a lecture to a packed auditorium in the local cultural center on the life of Father José Bonifacio Bonafont. Unlike many lectures of this sort, Gärtner's talk was not merely a recounting of familiar anecdotes. Rather, he himself had read and transcribed several Independence-era archival documents, and he used these documents to poke holes in some accepted myths. He held the audience's rapt attention as he spoke for over an hour, and he then led a spirited question-and-answer session. Many of the audience comments centered around one specific assertion by Gärtner Posada: He had found no documentary proof that Riosucio was actually founded on 7 August 1819; the date was most likely apocryphal. The gist of the questions asked by several members of the audience was: If 7 August is not really our founders' day, then where does that leave our celebration? Where does that leave us?

REMEMBERING RIOSUCIO

The period covered by this book closes with efforts by local twentieth-century intellectuals to consolidate Riosucio's collective identity as a community with its own particular history. As Riosucio became part of Caldas and was subordinated to Manizales, and as Antioqueños continued to flood into Riosucio, early-twentieth-century local intellectuals expressed second thoughts about the benefits of Antioqueño migration. As we have seen, some Riosuceños even sought to secede from Caldas and form a separate department, which they justified by claiming that they belonged to a race different than that of the Antioqueño–Caldenses.

To identify themselves as a distinct race, they not only emphasized their distinct cultural and biological characteristics, they also emphasized their own separate historical origins. This chapter traces their elaboration of a narrative of Riosucio history. Beginning in the early twentieth century, at the same time that they found themselves economically and politically subordinated to the new department of Caldas, local intellectuals started writing the history of Riosucio town and district. By reconstructing and reclaiming a rich past prior to the colonización Antioqueña, they challenged aspects of the homogenizing discourse of the new regional elite. They portrayed their town as more historically rooted, and implicitly more important, than the rest of Caldas. According to this story, diverse and opposed communities united on the eve of Independence to create the community that historian Germán Arciniegas would later refer to as a microcosm of Colombia, the very "image of the republic."[1]

This chapter draws heavily on writings first published in the second decade of the twentieth century. It also moves forward in time to encompass the contributions that several generations of local intellectuals, based in the town center, made to the narrative of Riosucio's history over the course of the century. At the beginning of the twentieth century, at the same time that literate Riosuceño townspeople were struggling to define themselves apart from Caldas, two brothers, Nicanor and Jesús Antonio Salazar, wrote down some notes about the history of Riosucio. The first known published version of the local narrative appeared in *La Opinión* during 1911. During the next few years, *La Opinión* would occasionally print other local historical pieces as well, alongside its usual editorials in favor of separating from Caldas. From the beginning, therefore, the creation and diffusion of a local historical narrative went hand in hand with assertions of a distinct collective identity and with demands for greater economic resources and political autonomy.[2]

The same story told in *La Opinión* would be repeated time and again over the course of the twentieth century, with various additions and changes. In 1923 a local mining investor, magistrate, and politician, Rómulo Cuesta, published a historical melodrama, *Tomás*, set during the civil war of 1876, which also incorporated snippets of local history dating back to the Conquest. Purificación Calvo de Vanegas, an educator and prominent town intellectual in Riosucio, wrote a local historical account during the 1950s, for which she consulted various prominent townspeople, including the Salazar brothers. Prominent members of the elite edited and secured the posthumous publication of her book and elaborated upon her stories.

These twentieth-century intellectuals recounted a history that went back to the colonial and early independence eras, before the period that is the subject of this book. This chapter thus leaps backward in time, as well as forward, in order to explore the meanings that Riosuceños have ascribed to their town's founding. Proving or disproving the historicity of their narrative is not my goal, yet a comparison of twentieth century accounts with earlier archival documents does reveal the ways in which the local historians themselves elaborated upon the "facts" that they were ostensibly merely reporting. Drawing on Joanne Rappaport's approach to indigenous narratives, I seek to uncover not so much what *did* happen in 1819, but what Riosucio's local historians, a century later, thought *should* have happened. The chapter provides insights into twentieth-century Riosuceños' notions of what they wanted their history and their community to be. Riosucio's founding story, as told in the *La Opinión* series, as well as in the subsequent accounts by Cuesta and Calvo, and in the more recent interpretations provided by Otto Morales Benítez and Julián Bueno, features several episodes: the Conquest; the colonial-era visita of Lesmes de Saravia y Espinosa; the founding of Riosucio town as a divided community on the eve of Independence; and the final unification of two parishes into one in 1846, which gave rise to the raza riosuceña.[3]

THE NARRATIVE

La Opinión's chronicle began with the arrival of the Spaniards in 1540 and the founding of the first local colonial settlements. Riosucio's early-twentieth-century historians were clearly immersed in the favorable White Legend of the Iberian conquest. According to *La Opinión:* "The Spaniards with altruism that honors them, proceeded to the civilization of the indigenous race." Calvo would later expand on the beneficence of the Spaniard: "In a genteel manner they attended to the advancement, education, and above all the literacy of the indígenas, without distinctions of any class."[4]

Yet these same writers also celebrated the bravery and resistance carried on by these "wild Indians." *La Opinión* described the pits and spikes that the Pirsas had used to ward off the mounted Spaniards. Cuesta would recall the neighboring Quinchías as cannibals, who crowned their fences with human heads. *La Opinión* characterized the Pirsas as protonationalists: "The indígenas of these parcialidades in their barbaric state had a noble notion of love for the patria, while they surrendered their native land to the conquerors, it was drenched in their blood, leaving in this manner a fine example for civilized generations to imitate." Thus, even while affirming a contrast between civilization and barbarism, the anonymous writer argued that Riosucio boasted a precolonial tradition of patriotism.[5]

The narrative goes on to describe the emergence of the royal mining concession of San Sebastián of Quiebralomo to Spanish miners. The writers in *La Opinión* and the other accounts traced common local surnames to the Spanish families. By emphasizing that Quiebralomo was settled by Spaniards, and that Riosucio originated primarily in Quiebralomo, rather than La Montaña, the narrators emphasized Riosucio's Spanish heritage.[6]

The next seminal moment in these published narratives was the official visit (*visita*) of colonial official Lesmes de Espinosa y Saravia in 1627. Indigenous intellectuals of La Montaña and the other neighboring parcialidades have long remembered and celebrated the 1627 visita because it provides a documentary basis for their land claims. For the town historians of Riosucio, however, the importance of Espinosa y Saravia's visit was that he certified the official existence of Quiebralomo. They recounted that he gave land to sixteen families in Quiebralomo, excluding free unions and workers (*la peonada*). Slaves were not mentioned. According to Calvo, who was clearly preoccupied with sexual propriety, Espinosa y Saravia favored only such families who boasted "well-constituted homes"—in other words, legitimately married couples with paternally recognized children. Calvo noted that many of the surnames of families favored by Espinosa y Saravia still figured prominently in mid-twentieth-century Riosucio. Not surprisingly, these lineages included those of the local historians, such as Salazar and Calvo.[7]

The accounts showed considerable confusion as to the date of the visita. Updating Espinosa y Saravia to the eighteenth century, some accounts recast him as a predecessor to José Bonifacio Bonafont, the priest they credited with unifying La Montaña and Quiebralomo into one community. Thus, according to La Opinión, Espinosa y Saravia arrived in 1750 to settle disputes raging between La Montaña and Quiebralomo. As a result of his mediation, "exalted passions were calmed" and "true peace" endured for many years. Nicanor Salazar recalled that during the visita, general happiness reigned. Calvo, who dated his visit to 1727, argued that he assigned boundaries, separated by a ditch, between the communities of Quiebralomo and La Montaña, in the same place that she and other historians also claimed that a dividing fence would later be erected in the nineteenth century.[8]

More than any other chapter in their collective history, the early-nineteenth-century founding of Riosucio town continues to live most vividly in the townspeople's imaginations. The character who most endures is the maverick priest, Father Bonafont. He was reportedly exiled from his native province of Santander for pro-Independence political activities, ending up as the parish priest of La Montaña. Early-twentieth-century historians cast Bonafont as a pious and patriotic founding father, thus providing a somewhat sanitized portrayal of his virtues. According to a contemporary observer, the French engineer Jean Boussingault, Father Bonafont lived openly with a woman, Manuela, with whom he had at least one child. Documents from the 1820s unearthed by Gärtner show that Bonafont was embroiled in multiple lawsuits with other priests and local judges and mayors. Boussingault, meanwhile, described Bonafont's parish at that time as a "mission." Bonafont was a missionary in the colonial tradition, a theocrat who wielded both religious and political authority over his Indians, "civilizing" them while promoting agriculture and industry.[9]

According to the twentieth-century published accounts, Bonafont arrived in the parish of La Montaña in 1814. He found that the tribute-paying indios of La Montaña and the non-tribute paying libres of Quiebralomo had been fighting for at least a century over the area known as Río Sucio. (Espinosa y Saravia's supposed "reign of happiness" had apparently proved ephemeral.) Disturbed by such un-Christian animosities, Bonafont decided to found a united community at Río Sucio, under the shadow of the Ingrumá peak. He enlisted the support of Father Ramón Bueno of Quiebralomo. They convoked two meetings, in 1814 and 1816, between the leaders of the opposing communities, but both sides engaged in mutual recriminations and each meeting ended unsuccessfully. According to La Opinión, however, the "enlightened and progressive priests" persisted. Finally, at the third and final meeting, in July of 1819, "Dr. Bonafont made an eloquent and expressive speech, elaborating with prophetic vision the future of this new society, making predictions that have been fulfilled. He said 'I want the union of these two races because from them will come generations [who will be] full of vigor for work, intelligent for science and arts, and moreover valiant, to defend the republican idea.' " Thus, Bonafont obtained "the union of two entirely antagonistic races." Moved by his speech, the two sides reached an agreement: They would move their parishes to Riosucio. Happiness again reigned.[10]

Purificación Calvo provided an explanation as to why the inhabitants of La Montaña ended up with the lower eastern plaza rather than the western plaza to which they had the greater claim, as it lay more clearly within or close to their resguardo: "Father Bonafont resolved the affair with this explanation: 'the lower part has no impediments for construction; there the indígenas can construct their homes easily; the ground on the upper part requires works of terraces; the Quiebralomeños are workers who will overcome the defects of the terrain.'" Thus, Calvo emphasized the technological superiority and industriousness of the Quiebralomeños, while she cast the Indians as technologically inferior.[11]

As noted in chapter 3, Bonafont's actual role in unifying the town was ambiguous at best. Calvo argued that he sought the unification of two parishes into one. Yet, as we have seen, the indígenas of La Montaña also long remembered Bonafont as looking out for their own interests, as opposed to those of the Quiebralomeños. Historical archival documents, including the documents transcribed by Gärtner, support the indígenas' view. In response to a petition by civil authorities to annex La Montaña to Quiebralomo, Bonafont wrote a document in 1825 in which he argued that the two parishes should remain separate. He had favored moving the communities close together, he said, in order to facilitate religious worship and instruction, but he dismissed the Quiebralomeños' legal claims to the site of Río Sucio. He argued that Quiebralomo was a mere agglomeration of mining sites with no land titles, and therefore had no rights to the land in question, which belonged to La Montaña. As the slaves of Quiebralomo had gradually bought their own freedom, he argued, they had expanded onto indigenous lands; Quiebralomeños were now occupying La Montaña lands. He also stated that the original plan to join the two communities in one place had been proposed to him by a civil authority, the Juez Mayor of Quiebralomo, Manuel José Lozano, who had taken all the initiative in the project. Bonafont was writing in the context of a dispute over administrative jurisdiction. He did not want his parish to be annexed to that of Quiebralomo because such an outcome would have cost him his job. His immediate personal interests in 1825 no doubt colored his recall of the events of the previous decade, but in any case he painted a picture far different from that of his twentieth-century biographers, who stressed his initiative in the move as well as the legality and economic necessity of Quiebralomo land claims.[12]

La Opinión also reported that Bonafont actively promoted marriages between the opposing bands in order to ameliorate continued conflicts. He even exalted the graces of the women of each neighborhood to the men of the other, thus ending the disagreements between neighborhoods. These claims may be based on Bonafont's own account of the increase of marriages among his flock. Priests throughout the nineteenth century would often make such claims as proof of their success in improving the moral customs of their flock. And Bonafont did make a reference to marriages of people from different neighborhoods:

> The frequent conflicts over possession of the lands have ceased. . . .
> The population has increased with the many marriages that have
> been contracted among some and other neighbors . . . and today they
> are more civilized . . . which leads us to hope that within a short time,
> these two neighborhoods will grow considerably, not only from natives, but also from other outside people, attracted by the fertility of
> the lands and the abundance of mines . . . to the extent that each priest
> will not be able to administrate his curacy all alone.[13]

Bonafont's prediction of an influx of outside settlers anticipated the pro-Antioqueño migration discourse of his successors.

The celebratory twentieth-century narrative also obviates the extent to which the founding of Riosucio followed a colonial policy of forcibly "reducing" dispersed populations into new villages in order to facilitate indoctrination and exploitation. In the early colonial period, these reducciones had been aimed at creating separate Indian towns. The colonial state and church had long sought to establish Indian villages apart from white and mestizo settlements, in order to protect the Indians' souls and morals. The local authorities' decision to unite both of the communities at Río Sucio, rather than preserve that site exclusively for the indígenas (which the leaders of La Montaña had long desired), conformed with some partial policy shifts that Safford notes for eighteenth-century New Granada. During the 1750s, some (though not all) colonial *visitadores* began to argue that the non-Indian population of New Granada needed access to lands monopolized by the Indians. These authorities began to describe the Indians as lazy, alcoholic, and unproductive—in other words, as miserable beings who would benefit, rather than suffer, from the influence of their enterprising neighbors. Meanwhile, authorities in some areas of New Granada forcibly reduced dispersed populations into multiracial towns. Historical research thus challenges twentieth-century assertions that Bonafont, acting on his own initiative and out of purely beneficial motives, convinced the two parishes to unite voluntarily. Likewise, the date of the transfer is also thrown into question. Gärtner Posada transcribed archival documents that suggested that the parishes moved sometime between 1815 and 1819, rather than concurrent with the Battle of Boyacá in August 1819.[14]

A last episode in the founding narrative concerns the official unification of two parishes into one municipal and parish district. Calvo wrote
that until the 1840s the parishes of Quiebralomo and La Montaña were
still separated by a fence. Each parish boasted its own government and a
rustic church named for its respective patron saint: Nuestra Señora de
la Candelaria below and San Sebastián de Quiebralomo above. On 27 May
1846 the governor of Cauca created a unified administrative district.
The diocese of Popayán followed suit, unifying the two parishes into one
under the leadership of the priest Manuel Velasco. Calvo lamented that
Bonafont had died suddenly the year before, and thus was never able to
see his supposed dream realized. The historical documents unearthed by
Gärtner paint a different picture: Bonafont posed possibly the greatest
obstacle to parochial unification; Velasco was his rival; Bonafont's death
in 1845 facilitated the unification of Riosucio parish.[15]

The unification of the two rival entities as one parish, one town, and
one electoral district would be recalled in the twentieth century as the
culmination of Riosucio's founding. Julián Bueno Rodríguez, the municipal cultural director, has particularly emphasized the historic and symbolic importance of the fence coming down and the mixing between two
communities, leading to the creation of a unique Riosucio raza. He recounts how a new generation of youthful inhabitants, unhampered by the
caste enmities of their elders, circumvented the fence at night to engage in
covert sexual trysts. Covert sexuality gave way to open unions, eventually leading to intermarriage among long-opposed families, and the fence
became obsolete. Bueno even goes so far as to trace to the unification the
"symbolic" beginning of Riosucio's famous biennial Carnaval.[16]

THE NARRATIVE RECONSIDERED

This collective narrative illustrates what several generations of literate
townspeople in Riosucio's urban core, living in the twentieth century,
thought *should* have happened. The past they longed for was a product of
their own twentieth-century aspirations. I have used some older historical documents to suggest the extent to which some of their facts have
blurred into fantasy. The subject of this chapter is not the original creation
of Riosucio per se, but rather the subsequent elaboration of Riosucio's
predominant historical myths. My assumption is that historical narratives, like any creative interpretations (be they ostensibly factual or fic-

tive) often tell us as much or more about the concerns of the era in which they are created than of the era about which they are written. So what do these narratives, with their obvious inconsistencies and elaborations, suggest to us about the aspirations of urban townspeople in the 1900s? What do they tell us about the discursive construction of Riosucio, as an entity within and yet apart from, and even opposed to, the rest of Caldas? Moreover, what are the implications for social and political conflicts over the course of the twentieth century?

The Riosucio narrative has some characteristics common to locally produced monographs of Colombian municipios and to traditional nine-teenth- and twentieth-century historiography more generally, such as the personification of history in the lives of a few "great men." Complicated historical processes involving many actors were reduced to the initiatives of a few idealized white male individuals, such as Bonafont and Espinosa y Saravia, while the actions of other actors were obscured and forgotten. The colonial caciques and republican cabildos of La Montaña and neigh-boring indigenous communities, who had petitioned and fought for the land of Riosucio for over a century, were either barely mentioned in the published narratives or entirely ignored. Bonafont, with his mix of local paternalism, Catholicism, and republican political ideology, was an espe-cially appealing hero for Conservatives. During the Regeneration of the 1880s–1890s and during the era of Conservative rule that followed, politi-cians sought to consolidate national unity based in part on explicitly anti-Liberal social policies and the memory of Bolívar. Conservative social policies placed responsibility for "civilizing" the Indians in the hands of missionary priests. Accordingly, the Conservative La Opinión reported that Bonafont was avidly pro-Bolívar and anti-Santander. The legacy of Bonafont, however, like that of Bolívar himself, could be molded to suit the needs of various political factions. Liberals could emphasize his re-publicanism, rebelliousness, and economic ingenuity. The indigenous in-habitants of La Montaña also remembered him as their hero, stressing his avid defense of their autonomy and land rights.

It is remarkable that any indígenas appeared in these narrative at all, and moreover, that they appeared as actors as late as the Independence era. Many towns and cities of Colombia have stories and monuments commemorating some cacique or cacica from the early colonial era who bravely resisted the Spanish invaders, only to perish, making way for a new society. Many of the mountains around Riosucio, including Ingrumá, are rumored to have secret caves where some Indian prince or princess buried themselves with their gold and gems rather than surrender to the Spaniards. Thus, the inhabitants of most towns in the region tend to remember Indians as inhabitants of the deep past, supernatural and alluring, but rarely to consider Indians as more recent historical actors. The local monographs that intellectuals throughout Colombia have written about their own towns tend to read as the collective genealogies of local elites, with no modern-era Indians and few popular forces beyond some picturesque anecdotes about well-known local characters. Calvo's monograph likewise focuses on elite leaders, but, building on earlier accounts, she does include the Indians of La Montaña as one half of the original dual community, one of the founding elements of local society. The Indians were not elevated to the importance of a Bonafont or an Espinosa y Saravia; their own agency as political actors was minimized. But they were described as forebears, and even participants, in the founding of the community. Intermarriage and mestizaje was recognized. Indigenous ancestry, for some Riosucio writers, was a source of pride and distinctiveness.

Afro-Colombian heritage was another matter. In emphasizing the Spanish lineages of Quiebralomo, writers obliterated Afro-Colombian contributions to Riosucio's history. Even as some local town intellectuals ambiguously tried to incorporate elements of their Indian heritage, they whitewashed Quiebralomo's slaves and mixed-race community leaders out of their historical narratives altogether. A character in Rómulo Cuesta's novel *Tomás*, for example, recalls the Quiebralomeños as the white "nobility." Drawing on Cuesta, Julián Bueno later wrote: "From La Montaña came the wild Indian, lover of the forest and liberty, agriculturalist by nature; from Quiebralomo the elegant white, friend of the urban environment, aficionado of modifying nature for his own use, miner for expedience."[17]

The colonial black presence was greater than the twentieth-century writers would admit. The mines of the Real de Quiebralomo, like the surrounding mining areas, were worked in part by slaves and the free descendants of slaves. Moreover, contemporary observers did not consider the leading families of Quiebralomo to be quite as white as their descendants later remembered them. Bonafont referred to the Quiebralomeños as slaves who had bought their own freedom. Indígenas in La Montaña and their protectors also referred to the Quiebralomeños as mulattos in their correspondence with ecclesiastic and state officials. These sources were likely slanted by the segregationist impulses of the writers; by characterizing non-Indians as "mulattos," they drew upon racist assumptions to imply that the Quiebralomeños were a contaminant from which the Indians needed to be protected.[18]

French visitor Jean Boussingault, meanwhile, noted in his humorous memoir that the local authorities of Quiebralomo threw a sumptuous banquet in his honor in 1829. He reported that these leading citizens dressed elegantly and ate from fine English china. To his European eyes, however, his hosts were all "people of color." He found comical their efforts to impress him with their civilized hospitality. Despite their fine clothes, the ostensible "nobility" of Quiebralomo all went barefoot. And the elegant Wedgwood soup tureens from which they ate were actually chamber pots. (He noted with relief that the pots were "virgin" because the locals were unaware of their intended use.)[19]

In addition to cleansing possible racial stains from their lineages, many of the twentieth-century writers tried to make Riosucio more important than it had been by linking their relatively insignificant nineteenth-century backwater to the birth of the Colombian nation and the independence of Latin America as a whole. Most significantly, they dated Riosucio's founding to the day of the Battle of Boyacá, the victory that made way for the liberation of New Granada, Venezuela, and ultimately the rest of Andean South America from Spain. The narratives also referred to the participation of Rodulfo Largo, an indígena from La Montaña, in the culmination of the independence wars at Ayacucho, Perú, alongside Simón Bolívar.[20]

Although ostensibly written about the past, the local histories also addressed the authors' contemporary concerns. These chronicles were all written in times of continued social strife. Colombia has long been a notoriously violent and divided country. The often-idealized recollections of the past seem to reflect the desires of their authors to overcome rifts that were continuing to divide Riosucio. At the same time that early-twentieth-century writers contested their administrative subordination to Manizales, they faced litigation from increasingly assertive indigenous communities. Facing pressures from above and below, from Antioqueños and indígenas, and writing in the context of the regenerated white republic, urban intellectuals traced their own lineages, from the upper plaza back through Quiebralomo to Spain, and argued that the essential identity and history of Riosucio—like that of the nation—was rooted in its Spanish heritage.

Twentieth-century writers tried to link the unification of Riosucio with that of the nation as a whole—a unity that by the mid–twentieth century was still far from realized. Cuesta's novel, *Tomás*, for example, purported to describe the history of the bitter 1876–77 war through the experiences of a Romeo-and-Juliet pair whose love was tragically thwarted by partisan politics. Divisions between Liberals and Conservatives were once again becoming violent during the 1920s. The novel may be read as a call for reconciliation on a local and national level. As in the nineteenth- and early-twentieth-century "foundational novels" analyzed by Doris Sommer, romantic love provided a metaphor for national consolidation in an era of internecine conflict. Julián Bueno's version of Riosucio's founding as the forging of one raza through intermarriage is also "foundational" in this sense, even if it does not purport to be fiction.[21]

Purificación Calvo recalled that the fence that divided Riosucio was torn down upon orders of the President of the Republic, who did not want archaic divisions of colonial caste to divide republican citizens. Calvo's manuscript, moreover, was produced during the period when partisan violence between Liberals and Conservatives reached its most atrocious levels. During La Violencia (from the late 1940s to the early 1960s) some two hundred thousand Colombians are said to have killed each other, mainly in rural districts. The departments of Antioquia and Caldas were among those that suffered the highest casualties. Riosucio both suffered its own deadly partisan violence and served as a refuge for people fleeing even more horrific neighboring districts. Calvo's good-natured monograph, which lauded both Liberal and Conservative contributors to Riosucio's patrimony, studiously avoided any reference to the violence of her own era; she preferred to write of past conflicts that had been resolved and past peoples who had been united. The fence was ultimately torn down, various versions of the foundational narrative attest, in the interests of the unified nation (i.e., on orders of the president) or through love (Julián Bueno's young lovers, who forged a new race by overcoming the barriers of caste).[22]

Otto Morales Benítez, Riosucio's most prominent native son, edited and published Calvo's manuscript. Morales Benítez has been an influential national political and intellectual figure in Colombia for over half a century. He has written extensively on Colombian, Latin American, and Caldas history. As a young Liberal politician, he participated in early official inquiries into the causes of La Violencia and helped negotiate a truce between the two warring parties. At the same time, he was involved, in the 1940s, in privatizing the indigenous resguardo of Quinchía. As a cabinet minister in the 1960s, he played an active role in some populist initiatives, particularly land reform and labor legislation. He professes an inclusive vision of Colombian nationhood.

The national divisions that writers and politicians such as Morales Benítez hope to overcome are not, of course, exclusively based on partisan political affiliation. Rifts between ethnic or racial groups have also divided Colombia. In Riosucio and the surrounding districts, as elsewhere in Colombia, La Violencia took on racial overtones that have yet to be fully researched. Among the groups most remembered for their participation in partisan vendettas were the Liberal campesinos of what had been the Quinchía resguardo (led by the bandit known as "Captain Vengeance" [*Capitán Venganza*]) and Conservative paramilitary bands from the highland Antioqueño enclaves. Race became an even more explicitly politicized concern during the 1970s and 1980s with the emergence of a nationwide indigenous rights movement. In casting Riosucio as a metaphor for the nation he hopes to unify, Morales Benítez has emphasized that Riosucio, and by extension the nation (and the whole continent), are essentially mestizo. Riosucio is a microcosm of a racially mixed nation. The mixing of two opposed races to form the "Riosucio race" is a trope for a national process of mestizaje and hoped-for unification. As historian W. John Green perceptively suggests, "Many modern Colombian writers have emphasized [Colombia's] high degree of race mixture in part because of their wistful desires to portray the nation as a unified whole . . . based on the questionable assumption that a racially mixed society is a more harmonious one."[23]

Morales Benítez argues that Colombia is a mestizo nation, that Latin America is a mestizo continent, and that "the mestizo" is the social actor who has shaped Latin America's past and will lead its future. His vision of the Colombian nation as inclusively mestizo draws on the legacy of Jorge Eliecer Gaitán, a populist Liberal who built strong bases of support among urban mestizo masses in the growing cities of the 1940s. Morales Benítez and like-minded Liberals offer a more democratically racialized national project than that of the racially exclusive white republic of the Conservatives. By publicizing the case of Riosucio, he has chipped away at the myth of Caldas as entirely white and Antioqueño. Even Caldas, Morales Benítez argues, is mestizo rather than white. Yet the usefulness of Morales Benítez's vision for Riosucio's rural indígenas is limited by his tendency to view the Indian as part of the past, an element that was absorbed by mestizaje, rather than as a vibrant identity claimed by poor rural Rio-suceños today.[24]

The publication of Calvo's monograph in 1961, along with the work of Otto Morales Benítez as a politician and writer, and the appointment of Julián Bueno Rodríguez as the officer of municipal culture, have helped to enshrine their combined narrative of Riosucio history, which they based largely on the earlier versions published at the beginning of the century, as its official local history. Yet, this official history does not explain why most rural Riosuceños continue to affirm an indigenous identity (along with indigenous land rights). Nor does the narrative of mestizaje explain how indigenous identity has been changed and reconstructed over time. Bueno, Morales Benítez, and other theorists of Riosucio's racial fusion have not successfully incorporated the aspirations and memories of present-day rural inhabitants of Riosucio into their more inclusive narrative. The indígenas did not figure at all in the regional myth of white Caldas. But even the countermyth of mestizo Riosucio (and, by extension, mestizo Colombia) homogenizes the population; it allows little space for any assertion of indigenous identity.[25]

The official narrative of local history has been shaped by the political and economic interests of its creators. The narrative, as it was first published in the local press, reflected the desires of an early-twentieth-century elite to contest the aspirations of Manizaleños, whom they viewed as trespassing upon local interests and sensibilities. When these and successive generations of Riosucio intellectuals incorporated indígenas in a subordinate role into the local historical narrative, they imagined Riosucio as a unified community, with the urban townspeople at its head. Townspeople have sought to ensure that the cabecera would maintain control over dependent rural precincts (*veredas*). More specifically, they want to assure that the cabecera maintains control over the electoral machinery, patron-client networks, and the disbursement of state revenues. Attempts to color the indígenas as mestizos have reflected ongoing efforts on the part of the same local elite to dissolve the increasingly assertive indigenous cabildos, privatize the indigenous landholdings, and hold on to disputed private properties in the resguardo. If Riosucio is one community, and Riosuceños are one race with a common history, as the official narrative implies, then there is no need for autonomous forms of indigenous governance that threaten the economic and political interests of private landholders and municipal officials.

Imagining community and defining identity involves power; governing elites (and would-be elites) narrate their past in such a way as to form unifying bonds without undermining hierarchy. Legal arguments about the legitimacy or illegitimacy of indigenous institutions contain arguments about history and racial identity. Control over resources has often been at stake; the dissolution of the Quinchía and San Lorenzo resguardos in the 1940s occurred in part as a response to demands from local political leaders seeking to privatize indigenous-held lands. Moreover, it is no accident that allusions to the mestizo nature of Riosucio's population—the raza riosuceña—were explicit in the 1970s–1980s. At that time, left-wing guerrilla groups started recruiting among the rural population, while Riosucio's indigenous leaders became involved in a nationwide indigenous rights movement. The indígenas became increasingly confrontational in pressing their land claims against the interests of local elites. In 1988 an activist from La Montaña, Jose Gilberto Motato Largo, ran for alcalde of Riosucio on an indigenous rights platform. Barefoot, dressed in campesino clothing, identifying as indigenous rather than mestizo or white, he directly challenged both the Liberal and Conservative cliques that continued to vie for control of the district government. Like many other leftist and alternative candidates that year, he was assassinated for his efforts. As in the vast majority of Colombian murders, no one was tried for this crime.[26]

Riosucio's official history, written by successive generations of educated intellectuals based in the town center, is not the only historical narrative about Riosucio. Previous chapters have shown how indigenous intellectuals in Riosucio district also wrote local history; they drafted and commissioned legal documents and petitions that recounted versions of the local narrative that differed in subtle and yet significant ways from the official narrative examined here. These unofficial histories were not published in newspaper series and monographs. Rather, they have been scattered over time and space in decaying documents and oral accounts.

The next chapter looks at the history of Riosucio district from an unofficial viewpoint, by examining the history and historical memory of the community of San Lorenzo. San Lorenzo's very existence complicates the binary origin story. San Lorenzo indígenas rarely appeared in the official narrative of Riosucio as the melding of two razas because San Lorenzo was neither of La Montaña nor of Quiebralomo. Nor, for that matter, did San Lorenzo meld into the whole. The indígenas of San Lorenzo continued to refer to themselves as indígenas despite pressures to conform and become mestizos. Moreover, like all of the indigenous inhabitants of the outlying veredas (including even those of La Montaña), the San Lorenzo inhabitants fit uncomfortably in the town-centered community that Riosucio's urban elites have tried to promote. The indígenas of San Lorenzo, and of Riosucio district more generally, have elaborated their own communal imaginings.

CHAPTER EIGHT

Remembering San Lorenzo:

Imagining an

Indigenous Community

While regional elites in Manizales were creating the myth of white Caldas and Riosucio town intellectuals were countering with the myth of mestizo Riosucio, the indigenous community of San Lorenzo was attracting scholarly attention. Anthropologist Luís Duque Gómez visited Riosucio in the early 1940s and expressed surprise at finding indigenous communities in white Caldas. San Lorenzo was the community that most impressed him for its "extraordinary group spirit." San Lorenzo had "a collective consciousness as one of the most advanced comunidades." Duque Gómez marveled at the community's repudiation of intermarriage and its resistance to settlement by outsiders. He also found that San Lorenzo was marked by a greater degree of racial purity than the surrounding parcialidades.[1]

Duque noted that San Lorenzo's endogamous kinship tendencies and aversion to interlopers were related to the strength of the community's internal organization. Equating racial purity and "vigor" with women's sexual purity, he also emphasized the "Christian morality" of San Lorenzo's women:

Where the community is more vigorous, better organized in relation to the significance of its juridical boundaries with respect to the rest of the ethnic groups, mestizaje is naturally affected, because white penetration is made more difficult. Such Indians have a certain disdain for the "whites" and when they refer to those natives who have mixed a little, they say pejoratively "they are very scrambled [re-

vueltos]." . . . The conduct of the Indian women in this resguardo is highly in accord with Christian morality, they are unlikely to engage in sexual contact with individuals of other ethnic groups, they only do so with members of their race and only after entering into Catholic matrimony.[2]

This chapter is about San Lorenzo, which, compared to neighboring parcialidades, sold off relatively little of its land during the late nineteenth and early twentieth centuries. When I first noted San Lorenzo's success in keeping its resguardo largely intact, I initially assumed that the community had maintained its integrity by remaining culturally and politically aloof, by turning its back on dominant society. But San Lorenzo's history turned out to be far more complicated. San Lorenzo was far from isolated; its relative autonomy was contingent upon the relationships that its leaders formed with outsiders. As in the cases of La Montaña and Supía-Cañamomo, such relationships implied compromises and sacrifices. Indigenous identity, moreover, was not the only glue that held the community together: Catholicism and Conservative party affiliation were also important aspects of communal life.

San Lorenzo's integrity and relative autonomy for conducting its internal affairs were achieved through negotiations with civil and ecclesiastic authorities. The community was particularly successful in carving a place for itself within the institutional structures and political alignments created by the Regeneration at the end of the nineteenth century. After the ouster of Conservatives from national power by Liberals in 1930, however, San Lorenzo was left vulnerable to new political and economic forces. The cabildo was largely helpless when faced with top-down interference in 1944 from the national Liberal government, which suppressed the cabildo and divided the community's lands into private parcels.

Most of this chapter is about the history of San Lorenzo during the late nineteenth and the early twentieth centuries, based in part on documentary sources similar to those consulted for the cases of Supía-Cañamomo and La Montaña in parts 1 and 2. The chapter traces how one community, over time, experienced some of the long-term historical processes examined in previous chapters. The chapter concludes with a discussion of memory and identity. The suppression of San Lorenzo's indigenous institutions and the subsequent restoration of those institutions during the 1980s and 1990s have affected the way that local inhabitants (and scholars) remember San Lorenzo's history, as is evident in transcripts of a series of interviews with indigenous elders carried out by sociologist Angela Gómez in the early 1990s. These transcripts, upon which this chapter draws, contain personal recollections going back to the first half of the twentieth century as well as some stories about earlier times. Such memories were influenced by the inevitable distortions of time and aging. And, as is commonly the case in oral history, these recollections were vague and contradictory as to chronology. As shown below, the personal narratives were also influenced by the dissolution and the resurrection of the indigenous cabildo and by the changing degrees of validity accorded to Indian identity over time. In short, this chapter tells a story about how San Lorenzo maintained, lost, and then re-created its identity as a pueblo indio. While the previous chapter was, to borrow a phrase from Otto Morales Benítez, about "memories of mestizaje," this chapter analyzes memories of Indianness.[3]

COMMUNAL PATRIARCHY AND ENDOGAMY

The chapter begins toward the end of the nineteenth century, by which time San Lorenzo had become known as the most "Indian" of the local indigenous communities. San Lorenzo's indigenous authorities used the coercive mechanisms that the state placed at their disposal to police the ethnic boundaries of their community and to maintain their relative autonomy from outside interference. They regulated the sexual behavior and marital choices of members, particularly of women. Members of the community agreed upon these norms and vested their cabildo with the authority to enforce them. The community was patriarchal, conceived by its members as an extended version of a male-headed family.[4]

The patriarchal norms they followed and enforced were the product of centuries of negotiation and interaction with the state and the church. The indígenas of San Lorenzo trace their ancestry to several families that the colonial visitador Lesmes de Espinosa y Saravia brought from what is now Sonsón, Antioquia, and settled in the area in 1627. (One might say that the Indians of San Lorenzo were Riosucio's first "Antioqueño migrants.") Although identified as an Indian village, theirs was a community very much shaped by the religious and state institutions of the colonial and then republican regimes. In dialogue with these institutions, they developed forms of dress, crafts, food consumption, beliefs, and other cultural markers which were not always dramatically different from those adapted by Indians and non-Indians of the area, but which they considered part of their own heritage and identity nonetheless. At the same time, they learned to speak Spanish and practice Catholicism.

By the 1870s, this community reportedly numbered almost four hundred individuals, who lived in a resguardo that straddled the districts of Supía and Riosucio. The resguardo had been part of Riosucio district until 1866, when it was separated by order of the chief of Toro and annexed to Supía. Around 1905, it would be re-annexed to Riosucio. Although the exact residential pattern and chronology remain unclear, by the end of the nineteenth century the main village had a chapel and central square, around which communal life centered. To the north of the main village, some of the indígenas lived in outlying hamlets and scattered farms. Elders recalled that in San Lorenzo, up until the mid–twentieth century, people drank herb beverages and homemade liquors called *guarapo* and *chicha* (made from cane and maize, respectively, and common in the Colombian Andes). They cultivated sugarcane, maize, and beans. The basis of their diet was probably plantain, especially a highly nutritious type known as *guineo* (reflecting its African origin). The highland portions of the resguardo served as common reserves, where a family might clear a small plot, collect wild tubers and plants, and hunt.[5]

The 1874 communal census (discussed in chapter 3) provides one of the few archival sources for nineteenth-century marital practices and racial identity. The most outstanding feature of the 1874 padrón was just how "Indian" San Lorenzo was thought to be (and thought itself to be). In neighboring Supía-Cañamomo, the communal census referred to members as "descendants of indígenas" by one or two lines, suggesting a certain distancing of the enrolled members with their indigenous ancestry. In San Lorenzo, however, the racial labels were clear, unambiguous, and immediate. Over 90 percent of the individuals listed were clearly defined with the label "indígena puro[a]." The few of mixed heritage were labeled mestizos, and a few women's names carried the annotation: "No es india." In San Lorenzo, a person was either Indian, mestizo, or not. Colonial-era caste labels such as mestizo and indio were obviously still in use in the community. Terms such as indio, "pure," and mestizo did not merely refer to an inherited status from a distant past, but to identities that were apparently still valid.[6]

Their unambiguous racial identity was reflected in the extent to which they kept both the demographic and geographical boundaries of their community intact. San Lorenzo's resistance to mixing with outsiders was especially striking in comparison to the overwhelming mestizaje of Supía-Cañamomo. The reportedly high proportion of "pure" Indians in San Lorenzo as late as the 1870s suggests that they had maintained endogamous kinship patterns throughout the nineteenth century by restricting the reproductive options of members, especially women. In 1874 no indigenous San Lorenzo women were listed as having married non-Indians, although three had married mestizos. Two "pure" indigenous men and one mestizo man had married non-Indian women. Any women who might have married outsiders, if such existed, were no longer listed as members, a sanction that apparently did not apply to men. San Lorenzo indígenas, moreover, were expected to marry. In comparison to other neighboring indigenous communities, the inhabitants of San Lorenzo were much more likely to live in male-headed households. Cabildos reportedly enforced the laws of the state against "scandalous" extramarital cohabitation (amancebamiento escandaloso) as well as the community's even stricter prescriptions regarding marital choice.[7]

Regeneration legislation, especially Law 89 of 1890 and Decree 74 of 1898, provided the indigenous leaders with tools for maintaining communal boundaries. In the 1890s and early 1900s, other communities, such as La Montaña, complained that Antioqueños and other male outsiders were gaining control over communal lands by marrying indigenous women, but only in the case of San Lorenzo have I found actual court documents whereby the cabildo, citing Decree 74, brought legal proceedings against such men and sought to have them expelled from communal lands. These proceedings apparently formed part of a defensive legal strategy on the part of the cabildo, which sued other interlopers as well. (The cabildo also sought to expel at least one male indígena who, the cabildo claimed, had lost his membership rights because of his prolonged absence from the community.) Forcing indigenous women who married outside the community to forfeit their rights prevented their non-Indian husbands from taking over their shares, and brutally preserved the integrity of the community.[8]

Previous chapters discussed how regions, like nations, have been imagined as communities and as families. The comunidad of San Lorenzo also imagined itself as a patriarchal family. The cabildo represented and embodied the collective padres de familia of the community. In practice, the cabildo was always (until very recently) composed of and chosen by men. As an elderly woman would recall, "They say that there was a Cabildo, I don't remember very well because the men went there to the Monday meetings, only men went." Or, as one man put it: "The maximum authority and that which the people obeyed, man or woman, was the Cabildo, those who would go to vote were men."[9]

The governor embodied and represented the collective paternal authority of the parents; he was the patriarch. His authority was reinforced by departmental and national legislation that cast the indígenas as legal minors. Of course, as indígenas, the governor and the cabildo were included within the category of non-adults, but within the confines of San Lorenzo they exercised considerable power. Rafael Bueno noted that the governor had to be experienced and around thirty years old at least. He had to be of sufficient age to exercise fatherlike authority. When parental authority broke down within a household, moreover, the governor's paternal role became even more evident; Bueno recalled that the cabildo and the governor instructed youth to obey their parents.[10]

As previous chapters have shown, Cauca Law 90 of 1859 and the subsequent legislation of the Regeneration era conferred upon governors and cabildos the authority to arbitrate certain kinds of disputes and punish minor "moral" infractions with up to two days of confinement. In San Lorenzo, the indigenous authorities took these responsibilities seriously. Duque Gómez asserted that, until sometime before his visit, the governors reportedly would order errant Indians who had abandoned the community brought back by force. Angela Gómez's elderly informants recalled that the governor disciplined people for disorderly behavior, such as excessive drunkenness and fighting, by tying them up and locking them in stocks. According to Rafael Bueno, the cabildo extended its coercive authority to the outlying precincts, or veredas, by delegating indígenas to act as commissaries and relying upon neighbors to maintain surveillance over each other.[11]

Indigenous authorities in San Lorenzo have preserved some scattered nineteenth-century cabildo documents, including minutes of cabildo meetings and a few fragments of arbitration proceedings. In those proceedings, the governor tried to restore familial and communal peace that had been perturbed by problems such as domestic violence, youthful rebellion, unpaid debts, and neighborly disputes. Following are excerpts from two such proceedings in 1894.[12]

We summoned the Señores Evangelista Gañan for the crime against Nicolás Gañan and made the agreement that neither the one nor the other would again cause another crime that [Evangelista] would not accuse Señor Nicolás with the wife of Evangelista and [Evangelista] promised not to continue being jealous of his wife and to live in peace and well, and he told me that from now on he would set up a good plot and he also committed to setting up a good house for his wife to work.[13]

Señora Liandra Betancur presented herself and said that she claimed the daughter Dorotea who had run away with Ramos Andica and they had been found in the house of Señor Clímaco Lemos, having gone to the Commissary. . . . Señor Lemos told them that he would bring them [before the Governor] and being present today the mother received the daughter . . . the said daughter answered that she would not again commit the same crime with the understanding that the punishment if she were to do it again would be the worst punishment.[14]

The governor appeared concerned with preserving familial peace and parental authority; parents and husbands were expected to make certain concessions to their charges (the husband had to provide for his wife, and the mother would receive her errant daughter back into the home) in return for which their charges would accept parental authority (Dorotea accepted that her mother would beat her if she erred again). Neighborly peace was also important; Evangelista agreed not to make accusations against his neighbor. At the same time that governors and cabildos enforced patriarchal family relationships, they used these proceedings to preserve their own authority and thus their community's autonomy. When disputes could not be resolved by the indigenous authorities, the state would become involved. In the second excerpt cited, the dispute was already beginning to transcend the borders of the community when the runaway lovers took refuge with Clímaco Lemos, a non-Indian official. Lemos cooperated with the cabildo and reinforced its authority by bringing the dispute to the governor.

When arbitration proceedings failed, the district mayor was the next recourse, followed by the circuit court judge. These officials could impose fines, confiscations, and prison sentences. Any act of expulsion, expropriation, or extended confinement undertaken by the state in such a case could prove costly, not only to the individual culprit but to their dependents and other family members, and even to the community as a whole. To the extent that the San Lorenzo cabildo was able to resolve some of these problems itself, it kept the coercive and potentially destructive forces of the state at bay. Thus, the cabildo, through the application of its legal authority and the enforcement of patriarchal and Catholic norms, maintained a certain degree of authority and autonomy. In part, the cabildo's success could have had to do with the relatively small size of San Lorenzo (compared to La Montaña and Supía-Cañamomo), where communal life revolved around the village square, market days, religious practice, and communal work rotations organized by the cabildo.[15]

LABORING TO BUILD A COMMUNITY

Regarding the cabildo there were functions that everyone had to carry out, all of the community had to obey the obligations . . . which included labor to open roads, ditches to mark boundaries . . . and one had to be ready for the meetings. Every two weeks they had meetings.—Constantino Betancur, ca. 1991

The cabildo reinforced its own authority by organizing the productive life of the community and directing the community's surplus inward, so as to avoid the trap of continually having to sell off portions of their communal resources. The cabildo's ongoing authority and prestige, manifest in its ability to mobilize communal labor, was essential to preserving the communal landholding. Several of Gómez's informants described the cabildo mainly as an institution that served to organize labor: "What the cabildo did was distribute the personnel to fix the paths, to make the streets and the pueblo of San Lorenzo." San Lorenzo belied stereotypes of "lazy" or "stupid" Indians. By the late 1890s, the community derived income from lands rented to non-indígenas. It also ran communal enterprises, most notably a roof-tile workshop, the profits from which went to maintaining the chapel, paying the priest, and covering the legal and land-surveying costs incurred in defending and managing the communal lands. Male indígenas were obliged to provide rotating labor for these enterprises and for the chapel, under threat of a fine or detention. At some point around the turn of the century, the cabildo initiated construction of a school.[16]

For a poor community to expend so much of its most abundant resource—labor—on the church was a significant sacrifice. In addition, San Lorenzo conducted regular collections to pay for chapel upkeep and religious rituals. But labor for the church was tightly bound up with labor for the community, and by focusing communal labor and other resources on the church as well as communal enterprises and village infrastructure, the community kept these resources within its own boundaries. Moreover, the chapel became the centerpiece of the village and the community and further served to enforce a sense of unity and belonging.

Informants generally agreed, and the archival documents also reflected, that the rotating work gangs organized by the cabildo were exclusively male. Yet the division of labor according to gender showed some flexibility. Some of the oral narratives mentioned that women tied up their skirts under their legs "in the form of pants and they went out to work." Women participated in labor specifically assigned to men, particularly in the context of informal work parties known as *convites*. In addition to the formal work teams organized by the cabildo, the indígenas of San Lorenzo mobilized convites to accomplish specific agricultural or building tasks on behalf of individual families (a practice still common among rural inhabitants, particularly for house-raising).[17]

Communal authorities negotiated with district officials to ensure that San Lorenzo's labor resources were primarily directed inward. In particular, they haggled over the allocation of forced labor. Poor peasant men, including indígenas, had to provide a tax consisting of physical labor on a rotating basis to their district government. Such labor (known as *trabajo personal subsidario*) was particularly important in building and maintaining the trails between towns and hamlets. San Lorenzo's cabildo, in the early twentieth century, negotiated with district officials in Riosucio, apparently with some success, to use the "subsidiary labor" within the village and to maintain the paths leading from San Lorenzo to the towns of Riosucio and Supía. Such arrangements underscore the extent to which San Lorenzo's relative autonomy depended not only on the hard work and "Catholic morality" of its members, but also on the ability of its cabildo to negotiate successfully with local representatives of the state.[18]

In addition to organizing labor, the cabildo adjudicated land rights. "The lands were of the Parcialidad . . . then later the people were forming more and the Governor of the Parcialidad would give an adjudication, fifteen *almudes* of land to each indígena and they would go to work what they had been adjudicated, this was how all of this was formed." Even though the cabildo apparently adjudicated portions of land to individual men or families, it maintained sufficient control over the allotments so that members did not sell off their "shares" as did the residents of neighboring communities in the 1870s–1880s. The cabildo seemed able to keep most outside leaseholders from claiming permanent land rights in the community. San Lorenzo's leaders did not, however, eschew all dealings with outsiders. San Lorenzo's cabildos, like those of the surrounding communities, had little choice but to engage in relationships with outsiders in order to gain access to loans and to the courts and to ameliorate the labor demands imposed by the state upon the community.[19]

POLITICAL PATRONAGE AND THE LIMITS OF AUTONOMY

San Lorenzo's indígenas did not preserve their lands and their self-identity by simply closing themselves off from the outside world. Like their neighboring communities, they participated in patron-client relationships. Their principal patrons for many years were the Cauca Liberal Francisco Senen Tascón, an ally of Ramón Palau, and his National-Conservative son, Francisco Tascón de la Roche. During the last half of the nineteenth century, the elder Tascón was one of the area's bigger miners and land dealers. His relationship with San Lorenzo dated back at least as far as the 1850s, when the indígenas, in one of their few recorded nineteenth-century land sales, sold him a plot of land and hired him as their legal representative. In 1882 forty-five men from San Lorenzo, probably representing the community as a whole, sold Tascón another plot of land. In May 1889 indigenous governor Pascual Gañan and administrator Salvador Bueno registered, along with Tascón, a joint claim to a silver mine and a gold mine. While Tascón clearly benefited from these arrangements, he apparently managed to stay on friendly terms with the cabildo.[20]

The younger Tascón's influence became evident in the late 1890s as the country became embroiled in the factional disputes leading up to the Thousand Days War. In 1897, for example, a politician in Riosucio ordered the indigenous governor of San Lorenzo to prepare to send men to defend the national government in the event of an uprising by Historical Conservatives. To be sure that the governor understood and complied, this boss sent a note to Tascón de la Roche, asking him to read, explain, and enforce their instructions to the indigenous governor. Political bosses treated the governor of San Lorenzo as an electoral precinct-captain as well as military recruiter. He was responsible for making sure that the members of the community rallied to the Conservative cause, electorally as well as militarily. San Lorenzo had become a reliable source of National Conservative military support and votes, although, the note suggests, there were still "recalcitrants"—either Liberals or dissident Conservatives—present in the resguardo. Scattered evidence suggests that Liberalism had been a force in San Lorenzo. For example, Liberal leaders disseminated broadsheets to obtain support in San Lorenzo in the 1880s. By the early twentieth century, San Lorenzo had become known as solidly Conservative.[21]

Earlier, in the 1870s, internal political controversies had arisen in San Lorenzo. In July 1875, during the Ramón Palau era and amidst a general climate of tension, a resident of Riosucio complained of a wave of growing hatreds and unspecified crimes in San Lorenzo. Soon after, another document, dated 8 September 1875 and signed by Governor Rufino Gañan along with various members of his cabildo, also referred to disputes regarding the cabildo. Unfortunately, all that exists of that document is a faded, ripped, and almost completely illegible fragment, so we can only guess at the context of the dispute. In the fragment, Gañan and his allies affirmed that they longed to remain in their posts but had been pushed out by "a few persons who do not know what is good." Clearly, some leaders of San Lorenzo were not above calling for outside intervention when their own internal authority was threatened. This particular dispute occurred at the same time that Palau and his Liberal allies in the town of Supía were trying to dismember the Supía-Cañamomo resguardo, while Conservative leaders in Riosucio town were taking a portion of La Montaña for the Quiebralomeños. Partisan alignments and patronage arrangements were apparently contested within San Lorenzo, but the contestations have been largely erased from the historical record of the nineteenth century, leaving us with little more than yellowed fragments to suggest the existence of dissent.[22]

Oral narratives provide contradictory accounts of San Lorenzo's partisan past. One informant noted that in the early-to-mid–twentieth century, Liberals as well as Conservatives campaigned actively in San Lorenzo. The same informant noted that the cabildos were elected popularly with ballots, as in any official election, and that there were often two opposing candidates—implying that the candidates may have been allied with opposing political parties. Some informants, however, claimed that San Lorenzo was historically Conservative except for some outlying, low-altitude areas near the Liberal black village of Guamal: "The only Liberals lived in the lower part toward Guamal, San Cayetano, La Playa, those [veredas] had been a Liberal hotbed, the rest were Conservatives." This quote suggested that even within such a small community as San Lorenzo, political alliances were often understood to follow topographical and racial configurations, as in the district and the nation at large. Another common story was that San Lorenzo was historically Liberal. According to this version, San Lorenzo only converted to Conservatism as a result of proselytizing by a priest who also changed the ways that Indians ate and dressed.[23]

San Lorenzo's cabildo likely reached some sort of accord with Mosquera Liberals such as Palau and Tascón and then, like many of this faction, entered into the Regeneration coalition from the Liberal rather than the Conservative side. The Thousand Days War, which divided the Nationalist coalition of Liberals and Conservatives and embittered Liberal–Conservative hatreds throughout Colombia, may have had similar effects in San Lorenzo. The men and boys of San Lorenzo went to war on the Conservative side, led into battle, according to one version, by one of Riosucio's preeminent turn-of-the-century Conservative bosses, Clemente Díaz.[24]

By the late 1890s, communal authorities were vociferously proclaiming their loyalty to the Conservative Party. This posture was reflected in a petition by San Lorenzo's then-governor Manuel C. Gañan, his cabildo, and about twenty other male indígenas regarding a jurisdictional dispute. In their letter to the government of Cauca, they complained of abuses by Supía district officials (to whom they were still at that time subordinated) and asked to be separated from the district of Supía and to be placed once again under the jurisdiction of the district of Riosucio. They made their argument by appealing to the partisan interests of the government and citing their historical loyalty to the National Conservative cause: "The majority of the people of Supía are radicals and perhaps from this comes the dislike, for them to treat us like this, we were always shouldering our rifles in defense of the Government that today rules, with the people of Riosucio." Their strategy was not immediately successful, but by 1905 the community of San Lorenzo was redistricted and attached to the more Conservative district of Riosucio, with whom San Lorenzo's leaders apparently enjoyed a more harmonious political relationship.[25]

The cabildo's political tactics and alliances demonstrate that their political autonomy was relative and compromised. San Lorenzo was culturally conservative. Moreover, it became more politically conservative and more church-oriented over the course of the period under discussion, from the 1870s through the Regeneration and into the twentieth century. The inhabitants' collective identity as Conservative and their identity as Catholic as well as indigenous, reinforced a sense of unity and helped keep the community together. Attaining this unity, however, involved recurring to outside authorities to help suppress dissent and overcome internal factional divisions. The sacrifices demanded by communal solidarity were not small. Keeping the faith entailed sacrifices in terms of labor and other communal resources directed toward the chapel and religious worship. Political parties, moreover, made demands in labor and, most painfully, in the sacrifice of young men drafted to fight in the civil wars of the nineteenth century.

San Lorenzo did manage to avoid the partisan massacres that plagued the country during La Violencia that started in the late 1940s. At least internally, "one does not hear that the violence reached here." By then, the indígenas of San Lorenzo were overwhelmingly Conservative, as were those few outsiders who were able to gain a foothold in the community, and the national government was once again, after the Liberal interlude of 1930–45, in Conservative hands. No internal Liberal force existed that was sufficiently strong to mount a challenge that might provoke retaliatory violence by Conservative inhabitants or the military. While the inhabitants of San Lorenzo were fortunate in escaping the partisan massacres, however, they did suffer another rupture that left deep marks on collective memory. In 1944 the Liberal national government, in collaboration with local politicians, partitioned the San Lorenzo resguardo and dissolved the cabildo. For the next four decades—the period in which Gómez's informants lived out most of their lives—the cabildo ceased to exist. Antioqueño migrants poured in, some of them fleeing La Violencia in other zones.[26]

DISSOLUTION OF THE INDIGENOUS COMMUNITY

My papa would tell how in that time the land was for whoever wanted to work it, for whoever grabbed a plot, wherever he wanted. . . . There was such a horrible commission that they say was going to divide up the mountains. . . . This all belonged to us, the poor, and now they were coming, they came . . . to rob the poor fools who were selling them the land for nothing. Those who ended up with the land were the [relatives of] the late Santiago González. . . . They bought what was ours for nothing.—Felipa Bueno, ca. 1991

The early 1940s marked the end of the fifty-year moratorium on dividing indigenous resguardos. In 1940 Liberal President Eduardo Santos decreed the partition of indigenous communal lands. As on all previous occasions when the government undertook to extinguish resguardos, however, these legal provisions were implemented unevenly. Local political alliances, the influence of local politicians in the national government, the commercial value of the lands in question, and resistance and negotiation on the part of the Indians themselves determined which communities were partitioned and which were not.[27]

San Lorenzo was targeted for dissolution rather than either of the other two resguardos that formed part of Riosucio district, La Montaña and Cañamomo-Lomaprieta (as Supía-Cañamomo had come to be known). Local private landowners were frustrated at their inability to gain access to San Lorenzo's fertile land, much of which was located at an ideal altitude for coffee. In La Montaña and Supía-Cañamomo, as we have seen, the cabildos had not constituted as great an impediment to the encroachment of miners, cattle ranchers, and farmers. In addition, San Lorenzo's relationship with Conservative politicians seem to have left it vulnerable to national changes in political administration after the Conservative government fell in 1930. The patriarchal indigenous authority structure of San Lorenzo, moreover, seemed to have entered a moment of crisis.[28]

Anthropologist Duque Gómez noted the enthusiasm of the functionaries of the public lands section of the Ministry of the Economy for the partition of San Lorenzo in the 1940s. They argued that private titling of Indian lands would provide a beneficial method for alleviating indigenous problems. San Lorenzo's relative "progress," compared with other neighboring parcialidades, ironically may have worked to the cabildo's disadvantage. State functionaries seem to have viewed the community as an ideal proving ground for its partition policy; San Lorenzo would be a model for others to follow.[29]

The expansion of coffee production had made these lands particularly appetizing. Coffee, according to oral narratives in San Lorenzo, had arrived through the initiatives of an Antioqueño priest assigned to Riosucio parish, Father José Gonzalo Uribe, who began preaching in the village chapel around the second decade of the century. Andrea recalled: "Coffee arrived. . . . A Father Uribe arrived and told them to plant coffee, if they confessed the penitence was to plant coffee because later that would provide for them to maintain themselves." A prototypical Antioqueño Catholic priest, according to the oral narratives, Uribe promoted commercial development and modified indigenous consumption habits as part of his religious mission. "He told the indigenous people to dress: he said, I am going to bring you a store to sell you shirts and pants, plant Coffee, don't plant guineo, plant other plantains that aren't colored but rather good plantain."[30]

The merchant that Father Uribe reportedly brought to San Lorenzo to sell respectable clothes to the Indians was an Antioqueño by the name of Santiago González, who set up a mule train between Medellín and San Lorenzo. The wily Antioqueño mule driver/merchant is a regional archetype, and González did his best to conform to type—at least in the memories of San Lorenzo indígenas. He reportedly bought coffee at low prices, sold merchandise, and after the partition he provided credit to the new indigenous property owners. He, along with his brothers and other merchants and investors from Riosucio and Antioquia, gained landholdings in San Lorenzo by buying titles and foreclosing on mortgages and crop liens. Felipa Bueno's father lost his plot to González through a foreclosure. María Jesús Díaz recalled: "The first to arrive were the Gonzálezes, they would get some poor guy and for a few bags of coffee they would take his lands . . . they would provide credit to plant a field of maize and . . . they took the land." The changing consumption and production habits encouraged by the priest and the merchants, whereby indígenas were to plant marketable corn, coffee, and "good" plantains rather than their staples, left San Lorenzo cultivators even more vulnerable to foreclosures and land loss, as well as to malnutrition.[31]

The resguardo partition apparently coincided with an internal crisis of authority within San Lorenzo. San Lorenzo had been enmeshed since 1905 in a long-running lawsuit with the neighboring parcialidad of La Montaña. Such lawsuits usually proved costly to indigenous communities, and this one apparently cost San Lorenzo in terms of land as well as morale. The San Lorenzo cabildo, following a pattern established in the other parcialidades, paid their apoderado, Emiliano García, in land. Constantino Betancur recalled:

> The cabildo ended in the two last suits between the parcialidad of La Montaña and the parcialidad of San Lorenzo. . . . They litigated over a piece of land, now there wasn't anyone left who would work for the Cabildo. . . . My father recounted that he was seventeen years at the time of this last lawsuit but he could not be Governor, only Acting Governor, because he was young.[32]

Betancur described such lawsuits as having fatally weakened the cabildo. Moreover, he implied that his young father had opposed some of the cabildo's actions but had been prohibited by the patriarchal structure of communal authority from challenging the cabildo or exercising effective leadership. Although the details are obscure, it seems that the cabildo was having difficulty adapting to changed economic and political circumstances, particularly the end of the era of one-party Conservative rule. Rafael Bueno recalled: "The Liberal Party was that which ended up in power and for this reason ended the cabildo because they could not tolerate Conservatives and San Lorenzo was Conservative."[33]

The dissolution of the resguardo of San Lorenzo opened the floodgates to forces that generations of cabildos had successfully kept at bay: indebtedness and landlessness among growing numbers of Indians, along with increased Antioqueño settlement and intermarriage. By the 1940s, many San Lorenzo indígenas had taken part in the export boom by growing coffee, but they were at the mercy of local "monopolizers" (acaparadores) who controlled coffee purchasing in the village. Felipa Bueno recalled that her elders sold their agricultural products very cheaply due to lack of access to transport out of San Lorenzo. One long-range result of land loss combined with population growth was increased out-migration. By the 1970s, the youth of San Lorenzo were migrating—the men to pick coffee seasonally and the women to serve as domestic laborers—throughout the Coffee Region.[34]

The suppression of the cabildo and the partition of communal lands were remembered, four decades later, as a rupture: the end of a well-defined and generally accepted, though discriminatory, structure of patriarchal authority. The concluding section of this chapter moves forward in time to consider the extent to which events since the 1940s have influenced collective memory and identity.

REMEMBERING AND RECREATING THE COMMUNITY

These oral histories were recorded in the 1990s, after the cabildo had been reinstated by a new generation of indigenous activists. During the 1970s, a wave of agrarian conflict had surged over Colombia, as landless and land-poor campesinos engaged in direct confrontations with large landholders. The peasant movement was spurred by the government's creation of a land reform agency and a peasant organization, known by its Spanish acronym as the ANUC. One offshoot of the peasant land movement was an indigenous land movement organized around the goal of regaining possession of communal territories. ANUC activists from San

Lorenzo, including Silvio Tapasco, organized to reconstitute the San Lorenzo cabildo in the early 1980s. They initially encountered resistance among inhabitants. "At the beginning [the inhabitants] didn't want to . . . they thought it was Communism, socialism." Tapasco and his allies reinstated the cabildo in 1984 according to the regulations laid out in Law 89 of 1890, and it continues to function to this day, complete with subcommittees, elections, and a cinder-block headquarters built on the site of the old roof-tile workshop. The cabildo adjudicates land to indígenas and to longtime colonos and their descendants, whom it attempts to incorporate as members of the community, and it works with the national land reform agency in an effort to obtain and redistribute private estates that remain within the communal boundaries. During my research sojourn, the cabildo was in the midst of surveying its boundaries and assembling documentation in an effort to prove legally the existence since the colonial period of a resguardo—a project resisted by the municipal government of Riosucio. At present, the cabildo's control over the resguardo is still disputed.[35]

The indigenous leaders of San Lorenzo, like those in the neighboring communities, have once again become political power brokers. Unlike in the era before the resguardo was partitioned, they now work with a series of organizations and institutions created to assist indígenas and other peasants—including the Regional Council of Caldas Indígenas (Consejo Regional de Indígenas de Caldas, or CRIDEC); non-governmental development organizations (NGOs); state-sponsored agricultural assistance projects; the Coffee Federation; and the governmental Office of Indigenous Affairs—all of which provide support and training to indigenous leaders and reaffirm indigenous identity as such. Under the new 1991 Constitution, the cabildos have the right to receive and disburse state revenues. On the mornings that the cabildo holds office hours, inhabitants form long lines in the cabildo headquarters, waiting to discuss their land allotments and related affairs with the governor and the secretary.

San Lorenzo's weekly market bustles with produce vendors, and the Coffee Cooperative does a brisk business on the central plaza of the village, buying top-quality coffee for foreign export. San Lorenzo also produces dark sugar (panela) and plantains for regional markets and is known for its basketry. Yet, at the same time, San Lorenzo remains mired in poverty, and most of its young men and young women migrate to find low-wage work. Underemployed and mobile, the youth of San Lorenzo are also recruited by the guerrillas.[36]

The principal guerrilla armies (known by their Spanish acronyms as the FARC, ELN, and EPL) have all operated in the mountains of western Caldas and Risaralda, claiming to support indigenous land rights. Indigenous leaders do not want to antagonize either side in the armed conflict and have attempted to stake out a public position of neutrality. But this stance has not protected them from repression. Military personnel and paramilitary groups, allegedly backed by landowners and politicians, have murdered indigenous activists, a pattern that has been repeated across the country. According to an internal report by the land reform agency in the early 1990s, "these actions had a clear goal: to exterminate the Resguardos, destroy the organization of the Cabildo, and appropriate the better part of its lands." By the end of the decade, paramilitaries associated with the national organization known as the AUC had entered the indigenous resguardos, carried out political assassinations, and threatened to massacre indígenas whom they accused of collaborating with the guerrillas.[37]

These developments affected the way that people in San Lorenzo remembered and represented their collective past. Angela Gómez's interviews with elders took place on the eve of the 1992 Quincentenary celebrations, a time when Indian contributions to Colombian identity were publicly debated and discussed. No doubt, she was not the first to ask these men and women about their indigenous heritage; Silvio Tapasco and his cohort had done much the same when they sought to resurrect the cabildo a decade before. The cultural climate of recent decades—in which indigenous culture is increasingly valued rather than universally disparaged—might have encouraged the elderly informants to relate their own Indian past in a favorable light. Had they been asked similar questions during the 1970s, when rural activists preferred a model of class rather than ethnic solidarity, the tone of their remembrances would have differed.

Moreover, given the present-day context of proletarianization, poverty, and rural violence, it is not surprising that these elders, like older people throughout Colombia, looked back at their youth with a certain nostalgia and characterized it as a period of greater peace, social order, natural abundance, and even semi-utopian communitarianism. (In this sense, their nostalgia shows similarities with that of Antioqueños who long "for the time of our grandparents.") Rosario Bueno recalled that "among those I am telling you about there were never any problems, they lived as siblings, all were like one's papá, one didn't see fights over land or boundaries either among families . . . not even when they had fiestas and they drank guarapo, all together they collaborated to work their plots and to gather wood in the tierra fría." According to Constantino Betancur: "The land had no owners rather it was only for he who wanted to take a plot and work it." Israel Rojas claimed that "around here one did not see . . . differences among families until now."[38]

These accounts contrast the rustic idyll of an imagined past with a present of private property and class differentiation accompanied by poverty, violence, and migrant labor: "The people went out to work . . . to look for day wages. Do you know how they pay those people down there? They would go for a whole week or a month to work, and earned a pathetic five centavos per day . . . one ended up in ruins." The informants portrayed the past as freer, in terms of access to natural resources, yet they also recalled the earlier era as socially more orderly and peaceful. With the end of the cabildo, patriarchal structures of communal authority broke down, leading to greater vice, disorder, and violence: "After the cabildo ended, one started seeing vices, robberies of cattle and crops."[39]

The nostalgia that colored these remembrances should not blind us, to the extent to which some of their content is substantiated by the archival evidence cited earlier in this chapter, even though other aspects are disputed. Conflicts over land and authority clearly did take place, yet nineteenth- and early twentieth-century padres de familia exercised patriarchal authority through their cabildos in such a way as to preserve the geographic and demographic integrity of their community. What some of the more rose-colored anecdotes obscure is the extent to which communal self-policing involved coercion and exclusion along gendered, generational, and partisan lines.

Gómez's interviews with indigenous elders were carried out as part of a larger effort by indigenous leaders, some national government officials, and NGOs to "recuperate memory" of cultural practices considered "authentically" Indian. This project emphasizes those markers of difference that might justify, from a cultural standpoint, the legal existence of the resguardos. The Office of Indigenous Affairs, for example, holds conferences for local practitioners of herbal medicine. In the oral narratives, informants were encouraged to go into detail about "indigenous" practices such as herbal medicine, weddings, funerals, communal work parties, beliefs about cave-dwelling spirits, consumption patterns, and former modes of dress. Yet, as Riosucio folklorist Julián Bueno has noted, many supposedly "Indian" practices are common not only among the resguardo indígenas, but among the rural inhabitants of these districts more generally. As Joanne Rappaport has similarly noted for present-day Cumbal indígenas in southern Colombia, "they frequently cite life ways common to their mestizo neighbors as evidence of their cultural distinctiveness."[40]

Rappaport has also suggested recently that scholars of Colombia should examine how Antioqueño colonization has affected indigenous identity in Colombia (as distinct from indigenous ethnicity in other Andean countries). In defining their own cultural practices, the indigenous informants of San Lorenzo defined themselves not so much in opposition to blacks, mestizos, or even whites, per se, but in opposition to Antioqueños. Increased Antioqueño colonization in San Lorenzo coincided with the suppression of the indigenous cabildo and the loss of communal indigenous identity—a rupture that split the lives of those who lived through it in two. What was before was Indian; what came after was not. Indígenas defined themselves against the Antioqueños. They contrasted Antioqueño mercantilism with indigenous communitarianism, for example, and they contrasted Antioqueño consumption preferences, such as commercial *aguardiente*, with their local foods and homemade liquor.[41]

As this book has argued repeatedly, the discourse of regional differentiation has associated Antioqueño practices with progress. The inhabitants of San Lorenzo have not been immune from this discourse. For four decades, beliefs and practices not associated with the Antioqueños were locally castigated and marginalized as indio, in the most pejorative sense of the word, connotative of backwardness. Even in the 1980s and 1990s, when indigenous identity and practice were increasingly reaffirmed and valued, decades of shame and ambivalence were not easily overcome. The oral narratives of elders reflect some of this ambivalence. Thus, even as they recall the past in utopian terms, indígenas such as Constantino Betancur recall that "the first primitives did not love to work" *(no le pusieron mucho amor al trabajo)*, a statement that is contradicted by his and others' detailed narratives about communal work parties and cabildo labor. The indigenous inhabitants of San Lorenzo even now are understandably somewhat ambivalent about asserting an identity that is still associated in popular parlance with backwardness, especially because the foil against which that identity has been reconstituted is *lo antioqueño*— which they associate with respectability, progress, and hard work. Such values are hardly alien to San Lorenzo, with its long history of devout

Catholicism, Conservative politics, patriarchal authority structures, and rotating labor obligations.[42]

By asserting an indigenous identity, however ambiguously, the elders, leaders, young activists, and other members of San Lorenzo resist Riosucio townspeople's and Antioqueño settlers' pretensions to the contrary. While the official history of Caldas became one of white settlement, and the official history of Riosucio became one of mestizaje, indígenas in communities such as San Lorenzo preserved and reconstructed "unofficial" histories of Indianness. What is unofficial history in one context, however, serves as official history in another. Even San Lorenzo's Indian challenge constitutes official history in another sense. The political power base of present-day indigenous leaders (as well as their access to resources that NGOs and the state provide to indigenous communities) depends on maintaining a general consensus in San Lorenzo as to the validity and worthiness of identifying as indigenous. Even the apparently primordial peasant village is an "imagined community" with its own dynamics of power that affect how it remembers its past and racializes its identity.[43]

This chapter has shown that San Lorenzo survived as long as it did and as well as it did because of the initiative, hard work, efficiency, and cohesiveness of its members, who organized their labor collectively and negotiated with external forces while maintaining a relative degree of internal autonomy. Their cohesion and autonomy were reinforced not only by a sense of their own racial difference but also by patriarchal familial norms, religious practice, and a web of mutual obligations. Voices of dissent were silenced, absorbed, or expelled from San Lorenzo and largely erased from its own official history. The dissolution of the resguardo in the 1940s by a Liberal government, however, suggests that San Lorenzo's patriarchal conservatism and its ties to Conservative politicians had limitations in terms of promoting permanent communal viability.

This chapter demonstrates some negative consequences for the indigenous inhabitants of the "progress" heralded by local promoters of privatization and Antioqueño settlement. It is hard to gauge to what extent land privatization itself was responsible for San Lorenzo's poverty, given that the two adjoining indigenous communities, which were never dissolved, suffered many of the same economic and social problems over the second half of the twentieth century. All of the indigenous communities of Caldas, those that were partitioned and those that were not, have been impoverished by land loss, erosion, colonization, unemployment, and out-migration, compounded by population growth, falling coffee prices, and violence.

Remarkably, older inhabitants of San Lorenzo retained strong memories of their Indianness. For four decades, they quietly maintained an indigenous identity, which they contrasted with all that was Antioqueño. On the basis of such clandestine recollections, a younger generation of activists, imbued with a new discourse of Indian ethnic solidarity, succeeded in reconstituting San Lorenzo's institutions and re-imagining their community.

CONCLUSION

Reimagining Region and Nation

Recent scholarly overviews of Colombian history tend to assume that the mountainous topography of colonial New Granada gave rise to autonomous regions. Entrenched regionalism, according to this reasoning, impeded republican efforts to modernize the state and integrate the fragmented nation, leading to endemic violence and a weak national government. There is much truth to this narrative of truncated nation-state formation, but it overemphasizes continuity and essentializes geography. This book shifts the emphasis away from how geography shaped history, focusing instead on how history shaped geography. Rather than envision regionalism as a colonial holdover that impeded national integration, I view Colombian nation-state formation as a process of creating a national geography composed of regions. Regions thus emerged as part of the process of Colombian nation-state formation. This change in focus reveals the historical dynamism of regional identities.[1]

The case of Riosucio, a town founded on the eve of Independence and named for a muddy creek, demonstrates the mutability and contested nature of regional boundaries. Over time, Riosucio belonged to several shifting and overlapping regions: el gran Cauca, Antioquia la grande, el viejo Caldas, la región cafetera. In Riosucio—and throughout postcolonial Colombia—seemingly timeless and primordial geographical identities were constituted and reconstituted through colonization and myth-making. Competing groups fought and negotiated over control of natural resources and local governments. The winners in these struggles consolidated local and regional discourses of identity that expunged dissonant identities or relegated them to the distant past.

This concluding chapter reflects briefly on the ways that Colombians have referred to race and region in narrating their past, mapping their present, and expressing their aspirations for the future progress of the nation. Defining Colombia as a "country of regions" served as a way for nineteenth-century nation-builders to organize and comprehend a scattered and diverse population that did not conform to idealized visions of a racially unified modern nation. The regional mystique of the Coffee Region, in particular, is a spatial manifestation of racialized notions of modernity that associate progress with whiteness. Excluded from the "white legend," black and indigenous campesinos in the Coffee Region have nonetheless found ways to reformulate the racialized discourse of progress in their efforts to make a space for themselves within the modern nation.

A NATION OF RACIAL REGIONS

Anthropologist Peter Wade's most recent research on Colombian musical culture emphasizes a tension in contemporary Colombia between heterogeneous and homogeneous conceptualizations of the nation: "In Colombia . . . official or other public discourse on the nation includes claims both to the supposed homogeneity brought about by centuries of cultural and physical mixing and to the tremendous ethnographic diversity of a 'country of regions.'" For Wade, this tension reflects one of the central paradoxes of modern nationalism: "The attempt to present the nation as a unified homogeneous whole conflicts directly with the maintenance of hierarchies of class and culture—and their frequent corollaries, region and race—that is wanted by those who are located in the higher echelons of those hierarchies." In other words, elites promote nationalist ideals of both unity and regional diversity that maintain the legitimacy of the nation as an imagined community. Yet nationalist ideals can also serve to undermine the hierarchies that undergird elite privilege.[2]

This book opens in the mid-nineteenth century, when Colombian geographers and costumbrista writers were construing New Granada as a territory composed of distinct ethnographic and climactic regions. Building on Wade, I would argue that their racialized discourse of regional differentiation served to mediate between the evident heterogeneity of the republic and the presumed homogeneity of an ideal nation. As Benjamin Orlove has noted for Peru, nineteenth-century efforts to organize national geography by region and race allowed scientists and statesmen to reduce a complex cultural and environmental heterogeneity into a comprehensible and governable order. In Colombia, late-nineteenth-century writers glossed regions as homogeneous races. The Antioqueño, the Costeño, the Caucano, the Santandereano, the Llanero, and the Bogotano all became known as "racial types" in their own right, and each was described according to its customs, ancestry, and relative level of progress.[3]

Regionalism, however, was not simply imposed from the center by elite intellectuals, any more than it represented a premodern folk authenticity superseded by the modern nation. The varying cultural practices of Colombia's scattered population (such as architecture, art, food, worship, clothing, stories, music) provided the raw material that elite writers used in diagramming and diagnosing the nation. Moreover, aspiring regional elites performed these costumbres in constituting their leadership and delineating their domains. Political alliances, cultural practices, transportation routes, and trade patterns bound subordinate towns and ascendant cities into nineteenth-century regional blocs that proved powerful but were far from static. Competing political factions continually jockeyed for regional hegemony, shaping and reshaping regional administrative boundaries. From the late 1850s to the mid-1880s, the national state was organized as a federation of regional states, further reinforcing regional identities, power blocs, and interregional animosities. The regional community proved easier to "imagine" than the national community.

All regions were not created equal. Racial hierarchy was evident in this geographical order. The racial types according to which the Colombian nation was defined were themselves laden with the stereotypes of a modern world that prized fair skin and European culture. Racial hierarchy, moreover, was institutionalized in the geographical ordering of the modern Colombian state, most explicitly in the Regeneration. Regeneration leaders exalted Colombia's Spanish heritage and tried to create a Conservative white republic. Regeneration-era legislation ranked indígenas by their relative level of savagery, classified them as legal minors, and entrusted the Catholic church with the evangelization and governance of the "savage" indigenous groups located in frontier spaces defined as uncivilized. In parts of Cauca, towns dominated by "white people" gained administrative control over districts inhabited by Indians and blacks. The creation of the new department of Caldas in 1905 administratively unified the emerging western Coffee Region under the jurisdiction of the Conservative Antioqueño city of Manizales. Coffee provided the country's most stable nexus with the world market. Coffee revenues facilitated the modernization of the country's fragmented transportation infrastructure—but without obliterating regionalism or racism. Caldas developed a strong regional mystique as a progressive white region.

Manizales literati recounted a white legend, according to which their fair-skinned race of Antioqueños had built the region by domesticating and populating a wild frontier. In making racial and regional identity synonymous, this narrative minimized conflict and obscured the key roles played by "other races"—Caucanos as well as migrants and investors from other regions—in the colonizing process that created the Coffee Region. Local intellectuals in towns such as Riosucio disputed Manizales's regional dominance without disputing the equation of race with region. The Riosuceños claimed to belong to a separate race, and thus a separate region.

Cultural practices, along with historical narratives, provided venues for "performing" regionalism. These performances, however, left some inhabitants out. The cultural symbols of Antioquia and Caldas regional identities (such as the carriel shoulder bag and mazamorro gruel) had originated in gold mines. Yet, the black and mixed-race mining areas of Antioquia and Caldas were barely acknowledged in the foundation myths that idealized the white agricultural settlements. With the consolidation of the Coffee Region, the black, Indian, and mestizo inhabitants were largely whitewashed out of the regional historical narrative. Riosucio muddied this clean white legend of homogeneous Antioqueño settlement. And yet, the countermyth of an inclusive mestizo history, elaborated and performed by cabecera intellectuals in Riosucio, obviated the distinct concerns and identities of the rural district's indigenous inhabitants.

The Riosucio discourse of a mestizo town challenged the white region, just as the populist Liberal ideal of the mestizo nation challenged the idealized Conservative white republic. But, as scholars have pointed out in many Latin American cases, the exaltation of mestizaje was not necessarily the antithesis of "whitening." Historically, the ideology of mestizaje was often predicated on the assumption that the whiter races would absorb and improve the darker ones. Throughout Latin American history, most nationalist thinkers (both elite and popular, liberal, conservative, and even Marxist) had a hard time envisioning a modern nation in which blacks and Indians, as such, would play an equal role. Back in the 1850s, Manuel Ancízar optimistically predicted that the industrious and democratic *raza granadina* would one day replace the blacks and Indians. His hopes were echoed in the twentieth-century Brazilian and Mexican theories of "racial democracy" and "the cosmic race." Most elite intellectuals of the nineteenth and twentieth centuries assumed that national progress would involve either the cultural transformation or physical whitening—or even the annihilation—of the presumably backward darker races.[4]

This book examines the implications, for rural campesinos and small-town inhabitants, of Riosucio's ambivalent incorporation into Colombia's most "progressive" region. Indian and black villages with communal land holdings, and their own historical narratives, deviated from elite notions of what a proper town or modern nation should be. Twentieth-century Riosucio was not located in a peripheral frontier such as the Amazonian basin or the Pacific Coast. In the case of Riosucio, racial deviance flourished in the Andean heartland. Caldas was the model of respectability—the most densely populated and one of the most prosperous and whitest regions of the country. The vitality of indigenous and black identities, even in the "model department," suggested the disturbing possibility that the "Granadan race" had failed to absorb everyone, that "progress" was not yet fully attained, and that the nation was neither a melting pot nor even an array of clear-cut homogenous regions. The persistence of racial distinctions and ethnno-linguistic minorities reflected a complex racial and spatial heterogeneity and has raised the disturbing possibility that the true nation, as Colombians today sometimes lament, does not really exist at all.[5]

MUDDYING THE WATERS OF CONTEMPORARY COLOMBIA

The frightening imagery of national fragmentation, of a country haunted by disintegration and terror, reproduced in countless scholarly texts, news media, and daily conversations throughout Colombia, has been aggravated in recent years. Colombians suffer extremely high levels of political and criminal violence, pervasive class and ideological divisions, economic crisis, paramilitary and guerrilla warfare, drug trafficking, and a weak state unable to consolidate territorial control. The questions of how to define and understand the Colombian nation, and, moreover, how to achieve the elusive goals of unity, progress, and peace, worry Colombians today just as much as in the 1850s, if not more so. One response to Colombia's seemingly endemic fragmentation has been a resurgent regionalism. Politicians and scholars have put forth proposals to reorganize the national territory administratively according to its "real" regions. Meanwhile, some peacemakers have advocated regional-level negotiations with armed rebels. Regional television stations, research centers, educational institutions, and economic development projects (often funded by international organizations) have proliferated. Grassroots politics on a regional level, some reformers argue, is the best counterpoint to both the weakness of the national state and its authoritarian and oligarchic tendencies.[6]

Given the amount of energy that Colombians are often willing to expend in efforts to advance their beloved towns and regions—as opposed to their abstract and often incomprehensible nation—regionalism has tremendous potential in terms of mobilizing civil society and, perhaps, in democratizing some aspects of the state. The contested and racialized history of the Coffee Region, however, suggests a cautionary note: Regions, like all communities in Colombia, have been imagined and constructed through power-laden processes that privilege some groups while subordinating and excluding others. Regions and localities are imagined communities; as such, they are not necessarily more "authentic" than the nation, nor are they necessarily democratic or egalitarian. The nation-state is not obsolete. The national government has an important role to play in mediating among factions at the local level and preserving the rights of minorities within regions and municipal districts. In Colombia, the state has too often abdicated this role, except when pressured to act by assertive citizen activists such as the indígenas of Riosucio.

The effects and causes of racialized assumptions regarding progress and the nation are not merely confined to some ideal discursive sphere. Now, as in the past, political economy and cultural discourse are inseparable. Throughout Latin America, assumptions and theories about racial superiority and inferiority have directly affected government policy on issues such as foreign immigration and interregional migration (as well as jurisdictional boundaries, land tenure, urban planning, and public health, just to name a few policy areas). Racist policies and practices resulted in the whitening of certain regional and national populations. The most prosperous regions and countries—Cuba, Argentina, São Paulo—could afford to attract and subsidize European immigration in the late nineteenth and early twentieth centuries, whereas others—like Cauca—had to make do, at best, with migrants from neighboring regions and countries. The result has been a rough correlation between the racial definition and economic condition of regions. Regions that have attained relatively higher standards of living—such as coastal Peru, São Paulo, Buenos Aires, and northern Mexico—have achieved a whiter status than the more "backward" regions that are still considered the domain of Indians, mestizos, and blacks—such as the *sierra* and *selva* of Peru, northeastern Brazil, parts of the Argentine interior, and southern Mexico.[7]

Riosucio illustrates both the benefits and pitfalls of such regional progress. Despite living in the midst of a lucrative export economy tied to world markets in one of the most densely populated and prosperous regions of Colombia, indígenas (and the former indígenas of the nearby disbanded resguardos) remain poor. The Coffee Region is the country's agricultural heartland and now boasts a relatively developed infrastructure. Paved highways link Riosucio to Medellín, Manizales, the rest of the country, and beyond. Rural inhabitants, including indígenas, have gained unprecedented access to primary-school education, though most indigenous children do not go on to finish high school. Their families grow coffee and food crops on ever-smaller, ever-more-eroded plots of land that have not supported the booming population. Youth migrate to work in the farms and houses of middle-class and wealthy Caldenses at below-minimum-level wages, broadening their horizons and expectations but also finding themselves, for the most part, trapped in poverty. Since the 1990s, declining international prices for coffee have reduced their options even further. Their economic and educational disadvantages reflect the extent to which indígenas have been largely excluded from the cultural mystique of the Coffee Region, as well as from its economic benefits. The resguardos and former resguardos supply much of the seasonal labor force for the coffee harvest, but regional folklore, television *novelas,* and international advertising campaigns portray coffee pickers and small farmers as fair-skinned descendants of Antioqueños.[8]

And yet, progress also provides indigenous activists with tools to revive their communal institutions. This book has shown how indigenous communities have made use of the institutions of their colonization—cabildos, pueblos indígenas, court documents, resguardos, legislation, censuses, even churches—to maintain and revitalize their collective identities. The coffee economy, while adding to the problems of the indígenas,

Figure 8. Miguel Antonio ("Miguelito") Largo, Governor of La Montaña, 1995, giving a speech at an inauguration ceremony for a new governor in the neighboring resguardo of Cañamomo-Lomaprieta, at the cabildo headquarters in La Iberia, District of Riosucio. Seated behind him are the then-alcalde of Riosucio and a politician from Supía district.

has also widened their opportunities. In the 1970s, some young men who migrated to pick coffee became members of militant peasant organizations and returned to their communities with ideas about reviving their indigenous identities and agitating for land reform. By the 1990s, indigenous cabildos were working with European importers of organic coffee, whose mission included aiding self-sustaining, environmentally friendly development projects in indigenous communities.

Poor mestizo, indigenous, and black Colombians have often framed their aspirations in terms of progress, just as the elite (both liberal and conservative) has done. The indígenas of Riosucio have not been immune from the association of progress with whiteness and Antioqueños. I once asked a senior indigenous leader of La Montaña, Miguel Antonio Largo Pescador, about Antioqueño colonization in his resguardo (see figure 8). He said that settlers caused problems, but that they "also brought progress." By "progress," he referred to material and economic benefits: infrastructure, trade, schools. He saw his community as progressing in part through market integration and colonization. He viewed progress itself as beneficial, and he associated it with Antioqueños, but his understanding of progress was nonetheless different from that of the national and local elite, who have so often described progress as inimical to communal landholdings, Indians, and blackness.[9]

On a national level, indigenous activists were successful in forcing a redefinition of the Colombian nation in the Constitution of 1991. Their objective can be interpreted as re-defining the very concept of progress. Indigenous delegates, in collaboration with parties of the left, successfully pressured the assembly to replace the white republic enshrined in the 1886 Constitution with a multicultural blueprint for the state. The indigenous participants demonstrated through their own savvy politicking that Colombia does not have to be uniformly white or even mestizo to be modern. Nor does it have to be racially homogeneous to be a unified nation. The Constituent Assembly reflected and reinforced a growing recognition of the nation as ethnically and racially heterogeneous. The Constitution is widely considered to be a highly "progressive" document that, at least on paper, protects civil rights and decentralizes and democratizes the state. Unlike during the Regeneration, unity and progress now connote equality, which under the new Constitution implies respect for difference.[10]

The new "pluricultural" definition of Colombia enshrined in the Constitution reflected the vibrancy of the indigenous rights movement by the early 1990s, and helped to invigorate the much weaker Afro-Colombian movement. Each of these movements has sought to create a pan-communal ethnic identity that transcends local and regional affiliations. The creation and implementation of the 1991 Constitution coincided with the commemoration of the 1492 Quincentenary, which provoked continent-wide dialogues concerning the conquest and oppression of indigenous and African peoples. Out of this milieu emerged a vision of the nation as culturally and racially heterogeneous. By the mid-1990s, government offices in Caldas were plastered with official posters portraying female and male Colombians of varying phenotypes and regional and ethnic dress; the posters proclaimed *Unidad en la Diversidad*.[11]

The 1991 Constitution replaced Law 89 of 1890 with permanent guarantees for indigenous and, for the first time, black landholdings. It provides for indigenous and black communal authorities to govern their own territories and administer certain local programs and revenues. The Constitution explicitly recognizes the legitimacy of indigenous culture and guarantees the right to bilingual education. As has been the case with other innovative national charters in Latin America, however, the full implementation of Colombia's Constitution has been blocked by politicians whose interests it threatens. The current situation of civil strife, moreover, in which right-wing paramilitary armies and the national army battle leftist guerrilla insurgents for control over the national territory, has had an especially devastating impact on reform and civil rights. The subsequent legislative and practical implementation of the clauses regarding black and indigenous rights has thus been spotty and controversial, and in some cases thwarted by specific acts of violence, but the government has proceeded to transfer the administration of some revenues and programs to indigenous authorities in legally recognized cabildos.[12]

The implementation of these reforms raised the stakes in conflicts over resguardos. In Riosucio and neighboring Supía, disputes over the legal status and historical boundaries of the indigenous landholdings gained new urgency in the 1990s. The state's transferal of certain fiscal resources into the hands of indigenous authorities threatened the patronage networks upon which local and regional politicians depended for electoral support. Cañamomo-Lomaprieta and La Montaña have gained full legal recognition of their resguardos and their authority to govern them. They received the first resource transferals from the government and grappled with new bureaucratic challenges. The San Lorenzo authorities, meanwhile, have been fighting for legal recognition of their resguardo, of their status as indígenas, and of their right to administer fiscal resources. A fourth cabildo, located in the village of Bonafont in the southeastern corner of the district, has struggled to gain recognition of the resguardo of Pirsas y Escopeteras, the existence of which they trace to the early colonial period. The municipal governments of Riosucio and Supía have contested the validity of the resguardos of San Lorenzo and Pirsas y Escopeteras.

Critics of the transfers, and even indigenous authorities themselves, have voiced concerns that the indigenous cabildos will be corrupted by their increasing incorporation into the administrative structures of the state and will replicate the clientelism of other politicians. Inhabitants of the cabecera (echoing the complaints of previous generations) accuse the indigenous leaders of cynically assuming the label "indigenous" for personal gain. Townspeople express fears that the indigenous communities will use the Constitution to secede from the municipio. Indigenous authorities counter that they themselves are "100 percent Riosuceño." The indígenas claim that they do not want to separate from the district of Riosucio; rather, they want to run it.[13]

The meanings of race and progress are thus contested and negotiated at a local level. These debates are about more than abstract philosophical concepts such as "identity." In arguing about their past, inhabitants debate the material effects and very meaning of progress. Arguments about history, culture, and identity reflect ongoing controversies over land, revenues, and governance. These conflicts continue to pit rural indigenous campesinos against urbanized middle- and upper-class non-Indians in the town centers and cities. The rural poor, moreover, are divided among themselves over questions of identity and land tenure.

In order to provide some vivid examples of how rural racial identities have been contested at even the most intimate local level, I conclude with some local stories from my field research in the mid-1990s in two villages: Bonafont and Guamal. A hike I took in December 1994 through a coffee grove on the edge of Bonafont with an indigenous governor, Medardo Largo, provided insights into the twentieth-century politics of local history and about the inscription of racial identities onto the landscape. A small coffee farmer helped us find what we were looking for: a large flat stone etched with markings. An argument ensued between the farmer and the governor over the origin of several large flat holes on the stone's surface. The coffee farmer claimed the holes were the Devil's thumb prints. His interpretation was consistent with devil imagery that pervades the oral traditions of Colombia's Afro-Colombian and mestizo mining regions. The Devil is the symbol of Riosucio's biennial carnival celebrations, which Julián Bueno, Otto Morales Benítez, and other writers have described as a syncretic celebration of Riosucio's racially mixed heritage.

Governor Largo, on the other hand, argued that the holes were used by sixteenth-century indígenas for human sacrifice before they went to war against Spanish invaders. As we walked away, the governor muttered that the farmer was a "mestizo" and "colono" who "doesn't know anything." The governor's story, about the indigenous armies defending their territories, supported his controversial legal battle to gain recognition of the cabildo and resguardo of Pirsas y Escopetera. At that time, Largo had made little headway in proving his case; he was a governor without a parcialidad to govern.[14]

Even within more established resguardos, race, history, and space are contested. One strategy that indigenous cabildos in Colombia have employed in recent years to solidify their land claims and authority has been to take a broad view of who constitutes an "Indian" and who has rights to communal membership. Rather than employ criteria of bloodlines to determine indigenous land rights, Riosucio's indigenous authorities emphasize a racial identity defined by place. The cabildos invite all residents of the resguardos to be indigenous, to give up their private land titles in exchange for communally issued documents, to join the formal community, and to vote for communal officials. Some of the new members are admittedly opportunistic in their reasons for joining; a blue-eyed descendant of Antioqueño settlers in the highland of La Montaña smiled jokingly with me when he said that he was Indian now, and proud of it. By joining the parcialidad, he avoided having to pay certain real estate taxes. Members of indigenous communities can also avoid the military draft and qualify for targeted scholarships and economic development projects. But conflicts continue in the resguardos. Not everyone slides so easily from one identity into another, and not everyone is willing to alter property arrangements or to give up their own identities as Antioqueño or black in order to become an Indian.[15]

Nowhere has the demographic and land tenure situation been more muddied and contentious than in the resguardo of Cañamomo-Lomaprieta (formerly Supía-Cañamomo), which has a long history of competing property claims, mining, slavery, intermarriage, and manipulation of census rolls. In the 1930s disputes over land culminated in the assassination of a rancher by an indigenous man, now remembered by the community as a hero. In the 1970s, members of the parcialidad participated in takeovers of private property and agitated successfully for government-sponsored land reform. Today, residents without historical links to the parcialidad may petition for membership. While many inhabitants have joined, others hold back.

The historically black village of Guamal is located in Supía district, not far from Riosucio and within the boundaries of the Cañamomo-Lomaprieta resguardo. Guamal has survived since Emancipation as a tightly knit, self-consciously black community (*comunidad negra*). Guamaleños define themselves as a group apart from both the indígenas and the whites of Caldas. The Guamaleños sometimes use the word "white" to refer to non-indigenous Riosuceños, whom they also refer to as mestizos, but they mainly use it to refer Caldenses of Antioquia descent and to Antioqueños. The community of Guamal has repeatedly withstood legal challenges by private landowners, the indígenas of Supía-Cañamomo, and church officials by using many of the same resistant-adaptive techniques employed by its indigenous neighbors, such as allying with Liberal politicians.

Guamaleños, moreover, elaborated their own historical narrative, which they employed time and again to justify their land claims in place of a clear title. As is so often the case, this communal origin story involves a church. In the early nineteenth century, the slave owner and miner María Josefa Moreno de la Cruz left a third of her estate, which included the slaves of Guamal, for the upkeep of a chapel she had endowed and dedicated to Saint Anne. The descendants of the slaves of Guamal have since used the chapel land for their own sustenance, while taking responsibility for maintaining the chapel. As present-day Guamaleños Amanda Moreno and Aristóbulo Moreno explained it to me, they became the slaves of the Saint. Thus, they argue, they cannot be dislodged from the chapel land. When church officials had long ago tried to transfer the statue of Saint Anne to Supía, I was told, the river had swollen up and prevented passage; the Saint preferred to stay in Guamal, with her blacks.[16]

Long-simmering disputes with the indigenous cabildo of Supía-Cañamomo erupted in the 1970s. During the national wave of land invasions and agitation for land reform, Guamaleños divided over whether to ally with the cabildo or confront it; the disputes reportedly caused at least one death. By the 1990s, some members had joined the parcialidad and Guamal had an elected representative on the cabildo. Other communal leaders, however, refused to participate. They are blacks, they claim, not Indians.

One of these black elders is Aristóbulo Moreno, keeper of the Guamal archive (see figure 9). I used to visit him on Sunday afternoons to read the community's volume of nineteenth- and twentieth-century documents, known as El Libro, which is haphazardly sewn together in no particular order. I would sit on the front porch of his house, overlooking his coffee trees and the highway. The house was built in the classic style of the Coffee Region: wattle-and-dub walls, guadua posts, walls painted bright red and white. My research went very slowly, as I spent most of the time talking about history and life with him and his mestizo wife from Riosucio, Olga Uchima, and their children and grandchildren. One day, he surprised me by referring to himself as Antioqueño. I asked him if one could be both Antioqueño and black. Aristóbulo paused and then gestured

Figure 9. Aristóbulo Moreno, Guamal, 1995

with his arm to indicate the surrounding countryside: Of course he was Antioqueño, because "all of this used to be Antioquia." Time and again, people in Guamal, Supía, and Riosucio would repeat this phrase to me: Prior to the creation of Caldas, this was all Antioquia. They had even learned it in school. "No," I repeatedly insisted, "this was never Antioquia. These districts belonged to Cauca." I said I had seen thousands of nineteenth-century archival documents that proved my argument, emblazoned with the seal of the "Estado soberano del Cauca."

Moreno's remark shows how regional identities are constituted in time (collective historical memory) and space (geography) and disseminated through state institutions (school). Moreover, our conversation also illustrates that even the most hegemonic of regional identities are subject to challenge and reinterpretation. Discourses of Antioqueño regional identity refer to place; people are Antioqueño because they, or at least their parents or ancestors, were born in Antioquia. Aristóbulo Moreno, and his self-consciously black, Indian, and mestizo family members and neighbors, have not only pushed and expanded the geographical boundaries of Antioquia, they have also expanded the racial boundaries of Antioqueño by including themselves within it. Guamaleños, like neighboring Riosuceños, continue to narrate separate collective identities; they proclaim that Guamal is a community descended from slaves who lived there before the Antioqueños arrived. Thus, alongside the hegemonic regional discourse, counterdiscourses continue to flourish, producing dissonant local historical and geographical "truths." Various and contradictory notions of history and identity often coexist side by side in the same communities, even in the same individuals.

When self-identified indigenous and black inhabitants speak of their desire for progress, and when they inscribe themselves within progressive whitened regions (and when black villagers choose mestizo spouses), are they trapped by their own internalized racism? Clearly, they draw from racialized discourses that imply the inherent inferiority of certain groups. Yet, a more positive and optimistic interpretation would be that these historical actors are finding innovative ways to challenge the assumption that progress—in other words, modernity—is the sole possession of whites and whitened mestizos. When black villagers refer to themselves as both black and Antioqueño, and when indigenous leaders refer to themselves as both mestizo and indigenous, they break the conceptual link between race and progress as well as the conceptual link between race and region; they do not assume that the region (or by extension the nation or the local community) has to be racially or culturally homogeneous. They thus expand the phenotypical and even the geographical boundaries of the region to include themselves among the modern and progressive. Whether I choose to give a negative or positive slant in my interpretation of these conversations is less important than the overriding arguments of this book: Racialized geographies were produced by historical actors; history, geography, and the very notion of progress itself have been racialized at every level in Latin America. If my Sunday afternoons in Guamal and my experiences in the archives and homes and plazas of the Coffee Region taught me one thing, it was that the imagining of racial and regional communities was far more complex than I had ever foreseen. All communities, whether national, regional, local, or racial, are contested, which does not make them any less real, vital, or necessary for the people who dwell within them and claim them as their own.

NOTES

Introduction

1 Osborne, "Milton Friedman's Smile," 339.

2 The municipio of Riosucio extends just over 300 square kilometers and has a population of around 50,000. The 1993 national census counted a total of 43,511 inhabitants in the municipio of Riosucio, 15,915 of whom resided in the cabecera. When they were asked if they belonged to an "ethnicity, indigenous group, or community," 17,790 inhabitants (41 percent) identified themselves as indigenous; most of those who did so lived in rural, outlying areas rather than the cabecera. A total of 135 other respondents self-identified as black when asked the same question. The information on the 1993 census was provided by telephone and electronic mail, on 9 August 1999 and 18 August 1999, by Yolanda Bodnar and Tatiana Rojas of the Departamento Administrativo Nacional de Estadística (DANE); see also Colombia, DANE, *XVI Censo Nacional de Población y V de Vivienda, Caldas*. Riosucio, Caldas, should not be confused with another mixed-race and violently contested Colombian town, Río Súcio, which is in the Department of Chocó.

3 Quote is from Bueno Rodríguez, "Reseña histórica del Carnaval de Riosucio," 639. For a mid-twentieth-century example of a Colombian town in which Indian and mestizo barrios were separated by a fence, see Reichel-Dolmatoff and Reichel-Dolmatoff, *The People of Aritama*.

4 Germán Arciniegas to Otto Morales Benítez, in *VI Encuentro de la Palabra*, 29.

5 Human rights groups report more than 25,000 homicides annually out of a Colombian population of about 36 million. Amnesty International reports that in 1999, "more than 3,500 people were victims of politically motivated violence, scores 'disappeared,' and an estimated 250,000 people were forced to flee their homes. At least 1,000 people were kidnapped by armed opposition groups and paramilitary organizations" (Amnesty International, *Report 2000*).

6 "Informe . . . Alcaldía Provincial de Marmato, Riosucio 8 de Octubre de 1906,"

Registro Oficial (Manizales) 2, no. 188 (1 March 1907), 1178–80. The Antioqueños' qualities were so familiar to his readers, he noted, that he did not even need to spell them out.

7 Regarding "locative" racial identities in Colombia, see Wade, *Blackness and Race Mixture*, 4, 43–61; and Wade, "The Language of Race, Place, and Nation in Colombia," esp. 41–45. Race, in both English and Romance languages, has had many meanings; among other definitions, race has been used to refer to a line of descent, breed, stock, or species. All of these uses were evident in nineteenth-century Colombia. On the history of race and the categories developed by Carl Linnaeus and Johann Blumenbach, see Banton, *The Idea of Race*; Gould, *The Mismeasure of Man*, 391–424; Williams, *Keywords*, 248–50.

8 For example, to be *chocoano* (from the Pacific coastal department of Chocó) is virtually synonymous in Colombia with being black. Meanwhile, any Antioqueño, regardless of appearance, might assert his or her whiteness, although in some cases the assertion may be open to dispute (see Wade, *Blackness and Race Mixture*, 78).

9 On "racialization," see Appelbaum, Macpherson, and Rosemblatt, *Race and Nation in Modern Latin America*; Banton, *The Idea of Race*, 18–62; Wade, *Music, Race, and Nation*, 14.

10 Catherine LeGrand's pathbreaking book, *Frontier Expansion and Peasant Protest in Colombia, 1830–1936*, established Colombia's agricultural frontiers as sites of mobility and conflict. She assumed, based on research available at the time, that Antioqueño settlement was a relatively harmonious exception. See also Marulanda Alvarez and González Arias, *Historias de frontera*; and Rausch, *The Llanos Frontier in Colombian History, 1830–1930*.

11 The three departments constituting the Coffee Region are Risaralda, Armenia, and Caldas.

12 Parsons, *Antioqueño Colonization in Western Colombia*. Charles Verlinden points out that the word *colonization* derives from the Latin *colere*, meaning "to cultivate" or "to put to use" and that it initially referred to the expansion of agricultural cultivation (*The Beginnings of Modern Colonization*, ix–x). Marco Palacios observed that "since the sixteenth century, and with all probability until well into the twenty-first century, Colombian regional societies have developed and will develop *colonizando*" ("El espejo de los enigmas," 1:13). For examples of the "rosy legend," see Agudelo Ramírez, *El Gran Caldas*; and Santa, *La colonización antioqueña*.

13 Some of the best revisionist works include Christie, *Oligarcas, campesinos y política en Colombia*; Christie, "Antioqueño Colonization in Western Colombia"; Giraldo Zuluaga, *La colonización antioqueña y la fundación de Manizales*; and Valencia Llano, *Colonización, fundaciones y conflictos agrarios*.

14 The literature on the Iberian conquest of indigenous peoples and the participation of the latter in the institutions of their own colonization is vast. My analysis is especially influenced by Spalding, *Huarochirí*; Stern, "New Approaches to the Study of Peasant Rebellion and Consciousness"; and Stern, *Peru's Indian Peoples and the Challenge of Spanish Conquest*.

15 On whitening through international immigration, see Andrews, *The Afro-Argentines of Buenos Aires, 1800–1900*; Graham, *The Idea of Race in Latin America, 1870–1940*; and Skidmore, *Black into White*, among others. On whitening in

Caldas and Antioquia as a result of migration and myth-making, see Appelbaum, "Whitening the Region"; Christie, *Oligarcas, campesinos y política en Colombia*; and Christie, "Antioqueño Colonization in Western Colombia." Regarding frustrated Colombian efforts to attract foreign immigration, see LeGrand, *Frontier Expansion and Peasant Protest in Colombia, 1830–1936*, 12, 17; Samper, *Ensayo sobre las revoluciones políticas y la condición social de las repúblicas colombianas*, 233; Sánchez, *Gobierno y geografía*, 196–205. On elite racial attitudes, see Safford, "Race, Integration, and Progress," 32.

16 The dependency literature is vast and widely cited. Some classic works are Frank, *Capitalism and Underdevelopment in Latin America*; Cardoso and Faletto, *Dependency and Development in Latin America*; Stein and Stein, *The Colonial Heritage of Latin America*; Burns, *The Poverty of Progress*. "Internal colonialism" was largely an economic model, whereby state policies and unequal trade produced the development of some regions and the underdevelopment of others (see Frank, *Capitalism and Underdevelopment in Latin America*; González Casanova, "Internal Colonialism and National Development"; Havens and Flinn, *Internal Colonialism and Structural Change in Colombia*; Love, *Crafting the Third World*, 151–71). More recently, Walter Mignolo, from a perspective informed by world-systems and postcolonial theories, argues that internal colonialism is more accurate than the South Asian theories of subalternity for describing the condition of Latin American indígenas within the nation-state (*Local Histories/Global Designs*, esp. 197–201). I would argue that "internal colonialism" is useful only if it is conceptualized as a multilateral, rather than unilateral, process; otherwise we underestimate the agency of the colonized and re-create the "black legend."

17 Jeffrey L. Gould uses Partha Chatterjee's opposition between narratives of ethnic community and of capital in *To Die in This Way*, esp. 69–101, to explain the "death" of Nicaraguan indigenous communities in the face of state formation. Cf. neighboring Guatemala, as described by Greg Grandin, who argues that Guatemala's process of agrarian capitalism and modern state-formation served to intensify, rather than suppress, indigenous ethnic identities (*The Blood of Guatemala*, esp. 131–58). Partha Chatterjee and Florencia Mallon each argue that elite nationalist projects, in India and Latin America respectively, both repressed and incorporated elements of subaltern visions of the nation rooted in local communities (Chatterjee, *The Nation and Its Fragments*, 158–240; and Mallon, *Peasant and Nation*; see also Thurner, *From Two Republics to One Divided*, esp. 137–52).

18 Coronil, "Beyond Occidentalism"; Prakash, *After Colonialism*. On the technologies of colonialism, see Anderson, *Imagined Communities*, 163–85; Cohn, *An Anthropologist among the Historians and Other Essays*, esp. 224–54; Cohn, *Colonialism and Its Forms of Knowledge*; and Hirsch, "Empire of Nations." Claudia Steiner describes twentieth-century Antioqueño colonization on the Caribbean coast as a "colonial encounter" (*Imaginación y poder*, esp. xviii–xxi, 61–92). Regarding race and social hierarchy embedded historically in the geography of other Andean countries, see Chambers, *From Subjects to Citizens*; de la Cadena, *Indigenous Mestizos*; Orlove, "Putting Race in Its Place"; Radcliffe and Westwood, *Remaking the Nation*; Williams, "Negotiating the State."

19 On "regionalism" in the colonial and independence periods, see McFarlane, *Colom-*

bia before Independence; Múnera, *El fracaso de la nación;* Uribe de Hincapié and Alvarez, *Raíces del poder regional,* esp. 339. For a critique of the essentialization of regions, see Stoller, "Liberalism and Conflict in Socorro, Colombia, 1830–1870." Raymond L. Williams describes Colombian regional cultural divisions taking shape between the 1830s and 1850s in *The Colombian Novel, 1844–1987,* 13. On the post-independence formation of regions, see also Zambrano, "Región, nación e identidad cultural," esp. 150–51. Barbara Weinstein portrays regionalism as a modernizing discourse, "Racializing Regional Difference"; see also Orlove, "Putting Race in Its Place."

20 On the fragmentation of the early republic, see Bushnell, *The Making of Modern Colombia,* 101–39; Palacios, "La fragmentación regional de las clases dominantes en Colombia"; Safford and Palacios, *Colombia,* esp. 1–17, 80–187.

21 On the history of Colombian use of the word "region," which derives from the Latin *regere,* and of medieval European notions of "paises," see Fals Borda, "Ordenamiento territorial e integración regional en Colombia." On etymology and historical usage of the word "region" in the United States, see also O'Brien, "On Observing the Quicksand." O'Brien, referring to the U.S. South, cautions that historians should pay attention to when and how places become defined as regions of larger nations and not impose twentieth-century definitions of region on earlier periods.

22 Comisión Corográfica, *Jeografía física i política de las Provincias de la Nueva Granada;* Sánchez, *Gobierno y geografía.* The word "chorography" refers to the description and mapping of specific regions (Sánchez, *Gobierno y geografía,* 17). On novels and regionalism, see Williams, *The Colombian Novel, 1844–1987,* 3–184.

23 Ancízar, *Peregrinación de Alpha;* Samper, *Ensayo sobre las revoluciones políticas y la condición social de las repúblicas colombianas,* 70–72, 82, 282–331. On Ancízar, Samper, and other elite writers, see also Safford, "Race, Integration, and Progress," 20–33; and Rojas de Ferro, "Identity Formation, Violence, and the Nation-State in Nineteenth-Century Colombia."

24 López de Mesa, *De cómo se ha formado la nación colombiana,* 48–99. He divided the country into two broad zones separated by a diagonal line; the eastern zone was generally mestizo and the western zone mulatto, which he further subdivided into geographic regions. Gutiérrez de Pineda divided the country into four regions or "cultural complexes," each of which she purposely gave a "geographical" label as well as an "ethnic" label: the "complex of the Mountain or Antioqueño," the "littoral-fluvial-mining or Negroid complex" (encompassing scattered areas as diverse as the Pacific and Atlantic coasts and the Magdalena and Cauca Valleys), the "Andean or American complex," and the "Santandereano or neo-Hispanic" complex (see Gutiérrez de Pineda, *Familia y cultura en Colombia,* esp. 15–19). Raymond L. Williams also delineates four cultural–geographic regions, though they are not the same as Gutierrez's (see *The Colombian Novel, 1844–1947,* 3–54; see also Fals Borda, *Historia Doble de la Costa,* vol. 1). Safford and Palacios refer to three major regions: the East, West, and Caribbean (*Colombia,* esp. 1–17).

25 López de Mesa, *De cómo se ha formado la nación colombiana,* 48–99; Jiménez López, "Algunos signos de degeneración colectiva en Colombia y los países similares"; and Jiménez López, "Primera conferencia." Jiménez López, a medical doctor like López de Mesa, cited European eugenecists and argued that Antioquia was the

least racially "degenerate" region of Colombia. See also Helg, "Los intelectuales frente a la cuestión racial en el decenio de 1920"; Wade, *Blackness and Race Mixture*, 15–17. Regarding the "inheritance of acquired characteristics" and the popularity of "neo-Lamarckism" in Latin America, see Stepan, *"The Hour of Eugenics,"* esp. 67–101; Graham, *The Idea of Race in Latin America, 1870–1940*.

26 Gutiérrez de Pineda, *Familia y cultura en Colombia*.

27 Quotes are from Roldán, "Violence, Colonization and the Geography of Cultural Difference in Colombia," 6. See also Roldán, "Violencia, colonización y la geografía de la diferencia cultural en Colombia," 3–26; Roldán, *Blood and Fire*; and Steiner, *Imaginación y poder*, esp. 61–92. Conferences in Colombia in the 1990s on regionalism and culture brought together social scientists with critical perspectives on region, resulting in innovative anthologies, including COLCULTURA, *Imágenes y reflexiones*; and Silva, *Territorios, regiones, sociedades*.

28 Wade, *Blackness and Race Mixture*, esp. 43. For a provocative critique of the core–periphery model as a way of analyzing Colombian social conflict, see Serje, "The Reverse of the Nation." The innovative and sophisticated research on Colombia, much of which is little known outside of Colombian academia, illustrates the importance of the Colombian case for theorizing about regionalism in Latin America more generally. Colombian historiography has unfortunately occupied a peripheral place in relation to what some historians refer to as the "major" countries of Latin America. Key works on regionalism in Mexico, in particular, have ignored the insights provided by Colombia scholarship, e.g., van Young, *Mexico's Regions*; and Lomnitz-Adler, *Exits from the Labyrinth*.

29 Van Young sought to define region as an analytical concept even while finding it problematic and difficult to define. He says that "regions do not really exist as historical or cultural subjects," and then asks: "Who is loyal to a region but a geographer? Who weeps over it, poetizes it, is ready to die for it?" (*Mexico's Regions*, 9–10). For Colombians and scholars of modern Colombia, the answer is obvious: many Colombians, and many other Latin Americans and North Americans, have written poetry about, wept over, and even waged war for their regions. Part of the problem with van Young's approach may be that he attempts to impose region as an abstract model back in time to the colonial period, when "region" did not have the same cultural meanings. Edward Ayers and Peter Onuf differentiate between "regionalism" as identity and "region" as a scholarly category for organizing and interpreting data (Introduction to *All Over the Map*). On the difficulty of defining region, see Applegate, "A Europe of Regions"; see also the response by O'Brien, "On Observing the Quicksand," 1202–7.

30 Wade, *Blackness and Race Mixture*, 43. I use the term *discourse* in the sense that Foucault proposed: power operates through discourses to constitute "truths" and falsities (Foucault, *Power/Knowledge*, esp. 93, 131–33).

31 Marxist and postmodern geographers and other theorists of space have criticized social historians for demystifying everything short of space; see, e.g., Soja, *Postmodern Geographies*, 14, 26–27; Allen et al., *Rethinking the Region*. See Foucault on the need for a history of spaces and power (*Power/Knowledge*, 149; also quoted in Wade, *Blackness and Race Mixture*, 51). For an influential Marxist analysis of the "fetishization of space," see Lefebvre, *The Production of Space*, esp. 10–12, 21. See also

Coronil, "Beyond Occidentalism," 76–78. For a summary and brief bibliography of critical geographical approaches to space and region and their usefulness for historians, see Applegate, "A Europe of Regions," 1181. For innovative historical research on the relationship between cartography and the making of modern nations, see Craib, "A Nationalist Metaphysics," and Thongchai, *Siam Mapped.*

32 Bourdieu describes conflicts over regional identity as "struggles over classifications, struggles over the monopoly of the power to make people see and believe, to get them to know and recognize, to impose the legitimate definition of the divisions of the social world and, thereby, to make and unmake groups" (*Language and Symbolic Power*, 221).

33 Anderson, *Imagined Communities*, 6; Roldán, "Violencia, colonización, y la geografía de la diferencia cultural en Colombia," 8; Applegate, "A Europe of Regions," 1176. Colombian historian Eduardo Posada-Carbó suggests that "if nations are identified with 'imagined communities,' regions are, in contrast, linked to 'the reality of place,' insofar as they are directly concerned with the lives of men" (*The Colombian Caribbean*, 3). Posada-Carbó's emphasis on the reality of regional identities to the people (I assume he means women as well as men) who experience them is well taken, but I contend that the social reality of such identities should not blind us to the historical power struggles out of which regions emerged. Van Young, on the other hand, states that "regions are weak in their claims to affective loyalty as compared to experienced or 'imagined' communities, respectively localities or nations" (*Mexico's Regions*, 10).

34 Quotation is from Gupta and Ferguson, *Culture, Power, Place*, 7; cf. Anderson, *Imagined Communities*, 6. On internal power struggles in the construction of indigenous communal narratives and communal identity, see Rappaport, *Cumbe Reborn*. On communities as internally differentiated sites of struggle, see Chatterjee, *The Nation and Its Fragments*, 167. I draw on Mallon's approach of analyzing politics at local, regional, and national levels as "nested arenas of contestation" (*Peasant and Nation*, 6).

35 Gender extends far beyond direct male–female relationships to denote more general "relationships of power" (Scott, *Gender and the Politics of History*, 42). On familial metaphors in Latin American political discourse, see Felstiner, "Family Metaphors." For a critique of Anderson's imagined community of fraternal equals and a discussion of the imagined community as a patriarchal hierarchy in the patriotic discourse of Mexican peasants, see McNamara, "Sons of the Sierra." Steve Stern finds that gendered and racial stereotypes have been used in Mexico to distinguish regions and areas within regions (Stern, *The Secret History of Gender*, 290–93).

36 La Violencia, along with the diffuse violence that continues today, is simply too large a topic for this book. I do not believe that the processes of the nineteenth and early twentieth century that I analyze (many of which were not particularly exceptional in the Latin American context) explain Colombia's more unique history in the second half of the twentieth century; I am particularly suspect of facile generalizations that Colombia is violent because it always has been (what country has not been?). I do believe that attention to the racialized dynamics of conflict and geography will help us analyze the still-incomprehensible enormity of Colombia's ongoing strife, but I leave La Violencia, for now, to scholars whose research focuses on it. See, especially, Roldán, *Blood and Fire.*

1 Beauty and the Beast

1 Rojas de Ferro, "Identity Formation, Violence, and the Nation-State in Nineteenth-Century Colombia," 199 (she argues that antagonistic and mutually exclusive racial, regional, and gender identities were constituted within "regimes of representation"); and Zambrano, "Región, Nación e Identidad Cultural," 150–51.

2 On the jurisdictional confusion of the early nineteenth century, see Sánchez, *Gobierno y geografía*, 177–96. Regionalism did not necessarily coincide with state boundaries. Multiple regional identities would ultimately emerge out of Cauca, while the term *costeño* that emerged in the mid–nineteenth century referred to inhabitants of two adjoining states along the Atlantic Coast—Bolívar and Magdalena (see Posada-Carbó, *The Colombian Caribbean*, 234–35). Scholars of colonial and independence-era New Granada, especially of Antioquia and the Caribbean Coast, argue that regional or provincial identities preempted nationalist sentiment for New Granada as a whole (see Uribe de Hincapié and Alvarez, *Raíces del poder regional*, 339; McFarlane, *Colombia before Independence*; Múnera, *El fracaso de la nación*). The divisions and conflicts that marked the independence era were significant, but one should not assume that regional identities had fully consolidated prior to the nation-state. The localism of the 1810s was not the same as the regionalism of the late nineteenth century; regions of a colony are not the same as regions of a nation. Regarding how, "without the nation there could be no regions; without the whole there could be no parts," see Ayers and Onuf, Introduction to *All Over the Map*, vii.

3 The discursive division of Colombia into regions was thus laden with the biases of an era in which capitalist European nations were building international empires in Africa and Asia, and the United States was expanding in size, economic power, and influence.

4 See Pombo, *De Medellín a Bogotá*, 115–16, and, for quotation, Carlos S. de Greiff, *Apuntamientos topográficos i estadísticos de la provincia de Medellín* (1852), 76, quoted in Alvarez, "Visión e imágenes del antioqueño y lo antioqueño." De Greiff also influenced Agustín Codazzi's impressions of Antioquia; see Comisión Corográfica, *Jeografia física i política de las Provincias de la Nueva Granada*, 206–12. The appellation "Yankee" would stick; Parsons mentioned it a century later in the first sentence of his seminal book, *Antioqueño Colonization in Western Colombia*, 1.

5 Gosselman, *Viaje por Colombia*, 209 (quotation), 182, 247. Some of the citations from Gosselman are also included in Alvarez, "Visión e imágenes del antioqueño y lo antioqueño." See also Brisson, "A pie de Cali a Medellín en 1890," 4:200–203; Comisión Corográfica, *Jeografía física i política de las Provincias de la Nueva Granada*, esp. 137–244. On red cheeks as a marker of race, health, and beauty in Eastern Colombia, see Ancízar, *Peregrinación de Alpha*; and Safford, "Race, Integration, and Progress," 28.

6 Codazzi quoted in Sánchez, *Gobierno y geografía*, 307. For critiques of patriarchs who coerced their children into loveless marriages for economic reasons, see the 1851 poem "Felipe" by Gregorio Gutiérrez González, excerpted in Twinam, *Miners, Merchants, and Farmers in Colonial Colombia*, 10–11, and the mid-twentieth-century essay by Sofía Ospina de Navarro, "La casa antioqueña," 380. For refutations of the Jewish myth, see Twinam, *Miners, Merchants, and Farmers in Colonial Co-*

lombia, 8–13; Safford, "Significación de los antioqueños en el desarrollo económico colombiano," 75–116.

7   Juan de Dios Restrepo quoted in Pombo, *De Medellín a Bogotá*, 67. On Antioqueños' reputation for hard work, see also Safford and Palacios, *Colombia*, 176–77.

8   Samper, *Ensayo sobre las revoluciones políticas y la condición social de las repúblicas colombianas*, 84–103. On tensions between sameness and difference in Colombian national culture, see Wade, *Music, Race, and Nation*, 5, and the conclusion to this book.

9   Pombo, *De Medellín a Bogotá*, 66–69. Images of motherhood and female virtue were already noted before the 1850s in defining Antioquia. A French mining engineer reported with skepticism in the 1820s that Antioqueñas were reputed to be virtuous wives and mothers (Boussingault, *Memorias*, 2:139). Another Frenchman reiterated the point with less doubt in 1863 (see Charles Saffray, quoted in Alvarez, "Visión e imágenes del antioqueño y lo antioqueño") See also Gutiérrez de Pineda, *Familia y cultura en Colombia*, 320–27.

10 Pombo, *De Medellín a Bogotá*, 154–55. The sensual, violent dance involving blacks, mulattos, or zambos was a common scene in novels and memoirs. See, e.g., Gregorio Sánchez Tómez, *La bruja de las minas*, quoted in Díaz López, "Antropología y economía del oro en Marmato, Caldas," 89–90; Cuesta, *Tómas*, 161–64; Samper, *Ensayo sobre las revoluciones políticas y la condición social de las repúblicas colombianas*, 98–99. Bernardo Arias Trujillo provided yet another highly stereotyped portrayal of sexuality and gender relations in a black community (see *Risaralda*, 31–47, 205–7). See also Antioqueño administrators' descriptions of black Costeños in early-twentieth-century Urabá, as depicted in Steiner, *Imaginación y poder*, 61–92.

11 Pérez, *Jeografía física i política de los Estados Unidos de Colombia*, 1: 290–93, 327; Ancízar, *Peregrinación de Alpha*, esp. 1:81, 2:185–86. See also Safford, "Race, Integration, and Progress," 20–33; Rojas de Ferro, "Identity Formation, Violence, and the Nation-State in Nineteenth-Century Colombia," 205–6. On Cauca, see Taussig, *The Devil and Commodity Fetishism*, 57–58; Hyland, "A Fragile Prosperity," 380; and Valencia Llano, *Estado soberano del Cauca*, 144–45. On "hot" versus "cold" regions in Mexico and accompanying stereotypes, see Stern, *The Secret History of Gender*, 285–94. Taussig found that highlanders and mestizos of southwestern Colombia both feared and desired the supernatural powers they associated with the indigenous and black inhabitants of the tropical lowlands, reflecting a "moral topography" that inscribed complex social hierarchies (*Shaminism, Colonialism, and the Wild Man*, 287).

12 Von Schenck, *Viajes por Antioquia en el año de 1880*, 18.

13 Ibid., 18–20, 49–53, 57. Subsequent geographers and travelers echoed von Schenck's opinions; see Röthlisberger, *El Dorado*, 346–48, 357; Hettner, *Viajes por los Andes colombianos (1882–1884)*, 248–52. See also Uribe Angel, *Geografía general del estado de Antioquia en Colombia*, 469–70.

14 One aspect of defining their own whiteness against others' blackness was, as in the antebellum United States, defining themselves as free rather than enslaved. For example, in 1913, in commemoration of the centennial of Antioquia's declared independence from Spain, periodicals in Bogotá and Manizales published a popular poem by the Antioqueño poet Epifanio Mejía that contrasted the iron axe of the indepen-

dent Antioqueño frontier settler with the iron shackles of the postrate slave (reprinted from *El Tiempo* [Bogotá] in *El Criterio* 6 [Manizales], no. 122 [23 August 1913]).

15 Hettner, *Viajes por los Andes colombianos (1882–1884)*, 246–57. On Indians and Antioqueños see also Samper, *Ensayo sobre las Revoluciones políticas y la condición social de las repúblicas colombianas*, 84–90; Comisión Corográfica, *Jeografia física i politica de las Provincias de la Nueva Granada*, 202–11.

16 Von Schenck, *Viajes por Antioquia en el año de 1880*, 38. This dichotomy was also used to characterize subregions of Antioquia; see Arango, *La mentalidad religiosa en Antioquia*, 212–16; Roldán, "Violencia, colonización y la geografía de la diferencia cultural en Colombia," 5–8; and Roldán, *Blood and Fire*, esp. 35–40, 295–98. On the use of regional/racial stereotypes to differentiate areas within regions in Mexico, see Stern, *The Secret History of Gender*, 289–90.

17 Rojas de Ferro refers to elite Colombian writers as the "literati." They constituted a "white and small minority in an almost illiterate population composed of blacks, indigenous, and mulattos." It was their literacy and their claim to be "civilized," as much as their (often very modest) wealth, that made them an elite. These same men, moreover, were also leading statesmen and entrepreneurs ("Identity Formation, Violence, and the Nation-State in Nineteenth-Century Colombia," 196–224). Regarding the common use of specific cultural traits to characterize entire regions in Colombia, see anthropologist Myriam Jiméno's essay in Silva, *Territorios, regiones, sociedades*, 67. On the importance of the "other" in defining regional identities, see also Stern, *The Secret History of Gender*, 217–21.

18 On Antioquia's mining economy, see Twinam, *Miners, Merchants, and Farmers in Colonial Colombia*, 149; Brew, *El desarrollo económico de Antioquia desde la Independencia hasta 1920*, 35–43, 85–132; Poveda Ramos, "Breve historia de la minería," 211–12; Restrepo, *Estudio sobre las minas de oro y plata en Colombia*, 74; Botero, "La comercialización de los metales preciosos en una economía primaria exportadora."

19 For the social scientists' explanations, see Parsons, *Antioqueño Colonization in Western Colombia*; Hagen, *On the Theory of Social Change*, 353–84; Gutiérrez de Pineda, *Familia y Cultura en Colombia*, 265–403.

20 Patiño Millan, "Riqueza, pobreza y diferenciación social en la Antioquia del siglo XVIII"; Patiño Millan, "La provincia en el siglo XVIII," 67–89; Uribe de Hincapié and Alvarez, "El parentesco y la formación de las élites en la Provincia de Antioquia," 49–94; Uribe de Hincapié and Alvarez, *Raíces del poder regional*, 187–292; Brew, *El desarrollo económico de Antioquia desde la Independencia hasta 1920*, 39–44, 90–92; Twinam, *Miners, Merchants, and Farmers in Colonial Colombia*, 91–141.

21 *Mazamorro*, or "Moor-meal," refers to the popular maize-and-milk porridge that formed the basis of their diet (see Restrepo, *Estudio sobre las minas de oro y plato en Colombia*, 74; Melo, "La economía neogranadina en la cuarta decada del siglo XIX," 114–18; Brew, *El desarrollo económico de Antioquia desde la Independencia hasta 1920*, 44–93). Patiño Millan emphasizes the racially mixed nature of Antioqueño popular sectors, in order to counter those traditional regionalist intellectuals, whom she accuses of trying to erase blacks and Indians from Antioquia history (see "Riqueza, pobreza y diferenciación social en la Antioquia del siglo XVIII," x, xiii, 65, 67,

297; and "La provincia," 70–85). I am indebted to anthropologist Jaime Arocha and historian Víctor Alvarez, who both pointed out to me the overlooked presence of Afro-Colombians among Antioqueño migrants.

22 Colmenares, *Cali*, 55–101, 159–82; Bushnell, *The Making of Modern Colombia*, 98. The Conservative rebellion was in part a response to popular revolts (Hyland, "A Fragile Prosperity," 381–82; and especially Sanders, "Contentious Republicans," 157–76).

23 Colmenares, *Cali*, 55–108, 169–82; Taussig, *The Devil and Commodity Fetishism*, 41–67; Hyland, "A Fragile Prosperity," 383–86, 398; Valencia Llano, *Empresarios y políticos en el Estado Soberano del Cauca, 1860–1895*.

24 For an example of the myth of master–slave fraternity in Antioquia, see Uribe Angel, *Geografía general del estado de Antioquia en Colombia*, 465. Sanders shows that Liberals actively campaigned for the support of slaves and former slaves ("Contentious Republicans," 113–91). On the 1840s–1850s, see also Delpar, *Red against Blue*; Bushnell, *The Making of Modern Colombia*, 91–92; Pacheco, *La fiesta liberal en Cali, 1848–1854*; Hyland, "A Fragile Prosperity," 381–99.

25 For a comparison of Antioquia and Cauca, see also Safford and Palacios, *Colombia*, 170–79.

26 Ibid., 132–56; Sanders, "Contentious Republicans"; Delpar, *Red against Blue*.

27 Bushnell, *The Making of Modern Colombia*, 104–14. Draconians, particularly the urban artisans of Bogotá and other eastern Andean towns, parted company with some Radical Liberals, in part over the issue of tariff reforms and free trade. The division led to José María Melo's coup attempt in 1854, backed by artisans. Obando and several other leading Draconians repudiated the uprising. A coalition of "Constitutionalist" Conservatives and Liberals militarily defeated Melo's forces and took Bogotá (see Delpar, *Red against Blue*, 9–10; Bushnell, *The Making of Modern Colombia*, 104–13; Safford and Palacios, *Colombia*, 197–215).

28 Quote is from Bushnell, *The Making of Modern Colombia*, 115. The first sovereign state was Panamá, founded in 1855. See also González Scarpeta, "Los distritos del departamento," 172–73; Delpar, *Red against Blue*, 11–13; Bushnell, *The Making of Modern Colombia*, 19–122.

29 Bushnell, *The Making of Modern Colombia*, 19–22; Palacios, "La fragmentación regional de las clases dominantes en Colombia," 1663–89; Uribe de Hincapié and Alvarez, "Algunos elementos para el análisis de la configuración del poder regional," 81.

30 By the mid–nineteenth century, according to regional historians, the colonial towns of Santa Fé de Antioquia (the original provincial capital of Antioquia) and Rionegro were known as Liberal strongholds, with the first dominated by Obandistas and the latter by Radicals. The former found adherents in black mining communities, indigenous communities, some frontier settlements, and among some contraband *aguardiente* distillers. Certain towns such as Marinilla and Sonsón boasted predominantly Conservative elites (see Uribe de Hincapié and García, "La espada de las fronteras," 35–36; Ortiz Mesa, *El federalismo en Antioquia, 1850–1880*, 14–39). Ortiz Mesa comments perceptively with regard to these conflicts over administrative divisions that "para controlar un territorio también era necesario saber dividirlo" (ibid., 47). Regarding the parallel process of intermunicipal rivalry, whereby

Santander, in eastern Colombia, was consolidated as a Liberal state, see Stoller, "Liberalism and Conflict in Socorro, Colombia, 1830–1870," 298–99.

31   Palacios, "La fragmentación regional de las clases dominantes en Colombia," esp. 1677–78. On the concept of hegemonic "balance" or "pact," see Mallon, *Peasant and Nation*, 1–22. On Antioquia, see also Uribe de Hincapié and García, "La espada de las fronteras," 38; Bushnell, *The Making of Modern Colombia*, 123; Delpar, *Red against Blue*, 94–96; Ortiz Mesa, *El Federalismo en Antioquia, 1850–1880*, 64–70; Uribe de Hincapié and Alvarez, "Algunos elementos para el análisis de la configuración del poder regional," 87–88. Historians commonly refer to the "Conservative Hegemony" of nineteenth-century Antioquia (and early twentieth-century Colombia as a whole) without a full discussion of what hegemony means. For an explicit theorization of the consolidation of the "hegemonic project" of Antioquia elites, see Roldán, "Violencia, colonización y la geografía de la diferencia cultural en Colombia," 6–7; and Roldán, *Blood and Fire*, 29–35. On surveillance, see Foucault, *Discipline and Punish*.

32   On consent, coercion, and hegemony in Antioquia, see Roldán, "Violencia, colonización y la geografía de la diferencia cultural en Colombia," esp. 7, 24. Quotation is from Uribe de Hincapié and García, "La espada de la frontera," 38 (emphasis in original). The vagrancy code is reproduced in Ortiz Mesa, *El federalismo en Antioquia, 1850–1880*, 90–91. The code defined as vagrants anyone who could not prove at least a subsistence-level income from property or from a full-time occupation defined as "legitimate" and "honest." "Vagrants" included women who were known to be prostitutes and "public women," their male consorts, disobedient youth, and couples who lived together openly without marriage, the implication being that such behavior threatened the family and thus the social order. On complaints in Cauca about migrants, see Valencia Llano, *Empresarios y políticos en el Estado Soberano del Cauca, 1860–1895*, 67–69. The Antioquia Liberal press (the principal escape valve for dissent under the Conservative administration) complained that vagrancy laws were also used to punish political dissidents (Ortiz Mesa, *El federalismo en Antioquia, 1850–1880*, 88–96).

33   Regarding Mosquera's disdain for the masses who often supported him, see Delpar, *Red against Blue*, 92; Taussig, *The Devil and Commodity Fetishism*, 57; Valencia Llano, *Manizales en la dinámica colonizadora, 1846–1930*, 130. On indigenous and Afro-Colombian alliances with Mosquera, see Sanders, "Contentious Republicans"; Findji and Rojas, *Territorio, economía y sociedad Páez*, 71–73; Pacheco, *La fiesta liberal en Cali, 1848–1854*; von Schenck, *Viajes por Antioquia en el año de 1880*, 53–55.

34   Historian Alonso Valencia Llano astutely argues that the negative image of *el caucano* as excessively bellicose and passionate about politics, which emerged and prevailed during this era, was precisely the result of militarism on the part of Mosquera's faction. He ignores, however, the threatening popular aspects of Mosquera's Liberalism, which Sanders emphasizes (see Valencia Llano, *Estado Soberano del Cauca*, 47–52, 141–52; Sanders, "Contentious Republicans").

35   Valencia Llano, *Manizales en la dinámica colonizadora, 1846–1930*, 150–55; Sanders, "Contentious Republicans," 278–80. On the racialization of Colombian Liberalism, see also McGuinness, "In the Path of Empire"; Green, "Left Liberalism and

Race in the Evolution of Colombian Popular National Identity." On the implications of racializing an army as black, and thus inciting fears of race war, see Ferrer, *Insurgent Cuba*, esp. 70–92.

36 Palacios, "La fragmentación regional de las clases dominantes en Colombia, 1678"; von Schenck, *Viajes por Antioquia en el año de 1880*, 19.

37 The Cauca Valley was segregated from the department of Cauca in the early twentieth century to create the department of Valle.

2 *"Accompanied by Progress"*

1 Quote regarding white race is from Pinzón, "Informe del Secretario de Relaciones Exteriores al Congreso Constitucional de 1849," 9–10, quoted in Sánchez, *Gobierno y geografía*, 197. Much of the material in this chapter was published previously in Appelbaum, "Whitening the Region."

2 Parsons discusses the area around Riosucio briefly in his classic account, *Antioqueño Colonization in Western Colombia*, 86. Santa barely mentions the northern districts and makes no mention of their non-Antioqueño populations (*La colonización antioqueña*, 17). Recently, however, local and regional scholars and activists have shown increasing interest in the history of the indigenous communities; see Valencia Llano, *Colonización, fundaciones y conflictos agrarios*, 335–61; Zuluaga Gómez, *Documentos inéditos para la historia de Caldas, Choco y Risaralda*; Zuluaga Gómez, "Resguardo indígena de Cañamomo y Lomaprieta"; and Zuluaga Gómez, *Vida, pasión y muerte de los indígenas de Caldas y Risaralda*.

3 Parsons, *Antioqueño Colonization in Western Colombia*, 69–76. On land conflicts in the central cordillera, see Valencia Llano, *Colonización, fundaciones y conflictos agrarios*, 28–91, 197; Ocampo, "Historia y dominio de clases en Manizales," 5–10; Christie, *Oligarcas, campesinos y política en Colombia*; and Christie, "Antioqueño Colonization in Western Colombia."

4 On land entrepreneurs, see LeGrand, *Frontier Expansion and Peasant Protest in Colombia, 1830–1936*, 35; Valencia Llano, *Empresarios y políticos en el Estado Soberano del Cauca, 1860–1895*, 53–67; Sanders, "Contentious Republicans," 54; and Londoño, "Un empresario territorial caucano." The Palau family participated in every partisan faction in Cauca. Ramón Palau's eldest brother was a prominent Radical; another brother was a Riosucio Conservative (see Arboleda, *Diccionario biográfico y geneológico del Antiguo Departamento del Cauca*, 480–83; Delpar, *Red against Blue*, 56). Some of Palau's nephews became lawyers/politicians/land entrepreneurs in and around Riosucio. Also, see the following letters from Ramón Palau to Tomás Cipriano de Mosquera in the Archivo Central del Cauca [hereafter cited as ACC], Archivo Mosquera: 3 March 1858, carpeta 19-P-1, no. 35.827; 9 March 1858, carpeta 19-P-1, no. 35.828; 2 October 1859, carpeta 28-P, no. 36.827; 23 October 1859, carpeta 28-P, no. 36.828; 1 October 1866, carpeta 43-P, no. 48.973; and 10 May 1871, carpeta 24-p, no. 53.146. Many of Palau's political activities and economic ventures either directly or indirectly fostered Antioqueño migration. During the late 1850s, he was provincial governor of a territorial subdivision that included Santa Rosa. In 1860 Palau received a concession from the state government to maintain the trail over the Quindío pass of the central cordillera, along with a land grant

(Valencia Llano, *Empresarios y políticos en el Estado Soberano del Cauca, 1860–1895*, 57 n. 12, 105). Palau also represented the Governor of Cauca in negotiating a treaty in 1867 between the hostile states of Cauca and Antioquia (see "Documentos relativos al convenio de paz, amistad i comercio . . . ," December 1867, ACC, Archivo Muerto, paq. 98, leg. 49). On lawyers as key political actors in Colombian history, see Uribe-Urán, *Honorable Lives*.

5 Vecinos of Santa Rosa to Legislators, 10 August 1859, ACC, Archivo Muerto, paq. 74, leg. 51; Valencia Llano, *Colonización, fundaciones y conflictos agrarios*, 145–54; Parsons, *Antioqueño Colonization in Western Colombia*, 77–78; Valencia Llano, *Empresarios y políticos en el Estado Soberano del Cauca, 1860–1895*, 57 n. 12; Duque Gómez, Friede, and Jaramillo Uribe, *Historia de Pereira*, 351–81; Sanders, "Contentious Republicans," 52–53.

6 Valencia Llano, *Empresarios y políticos en el Estado Soberano del Cauca, 1860–1895*, 57, 105, 159; Palau to Mosquera, 9 March 1858, ACC, Archivo Mosquera, carpeta 19-P-1, no. 35.828. On the Pereira family, see Arboleda, *Diccionario biográfico y geonológico del Antiguo Departamento del Cauca*, 347–49; Uribe-Urán, *Honorable Lives*, 146–47; Delpar, *Red against Blue*, 53.

7 Ordenanza No. 9, 26 October 1855, transcribed in Cardona Tobón, "Exención para los pobladores de Oraida," 11. For the full text of the 1873 law, see "Ley Número 371 de 8 de septiembre de 1873 que fomenta la inmigración," *Registro Oficial* (Popayán) 1, no. 13 (13 September 1873), 2. This law was signed by Ramón Palau's Radical brother Emigdio, who presided over the legislature at that time (Ramón Palau to Legislature, 3 October 1874, ACC, Archivo Muerto, paq. 124, leg. 57; Emigdio Palau to Deputies, 1875, ACC, Archivo Muerto, paq. 130, leg. 15). For the proposed 1883 legislation, see "Proyecto de ley sobre inmigración," 6 July 1883 and 27 July 1883, ACC, Archivo Muerto, paq. 164, leg. 49. The attorney general of New Granada commented in 1858 regarding the presence of whites in the states of Santander, Boyacá, Cundinamarca, and Antioquia. He noted that these states would therefore benefit from a proposed annexation to the United States (quoted in McGuinness, "In the Path of Empire," 15).

8 Regarding the Toro-Anserma trail, see Alejandro Carvajal, Jefe Municipal of Toro, "Informe del Jefe Municipal de Toro al señor Presidente del Estado Soberano del Cauca," *Gaceta Oficial* (Popayán) 8, no. 338 (1 October 1870). "Districts" refers to what are now municipios, each of which includes a town center of the same name and its surrounding rural hinterland. Nineteenth-century local administrative boundaries and names often shifted. During most of the period covered in this article, Riosucio and each of the surrounding districts constituted a separate parish. Each had its own alcalde but was administratively subordinate to the distant town of Toro in the Cauca Valley, overseen by the jefe municipal of Toro. The locus of authority in Toro shifted over this period from Toro to the more populous Riosucio. Once segregated from Toro in the 1880s, the whole area was called variously Supía Canton, Riosucio Province, and Marmato Province, until its component districts became autonomous municipios in the twentieth century (see González Scarpeta, "Los Distritos del Departamento," 173).

9 Archivo General de la Nación [hereafter cited as AGN], Sección República, Fondo Censos de Población, Census of 1851, fol. 55; Ordenanza, Municipio de Toro, 23

March 1866, ACC, Archivo Muerto, paq. 94, leg. 40. What I call Supía-Cañamomo was variously referred to as either "Cañamomo," "Supía," or "Supía y Caña-momo." Today the community is known as Cañamomo y Lomaprieta or, simply, Cañamomo-Lomaprieta.

10 The Chamí are part of the larger ethnolinguistic grouping known as the Embera. Boussingault described them in the 1820s (*Memorias*, 2: 193, 233–49). The eth-nolinguistic origins of the other communities discussed in this book are murky. Indigenous leaders of La Montaña and Cañamomo identify as Embera-Chamí. The Bureau of Indigenous Affairs classifies them as such and labels the San Lorenzo indígenas (who trace their origins to the area of Sonsón, Antioquia) as Embera-Catío (Dora Inés Loaíza Marín, internal report, August 1992, Oficina de Asuntos Indígenas [hereafter cited as OAI]). See also the official censuses of 1835, 1843, 1851, and 1871, AGN, Sección República, Censos de Población. On the "refounding" of Anserma, see Parsons, *Antioqueño Colonization in Western Colombia*, 86.

11 According to the official 1843 census, Riosucio, Supía, and Marmato together still had 442 Afro-Colombian slaves (not including their children born since 1821, who were technically free but still subject to coerced labor). On Guamal, see Appel-baum, "Guamal"; and the concluding chapter to this book. See also Duque Gómez, "Grupos sanguineos entre los indígenas del Departamento de Caldas," 645; Boussin-gault, *Memorias*, 2: 107–8; and Zapata Bonilla, *Historia de Supía*. Regarding Mar-mato, see Díaz López, "Antropología y economía del oro en Marmato, Caldas."

12 Documents from 1805 are from AGN, Sección Colonia, Fondo Poblaciones del Cauca, vol. 2, fols. 985–1022, excerpted and quoted by Valencia Llano, *Colonización, funda-ciónes y conflictos agrarios*, 339–43.

13 Officials and residents of Riosucio to Constituent Assembly, 27 August 1857, ACC, Archivo Muerto, paq. 64, leg. 41. See similar requests: Vecinos of Supía to Constitu-ent Assembly, 27 September 1857, and Cabildo Parroquial of Supía to Constitu-ent Assembly, 28 September 1867, both in ACC, Archivo Muerto, paq. 64, leg. 41; Vecinos of Riosucio to Legislative Deputies, 13 July 1857, and Employees and citi-zens of Ansermavieja to Legislators, 31 July 1859, both in ACC, Archivo Muerto, paq. 74, leg. 51.

14 Cardona Tobón, "Las guerras civiles en el alto occidente de Caldas," 97–99; Ramón Palau to Tomás Cipriano de Mosquera, 9 March 1858, ACC, Archivo Mosquera, car-peta 19-P-1, no. 35.828; correspondence between Ramón Rosales, Jefe Municipal of Toro, and Secretary of the Government of Cauca, June–July 1864, ACC, Archivo Muerto, paq. 89, leg. 64; "Un decreto de Junio 24 de 1864"; C. Piedrahita to Secre-tary of the Government, 26 December 1865, ACC, Archivo Muerto, paq. 92, leg. 81. The state government subsequently pardoned the Conservatives, and efforts to join Antioquia continued for at least a decade (see Ramón Palau to Tomás Cipriano de Mosquera, 10 May 1871, ACC, Archivo Mosquera, carpeta 24-P, no. 53.146).

15 The earliest references to El Oro that I found are Pablo Molano to Bishop, 25 July 1850, which mentioned sixty families, and Manuel Velasco to Bishop, 3 Septem-ber 1850, which counted only thirty-six; both documents are in the Archivo del Arzobispado de Popayán [hereafter cited as AAP], leg. 216, no. 7. That year, the priest of Quinchía asked the Bishop of Popayán for permission to minister to families living in a site known as El Oro in the highlands of La Montaña, but he lost out to Father Velasco of Riosucio, who contested Quinchía's jurisdiction over these set-

tlers. Velasco sought and received permission to take a portable altar up to the highland, and the village of El Oro has been part of Riosucio district ever since. See also Ordenanza No. 5, 30 September 1854, quoted in Cardona Tobón, "Las viejas aldeas de Riosucio"; Ordenanza No. 9, 26 October 1855, transcribed in Cardona Tobón, "Exención para los pobladores de Oraida." Regarding Antioqueño settlement in Arrayanal on lands of the Chamí Indians, see Census of Arrayanal, March 1859, ACC, Archivo Muerto, paq. 76, leg. 126; Víctor Zuluaga Gómez, *Historia de la comunidad indígena chamí*, 67–70.

16 "Solicitud de unificación de las parroquias de La Montaña y de Quiebralomo en el sitio de Riosucio," 1824–25, ACC, Sala Independencia, C-III, no. 6970, transcribed in Gärtner Posada, "Tras la huella del Padre Bonafont en el Archivo Central del Cauca." On Manuel Velasco, see Calvo de Vanegas, *Riosucio*, 174–83. See chapter 7 in this volume for local historical versions of Bonafont's role and the founding of Riosucio.

17 May 1865, Registro de Instrumentos Públicos de Riosucio [hereafter cited as RIPR], Sección Supía, no. 14, fol. 6. Silva was connected by marriage to one of the slave-owning families that had constituted a local elite in the colonial era. His wife, Juana Paula Montaño, was the "natural" (illegitimate) daughter of miner Francisco Lemos, an heir of the Moreno de la Cruz dynasty. That family, along with their relatives the Castros, had been the largest slave owners and miners in the Riosucio-Supía-Marmato mining zone during the late colonial period (see "Santiago Silva contra herederos de Francisco Gervacio Lemos," 1843, ACC, Sala República, no. 4064; Ramón E. Palau to Mosquera, 16 March 1859, ACC, Archivo Mosquera, carpeta 28-P, no. 36.825; "Juicio Guamal ó Benitez," 1894, Juzgado del Circuito Civil de Riosucios [hereafter cited as JCCR]). Silva bequeathed legal volumes, codes, and copies of the constitutions to his heirs, suggesting that he was well versed in the law, though it's not clear what formal legal training he had ("Partición de los bienes hereditarios del finado Santiago Silva," 2 March 1882, RIPR, Sección Riosucio, no. 17, fols. 7–11).

18 Palau to Mosquera, 10 May 1871, ACC, Archivo Mosquera, carpeta 24-P, no. 53.146; Miguel Abadía to Mosquera, 25 February 1872, ACC, Archivo Mosquera, carpeta I-A, no. 53.543; notarized documents, 4 and 11 March 1872, Notaría de Supía [hereafter cited as NS], fols. 19–23; "Aviso de matrimonio," *Registro Oficial* (Popayán) 3, 28 June 1882, 4; will of Felipe Ortiz, 7 August 1877, RIPR, Sección Riosucio, fols. 3–4.

19 Indígenas of Quinchía to President of State of Cauca, 10 June 1875, transcribed in Zuluaga Gómez, *Documentos inéditos para la historia de Caldas, Choco y Risaralda*, 118–20; the letter is also reproduced in Valencia Llano, *Colonización, fundaciones y conflictos agrarios*, 352–54.

20 "Ley de 1821 (11 de Octubre) . . . Resolución sobre que los indios colombianos paguen la contribución llamada contribución personal de indígenas (15 de Octubre de 1828)," "Ley 1832 (marzo 6) que da reglas para el repartimiento de los resguardos de indígenas y declara abolida la contribución personal," "Ley 1834 (junio 2) adicional a la del 6 de marzo de 1832," and "Ley de 1850 (22 de junio)," all reproducidos in Triana Antorveza, *Legislación indígena nacional*, 81–117, and discussed in Safford, "Race, Integration and Progress," 11–18. The 1850 law had a greater effect on indigenous communities in regions such as the Bogotá-Cundinamarca highlands (see Curry, "The Disappearance of the Resguardos Indígenas of Cundinamarca, Colombia, 1800–1863," 181, 200–201).

21 Safford, "Race, Integration, and Progress," 12, 15; Triana Antorveza, *Legislación*

indígena nacional, 26; Sanders, "Contentious Republicans," 214–24. See also comments of Andrés Cerón, president of Cauca in 1869, *Gaceta Oficial* (Popayán) 12, no. 303 (19 September 1869), 1022.

22 Palau's speech is in *Anales de la Legislatura* (Popayán) 1, no. 24 (8 October 1873), 189–90. Legislator José Hernández expressed similar sentiments, dismissing dissent by indígenas of southern Cauca. The very fact that these Indians were able to write in their own defense, he stated, suggested that they were sufficiently "civilized" that they no longer needed special legal protection (José Hernández to Deputies, ACC, Archivo Muerto, 23 August 1875, paq. 130, leg. 15; Indígenas of Túquerres, Cumbal, Muellanues, Guachual, Imues, and Potosí to Legislature, 31 July 1877, ACC, Archivo Muerto, paq. 112, leg. 14). Some legislators, however, expressed ambivalence (see Antonio Arquez to Deputies, 9 August 1873, ACC, Archivo Muerto, paq. 124, leg. 56).

23 "Ley Número 44 (de 17 de Octubre de 1873) sobre administración y división de los resguardos de indígenas," *Registro Oficial* (Popayán) 1, no. 13 (1 November 1873), 1–2. Ramón's Radical elder brother Emigdio presided over the regional legislative body at this time. Ramón Palau's legislative influence was such that in 1875 he also gained passage of a law that guaranteed the legality of all sales and concessions of indigenous lands to the municipal authorities in the northern districts (see "Ley Número 47 [de 23 de septiembre de 1875] Sobre administracion y division de los resguardos de indígenas," *Registro Oficial* [Popayán] 3, no. 121 [29 September 1875], 2–3; see also Ramón Palau to Legislature, 3 October 1874, ACC, Archivo Muerto, paq. 124, leg. 57; Emigdio Palau to Deputies, 1875, ACC, Archivo Muerto, paq. 130, leg. 15). Several legislators, including Ramón Palau and Carlos Gärtner, proposed unsuccessfully in 1879 to abolish the resguardos immediately ("Proyectos de leyes y decretos que fueron negados por la Legislatura," 8 August 1879, ACC, Archivo Muerto, paq. 146, leg. 3). Zuluaga Gómez describes Law 44 as "un festín para los abogados, compañías mineras y traficantes de tierras" (*Vida, pasión y muerte de los indígenas de Caldas y Risaralda,* 102). Indigenous resources in Riosucio were occasionally sold even before the 1873 law; thus Felipe Ortiz (Ramón Palau's father-in-law) obtained land in the heart of La Montaña (31 May 1865, RIPR, Sección Supía, no. 13, fol. 6).

24 See Zuluaga Vélez, "Causas de la desaparición del resguardo de los Tabuyos en Anserma (Caldas)." Local officials prematurely announced the demise of Tachiguí and Tabuyo as early as 1870 (Alejandro Carvajal, Jefe Municipal of Toro, "Informe del Jefe Municipal de Toro al señor Presidente del Estado Soberano del Cauca," *Gaceta Oficial* [Popayán] 8, no. 338 [1 October 1870]; on Tachiguí, see also Francisco J. Bueno to Modesto García, 11 October 1905, AGN, Sección República, Fondo Baldíos, vol. 24).

25 On Anserma, see Corrales G., "Tercera fundación e historia de Anserma."

26 Various transactions, 1857–92, RIPR, Secciónes Riosucio and Supía. For the years between 1857 and 1892, I counted 479 transactions explicitly involving indigenous resguardo landholdings listed in the RIPR, of which 40 percent corresponded to the resguardo of La Montaña and 30 percent to Supía-Cañamomo. In 1874, officials found it necessary to divide the Registry of Public Instruments in half. One set of books, maintained in Supía, contained most transactions involving the resguardos of San Lorenzo and Supía-Cañamomo. Another set was kept in Riosucio and covered

the other northern districts. A book for Riosucio for the crucial years of 1874–75 was missing, which means that the number of registered transactions referring to indigenous landholdings was actually higher.

27 Curry, "The Disappearance of the Resguardos Indígenas of Cundinamarca, Colombia, 1800–1863," 165–66, 200–201; Lauria-Santiago, *An Agrarian Republic*; Gould, *To Die in This Way*; Reeves, "Liberals, Conservatives, Indigenous Peoples"; Kourn, "The Business of Land."

28 The 1874 accord is contained in "Solicitud y documentos en el asunto de Quiebralomo," 13 December 1890, ACC, Archivo Muerto, paq. 191, leg. 57.

29 Leg. of measurements, 1875–76, Archivo de la Communidad de La Montaña [hereafter cited as ACM]; conversations with Girdardo Hoyos, 8 February 1994, at Riosucio, and Javier Naranjo, 28 January 1994, in El Oro.

30 May 1876, RIPR, Sección Riosucio, no. 74, fol. 43. The percentages of indigenous land transactions do not reflect all of the ways that indigenous resources were transferred to outsiders. My figures, moreover, do not include transfers of mining rights and shares of mines located within the resguardo that were not explicitly attached to transfers of real estate.

Most buyers were men. In 1880–81, only two women appeared as buyers of indigenous lands in the resguardos recorded in the Riosucio section of the registry. Silvana Ospina bought forty hectares in La Montaña in company with her husband Vicente Marín, whereas Teresa Salazar bought forty-seven hectares there (see documents registered in RIPR, Sección Riosucio: 10 May 1880, no. 31, fol. 64; 9 October 1880, no. 90, fol. 43; 4 December 1880, no. 112, fol. 56).

31 See documents registered in RIPR, Sección Riosucio: March 1876, no. 40, fol. 23; 12 August 1877, fol. 6; 21 August 1880, no. 83, fol. 40. See also "La Parcialidad de la Montaña contra el Sr. Juan de D. de los Rios," 1905, JCCR.

32 Census for Supía-Cañamomo, 1874, NS. Identifying and counting the communal members of Supía-Cañamomo, and even quantifying the extent of each individual's membership in the community (by "one line" or "two lines"), was intended to facilitate the community's dismemberment and governance. Scholars of India have shown that censuses were among the "technologies" of colonization employed by colonial and postcolonial regimes. The enumeration and fixation of previously "fuzzy" and fluid communal identities facilitated colonial era rule while also providing a framework for anticolonial and postcolonial communal mobilization (Chatterjee, *Nation and its Fragments*, 223; Cohn, *Anthropologist among the Historians*, 224–54).

33 10 and 14 October, 17 November, and 12 December 1874, RIPR, Sección Supía, nos. 52, 57–58, 66, 74, fols. 29, 32, 36, 72, respectively; 26 November 1874, NS, no. 93, fol. 194. See also Zuluaga Gómez, *Vida, pasión y muerte de los indígenas de Caldas y Risaralda*.

34 On the Betancurts, who held property together, see 10 May 1875, RIPR, Sección Supía, no. 103, fols. 59–60; 25 August 1879, no. 140, fol. 95; 13 June 1876, NS, no. 19, fols. 49–52.

35 Census of Supía and Cañamomo, 1874, NS; document dated 28 February 1891, Archivo de la Comunidad de Guamal [hereafter cited as ACG], fol. 199. See also ACG, fols. 37, 69–70, 88, 94, 174–76, 228, 231–33, and 285; 10 October 1874, RIPR, Sección

Supía, no. 53, fols. 29–31; Zuluaga Gómez, *Vida, pasión y muerte de los indígenas de Caldas y Risaralda*, 106–8, 111–12; Zuluaga Gómez, "Resguardo indígena de Cañamomo y Lomaprieta," 597–98; Valencia Llano, *Colonización, fundaciones y conflictos agrarios*, 350–51. In 1876, the cabildo of the resguardo of Quinchía also ceded a portion of their territory, valued at 100 pesos, to the district of Quinchía (5 February 1876, RIPR, Sección Riosucio, no. 15, fol. 6).

36 10 July 1876, RIPR, Sección Riosucio, no. 91, fols. 52–56. The squatters received the option to buy the rest of the land they occupied. One recipient who did claim to be indigenous was Marcelino Betancurt, one of the people who had sued to be included within the padrón. In 1879, before the rest of the resguardo was divided, Trejo adjudicated to Betancurt fifty-five out of eighty hectares that the latter was recognized to possess within the resguardo (see 25 August 1879, RIPR, Sección Riosucio, fol. 95, no. 140).

37 Quoted in Zuluaga Gómez, *Documentos Inéditos*, 117.

38 Law 47, 23 September 1875, "Sobre administracion y division de los resguardos de indígenas," *Registro Oficial* (Popayán) 3, no 121 (29 September 1895), 2–3.

39 "Averiguatorio del motin o azonada que pretenden ejecutar algunos individuos," Archivo Municipal de Supia [hereafter cited as AMS], 17 September 1875.

40 "Lei Número 41 (de 4 de Octubre de 1879)," *Registro Oficial* (Popayán) 1, no. 32 (25 October 1897), 1–3.

41 10 November 1880, RIPR, Sección Supía, no. 103, fol. 41; 20 February 1883, no. 168, fol. 61. While some internal class differentiation within the communities was evident, overall they remained poor. For analysis of much more pronounced class differentiation among the K'iche Indians of Guatemala, see Grandin, *The Blood of Guatemala*.

42 10 November 1880, RIPR, Sección Riosucio, no. 105, fol. 41.

43 An exact breakdown of buyers' background is not possible, because transactions did not list places of birth and some surnames (such as Hoyos) were common in Cauca and Antioquia. Among the many buyers were the Supía District procurador, Bonifacio E. Zabala, who briefly recused himself from office at one point so that he, too, could buy some of the land that the district was selling. European investors included men such as "Julio" Richter, "Henrique" Wagner, and Frank "Francisco" Stephens. Another European technician, an English man known as "Guillermo" Martín, would make use of his surveying skills in the 1880s to obtain some of the best resguardo lands in payment for his services to the cabildo. As procurador of Supía during 1878, Zabala sold portions of land obtained from the parcialidad to various individuals from Antioquia, Cauca, and Europe: Richter; Gonzalo Palau (Ramón Palau's nephew, acting on behalf of the Western Andes Company); Braulio Ortega and Rudescindo Ospina, both of Antioquia; and Ricardo de la Roche, Eustaquio Tascon, Celestino de la Roche, and Teresa de la Roche, all of Cauca origins, among others. Eustaquio Piedrahita took Zabala's place as procurador in March of 1878 and sold lots of about twenty hectares each to Zabala and to Luís Horacio Zabala (see 1878–79 RIPR, Sección Supía).

44 Restrepo, *Estudio sobre las minas de oro y plato en Colombia*, 46, 67. For examples of mining claims staked by Riosucio-area notables including Santiago Silva, Vicente de la Cuesta, Bartolomé Cháves, Francisco S. Tascón, Julio Richter, and others, see

Gaceta Oficial (Popayán) 1, no. 77 (2 October 1866), 615; *Gaceta Oficial* (Popayán) 3, no. 300 (11 August 1869), 1004; *Registro Oficial* (Popayán) 1, no. 231 (10 January 1874), 3; *Registro Oficial* (Popayán) 2, no. 96 (11 December 1880), 3; *Registro Oficial* (Popayán) 2, no. 133 (24 June 1881), 4; *Registro Oficial* (Popayán) 1, no. 65 (9 April 1887), 1; and *Registro Oficial* (Popayán) 4, no. 339 (13 November 1889), 4. Valencia Llano based his list on claims published in the *Registro Oficial*, which replaced the *Gaceta Oficial*. I refer to the number of mines in his list, not the number of titles or the number of individuals. Some titles referred to multiple mines, and some individuals shared titles. Valencia Llano also used the *Registro Oficial* to assemble data on gold production (see *Empresarios y políticos en el Estado Soberano del Cauca, 1860–1895*, cuadros PM.1 and PM.2).

45 Brew, *El desarrollo económico de Antioquia desde la Independencia hasta 1920*, 140–41. Shareholders generally included the mine's discoverer, someone responsible for providing labor, a merchant or two to provide startup capital and supplies, and a lawyer for necessary paperwork and lawsuits.

46 Restrepo, *Estudio sobre las minas de oro y plato en Colombia*, 67; Poveda Ramos, "Breve historia de la minería," 212–14; Botero, "La comercialización de los metales preciosas en una economía primaria exportadora"; Valencia Llano, "La colonización y el desarrollo del Gran Caldas (siglo XIX)," 23–25; Gärtner Posada, "Extranjeros en el occidente del Gran Caldas." For a fictionalized account of the experiences of a locally born manager for the English company, see Cuesta, *Tomás*, 126–81.

47 He is also remembered by the black residents of Guamal as a generous eccentric (conversations with Amanda Moreno, 1994, Guamal; and Conrado Cataño [Chávez's great-grandson] Supía, 1994). Chávez's wealth notwithstanding, his personal life had its ups and downs. He divorced his wife Ulpiana de la Roche after accusing her of having an affair with a priest while he was away working in Marmato, and then he left his own fortune to subsequent out-of-wedlock children. The lives of de la Roche, a relatively wealthy woman who also went on to have several children of her own, and Chávez may also reflect that moral codes in lowland mining communities such as Supía were more flexible than they were reputed to be in conservative highland Antioqueño agricultural towns (see "Juicio de sucesión testamentaria del Señor Bartlomé Chávez," 21 November 1904, NS, no. 121, fols. 357–482; "Diligencias mortoriales de Sra. Ana Josefa Chávez," 20 April 1893, NS, no. 42, fols. 159–202; see also "Juicio de sucesión testamentaria del Señor Bartolomé Chávez," 21 November 1904, NS, no. 121, fols. 357–482). Regarding Chávez's resguardo land purchases, most of which adjoined mines, see the following transactions registered in RIPR, Sección Supía and RIPR, Sección Riosucio: 60.5 hectares at the Taiza mine from administrator Trejo, on 18 December 1874; 150 hectares from Trejo at the Viringo mine, 22 December 1874 (sold by the community to pay some of their legal costs to Palau); 25 hectares at La Linea from Marcelo Vinasco, 6 September 1879; 30 hectares at La Linea from indígena Isidro Vélez, 6 October 1882; 362 hectares from indígenas Vicente and Inés Largo at La Linea on 21 November 1882; 100 hectares from Trejo and the Isidro Vélez (serving as governor) at La Linea, 11 August 1883, and 40 more hectares, 2 January 1884; 28 hectares in La Linea from Floriano Murillo, 25 July 1884; 69.5 hectares at Hojas Anchas from various individuals, 23 December 1886, and 32 more hectares at Hojas Anchas, 25 August 1889.

48 Gärtner de la Cuesta, *Mis memorias o devaneos de un desocupado*, 43–45; Arango Mejía, *Geneologías de Antioquia y Caldas*, 579–80, 582; Arboleda, *Diccionario biográfico y geneológico del Antiguo Departamento del Cauca*, 120, 136.

49 Gärtner de la Cuesta, *Mis memorias o devaneos de un desocupado*, 56. Domingo Hincapié of Pácora, Antioquia, had bought 552 hectares, known as "Palermo," from the administrator of the resguardo of La Montaña on 11 September 1876, along with another lot in El Oro of 92 hectares (RIPR, Sección Riosucio, 11 September 1876, no. 93, fols. 58, 11). Carlos Gärtner, the governor's father, co-sponsored the unsuccessful legislative initiative to rapidly dismantle the resguardos in 1879 ("Proyecto de ley por lo cual se hace forzoso el repartimiento de los Resguardos de indígenas del Estado," 8 August 1879, ACC, Archivo Muerto, paq. 146, leg. 3).

50 Gärtner de la Cuesta, *Mis memorias o devaneos de un desocupado*, 53, 55. Wills and probate documents provide information on material culture, religious practices, economic activities, and networks; see the will of Ana Josefa Chávez, dictated on 20 April 1889 and opened on 20 April 1892, NS, no. 211, fols. 17–31, and "Diligencias mortoriales de Sra. Ana Josefa Chávez," NS, no. 42, fols. 159–202; the wills of Benedicta León, 12 December 1879, NS, no. 132, fols. 845–48, and Margarita León Calvo, 7 January 1885, JCCR; "Sucesión testimentaria de Lisímaco de la Roche," 6 April 1892, NS, no. 30, fols. 75–110; wills of Julio Richter, 7 October 1899, NS, no. 73, fols. 202–10, and Saturnino Rojas, 20 March 1903, no. 49, fols. 124–27; "Sucesión intestada de Ricardo Sanz y Amalia Suárez," 8 December 1904, NS, no. 134, fols. 511–48. On regional architecture, see Tobón Botero, *Arquitectura de la colonización antioqueña*, esp. vol. 2, *Caldas*.

51 "Sucesión intestata de la señora Leonarda Botero de O.," 4 June 1893, NS, fols. 283–92.

52 Quote is from Cardona Tobón, "Las viejas aldeas de Riosucio," 12. See also "Sucesión de Juana H. Hurtado," 1884, JCCR. Ramírez is a surname long associated with Antioqueño migrants in El Oro, but Hurtado is not common in the area. Regarding contemporary kinship practices in El Oro, see Castaño C. and Gallego M., "Papel del parentesco en la familia como unidad de producción, circulación, y consumo," 50–53, 60–95. Tomás Medina bought and sold indigenous land shares in the Guática resguardo in the 1870s and 1880s. Buyers included his wife's Ramírez relatives. At the same time, he received shares in the Guática resguardo as payment for acting as the community's legal representative. He also bought some shares in the Arrayanal and Quinchía resguardos (see the following entries in RIPR, Sección Riosucio: 20 February 1876, fol. 3, no. 26; 19 March 1876, fols. 25–26, nos. 45–46; 12 May 1878, fol. 19, no. 20; 2 June 1878, fol. 22, no. 27; 18 September 1882, fol. 76, no. 174; 20 November 1882, fol. 89, nos. 212–13; 2 May 1883, fol. 147, no. 381; 13 September 1888, fol. 44, no. 140). See also "Radicación de títulos," 26 September 1878, RIPR, Sección Riosucio, fols. 4–6, nos. 34–35, in which Medina registered various shares and fractions thereof (described with terms such as *media acción* or *cuarto derecho*) that he owned in the resguardos of Guática, Arrayanal, and Quinchía. On Medina's mining venture, see RIPR, Sección Riosucio, 2 November 1882, fols. 17–18, no. 56. On Medina's ambiguous relationship with the indigenous community, see "Libro de actas," 24 February 1882, Archivo Familia Tunusco [hereafter cited as AFT], fol. 10, leg. 7; "Libro de Actas," 4 November 1894, AFT, fols. 32, leg. 12.

53 A married women did not legally administer her own properties and could not sell her land without her husband's permission until the 1930s, yet she retained legal ownership of anything she brought into the marriage as well as half of all property obtained by the couple. Lands were subject to subdivision through inheritance, and each generation had to labor anew to consolidate its own landholdings. For additional examples of nineteenth-century wills left by Antioqueños in Supía and the surrounding towns, see those of the following individuals, all in NS: Braulio Ortega, 31 July 1877, no. 64, fols. 164–68; José Maria Orrego, 27 September 1879, no. 111, fols. 91:794–95 and 91:797; Teodomiro Díaz, 7 August 1888, no. 23, fols. 270–73; Pedro Montoya, 22 March 1889, no. 30, fols. 123–25; Mercedes Betancur Ortega (widow of Braulio Ortega), 15 March 1894, no. 171, fols. 80–83.

54 On the origins of migrants in the District of Supía, see the marital registries of the Parish of Supía, 1858–75, books 4–5. Unfortunately, the parish priest of San Sebastián in Riosucio did not allow me to examine his books, and the books of Nuestra Señora de la Candelaria were lost in a fire.

55 Interviews with Miguel Girardo Hernández Trejos, Riosucio, 22 January 1994; and Girdardo Hoyos, Riosucio, 8 February 1994; as well as conversations with Lucía Jaramillo, Pedro Jaramillo, and Javier Naranjo, El Oro, 28 January 1994. On agricultural production and family structure in El Oro as of the late twentieth century, see Castaño C. and Gallego M., "Papel del parentesco en la familia como unidad de producción, circulación, y consumo," 50–53, 60–95. They found that the Oreños of the 1980s were middle-sized farmers, with landholdings between 6 and 60 hectares—holdings large enough to obtain subsistence and a marketable surplus yet not requiring great amounts of outside labor. A strict sexual division of labor, along with large families, endogamy among people of Antioqueño descent, Catholic unions, and patrilocality still predominated. For more on the lives of settlers throughout the region, see Valencia Llano, *Vida cotidiana y desarrollo regional en la colonización antioqueña*; Sanders, "Contentious Republicans," 49–65.

56 *El Iris*, 1 January 1884.

57 *El Iris*, 1 February 1884.

58 *El Iris*, 31 February 1884.

59 *El Iris*, no. 2, n.d., 1884.

60 Arboleda, *Diccionario biográfico y geneológico del Antiguo Departamento del Cauca*, 485.

61 Uribe-Uran emphasizes the similar interests and ideologies of Liberal and Conservative lawyer-politicians in mid-century New Granada (*Honorable Lives*, 148–49).

3 *"By Consent of the Indígenas"*

1 February 1855, RIPR, Sección Supía, no. 6, fol. 4; Officials and residents of Riosucio to Constituent Assembly, 27 August 1857, ACC, Archivo Muerto, paq. 64, leg. 41; 31 May 1865, RIPR, Sección Supía, no. 14, fol. 6. For politicians' views, see Alejandro Carvajal, "Informe del Jefe municipal de Toro al señor Presidente del Estado Soberano del Cauca," *Gaceta Oficial* (Popayán) 8, no. 338 (1 October 1870); Alejandro Carvajal, "Informe de la Comisión á cuyo estudio pasó el Mensaje del señor Gobernador del Departamento," *Anales de la Asamblea* (Popayán), no. 11 (21 July 1898),

86. Zuluaga Gómez argues that the indígenas opposed the partition but were tricked into signing documents that went against their wishes (*Vida, passión y muerte de los indígenas de Caldas y Risaralda*, 103). For an equally unequivocal argument that indígenas in Cundinamarca welcomed and benefited from the dissolution of the resguardos, see Curry, "Disappearance of the Resguardos Indígenas of Cundinamarca, Colombia, 1800–1863."

2 Stern, "New Approaches to the Study of Peasant Rebellion and Consciousness."

3 Santos Vecino, "Las sociedades prehispánicas de Jardín y Riosucio"; Escobar Gutiérrez, "La comunidad, unidad de reproducción y explotación." See also AGN, Sección Colonia, Fondo Visitas del Cauca, vols. 1–2. Some estimates put the indigenous population of the area at about 40,000 in the 1530s, declining to under 2,000 by 1850 (Christie, *Oligarcas, campesinos y política en Colombia*, 99). The institution of the *encomienda* lasted longer here than in the bigger mining centers of the Spanish empire.

4 On colonial-era disputes, see the following documents in AAP: Autos sobre la Agregación de los feligreses de Quiebralomo al Pueblo de la Montaña, 1712, leg. 457; Protector General for the Indians of La Montaña, 3 April 1772, leg. 375, no. 31; Protector General for the Indians of La Montaña to Bishop of Popayán, 2 April 1772, leg. 375, no, 31; Indígenas of La Montaña to Bishop of Popayán, 26 July 1790, leg. 30, no. 15; Pedro Danaviña to Bishop of Popayán, leg. 27, no. 8; Matias Motato, Cacique of La Montaña to Bishop of Popayán, 1804, leg. 5397. See also Valencia Llano, *Colonización, fundaciones y conflictos agrarios*, 341–43; Personero público protector de indígenas to Juez primero, 1 June 1844, Archivo Municipal de Supia [hereafter cited as AMS], tomo 1846.

5 See chapter 7 regarding the founding of Riosucio.

6 See chapter 2 and "Lei 90 (de 19 de octubre de 1859), sobre protección de indíjenas," reprinted in *Registro Oficial* (Popayán) 1, no. 32 (25 October 1879), 2–3; and in Triana Antorveza, *Legislación indígena nacional*, 26. See also Andrés Cerón, *Gaceta Oficial* (Popayán) 12, no. 303 (19 September 1869), 1022.

7 "Padron de la Parcialidad de Indígenas de San Lorenzo Año de 1,874," 28 June 1874, notarized on 28 September 1874, NS; a virtually identical copy is preserved in ACM, unclassified. Also, "Padron de los indijenas Naturales de la parcialidad de Supia I Cañamomo formado por la Junta de comuneros . . . ," 1874, NS. Also, "Senso de Poblacion del Antiguo pueblo de la Montaña de Nuestra Señora de la Candelaria, abitantes que hacen parte de las parcialidades . . . ," 1871, ACM. I was unable to locate the 1874 padrón for La Montaña, which apparently has been lost. The 1871 census in the cabildo archives was missing pages in the middle section, so for the purpose of compiling the statistics I used the first 241 out of a total of 1,443 names, which makes for a problematic sample. The first name on the list is the governor of the parcialidad. After that, it is not clear in what order the census was recorded; the sample should not be assumed to be random. The censuses for 1874, mandated by the repartimiento law of 1873, include information on lineage that the 1871 census excludes. The census for La Montaña, unlike that of Supía-Cañamomo and San Lorenzo, includes information on age and profession.

8 On the potential instrumentality of identifying as "indigenous" in censuses, see Chambers, "Little Middle Ground."

9 The censuses were roughly organized by family—generally but not always a two-

generation nuclear family—although it is not always clear if these groupings corresponded to actual households. A single parent and her children, or a grandparent, might be included with a nuclear family in the same family groupings, which ranged in size from 1 to 11.

10 I had expected, given the prevalent stereotypes, to find dramatic differences in regard to gender roles, family, and notions of morality between indígenas and Antioqueños, but in the indígenas' tendency to form nuclear households, along with their gendered division of labor, the indígenas followed patterns usually associated with Antioqueños: generally high rates of marriage and low rates of illegitimacy. Between one-fourth and one-third of the people (not including widows and widowers) were listed as "married" (28.6 percent in La Montaña, 31.8 percent in San Lorenzo, and 25.3 percent in Supía-Cañamomo). In the nearby black community of Guamal, on the other hand, the gendered division of labor was much less clear and the proportion of female-headed households was much higher (see ACG, fols. 42–45; Appelbaum, "Guamal"). Of the population of Supía-Cañamomo, 3.6 percent consisted of women who gave birth to "natural" children, or 7.2 percent of all women and girls. In San Lorenzo and the sample from La Montaña, the frequency was lower—1.7 percent and 1.6 percent, respectively.

11 We lack the lineage information for La Montaña because the communal census there was drawn up before the enactment of Law 44 and thus did not refer to land portions, and the 1874 census for that community has been lost.

12 AGN, Sección República, Censos de Población, 1869–1871, roll 3/11, fols. 538, 602. Of the reported 8,689 inhabitants of both districts, 4,156 (about 48 percent) were men (2,712 in Riosucio and 1,444 in Supía), and 4,533 were women, which suggests a lack of single male migrants coming in. If anything, single men, especially non-Indian vecinos without access to land, may have been migrating out of the area in search of land and work and to join military campaigns. In addition to agriculture, a small number of other occupations were represented in the two districts. There were 63 merchants and 148 artisans, the majority of whom (103) were men. A total of 129 residents were listed as servants, most of whom (96) were women. Of 228 miners in both districts, the majority (155) were women; placer mining was common among single women and female heads of household. Schooling was available for a few children. Supía district had 66 students in primary school, almost evenly divided between boys and girls. Riosucio district also boasted a high school, to which only boys had access. The district censuses cannot be taken at face value, however, any more than the indigenous padrones. Census-takers may have exaggerated the educational level of their citizenry in order to promote their district's efforts to attain the status of cabecera.

13 Pequeño Cabildo, Parcialidad of Riosucio, to Tomás Cipriano de Mosquera, 13 February 1863, ACC, Archivo Mosquera, no. 45.290. A total of 130 male indígenas' names were appended; most signed by proxy. The handwriting in the document is elegant, suggesting the services of a professional scribe.

14 Indígenas of La Montaña to Bishop of Popayán, 21 February 1863, ACC, Archivo Mosquera, carpeta 58-Varios-I, no. 45.367.

15 Such disputes were not unique to Riosucio. Disputes over parish churches between indígenas and vecinos also broke out in the neighboring Guática and the black village of Guamal (see Appelbaum, "Guamal," and the concluding chapter to this

book; see also assorted documents in ACG, and Zapata Bonilla, *Historia de Supía*). Regarding similar disputes involving the indígenas of Supía-Cañamomo and Guática, respectively, see "Una petición de los indijenas de la parcialidad de Supia," 12 June 1871, AMS; Cabildo of indígenas of Guática to Vicario Capítular, 15 October 1888, AAP, leg. 242, no. 18.

16 Officials and residents of Riosucio to Constituent Assembly, 27 August 1857, ACC, Archivo Muerto, paq. 64, leg. 41; assorted documents, 1857–59, ACC, Archivo Muerto, paq. 74, leg. 51.

17 Los vecinos de Riosucio disputan la Construcción de las dos Capillas, October-November 1867, AAP, leg. 2878. For a different version of these events, see Calvo de Vanegas, *Riosucio*, 187–88.

18 Officials and residents of Riosucio to Constituent Assembly, 27 August 1857, ACC, Archivo Muerto, paq. 64, leg. 41.

19 February 1855, RIPR, Sección Supía, fol. 4, no. 6; Officials and residents of Riosucio to Constituent Assembly, 27 August 1857, ACC, Archivo Muerto, paq. 64, leg. 41; 12 July 1857, RIPR, Sección Supía; 31 May 1865, RIPR, Sección Supía, fol. 6, no 14; 22 November 1882, RIPR, Sección Riosucio, fol. 91, no. 218.

20 "Una lista de empadronamiento . . . Libro copiador del Censo de la Poblacion del año de 1887 sacado de los indijenas del sentro de Riosucio," ACM; 1871 census manuscript, AGN, Sección República, Fondo Censos de Población, 1869–70, rollo 3/11, fols. 616, 177.

21 See the following records, all in RIPR, Sección Riosucio: 12 August 1877, fol. 2; 16 August 1888, fol. 44, no. 95; 3 April 1888, fol. 15, no. 30. The usual price for plots in the settled part of the tierra fría at that time was apparently about four pesos per hectare, which is what several Antioqueños paid for plots they obtained from Pedro Pescador, administrator of the resguardo of La Montaña (see, e.g., 21 November 1888, RIPR, Sección Riosucio, fol. 72, no. 153; and 11 March 1889, fol. 28, no. 60). These transactions do not indicate if the land was "improved" or not. Moreover, most transactions listed in the RIPR do not list the size of the plot or the nature of the land involved, so it is difficult to appraise land values and price variation. Nonetheless, Vicente Largo was most likely ripped off. He sold his plot near the headwaters of the Risaralda River at about the time that area was being opened up by the Antioqueño investors and squatters who founded Belalcázar, just to the south.

22 "Orden Público sucesos del municipio de Toro," *Registro Oficial* (Popayán) 2, no. 74 (31 July 1880), 2–3; "Efemerides," *La Opinión*, 24 December 1913.

23 On clientelism, see LeGrand, "Perspectives for the Historical Study of Rural Politics and the Colombian Case." Sanders prefers the term "political bargaining" to describe relationships between popular and elite liberals in nineteenth-century Cauca (Sanders, "Contentious Republicans"). Despite objections that the patron–client model minimizes agency, I still find it useful because it evokes both the reciprocity and inequality that characterized the relationships discussed in this chapter.

24 "Una petición de los indijenas de la parcialidad de Supia," 12 June 1871, AMS. The letter also complained that the indígenas were overburdened with providing the materials for the rebuilding of the parish church in the town of Supía, mentioning a dispute with the townspeople over the church. This document, which has been preserved in the haphazard archive of the Supía mayor's office, is compelling in

its immediacy. Even though the governor at that moment and the majority of the cabildo was illiterate, the document was apparently drafted by an indígena (probably the secretary José Toribio Largo, who judging from his last name was from La Montaña). Different themes in the letter tend to run together, constituting a text rife with misspellings and largely lacking in punctuation.

25 Ibid.

26 NS, 11 March 1872, fols. 22–23.

27 On the manipulation of the indígenas by lawyers, see Zuluaga Gómez, *Vida, pasión y muerte de los indígenas de Caldas y Risaralda*, 102–3.

28 James Scott's notion of a "backstage transcript" is both inspiring and frustrating for historians; inspiring because it suggests a whole range of clandestine resistant (or "counterhegemonic") discourse and actions on the part of people who often appear acquiescent, yet maddening because so much of this "resistance" remains hidden, obscured from historical documents that largely embody the "public transcript of the powerful" and thus out of our reach (Scott, *Weapons of the Weak*, 284–88).

29 "Proyecto por la cual se varia la capital del Municipio de Toro," August 1875, ACC, Archivo Muerto, paq. 130, leg. 15; "Ley número 38 de 15 de septiembre de 1875," *Registro Oficial* (Popayán) 3, no. 120 (25 September 1875), 2; "Ley número 1.0 de 17 de julio que señala la capital del municipo de Toro," *Registro Oficial* (Popayán) 4, no. 176 (1 September 1877), 1.

30 See chapters 1, 4.

31 Julio Meléndes to Mayor of Riosucio, 13 July 1875; Jefe Municipal to Alcalde, 5 June 1877, 12 July 1877, and 9 October 1878, AMS; Democratic Society of Marmato to Legislature, 12 August 1877, ACC, Archivo Muerto, paq. 137, leg. 28; *Registro Oficial* (Popayán) 5, no. 231 (27 July 1878), 1–3; Alfredo Quintero V. to President of State, 2 July 1880, ACC, Archivo Muerto, paq. 151, leg. 51.

32 Palacios, *Entre la legitimidad y la violencia*, 42.

33 Sanders, "Contentious Republicans," 343–46. On confiscated properties, see *Registro Oficial* (Popayán) 5, no. 229 (12 May 1878), 3; and *Registro Oficial* (Popayán) 5, no. 232 (23 August 1878), 2. Also, Juan José Hoyos to Governor of Bishopric, 30 June 1879, AAP, leg. 23, no. 27; "Orden público: sucesos del municipio de Toro," *Registro Oficial* (Popayán) 5, no. 74 (31 July 1880), 2–3.

34 At least one governor of La Montaña, Zoilo Pescador, fought and died for the Liberal side in the war of 1876–77 (Petrona Gaspar to Legislative Deputies, 23 July 1879, ACC, Archivo Muerto, paq. 147, leg. 63; "Telegramas Oficiales," *Registro Oficial* [Popayán] 5, no. 74 [31 July 1880], 3).

35 "Orden público: sucesos del municipio de Toro," *Registro Oficial* (Popayán) 5, no. 74 (31 July 1880), 2–3.

36 Ulpiano Quintero V. and others to President of State, 2 July 1880, ACC, Archivo Muerto, paq. 151, leg. 51.

37 "Telegramas Oficiales," *Registro Oficial* (Popayán) 2, no. 74 (31 July 1880), 3; "Memoriales relativos a la amnistía concedida a varios individuos," *Registro Oficial* (Popayán) 2, no. 90 (13 November 1880), 4.

38 The quoted phrase is from Scott, *Weapons of the Weak*, 288.

39 Regarding indigenous ethnicity, see Rappaport, *Cumbe Reborn*; Field, "Who Are the Indians?"

1　"Proposición aprobada por la Municipalidad de Toro . . . Enero 3 de 1885," *Registro Oficial* (Popayán) 5, no. 359 (24 January 1885), 3.

2　Melo, "Etnia, región y nación," 37–38; see also Urrego, *Sexualidad, matrimonio y familia en Bogotá, 1880–1930,* on urban life in Bogotá during this era.

3　Quoted in Valencia Llano, *Estado soberano del Cauca,* 238–39.

4　See Park, *Rafael Nuñez and the Politics of Colombian Regionalism, 1863–1886;* Palacios, *Entre la legitimidad y la violencia,* 47–60. For a more favorable view of the Regeneration than that of Palacios and most recent historians, see Posada-Carbó, "Limits of Power."

5　Park, *Rafael Nuñez and the Politics of Colombian Regionalism, 1863–1886,* 263–64; Delpar, *Red against Blue,* 110–39. Also, "Constitución de la República de Colombia (4 de agosto de 1886)," reproduced in Uribe Vargas, *Las constituciones de colombia* 3:1091–1133; Palacios, *Entre la legitimidad y la violencia,* 50.

6　Park, *Rafael Nuñez and the Politics of Colombian Regionalism, 1863–1886,* 194–98; Delpar, *Red against Blue,* 135–39, 158–84; Bergquist, *Coffee and Conflict in Colombia, 1886–1910.*

7　Urrego, "Control social, matrimonio y resistencia popular en Bogotá," 204. Regeneration politicians also mobilized the faithful in campaigns intended to strengthen the Conservative Party and legitimate the state's initiatives. For example, in 1891, Conservatives and church officials organized a movement to get municipal councils throughout the country to consecrate their districts, and thus the nation as a whole, to the Sacred Heart of Jesus (Henríquez, "El Sagrado Corazon," 36; Urrego, *Sexualidad, matrimonio y familia en Bogotá, 1880–1930,* esp. 39–44). Secular versus religious public education had been one of the main issues dividing Liberals and Conservatives in the nineteenth century. For an example of how Regeneration education was intended to socialize children to take their particular places within the gender, class, and racial hierarchy of regenerated Colombia, see, "Informe del señor Prefecto de la Provincia de Toro," (Popayán) 1, no. 2 (6 November 1889), 7.

8　On citizenship and class in the Regeneration, see Urrego, *Sexualidad, matrimonio y familia en Bogotá, 1880–1930,* 352–53.

9　My discussion of Law 89 is based primarily on the text of the original legislation, as published in *Registro Oficial* (Popayán) 2, no. 178 (18 March 1891), 709–10, among other places. On the missionaries' responsibilities for care of the "barbarous tribes," see "Convenio con la Santa Sede sobre Misiones," *Registro Oficial* (Popayán) 3, no. 77 (6 May 1903), 309–11. "Savages" entrusted to the missions were mainly lowland Indians of the coasts and the Amazon basin, but also included the mountain Indians of the Sierra Nevada de Santa Marta and those of the western side of the western cordillera, west of Riosucio.

10　Regarding a Cauca politician who supported protecting the resguardos, see, e.g., Julián Trujillo, "Observaciones al proyecto de ley sobre administración y división de los resguardos indígenas," quoted in Findji and Rojas, *Territorio, economía y sociedad Paéz,* 86.

11　Safford, "Race, Integration, and Progress."

12　"Decreto Número 74 de 1898 (enero 1.0) en desarrollo de la Ley 89 de 1890, por el cual se determina la manera como deben gobernarse los salvages que vayan reduciéndose á la vida civilizada y las comunidades de indígenas," *Registro Oficial* (Popayán) 9, no. 1213 (16 February 1898), 4889–93.

13 Ibid., articles 97–99.

14 See chapters 3 and 8. Also, Indígenas of Yumbo to President of Cauca, 20 August 1873, ACC, Archivo Muerto, paq. 124, leg. 63; Isaias Largo to Governor, 23 September 1899, ACC, Archivo Muerto, paq. 267, leg. 24. Feminist scholars who study the intersections of race and gender have argued that colonial and multiracial societies have often policed their racial and class boundaries by regulating women's sexuality and marital choices (e.g., Stolcke, *Marriage, Class, and Colour in Nineteenth-Century Cuba*; Alonso, *Thread of Blood*; Stoler, "Carnal Knowledge and Imperial Power").

15 Regarding ideological influences on the Regeneration, see Palacios, *Entre la legitimidad y la violencia*, 47. On liberalism and state-formation, see, e.g., Mallon, *Peasant and Nation*; Joseph and Nugent, *Everyday Forms of State Formation*. One new study that examines conservative state-formation and race is Williams, "Negotiating the State." René Reeves argues that the differences between Liberals and Conservatives in regard to indigenous policy have often been overdrawn ("Liberals, Conservatives, Indigenous Peoples").

16 Some important examples of the extensive historical research on coffee in Colombia include Palacios, *Coffee in Colombia, 1830–1970*; Jiménez, "The Limits of Export Capitalism"; Arango, *Café e industria, 1850–1930*; Bergquist, *Labor in Latin America*; Bergquist, *Coffee and Conflict in Colombia, 1886–1910*; Parsons, *Antioqueño Colonization in Western Colombia*; and Vallecilla Gordillo, *Café y crecimiento económico regional*.

17 Charles Bergquist argued that political divisions among the elite during the Regeneration era corresponded directly to their positions within the emerging coffee-export economy, and thus the war was a result of dependence on coffee exports, but his argument has been refuted by historians who emphasize such factors as regional divisions, longstanding traditions of warfare to resolve political power struggles, and conflicts in neighboring countries (see Bergquist, *Coffee and Conflict in Colombia, 1886–1910*, esp. 51; Delpar, *Red against Blue*, 158–59; Park, *Rafael Nuñez and the Politics of Colombian Regionalism, 1863–1886*, 268–69; Palacios, *Entre la legitimidad y la violencia*, 60–62).

18 Bergquist, *Coffee and Conflict in Colombia, 1886–1910*, 103–94. See also Delpar, *Red against Blue*, 158–91; Bushnell, *The Making of Modern Colombia*, 148–54.

19 On the Regeneration in Cauca, see Valencia Llano, *Estado soberano del Cauca*, 260–82. The other big regional loser, economically and politically, was Santander (see Palacios, *Entre la legitimidad y la violencia*, 66). Antioqueños Carlos E. Restrepo, Marco Fidel Suárez, and Pedro Nel Ospina served as presidents of Colombia in 1910–14, 1918–21, and 1922–26, respectively.

20 Bushnell, *The Making of Modern Colombia*, 155–80; Bergquist, *Coffee and Conflict in Colombia, 1886–1910*.

21 "Decrepitud," *El Iris*, 1 March 1884, 20; *El Iris*, 1 January 1884; *El Iris* no. 2, 1884; *El Iris*, 15 March 1884, 23–24. *El Iris* also called for an end to popular street celebrations. "Barbaric" and "savage" practices such as bull running and cockfights, the author argued, were symptomatic of underpopulated, "almost primitive" villages

("No mas fiestas!," *El Iris*, 1 March 1884, 19–20). Regarding how the Regeneration emerged as a reaction against popular mobilization of urban artisans, black Liberals, and other plebeians, see Palacios, *Entre la legitimidad y la violencia*, 54–60; Sanders, "Contentious Republicans," 304–96.

22 Belisario Caballero to Secretary of Government, 10 May 1882, reproduced in *Registro Oficial* (Popayán) 3, no. 189 (27 May 1882), 1–2; Benigno Gutiérrez, "Informe del señor Prefecto de la Provincia de Toro," *Registro Oficial* (Popayán) 1, no. 2 (6 November 1889), 5.

23 "Gobierno del Estado . . . Decreto Número 108 de 22 de junio de 1878," *Registro Oficial* (Popayán) 5, no. 228 (6 July 1878), 1–2; "Ordenanza no. 33 de 17 de Agosto de 1892 por la cual se determina los Distritos de cada una de las Provincias . . . ," ACC, Archivo Muerto, paq. 211, leg. 30.

24 See Jesús Constain to Secretary of Government of Cauca, 16 September 1897, ACC, Archivo Muerto, paq. 244, leg. 54; Clemente Díaz to the Secretary of Government, 27 May 1898, ACC, Archivo Muerto, paq. 295, leg. 92. The indígenas of Guática expressed their opposition in "Legajos de hactas . . . ," 18 February 1891, AFT, leg. 12, fol. 10; see also "Legajo de hactas . . . ," 6 July 1893, AFT, leg. 12, fol. 25; "Acuerdo No. 14 expedido por el Consejo Municipal de Nazareht," 1895, JCCR; and "Ordenanza no. 22 de 17 de Agosto de 1892 . . . ," ACC, Archivo Muerto, paq. 211, leg. 30. Quinchía historian Alfredo Cardona Tobón argues that priests along with Antioqueño settlers used these new districts to establish Conservative control over indigenous communities ("Colonizaciones y partidos políticos"). At the same time that Nazareth was created, the Antioqueño-founded settlement of Apia was given administrative authority over the historically black village of La Virginia near Pereira. Quotes regarding racial districting in the Province of Obando are in Miguel Medina y Delgado to President of Departmental Assembly, 12 July 1888, ACC, Archivo Muerto, paq. 181, leg. 36.

25 Rodolfo Velasco V., "Agricultura: Nota del Prefecto Provincial de Marmato é informe á que ella se refiere," *Registro Oficial* (Popayán) 3, no. 420 (22 August 1892), 1679. Carvajal was commissioned to study the feasibility of a route to the Pacific (Griseldino Carvajal, "Exposición descriptiva del camino de Chamí," *Registro Oficial* [Popayán] 7, no. 930 [19 February 1896], 3738). See also Díaz, "Informe del Prefecto de la Provincia de Marmato," *Registro Oficial* (Popayán) 10, no. 69 (28 June 1899), 273–74. Prefect Clemente Díaz even went as far as to publish a short-running official newspaper, *La Revista Oficial de Marmato*, modeled after the departmental official registers.

26 Benigno Gutiérrez, "Informe del señor Prefecto de la Provincia de Toro," *Registro Oficial* (Popayán) 1, no 2 (6 November 1889), 239, 241–42; Rodolfo Velasco V., "Agricultura: Nota del Prefecto Provincial de Marmato é informe á que ella se refiere," *Registro Oficial* (Popayán) 3, no. 420 (22 August 1892), 1679; Parsons, *Antioqueño Colonization in Western Colombia*, 130–33; Brew, *El desarrollo económico de Antioquia desde la Independencia hasta 1920*, 201–14. Also, Griseldino Carvajal, "Exposición descriptiva del camino de Chamí," *Registro Oficial* (Popayán) 7, no. 943 (31 March 1896), 3747.

27 Brew, *El desarrollo económico de Antioquia desde la Independencia hasta 1920*, 264, 264 n. 104; Griseldino Carvajal, "Exposición descriptiva del camino de Chamí," *Registro Oficial* (Popayán) 7, no. 930 (19 February 1896), 3738; Rodolfo Velasco V.,

"Agricultura: Nota del Prefecto Provincial de Marmato é informe á que ella se re-fiere," *Registro Oficial* (Popayán) 3, no. 420 (22 August 1892), 1679. See also Will of Leonarda Botero de Ospina, 4 June 1893, NS, fols. 283–392.

28 Rodolfo Velasco V., "Agricultura: Nota del Prefecto Provincial de Marmato é in-forme á que ella se refiere," *Registro Oficial* (Popayán) 3, no. 420 (22 August 1892), 1679; Francisco Trejos, "Informe . . . Alcaldía Provincial de Marmato . . . Riosucio, 8 de Octubre de 1906," *Registro Oficial* (Manizales) 2, no. 188 (1 March 1907), 1178; Griseldino Carvajal, "Exposición descriptiva del camino de Chamí . . . ," *Registro Oficial* (Popayán) 7, no. 930 (19 February 1896), 3738–39, and no. 943 (31 March 1896), 3747.

29 Rodolfo Velasco V., "Agricultura: Nota del Prefecto Provincial de Marmato é in-forme á que ella se refiere," *Registro Oficial* (Popayán) 3, no. 420 (22 August 1892), 1679.

30 Gould, *To Die in This Way*, 48. Twentieth-century Cuzco indigenous intellectuals faced a similar paradox (de la Cadena, *Indigenous Mestizos*, 306–14).

31 Benigno Gutiérrez, "Informe del señor Prefecto de la Provincia de Toro," *Registro Oficial* (Popayán) 1, no 2 (6 November 1889), 239, 241–42.

32 Gärtner de la Cuesta, *Mis memorias o devaneos de un desocupado*, 60–61. Riosucio native Carlos Gil pointed the cemetery out to me and told me the same story in 1994.

33 Ibid., 60–67.

5 Regenerating Conflict

1 "Acta No. 5 . . . 9 de Abril de 1899," registered 2 June 1902, RIPR, Sección Riosucio, fol. 35, no. 68. The document consisted of a copy of the minutes of a cabildo meeting presided over by acting Governor Braulio Largo. It is not clear how or why Largo was acting in this capacity.

2 For examples of land transactions in El Rosario, see the following entries in RIPR, Sección Riosucio: 3 March 1902, fols. 21–22, nos. 40–41 and fol. 34, no. 65; 27 October 1905, fol. 146, no. 220; 6 June 1906, fol. 60, no. 113; 3 July 1906, fol. 65, no. 124; 4 July 1906, fols. 65–66, no. 125; 6 September 1906, fol. 88, no. 168; 13 Septem-ber 1906, fols. 91–92, no. 173; 4 October 1906, fol. 99, no. 188; and similar trans-actions for the years 1907–1908.

3 Cardona Tobón, "Las viejas aldeas de Riosucio," 12–14. Also, Marco Antonio Tobón, "Bosquejo histórico de la población de El Rosario," excerpted in ibid.; Vecinos of Riosucio to Deputies of Assembly, 17 June 1904, ACC, Archivo Muerto, paq. 325, leg. 95; "Decreto No. 367 de 1904 (Noviembre 19) por el cual se fomenta la enseñanza industrial en el Departamento," *Registro Oficial* (Popayán) 4, no. 225 (1 December 1904), 904. See also Griseldino Carvajal, "Exposición descriptiva del camino de Chamí . . . ," *Registro Oficial* (Popayán) 7, no. 916 (16 January 1896), 3638–39. The emphasis on honorable labor was central both to the discourses of Antioquia region-alism and the Regeneration. On efforts of the Catholic church in Antioquia to form a disciplined working class, see Farnsworth-Alvear, *Dulcinea in the Factory*.

4 Marco Antonio Tobón, "Bosquejo histórico de la población de El Rosario," excerpted in Cardona Tobón, "Las viejas aldeas de Riosucio," 12–14.

5 "Remates" notices, *La Opinión*, 1911–19. Each of these sales took place under the

supervision of the Circuit Court. Thirty-five involved shares of land in Quinchía resguardo, while the remaining three included two in La Montaña and one in San Lorenzo. These numbers indicate the overall trend but do not necessarily account for all such sales. A few issues of *La Opinión* are missing.

6 I found thirty-seven unclassified documents in the JCCR, organized in piles loosely by year, from 1902 to 1920, and bearing labels such as "Solicitud de permiso para vender un derecho . . . ." The remainder were divided among La Montaña (three petitions), San Lorenzo (two petitions) and Cañamomo-Lomaprieta (one petition). The sellers emphasized their precarious economic situation and appear to have been among the most economically vulnerable members of the parcialidades: women and the elderly. Just under half of the petitioners were women, about half of whom appeared alone in the documents and were probably single or widowed. For a detailed analysis of the gender and age dynamics, as well as the extreme market inequities governing these land transfers, see Appelbaum, "Remembering Riosucio," chapter 7, and Appelbaum, "Las parcialidades indígenas de Riosucio y Quinchía frente a la ley 89 de 1890 (1890–1920)." On how gender inequalities contributed to the commodification of K'iche' indigenous lands in Guatemala, see Grandin, *The Blood of Guatemala*, 38–40.

7 Among the apoderados, Marcelino Betancurt, M. Valerio Díaz, and Aurelio Durán were the names that appeared most frequently. Buyers who were most likely Antioqueños included people with surnames such as Ocampo, Ibarra, Puerta, Estrada, Hoyos, and Osorio. Surnames of local origin among the buyers included Trejos or Trejo, Betancur or Betancurt, and Aricapa.

8 "Permiso para enajenar derecho proindiviso en la Parcialidad de San Lorenzo," 1913, and "Permiso judicial de Nemesio Gañan, 1920," both in JCCR.

9 Municipal official Jesús Güendica, who tried unsuccessfully to stop the flood sales in Quinchía in 1918, noted that by comparison the Riosucio indígenas only rarely sold their lands ("Permiso para vender un derecho en la Comunidad indígena de Quinchía," 1918–19, JCCR).

10 "Informe . . . Alcaldía Provincial de Marmato . . . Riosucio, 8 de Octubre de 1906," *Registro Oficial* (Manizales) 2, no. 188 (1 March 1907), 1178.

11 Justiano Pescador to Secretary of Government, 5 September 1895, ACC, Archivo Muerto, paq. 221, leg. 51.

12 The money was to pay a debt that Vargas claimed from the cabildo for sixty-six pesos. The cabildo also said it owed money to lawyer Gonzalo Palau and surveyor Jorge Gärtner, among others. The cabildo hired two additional surveyors to measure off two large plots to sell, thus alienating more land and incurring more expenses. Justiano Pescador, the governor, stood to benefit from the sale; he and another cabildo leader would receive forty pesos to pay for expenses they claimed to have made on the community's behalf ("Solicitud para vender unas acciones en la comunidad de la Montaña," 19 April 1897, JCCR). Accountability was a serious problem. Several years later, a new cabildo in La Montaña reviewed the expenses submitted by Vargas and attempted to sort out their outstanding debts, noting that several receipts and some communal funds were missing (fragment from Minutes of Cabildo Meeting, 21 January 1906, ACM).

13 Isaias Largo to Governor, 20 September 1899, ACC, Archivo Muerto, paq. 267, leg. 24.

14 "Juicio Ordinario Reivindicatorio de un lote de terreno situado en el Resguardo de la Parcialidad de indigenas de 'La Montaña,'" 1906, JCCR. See also transactions registered on 14 March 1886, RIPR, Sección Riosucio, fol. 9, nos. 17–18.

15 On the Mápura case, see the following JCCR documents: Clemente Díaz to Circuit Judge, 1877; Primitivo Fernández de Soto to Circuit Judge, 1877; "Interdicto de recuperar posesion de terreno," 1882; "Deslinde de Mápura," 1884; Indígenas of Quinchía versus owners of Mápura, 6 February 1888; and "Articulación al de Mápura," 1893.

16 The main source for the case of El Peñol is "Juicio de Deslinde-Avelina de la Roche-Demandado-La Comunidad de Cañamomo," 1891–94, JCCR. Regarding the sale by Ospina to Tascón, see 21 September 1874, NS, no. 43, fols. 100–103. Marco Tulio Palau played both sides in disputes involving settlers and indígenas in Guática, disputes in which Gärtner was also involved. Víctor Zuluaga has found documents showing that Palau then went on to cheat the Chamí indígenas of Arrayanal and Pueblo Rico out of most of their territory (see Zuluaga Gómez, *Vida, pasión y muerte de los indígenas de Caldas y Risaralda*, 116, 125–26; and *Documentos inéditos para la historia de Caldas, Choco y Risaralda*, 115–20).

17 Documents referring to El Peñol, Mata de Guinea, etc., August 1894, ACC, Archivo Muerto, paq. 217, leg. 96; also, "Juicio de Deslinde-Avelina de la Roche-Demandado-La Comunidad de Cañamomo," 1891–94, JCCR. Thurner argues for Peru that "unimagined political communities coalesced in the redeployment of colonial 'indigenous rights'" as an "avenue of political reinsertion in the postcolonial Republic and its history." Thus, "peasants redefined their relationship to the larger political community subject to Peruvian law and destabilized exclusionary, official notions of 'republican' citizenship" (*From Two Republics To One Divided*, 137, 139).

18 Ramón Marín and Emiliano García to Rafael Uribe Uribe, 18 August 1909, Academía Colombiana de Historia [hereafter cited as ACH], Fondo Uribe Uribe, fols. 9857–58. El Negro Marín, a working-class black from the mining enclave of Marmato, was an Uribe Uribe protégé famous for his military tactical brilliance in the war. His image graced the packets of Sello Negro cigarettes, but he nonetheless died in poverty. Emiliano García was a local Liberal politician who occasionally represented indigenous communities.

19 The deteriorated state of the JCCR, the even worse condition of Riosucio's municipal archives, and the fact that both the Riosucio notarial archive and the archives of the government of Caldas were burned down during La Violencia, impede the exact quantification of similar cases during the Regeneration and early twentieth century. The surviving documentation in the JCCR, however, does lend itself to qualitative analysis. For additional land disputes during this period involving local indigenous resguardos, see the following JCCR *sumarios*: "Interdicto de recuperar posesion de un terreno," 1882; "Interdicto la posesion de unas mejoras situadas en el punto de Arrayanal . . . ," 1883; "Juicio de oposición a la posesión de los terrenos de la comunidad de indigenas de Arrayanal," 1884; "Juicio de deslinde del terreno de Yarumal en Quinchía," 1894; "La Parcialidad de la Montaña contra el Sr. Juan de D. de los Rios," 1895; "Acción revindicatoria: Salinas de 'Quimaná y Guacamayero.' . . . Demandante—La Parcialidad de Indigenas de 'La Montaña'—'Demandados'—Juan Pablo y Odulfo Gómez—Carlos y Jorge Gärtner—Federico Delgado y Charles W.

Brandon," 1899–1912; "Indígenas of Quinchía versus Martin Trejos," 1905; "Demanda Reivindicatoria. Actor. La Parcialidad de La Montaña . . . ," 1906; "Juicio ordinario sobre servidumbre de un terreno de 'Mogan,'" 1912; "Juicio Civil Ordinario de la Parcialidad indígena de Quinchía, Bruno Tapasco y Mercedes Pescador, contra Benito Arce," 1914, JCCR; and "Tercería excluyente propuesta por el Doctor Enrique A Bercerra como apoderado de Antonio Morales, Juan Mateo Largo . . . ," 1920, among others. See also Bonifacio E. Zabala to Municipal Judge of Supía District, 17 September 1891, AMS, tomo 1891; Indígenas of Tabuyo to Governor, 27 February 1905, ACC, Archivo Muerto, paq. 332, leg. 89; Rejinaldo Hernández, Governor of Parcialidad of Cañamomo and Loma Prieta, to Minister of Public Works, 1907, AGN, Sección República, Fondo Baldíos, tomo 28, fols. 137–39; and Zuluaga Gómez, *Documentos inéditos para la historia de Caldas, Choco y Risaralda,* 115–20.

20 Rappaport, *The Politics of Memory,* 104–6; Troyan, "State Formation and Ethnic Identity in Southwestern Colombia, 1930–1991."

21 Rappaport, *Cumbe Reborn,* 25–27.

6 Riosucio on the Margins of the "Model Department"

1 *El Mensajero,* 15 April 1905, 1. The census for 1918 would count 43,203 inhabitants in the district of Manizales, up from 3,000 in 1851 (Palacios, *Coffee in Colombia, 1830–1970,* 180).

2 Quotes are from *El Mensajero,* 25 February, and 15 April 1905. See also *El Ruiz,* 15 April 1905, 1–2.

3 Bushnell, *The Making of Modern Colombia,* 154–60; de los Ríos Tobón, "La política," 443–48. The report from which the quote is taken is reproduced in Agudelo Ramírez, *El Gran Caldas,* 186–88.

4 Caldas was created by Law 17 of 1905. See *Registro Oficial* (Popayán) 5, no. 290 (17 June 1905), 1163; de los Ríos Tobón, "La política," 443–48; Giraldo Zuluaga, *Modernización e industrialización en el Antiguo Caldas, 1900–1970,* 38. Reyes subdivided the country into ever-smaller units. He briefly subdivided Caldas, awarding part of the Cauca section and the Quindío Valley to the old Cauca city of Cartago. Following the plebiscite, Reyes responded by suppressing Cartago and adding the Quindío to Caldas.

5 *La Voz del Sur,* 15 December 1889, 3. See also de los Ríos Tobón, "La Política," 443–48; Vilegas Vilegas and Aramburo Siegert, "Paisas," 12; and Uribe de Hincapié and García, "La espada de las fronteras," 39.

6 For the text of the Municipal Resolution of 14 August 1904, see Agudelo Ramírez, *El Gran Caldas,* 180–82. Quote is from *El Correo del Sur,* 17 August 1904, 2. In 1896 Rafael Uribe Uribe suggested in the National Congress that a new administrative entity might have Riosucio, Pereira, or Manizales as its capital (see de los Ríos Tobón, "La Política," 459; Morales Benítez, *Cátedra caldense,* 60–61).

7 By the second decade of the twentieth century, with the spread of eugenics, race was a key scientific, sociological, and medical category in Colombia. In 1912 racial labels such as "indigenous" and "black" were added to the national census. See Jiménez López et al., *Los problemas de la raza en Colombia.* See also Helg, "Los intelectuales frente a la cuestión racial en el decenio de 1920"; she notes the dissemination of the theories of the Argentines Lucas Ayarragary and José Ingenieros in Colombia by the

1920s. On the reputation of Caldas as white, see Duque Gómez, "Grupos sanguineos entre los indígenas del Departamento de Caldas," 623. For a racialized and stereotypical portrayal of Caldas by a foreign visitor, see Walter Röthlisberger, "El Occidente de Colombia" (Walter was the son of Ernst Röthlisberger, who wrote *El Dorado: Estampas de viaje y cultura de la Colombia suramericana*).

8   Rodrigo Jiménez Mejía, quoted in Morales Benítez, "La colonización antioqueña" (no page numbers). See also Bernardo Arias Trujillo's portrayal of Antioqueño migrants as white in his 1935 novel *Risaralda*.

9   Helg, "Los intelectuales frente a la cuestión racial en el decenio de 1920," 40–53. Quote is from *La Idea*, 22 November 13, 2–3. In an effort to debunk the white myth, Christie found that, according to the 1912 census, even in the heart of white Caldas, more than half of the populations of four towns was not classified as white (Christie, *Oligarcas, campesinos y política en Colombia*, 40; and Christie, "Antioqueño Colonization in Western Colombia," 270–71).

10   *El Ruíz*, 15 April 1905, 1–2; see also *La Idea*, 22 November 1913, 2–3. On the annexation of Pueblo Rico, see Governor's Message to the Department Assembly of 1913, published in *Gaceta Departmental* (Manizales) 9, no. 337 (12 March 1913), 203–7; and *El Conservador*, 5 May 1911, 2.

11   Regarding class conflict on the Caldas frontier, see Palacios, *Coffee in Colombia, 1830–1970*, 161–97; Bergquist, *Labor in Latin America*, 325–30; Christie, *Oligarcas, campesinos y política en Colombia*; Christie, "Antioqueño Colonization in Western Colombia"; and Valencia Llano, *Colonización, fundaciones y conflictos agrarios*.

12   *El Mensajero*, 25 February 1905, 1.

13   *El Mensajero*, 14 October 1905, 1.

14   *El Mensajero*, 14 October 1905, 1. The Quindío had gently sloping volcanic soils ideal for coffee. From the 1880s to the 1930s, businessmen from Cauca and Manizales fought against independent squatters. Manizales newspapers could have been emphasizing their ostensibly common heritage in an effort to ameliorate such conflicts. See Palacios, *Coffee in Colombia, 1830–1970*, 184–97; Christie, *Oligarcas, campesinos y política en Colombia*, 33–37; Christie, "Antioqueño Colonization in Western Colombia," 266–67; Valencia Llano, *Colonización, fundaciones y conflictos agrarios*, 227–94; Parsons, *Antioqueño Colonization in Western Colombia*, 81–82; Londoño, "Un empresario territorial caucano"; and Londoño, "Los conflictos por el deslinde de las tierras de Burila."

15   For examples of filial metaphors and Antioquia described as a loving mother, see *El Mensajero*, 29 March 1913; Juan Andrés Echeverri, *Registro Oficial* (Manizales) 1, no. 111 (20 June 1906), 549; *El Criterio* 23, August 1913; *La Mazorca*, 11 August 1913. Perhaps relevant to the image of Antioquia as a mother is the Antioqueños' famed devotion to their mothers. On maternal veneration, see Gutiérrez de Pineda, *Familia y cultura en Colombia*, 320–27.

16   Alejandro López, quoted in Valencia Llano, *Vida cotidiana y desarrollo regional en la colonización antioqueña*, 61. Cano was also known for his busts of regional Antioqueño heroes. The painting was widely reproduced and popular, according to Ortega Ricaurte, *Diccionario de artistas en Colombia*, 68–71; and Londoño Velez, *Historia de la pintura y el grabado in Antioquia*, 141–59, 179.

17   Typically, a family-owned (or rented) and operated Caldas farm would become a unit

of diversified production, with food crops for personal and local consumption grown between and among the rows of coffee. Labor-intensive cultivation practices involved all family members. Nostalgia notwithstanding, peasant households were the sites of considerable intergenerational and intergender power struggles and violence over issues such as land, labor, sexuality, and marital choice; even the most positive accounts often emphasize fathers' "austerity" (conversations in Riosucio, 1993–95, and with Dora de Rengifo, Bogotá, July–August 1992, September–October 1993; see also Valencia Llano, *Vida cotidiana y desarrollo regional en la colonización antioqueña*, 61–134; Bergquist, *Labor in Latin America*, 317–30).

18 Caldas split in 1957 into Risaralda, Quindío, and Caldas, due in part to the rise of new commercial and industrial elites in the booming cities of Pereira (the new capital of Risaralda) and Armenia (the new capital of Quindío). The three departments are often referred to together as Old Caldas and are served by one of Colombia's regional television stations: Telecafé. Even the section of the FARC guerrilla army that operates in this region is known as "The Coffee Front" (*El Frente Cafetero*).

19 According to London, the Coffee Growers' Federation worked with bishops and parish priests to promote coffee production ("From Coffee Consciousness to the Coffee Family," 12). The participation of priests in developing the coffee industry was described to me repeatedly in Riosucio, Supía, and Manizales during 1993–95.

20 Giraldo Zuluaga argues that Manizales's importance in the coffee trade was threatened in 1915 by the completion of the Pacific Railroad, which connected the middle Cauca Valley and the Quindío directly to the Pacific coastal port of Buenaventura, just after the Panama Canal was opened (*Modernización e industrialización en el Antiguo Caldas, 1900–1970*, 62–69). Brew notes that the British-built *cable teleférico* allowed the coffee traders of Manizales to circumvent Medellín (*El desarrollo económico de Antioquia desde la Independencia hasta 1920*, 98). The departmental legislature also ordered feasibility studies for an aerial cable system connecting Riosucio and Anserma to Manizales, but it was never built (Ordenanza No. 15, *Anales de la Asamblea* [Manizales] 12, no. 32 [22 March 1922], 1).

21 Giraldo Zuluaga, *Modernización e industrialización en el Antiguo Caldas, 1900–1970*; Díaz López, "Antropología y economía del oro en Marmato, Caldas."

22 The Western Andes Mining Company, which ran the major mines and refinery operations in Marmato in the late nineteenth century, sent its gold bars to agents in Medellín, who shipped it to London. The same merchants in Medellín also provisioned the Marmato mines with materials and supplies (see Botero, "La comercialización de los metales preciosos en una economía primario exportadora"). See also Giraldo Zuluaga, *Modernización e industrialización en el Antiguo Caldas, 1900–1970*, 53–70; and Vallecilla Gordillo, *Café y crecimiento económico regional*, 73–106.

23 British firms had obtained disputed titles during the early nineteenth century from Marmato's last local owner and from the new national government seeking to pay off its war debts (see Tulio Ospina, petition to Minister of Hacienda, July 1899, Fundación Antioqueña de Estudios Sociales [hereafter cited as FAES], AOH/M/3). After nationalizing the mines, the government awarded a rental contract to a Conservative political figure, Alfredo Vásquez Cobo, and reportedly signed over to him the title to 20 percent of the mines in question. See also Vélez L., *Alfredo Vásquez Cobo*,

"*El Candidato Reo,*" 87–89; "El Informe del doctor Carlos Gartner de la Cuesta y del Representante Héctor Moreno Díaz . . . ," and "Informe rendido por el mismo Representante Sanín Villa," both in Colombia, Congreso, *Supía y Marmato ante la Cámara,* 1–25, 31–41; as well as Díaz López "Antropología y economía del oro en Marmato, Caldas." Also, Ramón Marín T., Riosucio to Rafael Uribe Uribe, 14 July 1909 and 29 July 1909, reprinted in *Supía Histórico* 2, no. 12 (November 1990): 347–49; Vélez, *Alfredo Vásquez Cobo, "El Candidato Reo,"* 89; Telegram, vecinos of Riosucio (Carlos Gärtner et al.), 22 July 1908, AGN, Sección República, Fondo Baldíos, tomo 29, fols. 762–67; *La Opinión,* 23 March 1910, 2–3. The episode was debated in Congress in 1909, providing a forum for more general criticisms of the Reyes dictatorship. Antioquia representative and future president Carlos E. Restrepo, the head of a dissident Conservative faction known as the Unión Republicana who had ties to some mining investors in Supía and Riosucio, strongly criticized Vásquez Cobo (see Vélez, *Alfredo Vásquez Cobo, "El Candidato Reo,"* 96).

24 On the decline of gold mining, see García, *Geografía económica de Caldas,* 143–44; Díaz López, "Antropología y Economía del Oro en Marmato, Caldas," 112–18, 152–53, 125.

25 Agudelo Ramírez, *El Gran Caldas,* 209. On the conformation of a politically and economically dominant class in Caldas with little participation on the part of local elites from "marginal" areas such as Riosucio, see Christie, *Oligarcas, campesinos y política en Colombia,* 37–38; and Christie, "Antioqueño Colonization in Western Colombia," 268–70.

26 Statistics on coffee production in Riosucio and the core coffee areas such as Manizales, Chinchiná, and the whole Quindío zone are hard to come by until 1932, when the Coffee Federation took a census of the number of coffee trees planted in each district. By that time, some mid-altitude sections of Riosucio had become major coffee producing areas. The 1932 coffee census reported 2,028,985 coffee trees in Riosucio's 318 square kilometers; Manizales district, by comparison, had 5,190,027 in 257 square kilometers (García, *Geografía económica de Caldas,* 590–91).

27 Francisco J. Bueno, Riosucio, to Modesto García, Bogotá, 11 October 1905, AGN, Sección República, Fondo Baldíos, tomo 24.

28 For Restrepo's attack on Vásquez Cobo, see Vélez, *Alfredo Vásquez Cobo, "El Candidato Reo,"* 96. On Carlos E. Restrepo and the Unión Republicana, see Bergquist, *Coffee and Conflict in Colombia, 1886–1910,* 252–62.

29 On Reyes's threat, see Agudelo Ramírez, *El Gran Caldas,* 194–95. Quote is from "Memorial Excelentísimo señor Presidente de Colombia," *Registro Oficial* (Manizales) 1, no. 412 (7 November 1905). See also *Registro Oficial* (Manizales) 2, no. 193 (15 March 1907).

30 "La Reintegración," *La Opinión,* 23 March 1910, 1–2.

31 Eliseo Vinasco y Hoya to Carlos E. Restrepo, 31 July 1909, Universidad de Antioquia, Sala Antioquia [hereafter cited as UA], Archivo Carlos E. Restrepo, Cartas Recibidas, tomo 10, fol. 279:456 (emphasis in the original). On Eliseo Vinasco, see Alzate Valencia, "Notas biográficas para una aproximación a la tradición periodística del Ingrumá."

32 Francisco Trejos, "Informe . . . Alcaldía Provincial de Marmato . . . Riosucio, 8 de Octubre de 1906," *Registro Oficial* (Manizales) 2, no. 188 (1 March 1907), 1179.

33 "Memento," *El Conservador*, 8 September 1911, 3.

34 Calvo de Vanegas, *Riosucio*, 51; "Hispania no Riosucio," *La Opinión*, 9 July 1917. Quotes are from "Hispania," *La Opinión*, 25 December 1917.

35 El Lego Indio, "Asoma las Orejas del Lobo," *La Opinión*, 26 April 1919. See also "La Provincia de Marmato," *La Opinión*, 3 March 1910, 2–3; José Tasamá, "Remitido," *La Opinión*, 10 May 1919.

36 Nestor Bueno Cock, Riosucio, to President, Supía Council, 10 May 1927, unclassified document, AMS.

37 See, e.g., "Algo Gravísimo," *La Opinión* (Riosucio/Hispania), 23 March 1918; *El Minuto* (Riosucio), 10 September 1927, 1.

38 Gärtner de la Cuesta, *Mis memorias o devaneos de un desocupado*, 57–58.

39 Ibid., 58.

40 I use hegemony in the Gramscian sense, as it has been theorized by historians who look at either hegemony primarily in terms of political alliances through which nation-states are consolidated, as well as by anthropologists who emphasize how diffuse hegemonic beliefs or discourses construct "common sense." Jeffrey Gould describes these two approaches in *To Die in This Way*, pp. 12–13. One of the most sophisticated and influential theorizations of the former approach is provided in Mallon, *Peasant and Nation*, esp. 6–8. Regarding hegemony at the regional level, see Roldán, *Blood and Fire*; Mallon, *Peasant and Nation*, 137–75. For the original formulation, see Gramsci, *Selections from the Prison Notebooks*.

41 Bourdieu, *Language and Symbolic Power*, 223–24. Bourdieu also emphasizes the importance of the group in recognizing the authority that constitutes the region. The success and legitimacy of the discourse depends on the extent to which it is grounded in what he refers to as the "objectivity" and "cultural or economic properties" of the group being constituted as a region, hence the importance in Colombia of making use of existing cultural artifacts and practices in the performance of regionalism. The use of such symbols is, if anything, more evident among the elite of Antioquia than that of Caldas. I am thankful to Barbara Weinstein for calling my attention to this passage. See also Applegate, "A Europe of Regions," 1175.

Much more could be written about the myths, material culture, literature, and politics of Manizales and Gran Caldas, omitted here for the sake of brevity. See Agudelo Ramírez, *El Gran Caldas*; Christie, *Oligarcas, campesinos y política en Colombia*; Giraldo Zuluaga, *La colonización antioqueña y la fundación de Manizales*; Valencia Llano, *Manizales en la dinámica colonizadora, 1846–1930*. The distinctive regional architecture combined local building materials with Spanish formalism and stylistic accents patterned on the latest international trends (such as Art Nouveau) (see Tobón Botero, *Arquitectura de la colonización antioqueña*, esp. 2:60–77).

7 Remembering Riosucio

1 Letter from Germán Arciniegas to Otto Morales Benítez, *VI Encuentro de la Palabra*, 29.

2 "Datos históricos relacionados con la fundación del 'Real de minas de San Sebastián de Quiebralomo,'" *La Opinión*, 27 January 1911; *La Opinión*, 10 February 1911; *La Opinión*, 24 February 1911; *La Opinión*, 10 March 1911; *La Opinión*, 7 April 1911; *La Opinión*, 20 July 1911; *La Opinión*, 22 August 1911; José Gonzalo Uribe, "El Pbro.

Don José Bonifacio Bonafont," *La Opinión*, 23 October 1912; "Datos históricos," *La Opinión*, 6 November 1913; "Documento histórico," *La Opinión*, 10 December 1913. See also "Datos históricos," *La Opinión*, 19 June 1918; and "histórico," *La Opinión*, 8 December 1918. Authorship is unclear; the 1911 installments were signed with (probably pseudonymous) initials ("C.D.M."). See also Emilio Robledo, "Orígines de Riosucio," *Archivo Historial* (Manizales) 2 (August 1919): 42–49.

3 Rappaport, in studying the historical narratives produced by indigenous intellectuals in southwestern Colombia, argues that Indian intellectuals, like other "non-Western historians," tend to write history as it "should have been" rather than "what really occurred." "Non-Western" and "Indian" narratives involve mythic images or metaphors and are nonlinear. This chapter, however, illustrates that such characteristics are neither limited to Indians, non-whites, nor to oral history (as to "non-Western," that could depend on one's definition of "the West"). See Rappaport, *The Politics of Memory*, 10–11.

4 "Datos históricos relacionados con la fundación del 'Real de minas de San Sebastián de Quiebralomo,' " *La Opinión*, 27 January 1911; Calvo de Vanegas, *Riosucio*, 34.

5 "La Provincia de Marmato," *La Opinión*, 3 March 1910, 2–3; see also Cuesta, *Tomás*, 127–28.

6 "Datos históricos," *La Opinión*, 27 January 1911 and 10 February 1911.

7 Calvo de Vanegas, *Riosucio*, 63.

8 "Datos históricos (continuación)," *La Opinión* (Riosucio/Hispania), 24 February 1911; Nicanor Salazar, cited in Bueno Rodríguez, "Aspectos históricos del municipio," 81; Robledo, "Orígenes de Riosucio," 42; Calvo de Vanegas, *Riosucio* 61, 65–66. For the actual 1627 documents, see "Expediente sobre las investigaciones que practicara el Oidor Lesmes de Espinosa Saravia, en Anserma y demás poblaciones indígenas de su jurisdicción . . . ," AGN, Sección Colonia, Fondo Visitas del Cauca, tomos 1–2.

9 Boussingault, *Memorias*, 2:102, 109–248. On Bonafont's legal disputes, see Gärtner Posada, "Tras la huella del Padre Bonafont en el Archivo Central del Cauca."

10 "Datos históricos," *La Opinión*, 10 March 1911.

11 Calvo de Vanegas, *Riosucio*, 43.

12 "Solicitud de unificación de las parroquias de La Montaña y de Quiebralomo en el sitio de Riosucio," 1824–25, ACC, Sala Independencia, C-III, no. 6970, transcribed in Gärtner Posada, "Tras la huella del Padre Bonafont en el Archivo Central del Cauca." See also Fernando Cuero I Caicedo, Bishop of Popayán, 30 July 1846, AAP, leg. 96, no. 2.

13 "Solicitud de unificación," transcribed in Gärtner Posada, "Tras la huella del Padre Bonafont en el Archivo Central del Cauca" (no page number); "Datos históricos," *La Opinión*, 22 August 1911. Gärtner Posada also suggested that "civilized" meant that the indigenous population was being transformed into a "pueblo mestizo." The same could be said, he concluded, "of the mulattos [*mulatada*] of Quiebralomo." Thus, while an iconoclast in terms of dates, he still recounts the history of Riosucio as a history of mestizaje.

14 Calvo de Vanegas, *Riosucio*, 44; Safford, "Race, Integration, and Progress," 4–7; Safford and Palacios, *Colombia*, 60. Gärtner Posada believes that one meeting cited as having occurred in 1819 actually took place in 1814, and that a colonial document showing this date had been misread by Calvo de Vanegas or whoever originally

transcribed it ("Tras las huellas del Padre Bonafont en el Archivo Central del Cauca"; José Bonifacio Bonafont to Bishop, 27 November 1823, AAP, leg. 64, no. 7). Moreover, as Gärtner Posada points out, the documents do not refer to the two parishes as one unified town. The documents of the 1820s refer to Río Sucio as a geographical site at which two separate parishes were located. Boussingault did refer to Río Sucio in the late 1820s as one town, but he used the name interchangeably with that of Quiebralomo. Adding to the confusion, Boussingault mentioned only one church, the patron saint of which was San Sebastián, and reported that Bonafont presided over this congregation, which seems to contradict Bonafont's own documents (Boussingault, *Memorias*, 2:102, 113).

15   Calvo de Vanegas, *Riosucio*, 67–68. See also Fernando Cuero I Caicedo, Bishop of Popayán, Decree, 30 July 1846, APP, leg. 96, no. 2.

16   Bueno Rodríguez, "Reseña histórica del Carnaval de Riosucio," 638; Calvo de Vanegas, *Riosucio*, 68.

17   Cuesta, *Tomás*, 12; Bueno Rodríguez, "Aspectos históricos del municipio," 89.

18   As late as 1843 the official census still counted 21 slaves in Quiebralomo alone (and, moreover, a total of 442 in the combined districts of Quiebralomo, La Montaña, Supía, and San Juan de Marmato). These figures probably excludes slaves' children born after 1821, who were legally free but in practice still enslaved (AGN, Sección República, Fondo Censos de Población, Census of 1843, fol. 50). Safford notes that some colonial officials who favored the integration of Spanish and Indian towns tended to refer to the inhabitants of the former as white, while at least one official who favored keeping such towns separate referred to the vecinos with terms such as *gente de color* (Safford, "Race, Integration, and Progress," 6).

19   Boussingault, *Memorias*, 2:109.

20   On Rodulfo Largo, see "La Provincia de Marmato," *La Opinión* , 3 March 1910, 2–3; and Calvo de Vanegas, *Riosucio*, 107.

21   According to Sommer, "Romantic passion . . . gave a rhetoric for the hegemonic projects in Gramsci's sense of conquering the antagonist through mutual interest, or 'love,' rather than through coercion" (Sommer, *Foundational Fictions*, 6–7).

22   Calvo de Vanegas, *Riosucio*, 67. A full account of La Violencia in Old Caldas remains to be written. On selected aspects, see Cardona Tobón, *Quinchía mestizo*; Christie, *Oligarcas, campesinos y política en Colombia*; Ortiz Sarmiento, *Estado y subversión en Colombia*; Bergquist, Peñaranda, and Sánchez, *Violence in Colombia*; Oquist, *Violence, Conflict, and Politics in Colombia*. A local memoir recounting La Violencia in Riosucio is Vinasco Calvo, *Frente a la huella del tiempo*.

23   Regarding Capitán Venganza, see Sánchez and Meertens, *Bandoleros, gamonales y campesinos*, 177–86. Quote is from Green, "Left Liberalism and Race in the Evolution of Colombian Popular National Identity," 117. Colombia's national identity was never so strongly identified as mestizo as Mexico's, but nonetheless many intellectuals have identified Colombia as basically mestizo. For an optimistic view of race mixture, see Cuesta, *Tomás*, 169; cf. the more pessimistic racial theorizing in Jiménez López et al., *Los problemas de la raza en Colombia*. Historian Jorge Orlando Melo, drawing on earlier argument by Jaime Jaramillo Uribe, argues that Colombia is fundamentally mestizo ("Etnia, región y nación," 45). On racial aspects of La Violencia in Antioquia, see Roldán, *Blood and Fire*; and Roldán, "Violencia, colonización y la geografía de la diferencia cultural en Colombia."

24 Morales Benítez, *Cátedra caldense*, 40–41; Morales Benítez, "La colonización antioqueña"; Morales Benítez, *Revolución y caudillos*, 40–42; conversation with Otto
Morales Benítez, Bogotá, 9 March 1995. When I asked Morales Benítez why a large
proportion of rural Riosuceños today continue to identify themselves as members of
indigenous communities, he brushed off my question as irrelevant; they are all
mestizos, whether they admit it or not, he said—a sentiment often echoed by Riosucio townspeople. W. John Green argues that the popular masses of Liberals who
followed Gaitán in the mid–twentieth century conceptualized Colombian nationality as mestizo in opposition to the predominant elite portrayal of the Colombian
nation as essentially white (Green, "Left Liberalism and Race in the Evolution of
Colombian Popular National Identity," 114). See also Braun, *The Assassination of
Gaitán.*

25 Revisionist scholars have repudiated the inclusive aspects of nationalist discourses
of mestizaje and have instead emphasized the ways in which discourses of mestizaje
have functioned to repress difference and to invalidate the demands of black and
indigenous citizens. See, e.g., Gould, *To Die in This Way*; Stutzman, "El Mestizaje."
Deborah Poole, on the other hand, argues that the discourse of mestizaje can emphasize spatial and racial diversity while also reinforcing hierarchy ("Racial Diversity
and Racial Unity in Oaxaca"). For an overview of the scholarship, see Appelbaum,
Macpherson, and Rosemblatt, "Introduction: Racial Nations."

26 On Quinchía, see Cardona Tobón, *Quinchía mestizo*; Christie, *Oligarcas, campesinos y política en Colombia*, 100–106. For an example of another district in a
different region in which non-Indians describe neighboring Indians as mestizos in
the hopes of extinguishing the resguardos and freeing the lands for privatization, see
Rappaport, *Cumbe Reborn*, 36–37. Regarding Motato Largo's death, an indigenous
activist told me that he knew who was responsible but he enjoyed life too much to
risk his life by telling people. Toward the end of my research stay, I started to break,
or at least bend, the law of silence. I recounted various local political factions who
might have been responsible out loud to a local friend until he obliquely confirmed
my guess. Under the 1886 Constitution, alcaldes had been appointed rather than
elected. Mayoral elections in 1988 were to provide a "democratic opening" throughout the country for groups, including parties on the left, which had been closed out
of the two-party system. In some cases, paramilitary death squads funded by drug
traffickers, large cattle ranchers, and established political cliques closed this space
with violence. On leftist alcaldes, see Carroll, "Violent Democratization." By the
late 1990s, 3,000 members of the left-wing party, the Unión Patriótica, had reportedly been assassinated, yet no one had been convicted for these crimes. Over 300
indigenous leaders were assassinated during the 1990s. Another indigenous leader,
María Fabiola Largo Cano, ran for mayor in Riosucio in 2000 and lost. Two years
later, two gunmen on a motorcycle shot and killed her.

8   Remembering San Lorenzo

1 Duque Gómez, "Problemas sociales de algunas parcialidades indígenas del occidente de Colombia," 188; and Duque Gómez, "Grupos sanguineos entre los indígenas del Departamento de Caldas," 628, and esp. 638.

2 Duque Gómez, "Grupos sanguineos entre los indígenas del Departamento de Cal-

das," 638–39. He was not alone in associating racial purity with indigenous women's sexual purity. De la Cadena, e.g., notes that early-twentieth-century intellectuals in Cuzco, Peru, essentialized and idealized indigenous women's sexuality. Indian women's instinctual rejection of "foreignness," the indigenista intellectuals argued, preserved "the purity of the Indian race" (*Indigenous Mestizos*, 195–97).

3 The interviews were carried out in 1991 and early 1992 by sociologist Angela María Gómez. She also interviewed elders in some of the other communities. Later, she transcribed the interviews with the assistance of Gloria Cuellar, a process which they found difficult due to technical problems and had not completed. When I arrived in Riosucio in 1993, Gómez generously offered me the transcripts, which are kept on file in her office in the Casa del Campesino in Riosucio. By that point, most of the interviews transcribed were from San Lorenzo. The interviews consulted in this chapter were with "Andrea" (last name not recorded), age 70; María Jesus Díaz, age 80; Felipa Bueno, age 65; Israel Rojas, age 80; Rosario Bueno, age 83; "Filomena," age 90; Constantino Betancur, age 54; Rafael Bueno, age 73. All were interviewed in San Lorenzo Resguardo, Riosucio. My own mobility within San Lorenzo resguardo was limited due to the presence of guerrillas; thus, I was unable to replicate these interviews. Also, see Morales Benítez, *Memorias del mestizaje*.

4 Patriarchy, in this context, refers to social and political relationships patterned on an ideal of the male-headed extended family. In characterizing San Lorenzo as a "communal patriarchy," I am drawing on Stern's definition of patriarchy as both gendered and generational. Patriarchy involves power differentials among men as well as between men and women. He shows that patriarchal norms conditioned a variety of social and political relationships in late-colonial Mexico, including the governance of indigenous communities. Women and men shared patriarchal assumptions but negotiated and fought (often violently) over the implementation of patriarchal rights and obligations (see Stern, *The Secret History of Gender*).

5 Various interviews cited above by Angela María Gómez, especially Constantino Betancur, Rafael Bueno, Rosario Bueno, and María Jesús Díaz.

6 "Padron de los indijenas Naturales de la parcialidad de Supia I Cañamomo formado por la Junta de comuneros . . . ," 1874, NS; "Padron de la Parcialidad de Indigenas de San Lorenzo Año de 1,874," 28 June 1874, notarized on 28 September 1874, NS.

7 San Lorenzo reportedly had the lowest percentage of female-headed households among the three communities in Riosucio (18.5 percent, compared to 20.8 percent in the La Montaña sample, and 30 percent in Supía-Cañamomo) and one of the lowest percentages of mothers who admitted to having given birth out of wedlock (1.7 percent of the total population; in Supía-Cañamomo the figure was 3.6 percent—still low). See chapter 3; see also Gómez's interview with Rafael Bueno.

8 The thin archival record regarding San Lorenzo starts to thicken around the time of the Regeneration and during the succeeding decades of Conservative rule in Colombia. Regarding complaints against intermarriage in La Montaña, see Isaias Largo to Governor, 23 September 1899, ACC, Archivo Muerto, paq. 267, leg. 24. Regarding San Lorenzo, see the following documents: Minutes of Cabildo meeting, 30 January 1911, Archivo de la Comunidad de San Lorenzo [hereafter cited as ACSL]; Cabildo of San Lorenzo to Circuit Judge, 3 June 1911, JCCR; loose pages regarding the Cabildo of San Lorenzo versus Pedro Mina and José Antonio Romero, December 1912–February 1912, JCCR.

9　Gómez's interviews: "Andrea," Rafael Bueno.

10　Rafael Bueno interview; see also "Andrea" interview.

11　"Andrea" interview, Felipa Bueno interview, Rafael Bueno interview, Israel Rojas interview.

12　In addition to the cases cited below, see the "acta" from 25 September 1899, ACSL. Similar, earlier examples have been preserved for the now-defunct indigenous community of Guática, and more were likely to have once existed for San Lorenzo as well. For Guática, see documents labeled "transacciones entre los miembros," AFT, leg. 2, fols. 24–30, including documents dated 23 January 1882, 11 June 1888, 19 October 1889, and 28 January 1890.

13　March 1894, ACSL.

14　"Acta de prosedimiento," 28 April 1894, ACSL.

15　Regarding dispute resolution in twentieth-century Zapotec communities in Oaxaca, see Nader, *Harmony Ideology*. She argues that preserving communal "harmony" was an indigenous strategy for resisting state intrusion. See also Stern, *The Secret History of Gender*, 247–48.

16　Comments similar to Betancur's were provided by María Jesusa Díaz and Rafael Bueno. Quotes are from Gómez's interviews with Israel Rojas and "Andrea"; information on work rotations is gleaned from the following documents in ACSL: various lists, 1899; Governor Juan Mateo Bañol, "El gobernador de esta comunidad nombra para trabajar en el tejar" [1899?]; "Lista de Aguas Claras," 29 April 1912; "Lista de los individuos que deven pagar las maderas para la Casa Cural, Aguasclaras," 29 April 1912; "Listas Generales" (including "Lista de los individuos que deben pisar barro los de Aguasclaras" and "prestar sus cervicios"), 1928.

17　Quote is from María Jesús Díaz interview. See also interviews with Rosario Bueno and Rafael Bueno. Indigenous women took part in a variety of productive tasks, including agricultural labor, making baskets which men sold in markets in Antioquia, and panning for gold.

18　Petition by Governor and Cabildo to Consejo Municipal, 20 February 1911, ACSL.

19　María Jesús Díaz interview; "Permiso para enajenar derecho proindiviso en la Parcialidad de San Lorenzo," 1913, and "Permiso judicial de Nemesio Gañan," 1920, both in JCCR; Resolution of Cabildo, 30 October 1925, ACSL. Also, "Libro para asiento de arrendamientos," 1884; "Libro de cuentas de los arrendos," 1886; "Libro de Entradas para el año de 1912," all in ACSL.

20　September 1858, RIPR, Sección Supía, fol. 6, nos. 21–22, fol. 6; 17 June 1882, RIPR, Sección Supía, fol. 22, no. 43.

21　Copies of telegrams, Benigno Gutiérrez to Governor of San Lorenzo, and Benigno Gutiérrez et al. to Francisco Tascón, San Lorenzo, both dated 4 December 1897, ACC, Archivo Muerto, paq. 244, leg. 54. Regarding San Lorenzo's military contribution to the Thousand Days War, see list of twenty-seven men "que estan en la carrera militar" and a separate list of thirty-three men "que estan en el Servicio Militar Cauca," 1899, both in ACSL. On its electoral contributions, see "Lista de los capitanes que deben trabajar enérgicamente en la organisación de las listas para las elecciones de Mayo," n.d. [apparently first decade of twentieth century], ACSL. On Liberal efforts to recruit in San Lorenzo, see "Alerta! Liberales del Municipio de Toro, Despertad!" 1 February 1884, in "Comunicaciones de los vocales de la Municipalidad de Toro," ACC, Archivo Muerto, paq. 175, leg. 4.

22 Julio Meléndes to Mayor of Riosucio 13 July 1875, AMS; fragment, 8 September 1875, AMS.

23 Israel Rojas interview; Constantino Betancur interview. Also, conversations in Riosucio and Supía, 1993–95. See also the historical chronicle compiled by schoolteachers from Riosucio who taught in San Lorenzo (Cataño Trejos and Trejos González, "Historia de la educación en San Lorenzo y su influencia," 4–5). They attribute San Lorenzo's Conservative politics, coffee production, and changes in dress to the proselytizing of Father Gonzalo Uribe, who arrived around 1916. In the same text, however, the teachers note that some oral accounts trace the political conversion to the earlier Thousand Days War.

24 Cataño Trejos and Trejos González, "Historia de la educación en San Lorenzo y su influencia," 4–5. Also, see Rafael Bueno interview; and lists of men in military service, 1899, ACSL.

25 Indígenas of San Lorenzo to Governor [of Cauca], 1 July 1895, ACC, Archivo Muerto, paq. 231, leg. 34. The principal item of contention between the indígenas of San Lorenzo and the Supía district government, which led to violent confrontations, seems to have been the indígenas' production of home-brewed liquor, which the government claimed violated the aguardiente tax laws (see Indígenas of La Montaña to Governor, 6 September 1891, ACC, Archivo Muerto, paq. 195, leg. 58; Indígenas of Province of Marmato to Governor, 3 July 1895, ACC, Archivo Muerto, paq. 231, leg 51). On the relationship between municipal official in Riosucio and the San Lorenzo cabildo, see Letter to Municipal Council, 11 January 1911, ACSL.

26 Quote is from Gómez's interview with Israel Rojas. See also Patiño Pavas, "Estudio socioeconómico del resguardo indígena de Cañamomo y Lomaprieta," 7.

27 "Decreto número 01421 de 1940," 18 July 1940, Diario Oficial (Bogotá), 23 July 1940, 268. Santos ordered the Ministry of the Economy was to appoint a three-man commission to partition each resguardo. No provision was made for including indigenous authorities in the process, except for one clause that allowed communities to apply for the right to undertake the partition themselves at their own expense. The decree was signed by the President, the Minister of the Economy, and the Minister of the Government, who was Jorge Gärtner from Riosucio, the son of Carlos Gärtner. Afterward, Quinchía and Guática were also partitioned. Findji and Rojas note that the national government's frontal assault on indigenous resguardos of the 1940s ended in the 1950s, in favor of a policy after 1958 of economic development and integration of Indian communities (Territorio, economía y sociedad Paéz, 98). In the early 1960s, the government embarked on a land reform program and divided up some large estates among individual rural campesino men, including estates in Quinchía and the Riosucio area.

28 According to indigenous leaders in Cañamomo-Lomaprieta, the 1930s saw major encroachments by cattle ranchers on much of the lower, more accessible lands of the resguardo, pushing the indígenas onto the highlands and steeper slopes. Conflicts over land led to the assassination of one of the ranchers by a member of the parcialidad; the assassin is now remembered as a hero (interview with Gabriel Campeón, La Iberia, Riosucio district, 16 March 1994; conversations with various people in Riosucio town and La Iberia, January–February 1995). For local arguments in favor of partitioning, see "Las tierras de San Lorenzo son adjudicados," El Monitor, 8

April 1944; "¿Falsa política o mala fé?" *El Monitor*, 6 May 1944. Regarding Quinchía, Duque Gómez reported in 1945 that over two-thirds of Quinchía's communal lands were in the hands of outsiders. This would have facilitated its official dissolution (see "Problemas sociales de algunas parcialidades indígenas del occidente de Colombia," 192). See also, Cardona Tobón, *Quinchía mestizo*, 132.

29 Duque Gómez, "Problemas sociales de algunas parcialidades indígenas del occidente de Colombia," 189.

30 Quotes are from interviews with "Andrea" and María Jesús Díaz. Likewise, Rafael Bueno, Israel Rojas, and Constantino Betancur all noted Uribe's role in promoting coffee production. See also Cataño Trejos and Trejos González, "Historia de la educación en San Lorenzo y su influencia," 4–5. For biographical information on Uribe, see Calvo de Vanegas, *Riosucio*, 217–19. Other conversations in Riosucio during 1993–95 elicited references to priests instructing their parishioners to plant coffee in penance for their sins. See also Patiño Pavas, "Estudio socioeconómico del resguardo indígena de San Lorenzo en Riosucio, Caldas," 7.

31 Interviews with Felipa Bueno and María Jesus Díaz. Israel Rojas and Constantino Betancur recounted similar stories about González. The INCORA report mentions that some families could not afford the fee for the new titles (Patiño Pavas, "Estudio socioeconómico del resguardo indígena de San Lorenzo en Riosucio, Caldas," 7). Regarding malnutrition associated with the decline of subsistence crops, I had informal conversations in Riosucio during 1994 and 1995 with a dietician who works with indigenous communities and a medical doctor based in San Lorenzo, and conversations in Popayán and Silvia, Cauca, with dietician Magdalena Rengifo in 1994.

32 Constantino Betancur interview.

33 Rafael Bueno interview.

34 Duque Gómez argued against partitioning the resguardos ("Problemas sociales de algunas parcialidades indígenas del occidente de Colombia," 188–89). The local press accused district authorities of using their posts to benefit from the coffee boom (see *El Monitor* [Riosucio], 26 April 1940). Regarding the "dirty monopoly" of the coffee buyers, see "Los acaparadores enemigos del pueblo," *El Monitor* (Riosucio), 21 September 1946; and "Algo Grave," *El Monitor* (Riosucio), 8 May 1943.

35 ANUC stands for Asociación Nacional de Usuarios Campesinos. Tapasco and some other young men from San Lorenzo had already been involved in Catholic training courses in community organization in the 1960s. Having grown up after the partition, he and his generation had developed their identity in class terms as campesinos, not as Indians. Through their involvement with the radical dissident faction of ANUC in the 1970s, the young activists met leaders of the emerging indigenous rights movement and started defining themselves as indigenous. Eventually, they switched sides within ANUC, joining the pro-government faction, as part of a deal whereby the official ANUC and the government would support indigenous rights (interview with Silvio Tapasco, San Lorenzo, 13 February 1993). See also Patiño Pavas, "Estudio socioeconómico del resguardo indígena de San Lorenzo en Riosucio, Caldas," 7.

36 According to the INCORA report, the cabildo's own census of 1991, the majority of inhabitants between the ages of 14 and 55, about 40 percent of whom were female domestic workers, worked periodically outside of the resguardo. Causes cited in-

clude the fact that most families live on tiny plots and have more children than needed to work them; erosion and intensive farming have damaged soils; few local employment opportunities exist; and the best lands of the resguardo are devoted to coffee, which has long periods during the year when little labor is required (Patiño Pavas, "Estudio socioeconómico del resguardo indígena de San Lorenzo en Riosucio, Caldas," 10). Since this report was written, economic crisis has caused agricultural unemployment to rise. The labor power and reproductive potential of young migrant laborers is beyond the control of the communal elders, which has further contributed to a weakening of patriarchal communal structures and a loosening of rules regarding sexual contact with outsiders.

37 The quote is from Patiño Pavas, "Estudio socioeconómico del resguardo indígena de San Lorenzo en Riosucio, Caldas," 8. The full names of the guerrilla groups are Fuerzas Armadas Revolucionarias de Colombia, Ejército de Liberación Nacional, and Ejército Popular de Liberación. AUC stands for Autodefensas Unidas de Colombia. In 2001, several hundred indígenas living in the area of El Salado in the Resguardo of La Montaña fled because of paramilitary threats; many of them camped for over a month in Riosucio's municipal stadium. More fled from Cañomomo-Lomaprieta in 2001 and 2002.

38 Gómez's interviews with Rosario Bueno and Constantino Betancur.

39 Quotes are from interviews with Felipa Bueno and Rafael Bueno, respectively.

40 Rappaport, *Cumbe Reborn*, 36–37.

41 Rappaport, Commentary for the panel on "Black and Indian Identities in Comparative Perspective," presented at the 2000 Meeting of the Latin American Studies Association, Miami, Fla. 17 March 2000.

42 Constantino Betancur interview.

43 For an analysis of how another Colombian indigenous group negotiates with state agencies and NGOS, see Jackson, "Culture, Genuine and Spurious."

Conclusion

1 See, e.g., Bushnell, *The Making of Modern Colombia*; Green, "Left Liberalism and Race in the Evolution of Colombian Popular National Identity"; Safford and Palacios, *Colombia*.

2 Wade, *Music, Race, and Nation*, 5.

3 Ibid.; Orlove, "Putting Race in Its Place," 327. In Peru, the result was a new hierarchical tripartite order—coast, sierra, selva. For citations of nineteenth-century Colombian writers, see references for introduction and chapter 1.

4 Ancízar, *Peregrinación de Alpha*, 1:121. His contemporary, José María Samper, explicitly argued that resguardos indigenas were impediments to progress because they were socialistic, opposed to private property, and impeded the mestizaje that he argued would absorb the Indians and whiten the country (Samper, *Ensayo sobre las revoluciones políticas y la condición social de las repúblicas colombianas*, esp. 61–63). On these writers and their contemporaries' views of progress and race, see Safford, "Race, Integration, and Progress," 20–32. On how Peruvian geographers came to see Indians and Indian regions as obstacles to national progress, see Orlove, "Putting Race in Its Place." On mestizaje as a popular counterdiscourse in Colombia

that challenged more elitist definitions of nationality, see Green, "Left Liberalism and Race in the Evolution of Colombian Popular National Identity." On the racist and whitening implications of mestizaje and "racial democracy," see Gould, *To Die in This Way*; Graham, *The Idea of Race in Latin America, 1870–1940*; Whitten, *Cultural Transformations and Ethnicity in Modern Ecuador*; and Wade, *Blackness and Race Mixture*, among others. On "racial democracy" and Mexican "mestizophilia," see the Introduction and the essays by Sueann Caulfield, Gerardo Rénique, Alexandra Stern, and Barbara Weinstein in Appelbaum, Macpherson, and Rosemblatt, *Race and Nation in Modern Latin America*. For particularly nuanced discussions of mestizaje that move beyond simply understanding mestizaje as a whitening discourse, see de la Cadena, *Indigenous Mestizos*; and Poole, "Racial Diversity and Racial Unity in Oaxaca."

5   On the racialized construction of frontiers in Colombia as savage, uncivilized, and dangerous, see Serje, "The Reverse of the Nation"; Roldán, "Violencia, colonización y la geografía de la diferencia cultural en Colombia"; Roldán, *Blood and Fire*; Taussig, *Shamanism, Colonialism, and the Wild Man*.

6   See, e.g., Fals Borda, "El Reordenamiento Territorial."

7   On Mexico, Peru, Brazil, and Argentina, see Alonso, *Thread of Blood*; de la Cadena, *Indigenous Mestizos*; Orlove, "Putting Race in Its Place"; the essays by Gerardo Rénique and Barbara Weinstein in Appelbaum, Macpherson, and Rosemblatt, *Race and Nation in Modern Latin America*; Andrews, *Blacks and Whites in São Paulo, Brazil, 1888–1988*; and Andrews, *The Afro-Argentines of Buenos Aires, 1800–1900*.

8   On population density, see Arango Villegas, *Los Municipios de Caldas en 1931*, 5. On discrimination, violence, and unequal educational opportunities for Colombian Indians, see United Nations, Commission on Human Rights, "Report by Dr. Maurice Glèlè-Ahanhanzo. Addendum: Mission to Colombia." INCORA reports that between 85 and 90 percent of school-age children in the resguardo of Cañamomo-Lomaprieta receive primary-school education, and that the cabildo of Cañamomo-Lomaprieta in 1993 administered 4,592.7 of the 6,357 square hectares composing the resguardo; the rest still remained in private hands. The cabildo adjudicated lots of between 0.5 and 2.5 hectares to members. The report estimates that about one-fourth of the resguardo population migrates to work in agriculture and domestic labor (see Patiño Pavas, "Estudio socioeconómico del Resguardo Indígena de Cañamomo y Lomaprieta," 5, 9–10, 17–18). Regarding cultural imagery, the wildly popular *telenovela*, *Café con Aroma de Mujer*, of the mid-1990s celebrated the distinct culture of the coffee region, embodied by a beautiful, blonde, poor heroine with a heavy Antioqueño accent, who climbed her way up from coffee picker to become an executive and marry a wealthy coffee baron.

9   Interview with Miguel Antonio Largo Pescador, Riosucio, 27 November 1993. Regarding how indigenous intellectuals in Quetzaltenango, Guatemala, reconceptualized progress and the nation in the 1890s, see Grandin, *The Blood of Guatemala*, 130–58.

10   Van Cott, *The Friendly Liquidation of the Past*.

11   The indigenous movement in Colombia, though divided, has achieved remarkable recognition and influence given the relatively tiny percentage of the population (around 2 percent) that still identifies clearly as indigenous (see Rappaport, *Cumbe*

Reborn, 15–17; van Cott, *The Friendly Liquidation of the Past*, 46, 94, 245–46).
Colombians of African descent, though representing somewhere between 15 and 40
percent of the population, have had a much harder time constituting political movements based on a collective identity as "Afro-Colombians" (see Asher, "Constructing Afro-Colombia"; Wade, *Blackness and Race Mixture*). On black movements representing a challenge to how the nation and region are defined, see Grueso, Rosero,
and Escobar, "The Process of Black Community Organizing in the Southern Pacific
Coast Region of Colombia."

12 Van Cott, *The Friendly Liquidation of the Past*.

13 Conversations in Riosucio, 1993–95, especially interviews with Miguel Antonio
Largo Pescador, 23 and 27 November 1993; Miguel Antonio Morales, 31 May 1994;
Gabriel Campeon, 22 March 1994.

14 Conversation with Medardo Largo, Bonafont, December 1994. The folklorist Julián
Bueno, employed by the municipal government of Riosucio, had argued against the
historical claims of the cabildo, whereas an anthropologist from the University
of Antioquia had supported Largo's claims (see Marjorie Maya Gallego, "Estudio
antropológico"; Julián Bueno to Marjorie Maya Gallego, 11 December 1992, OAI; and
Bueno Rodríguez, "Bonafont").

15 As "Miguelito" Largo explained to me, the indigenous communities have been affected by biological *mestización*. And yet, Largo insists that this mixing does not
preclude a culturally and historically indigenous identity still tied to landholding
and location (interviews with Miguel Antonio Largo Pescador, Riosucio, 23 and 27
November 1993; cf. Gould, *To Die in This Way*, 134–76). De la Cadena finds that
Cuzco inhabitants often refer to themselves as both "mestizo" and "indígena"—
which they distinguish from the more pejorative "indio." She argues that their continuing denigration of the indio, however, is an internalized reflection of the dominant racism that continues to mark their "contradictory consciousness" (*Indigenous Mestizos*, esp. 1–43). In Riosucio, indigenous leaders such as Largo Pescador
increasingly prefer to use a more specific ethnic label than "indigenous," referring to
themselves as "Embera-Chamí." This is in accord with a larger trend throughout
Latin America.

16 On the history of Guamal's chapel and land claims, see Zapata Bonilla, *Historia de
Supía*, 81–89; escritura no. 88, 26 May 1879, NS; various documents in ACG, esp. fols.
94, 175–76, 199, 202, 207–8, 234–35. Because Guamal is outside of the boundaries of
Riosucio district, I did not include most of my research on that community in this
book. For more details, see Appelbaum, "Guamal."

BIBLIOGRAPHY

Archives

Academia Colombiana de Historia, Bogotá [ACH]
  Fondo Uribe Uribe
Archivo Central del Cauca, Popayán, Department of Cauca [ACC]
  Archivo Mosquera
  Archivo Muerto
  Sala Independencia
  Sala República
Archivo de la Comunidad de Guamal, Community of Guamal, Supía, Department of Caldas [ACG]
Archivo de la Comunidad de La Montaña, Village of El Salado, Riosucio, Department of Caldas [ACM]
Archivo de la Comunidad de San Lorenzo, Community of San Lorenzo, Riosucio, Department of Caldas [ACSL]
Archivo del Arzobispado de Popayán, Popayán, Department of Cauca [AAP]
Archivo Familia Tunusco, Village of Santa Ana, Guática, Department of Caldas [AFT]
Archivo General de la Nación, Bogotá [AGN]
  Sección Colonia, Fondo Poblaciones del Cauca
  Sección Colonia, Fondo Visitas del Cauca
  Sección República, Fondo Baldíos
  Sección República, Fondo Censos de Población
Archivo Municipal de Supía, Supía, Department of Caldas [AMS]
Fundación Antioqueña de Estudios Sociales, Medellín [FAES]
Juzgado del Circuito Civil de Riosucio, Riosucio, Department of Caldas [JCCR]
Notaría de Supía, Supía, Department of Caldas [NS]
Oficina de Asuntos Indígenas, Riosucio, Department of Caldas [OAI]
Registro de Instrumentos Públicos de Riosucio, Riosucio, Department of Caldas [RIPR]

Universidad de Antioquia, Sala Antioquia, Medellín [UA]
Archivo Carlos E. Restrepo

Primary Periodical Sources

Anales de la Asamblea (Manizales)
Anales de la Asamblea (Popayán)
Anales de la Legislatura (Popayán)
Archivo Historial (Manizales)
El Aviso (Manizales)
El Conservador (Riosucio)
El Correo del Sur (Manizales)
El Criterio (Manizales)
El Deber (Riosucio)
Los Ecos del Ruiz (Manizales)
Gaceta Departmental (Manizales)
Gaceta Oficial (Popayán)
La Idea (Manizales)
El Iris (Supía/Riosucio)
La Mazorca (Pereira)
El Mensajero (Manizales)
El Minuto (Riosucio)
El Monitor (Riosucio)
La Opinión (Riosucio)
Registro Oficial (Manizales)
Registro Oficial (Popayán)
Revista Judicial (Manizales)
La Revista Oficial de Marmato (Riosucio)
El Ruiz (Manizales)
La Unión (Riosucio)
La Voz del Sur (Manizales)

Books, Articles, and Essays

VI Encuentro de la Palabra. Manizales: Imprenta Departmental, 1990.
VII Encuentro de la Palabra. Manizales: Imprenta Departmental, 1991.
Agudelo Ramírez, Luis Eduardo. *El Gran Caldas: Portento del despertar de Antioquia.* Medellín: Ediciones Autores Antioqueños, 1989.
Allen, John, Doreen B. Massey, and Allan Cochrane, with Julie Charlesworth et al. *Rethinking the Region.* New York: Routledge, 1998.
Almario G., Oscar. *La configuración moderna del Valle del Cauca, Colombia, 1850–1940: Espacio, poblamiento, poder y cultura.* Cali: CECAN, 1994.
Alonso, Ana María. *Thread of Blood: Colonialism, Revolution, and Gender on Mexico's Northern Frontier.* Tucson: University of Arizona Press, 1995.
Alvarez, Sonia E., Evelina Dagnino, and Arturo Escobar, eds. *Cultures of Politics, Politics of Cultures.* Boulder, Colo.: Westview, 1998.

Alvarez, Víctor. "Visión e imágenes del antioqueño y lo antioqueño: Pistas hacia el asunto de la identidad regional (Selección y recopilación de textos)." Medellín, 1993. Manuscript.

Alzate Valencia, Conrado. "Notas biográficas para una aproximación a la tradición periodística del Ingrumá." *Supía Histórico* 7 (August 1994): 770–71.

Amnesty International. *Report 2000*. www.amnesty.org.

Ancízar, Manuel. *Peregrinación de Alpha*. 2 vols. Bogotá: Biblioteca Banco Popular, 1984.

Anderson, Benedict. *Imagined Communities: Reflections on the Origin and Spread of Nationalism*. Rev. ed. London: Verso, 1991.

Andrews, George Reid. *The Afro-Argentines of Buenos Aires, 1800–1906*. Madison: University of Wisconsin Press, 1980.

——. *Blacks and Whites in São Paulo, Brazil, 1888–1988*. Madison: University of Wisconsin Press, 1991.

Appelbaum, Nancy P. "Remembering Riosucio: Race, Region, and Community in Colombia, 1850–1950," Ph.D. diss., University of Wisconsin, 1997.

——. "Las parcialidades indígenas de Riosucio y Quinchía frente a la ley 89 de 1890 (1890–1920)." Trans. María Monterroso. 30 June 1999. Photocopy.

——. "Whitening the Region: Caucano Mediation and 'Antioqueño Colonization' in Nineteenth-Century Colombia." *Hispanic American Historical Review* 79, no. 4 (November 1999): 631–68.

——. "Guamal: Historia, identidad y comunidad." In *XII Encuentro de la Palabra*. Manizales: Imprenta Departmental, forthcoming.

Appelbaum, Nancy P., Anne S. Macpherson, and Karin Alejandra Rosemblatt. "Introduction: Racial Nations." In *Race and Nation in Modern Latin America*, ed. Nancy P. Appelbaum, Anne S. Macpherson, and Karin Alejandra Rosemblatt. Chapel Hill: University of North Carolina Press, 2003.

——, eds. *Race and Nation in Modern Latin America*. Chapel Hill: University of North Carolina Press, 2003.

Applegate, Celia. "A Europe of Regions: Reflections on the Historiography of Sub-National Places in Modern Times." *The American Historical Review* 104, no. 4 (October 1999): 1157–82.

Arango, Gloria Mercedes. *La mentalidad religiosa en Antioquia: Prácticas y discursos, 1828–1885*. Medellín: Universidad Nacional, 1993.

Arango, Mariano. *Café e industria, 1850–1930*. Bogotá: C. Valencia Editores, 1982.

Arango Mejía, Gabriel. "Algo sobre orígenes de los antioqueños." *Repertorio Histórico* 15 (January 1942): 297–304.

——. *Genealogías de Antioquia y Caldas*. Medellín: Imprenta Departmental, 1942.

Arango Villegas, Rafael. *Los Municipios de Caldas en 1931 (Estadísticas comparadas con las de 1930)*. Manizales: Imprenta Departmental, 1932. .

Arboleda, Gustavo. *Diccionario biográfico y geneológico del Antiguo Departamento del Cauca*. Cali: Arboleda, 1926.

Arias Trujillo, Bernardo. *Risaralda*. Medellín: Editorial Bedout, 1971.

Asher, Kiran. "Constructing Afro-Colombia: Ethnicity and Territory in the Pacific Lowlands." Ph.D. diss., University of Florida, 1998.

Ayers, Edward L., and Peter Onuf. Introduction to *All Over the Map: Rethinking Ameri-*

can Regions, by Edward Ayers et al. Baltimore: Johns Hopkins University Press, 1996.

Ayers, Edward L., Patricia Nelson Limerick, Stephen Nissenbaum, and Peter S. Onuf, eds. *All Over the Map: Rethinking American Regions*. Baltimore: Johns Hopkins University Press, 1996.

Banton, Michael. *The Idea of Race*. London: Tavistock Publications, 1977.

Bell Lemus, Gustavo, ed. *El Caribe Colombiano: Selección de textos históricos*. Barranquilla: Ediciones Uninorte, 1988.

Bergquist, Charles. *Coffee and Conflict in Colombia, 1886–1910*. Durham, N.C.: Duke University Press, 1978.

——. *Labor in Latin America: Comparative Essays on Chile, Argentina, Venezuela, and Colombia*. Stanford, Calif.: Stanford University Press, 1986.

Bergquist, Charles, Ricardo Peñaranda, and Gonzalo Sánchez, eds. *Violence in Colombia: The Contemporary Crisis in Historical Perspective*. Wilmington, Del.: Scholarly Resources: 1992.

Beyer, Robert Carlyle. "The Colombian Coffee Industry: Origins and Major Trends, 1740–1940." Ph.D. diss., University of Minnesota, 1947.

Botero, María Mercedes. "La comercialización de los metales preciosos en una economía primario exportadora: Antioquia, 1850–1890." Paper presented at the annual meeting of the Latin American Studies Association, Washington, D.C., September 1995.

Bourdieu, Pierre. *Language and Symbolic Power*. Cambridge, Mass: Harvard University Press, 1991.

Bourgois, Philippe. *Ethnicity at Work: Divided Labor on a Central American Banana Plantation*. Baltimore: Johns Hopkins University Press, 1989.

Boussingault, Jean Baptiste. *Memorias*. 2 vols. Bogotá: Banco de la República, 1985.

Braun, Herbert. *The Assassination of Gaitán: Public Life and Urban Violence in Colombia*. Madison: University of Wisconsin Press, 1985.

Brew, Roger. *El desarrollo económico de Antioquia desde la Independencia hasta 1820*. Bogotá: Banco de la República, 1977.

Brisson, Jorge. *Exploración en el Alto Chocó*. Bogotá: Imprenta Nacional, 1895.

——. *Viajes por Colombia en los años de 1891 a 1897*. Bogotá: Imprenta Nacional, 1899.

——. "A pie de Cali a Medellín en 1890." In *Las maravillas de Colombia: Sorprendentes y poco conocidos*, vol. 4, *El Chocó. Antioquia y Medellín. El "Viejo Caldas." El Río Cauca, Cartago y Cali. Popayán*, ed. Enrique Congrains Martín. Bogotá: Forja, 1979.

Bueno Rodríguez, Julián. "Aspectos históricos del municipio." In *Riosucio Caldas, Plan de Desarrollo*. Manizales: Gobernación de Caldas, 1977.

——. "Bonafont: Una historia desconocida." Riosucio, 1993. Photocopy.

——. "Reseña histórica del Carnaval de Riosucio." *Supía Histórico* 2 (December 1993): 638–44.

Burns, E. Bradford. *The Poverty of Progress: Latin America in the Nineteenth Century*. Berkeley: University of California Press, 1980.

Bushnell, David. *The Making of Modern Colombia: A Nation in Spite of Itself*. Berkeley: University of California Press, 1993.

Caldas, Department of. *Codificación de las ordenanzas y otras disposiciones de carácter permanente*. Vol. 2, *1915–1918*. Manizales: Imprenta Departmental, n.d.

Calvo de Vanegas, Purificación. *Riosucio*. Manizales: Imprenta Departmental, 1963.

Cardona Tobón, Alfredo. "Las guerras civiles en Riosucio." *Registros de Historia* (Manizales) 1, no. 1 (January–March 1987): 7–16.

——. "Colonización y poblamiento de Belalcázar." *Registros de Historia* 2 (Manizales), no. 3 (October 1988): 13.

——. "Las guerras civiles en el alto occidente de Caldas." *Supía Histórico* 1 (1989): 91–106.

——. *Quinchía mestizo*. Pereira: Fondo Editorial del Departamento de Risaralda, 1989.

——. "Documentos históricos de Riosucio." *Registros de Historia* (Manizales) 5, no. 6 (July 1990): 16–22.

——. "Exención para los pobladores de Oraida." *Registros de Historia* (Manizales) 5, no. 6 (July 1990): 11.

——. "Las viejas aldeas de Riosucio." *Registros de Historia* (Manizales) 5, no. 6 (July 1990): 4–16.

——. "Colonizaciones y partidos políticos." *Supía Histórico* 2 (November–December 1991): 449–67.

——. "Marginados y señores en la historia regional." *Supía Histórico* 2 (April 1994): 684–90.

Cardoso, Fernando Henrique, and Enzo Faletto. *Dependency and Development in Latin America*. Berkeley: University of California Press, 1979.

Carmagnani, Marcello. *El regreso de los dioses: El proceso de reconstitución de la identidad étnica en Oaxaca, siglos XVII y XVIII*. Mexico City: Fondo de Cultura Económica, 1988.

Carroll, Leah Anne. "Violent Democratization: The Effect of Political Reform on Rural Social Conflict in Colombia." Ph.D. diss., University of California at Berkeley, 2000.

Castaño C., Consuelo, and Gabriel Gallego M. "Papel del parentesco en la familia como unidad de producción, circulación y consumo." Thesis, Universidad de Caldas, 1989.

Castro Caycedo, Germán. *Colombia amarga*. Bogotá: Planeta, 1986.

Cataño García, Conrado. "Los caminos del mito y las supersticiones supieñas." *Supía Histórico* 2 (December 1993): 656–73.

Cataño Trejos, Jaime Diego, and Carmen Lía Trejos González. "Historia de la educación en San Lorenzo y su influencia." Photocopy.

Cayón Armella, Edgardo, and Ildefonso Gutiérrez. "Etnografía de los Embera-Chamí de Risaralda (Colombia)." Popayán. Manuscript.

Chambers, Sarah C. *From Subjects to Citizens: Honor, Gender, and Politics in Arequipa, Peru, 1780–1854*. University Park: Pennsylvania State University Press, 1999.

——. "Little Middle Ground: The Instability of a Mestizo Identity in the Andes, Eighteenth and Nineteenth Centuries." In *Race and Nation in Modern Latin America*, eds. Nancy P. Appelbaum, Anne S. Macpherson, and Karin Alejandra Rosemblatt. Chapel Hill: University of North Carolina Press, 2003.

Chandler, David L. "Family Bonds and the Bondsman: The Slave Family in Colonial Colombia." *Latin American Research Review* 16, no. 2 (1981): 107–31.

Chatterjee, Partha. *The Nation and Its Fragments: Colonial and Postcolonial Histories*. Princeton, N.J.: Princeton University Press, 1993.

Christie, Keith H. "Antioqueño Colonization in Western Colombia: A Reappraisal." *Hispanic American Historical Review* 58 (May 1978): 260–83.

——. *Oligarcas, campesinos y política en Colombia: Aspectos de la historia sociopolítica de la frontera antioqueña*. Bogotá: UNAL, 1986.

Cohn, Bernard. *An Anthropologist among the Historians and Other Essays.* Delhi and New York: Oxford University Press, 1987.

——. *Colonialism and its Forms of Knowledge: The British in India.* Princeton, N.J.: Princeton, University Press, 1996.

COLCULTURA (Instituto Colombiano de Cultura). *Imágenes y reflexiones de la cultura colombiana: Regiones, ciudades y violencia.* Bogotá: COLCULTURA, 1991.

Colmenares, Germán. *Cali: Terratenientes, mineros y comerciantes, siglo XVIII.* Cali: Universidad del Valle, 1975.

——, ed. *La independencia: Ensayos de historia social.* Bogotá: COLCULTURA, 1986.

Colombia. *Anuario estadístico de Colombia.* Bogotá: Imprenta de Medardo Rivas, 1875.

——. Congreso. *Supía y Marmato ante la Cámara.* Bogotá: Imprenta Nacional, 1936.

——. Departamento Administrativo Nacional de Estadísticas (DANE). *XVI Censo Nacional de Población y V de Vivienda, Caldas.* Bogotá: Centro Administrativo Nacional, 1996.

Comisión Corográfica. *Jeografía física i política de las Provincias de la Nueva Granada por la Comisión Corográfica bajo la dirección de Agustín Codazzi, Provincias de Soto, Santander, Pamplona, Antioquia y Medellín.* Bogotá: Publicaciones del Banco de la República, Archivo de la Economía Nacional, 1958.

Congrains Martín, Enrique, ed. *Las maravillas de Colombia: Sorprendentes y poco conocidos.* Vol. 4, *El Chocó. Antioquia y Medellín. El "Viejo Caldas." El Río Cauca, Cartago y Cali. Popayán.* Bogotá: Forja, 1979.

Congreso de Historia de Colombia. *Memorias.* Bogotá: Guadalupe, 1986.

Coronil, Fernando. "Beyond Occidentalism: Toward Nonimperial Geohistorical Categories." *Cultural Anthropology* 11, no. 1 (February 1996): 51–87.

Corrales G., Jaime. "Tercera fundación e historia de Anserma." *Supía Histórico* 2 (November–December 1991): 23–24.

Craib, Raymond B. "A Nationalist Metaphysics: State Fixations, National Maps, and the Geo-Historical Imagination in Nineteenth-Century Mexico." *Hispanic American Historical Review* 82, no. 1 (February 2002): 33–68.

Cuesta, Rómulo. *Tomás.* Manizales: Imprenta Departmental, 1992.

Currie, Lauchlin. *Programa económico y administrativo para el departamento de Caldas.* Manizales: Imprenta Departmental, 1952.

Curry, Glenn Thomas. "The Disappearance of the Resguardos Indigenas of Cundinamarca, Colombia, 1800–1863." Ph.D. diss., Vanderbilt University, 1981.

"Un decreto de Junio 24 de 1864." *Supía Histórico,* no. 2 (April 1988): 3–4.

De la Cadena, Marisol. "Women are More Indian: Ethnicity and Gender in a Community near Cuzco." In *Ethnicity, Markets, and Migration in the Andes: At the Crossroads of History and Anthropology,* ed. Brooke Larson and Olivia Harris, with Enrique Tandeter. Durham, N.C.: Duke University Press, 1995.

——. *Indigenous Mestizos: The Politics of Race and Culture in Cuzco, Peru, 1919–1991.* Durham, N.C.: Duke University Press, 2000.

De los Rios Tobón, Ricardo. "La política: Creación del Departamento de Caldas." In *V Congreso de Historia de Colombia: Memorias (Armenia 1985).* Bogotá: Guadalupe, 1986.

Delpar, Helen. *Red against Blue: The Liberal Party in Colombian Politics, 1863–1899.* Tuscaloosa: University of Alabama Press, 1981.

Díaz López, Lydia del Carmen. "Antropología y economía del oro en Marmato, Caldas." Thesis, Universidad Nacional de Colombia, Bogotá, 1985.

Duara, Prasenjit. *Rescuing History from the Nation: Questioning Narratives of Modern China.* Chicago: University of Chicago Press, 1995.

Duque Gómez, Luis. "Grupos sanguineos entre los indígenas del Departamento de Caldas." *Revista del Instituto Etnológico Nacional* (Bogotá), no. 3 (1944): 623–53.

——. "Problemas sociales de algunas parcialidades indígenas del occidente de Colombia." *Boletín de Arqueología* 1 (March–April 1945): 185–201.

Duque Gómez, Luis, Juan Friede, and Jaime Jaramillo Uribe. *Historia de Pereira (1863–1963).* Bogotá: Voluntad, 1963.

Errázuriz, María C. *Cafeteros y cafetales del Líbano: Cambio tecnológico y diferenciación social en una zona cafetera.* Bogotá: Universidad Nacional de Colombia, 1986.

Escobar Gutiérrez, María Elvira. "La comunidad, unidad de reproducción y explotación: El caso del resguardo de Cañamomo y Lomaprieta en el siglo XVIII." Paper presented at the Congreso de Antropología, Medellín, 1994.

Fals Borda, Orlando. *Historia doble de la Costa,* vol. 1, *Mompox y Loba.* Bogotá: Carlos Valencia Editores, 1979.

——. "Ordenamiento territorial e integración regional en Colombia." In *La Insurgencia de las Provincias,* ed. Orlando Fals Borda. Bogotá: Siglo Veintiuno, 1988.

——. "El Reordenamiento Territorial: Itinerario de una idea." In *Territorios, regiones, sociedades,* ed. Renán Silva. Cali: Universidad del Valle and CEREC, 1994.

——, ed. *La insurgencia de las provincias.* Bogotá: Siglo Veintiuno, 1988.

Farnsworth-Alvear, Ann. *Dulcinea in the Factory: Myths, Morals, Men, and Women in Colombia's Industrial Experiment, 1905–1960.* Durham, N.C.: Duke University Press, 2000.

Felstiner, Mary Lowenthal. "Family Metaphors: The Language of an Independence Revolution." *Comparative Studies in Society and History* 25, no. 1 (1983): 155–80.

Ferrer, Ada. *Insurgent Cuba: Race, Nation, and Revolution, 1868–1898.* Chapel Hill: University of North Carolina Press, 1999.

FICDUCAL (Fundación Para el Fomento de la Investigación Científica y el Desarrollo Universitario de Caldas and Gobernación de Caldas). *La colonización antioqueña.* Manizales: Imprenta Departmental, 1989.

Field, Les W. "Who Are the Indians? Reconceptualizing Indigenous Identity, Resistance, and the Role of Social Science in Latin America." *Latin American Research Review* 29, no. 3 (1994): 237–48.

Findji, Maria Teresa, and José María Rojas. *Territorio, economía y sociedad Páez.* Cali: Universidad del Valle, 1985.

Flórez, Lenin. *Estudios sobre la Regeneración.* Cali: Imprenta Departmental del Valle, 1987.

Foucault, Michel. *Power/Knowledge: Selected Interviews and Other Writings.* New York: Pantheon, 1972.

——. *Discipline and Punish: The Birth of the Prison.* New York: Vintage, 1979.

Frank, André Gunder. *Capitalism and Underdevelopment in Latin America.* New York: Monthly Review Press, 1967.

Gallego Estrada, Alberto, and Miguel Giraldo Rodas. *Historia de Marmato.* Bogotá: Gráficas Cabrera, 1984.

García, Antonio. *Legislación indigenista de Colombia.* Mexico City: Instituto Indigenista Interamericano, 1952.

———. *Geografía económica de Caldas.* 2d ed. Bogotá: Banco de la República, 1978.

Gärtner de la Cuesta, Jorge. *Mis memorias o devaneos de un desocupado.* 2d ed. Manizales: Imprenta Departmental, 1991.

Gärtner Posada, Alvaro. "Extranjeros en el occidente del Gran Caldas." *Supía Histórico* 2 (August 1989).

———. "Tras la huella del Padre Bonafont en el Archivo Central del Cauca (Elementos para una nueva visión de la fundación de Riosucio)." Paper presented in Riosucio, Colombia, 4 August 1994.

Giraldo Zuluaga, Luisa Fernanda. *La colonización antioqueña y la fundación de Manizales.* Manizales: Imprenta Departmental, 1983.

———. *Modernización e industrialización en el Antiguo Caldas, 1900–1970.* Manizales: Universidad de Caldas, 2001.

Gobernación del Cauca. *Recopilación de Ordenanzas del Cauca.* Popayán: Imprenta del Departamento, 1892.

Gómez, Fernando. "Los censos en Colombia antes de 1905." In *Compendio de estadísticas históricas de Colombia,* ed. Miguel Urrutia and Mario Arrubla. Bogotá: Universidad Nacional, 1970.

González Casanova, Pablo. "Internal Colonialism and National Development." *Studies in Comparative International Development* 1 (1965): 27–37.

González Scarpeta, José María. "Los distritos del departamento." *Boletín Histórico del Valle* (April 1934): 165–77.

Gosselman, Carl August. *Viaje por Colombia: 1825–1826.* Bogotá: Banco de la República, 1981.

Gould, Jeffrey L. *To Die in this Way: Nicaraguan Indians and the Myth of Mestizaje, 1880–1965.* Durham, N.C.: Duke University Press, 1998.

Gould, Stephen Jay. *The Mismeasure of Man.* Rev. and exp. ed. New York: W. W. Norton, 1996.

Graham, Richard, ed. *The Idea of Race in Latin America, 1870–1940.* Austin: University of Texas Press, 1991.

Gramsci, Antonio. *Selections from the Prison Notebooks.* Ed. and trans. Quintin Hoare and Geoffrey Nowell Smith. New York: International Publishers, 1971.

Grandin, Greg. *The Blood of Guatemala: A History of Race and Nation.* Durham, N.C.: Duke University Press, 2000.

Green, W. John. "Left Liberalism and Race in the Evolution of Colombian Popular National Identity." *The Americas* 57, no. 1 (July 2000): 95–124.

Grueso, Libia, Carlos Rosero, and Arturo Escobar. "The Process of Black Community Organizing in the Southern Pacific Coast Region of Colombia." In *Cultures of Politics, Politics of Cultures,* ed. Sonia E. Alvarez, Evelina Dagnino, and Arturo Escobar. Boulder, Colo.: Westview, 1998.

Gupta, Akhil, and James Ferguson, eds. *Culture, Power, Place: Explorations in Critical Anthropology.* Durham, N.C.: Duke University Press, 1997.

Gutiérrez, Benigno. "Informe del señor Prefecto de la Provincia de Toro." In *Informe del Gobernador del Departamento del Cauca a la Asamblea del Mismo en sus sesiones ordinarias de 1890.* Popayán: Imprenta del Departamento, 1890.

Gutiérrez de Pineda, Virginia. *Familia y Cultura en Colombia*. Bogotá: Tercer Mundo, 1968.

Hagen, Everett. *On the Theory of Social Change: How Economic Growth Begins*. Homewood, Ill.: Dorsey Press, 1962.

Hamilton, J. P. *Viajes por el interior de las Provincias de Colombia*. Bogotá: Banco de la República, 1955.

Havens, A. Eugene, and William L. Flinn. *Internal Colonialism and Structural Change in Colombia*. New York: Praeger, 1970.

Helg, Aline. "Los intelectuales frente a la cuestión racial en el decenio de 1920: Colombia entre México y Argentina." *Estudios Sociales*, no. 4 (Medellín) (March 1989): 39–53.

——. *Our Rightful Share: The Afro-Cuban Struggle for Equality, 1886–1912*. Chapel Hill: University of North Carolina Press, 1995.

Henríquez, Cecilia. "El Sagrado Corazon: ¿Una cuestión política o de religiosidad popular?" In *Los imaginarios y la cultura popular*, ed. José Eduardo Rueda Enciso. Bogotá: CEREC, 1993.

Hettner, Alfred. *Viajes por los Andes colombianos (1882–1884)*. Bogotá: Banco de la República, 1976.

Hirsch, Francine. "Empire of Nations: Ethnographic Knowledge and the Making of the Soviet Union." Unpublished manuscript.

Holton, Isaac. *New Granada: Twenty Months in the Andes*. Carbondale: Southern Illinois University Press, 1967.

Hyland, Richard P. "A Fragile Prosperity: Credit and Agrarian Structure in the Cauca Valley, Colombia, 1851–87." *Hispanic American Historical Review* 62, no. 3 (1982): 369–406.

INCORA (Instituto Colombiano de la Reforma Agraria). *Estudio regional de los municipios de Anserma, Quinchía, Ríosucio y Supía (Caldas y Risaralda)*. Bogotá: INCORA, 1967.

——. *Estudio socioeconómico en la parcialidad indígena de Cañamomo y Lomaprieta en el municipio de Ríosucio, departamento de Caldas*. Bogotá: INCORA, 1970.

——. *Situación social de la tenencia, tendencias y estratificación social en el noroccidente de Caldas y los municipios de Guática y Quinchía, Risaralda*. Bogotá: INCORA, 1972.

Jackson, Jean. "Culture, Genuine and Spurious: The Politics of Indianness in the Vaupés, Colombia." *American Ethnologist* 22, no. 1 (1995): 3–27.

Jaramillo, Hugo Angel. *Pereira: Proceso histórico de un grupo étnico*. Pereira: Gráficas Olímpica, 1983.

Jaramillo Meza, J. B. *Estampas de Manizales*. Manizales: Imprenta del Departamento, 1951.

Jiménez, Michael. "The Limits of Export Capitalism: Economic Structure, Class, and Politics in a Colombian Coffee Municipality, 1900–1930." Ph.D. diss., Harvard University, 1985.

——. "Class, Gender, and Peasant Resistance in Central Colombia." In *Everyday Forms of Peasant Resistance*, ed. Forrest D. Colburn. Armonk, N.Y.: M. E. Sharpe, 1989.

——. "Traveling Far in Grandfather's Car: The Life Cycle of Central Colombian Coffee Estates." *Hispanic American Historical Review* 69 (May 1989): 186–215.

Jiménez López, Miguel. "Algunos signos de degeneración colectiva en Colombia y los países similares." In *Los problemas de la raza en Colombia*, by Jímenez López et al. Bogotá: Biblioteca de Cultura, 1920.

——. "Primera conferencia." In *Los problemas de la raza en Colombia*, by Jímenez López et al. Bogotá: Biblioteca de Cultura, 1920.

Jiménez López, Miguel, et al. *Los problemas de la raza en Colombia*. Bogotá: Biblioteca de Cultura, 1920.

Jimeno, Myriam, Gloria Isabel Ocampo, and Miguel Angel Roldán, eds. *Identidad: Memorias del Simposio Identidad Etnica, Identidad Regional, Identidad Nacional.* Bogotá and Medellín: COLCIENCIAS and FAES, 1989.

Joseph, Gilbert M., and Daniel Nugent, eds. *Everyday Forms of State Formation: Revolution and the Negotiation of Modern Rule in Modern Mexico*. Durham, N.C.: Duke University Press, 1994.

Jurado Jurado, Juan Carlos. "Orden y desorden en Antioquia: Pobres y delincuentes entre 1750 y 1850." *Estudios Sociales*, no. 7 (June 1994): 67–84.

Kouri, Emilio H. "The Business of the Land: Agrarian Tenure and Enterprise in Papantla, Mexico, 1800–1910." Ph.D. diss., Harvard University, 1996.

Lauria-Santiago, Aldo A. *An Agrarian Republic: Commercial Agriculture and the Politics of Peasant Communities in El Salvador, 1823–1914.* Pittsburgh: University of Pittsburgh Press, 1999.

Lefebvre, Henri. *The Production of Space*. Trans. Donald Nicholson-Smith. Oxford: Blackwell, 1991.

LeGrand, Catherine. "Perspectives for the Historical Study of Rural Politics and the Colombian Case: An Overview." *Latin American Research Review* 12 (spring 1977): 7–36.

——. *Frontier Expansion and Peasant Protest in Colombia, 1830–1936.* Albuquerque: University of New Mexico Press, 1986.

Lomnitz-Adler, Claudio. *Exits from the Labyrinth: Culture and Ideology in the Mexican National Space*. Berkeley: University of California Press, 1992.

London, Christopher E. "From Coffee Consciousness to the Coffee Family: Reformation and Hegemony in Colombia's Coffee Fields." Paper presented at the annual meeting of the Latin American Studies Association, Washington, D.C., September 1995.

Londoño, Jaime Eduardo. "Un empresario territorial caucano: Lisandro Caicedo." *Región: Revista del Centro de Estudios Históricos del Suroccidente Colombiano* 1, no. 0 (August 1993): 33–50.

——. "Los conflictos por el deslinde de las tierras de Burila." *Región: Revista del Centro de Estudios Históricos del Suroccidente Colombiano* 1, no. 1 (November 1993): 33–50.

Londoño Velez, Santiago. *Historia de la pintura y el grabado en Antioquia*. Medellín: Editorial Universidad to Antioquia, 1995.

López, Libardo. *La raza antioqueña*. Medellín: Imprenta de "La Organización," 1910.

López de la Roche, Fabio E. "Colombia: La búsqueda infructuosa de la identidad." In *Identidad: Memorias del Simposio Identidad Etnica, Identidad Regional, Identidad Nacional,* ed. Myriam Jimeno, Gloria Isabel Ocampo, and Miguel Angel Roldán. Bogotá and Medellín: COLCIENCIAS and FAES, 1989.

López de Mesa, Luis. *De cómo se ha formado la nación colombiana*. Bogotá: Librería Colombiana, 1934.

——. "Análisis e interpretación del pueblo antioqueño." In *El pueblo antioqueño: 6 estudios diferentes de 6 autores de renombre*. Medellín: Editorial Granámerica, 1972.

López Toro, Alvaro. *Migración y cambio social en Antioquia*. Medellín: Hombre Nuevo, 1979.

Love, Joseph L. *Crafting the Third World: Theorizing Underdevelopment in Rumania and Brazil*. Stanford, Calif.: Stanford University Press, 1996.

Machado, Absalón C. *El café de la aparcería al capitalismo*. Bogotá: Tercer Mundo, 1988.

Mallon, Florencia E. *The Defense of Community in Peru's Central Highlands: Peasant Struggle and Capitalist Transition, 1860–1940*. Princeton: Princeton University Press, 1983.

——. *Peasant and Nation: The Making of Postcolonial Mexico and Peru*. Berkeley and Los Angeles: University of California Press, 1995.

Martinez-Alier, Verena. *Marriage, Class, and Colour in Nineteenth-Century Cuba*. 2d. ed. Ann Arbor: University of Michigan Press, 1989.

Marulanda Alvarez, Elsy, and José Jairo González Arias. *Historias de frontera: Colonización y guerras en el Sumapaz*. Bogotá: CINEP, 1990.

Massey, Doreen, ed. *Space, Place, and Gender*. Minneapolis: University of Minnesota Press, 1994.

Maya Gallego, Marjorie. "Estudio antropológico: 'Parcialidad de Bonafont.'" Report prepared for the Bureau of Indigenous Affairs, Ministry of the Government, Colombia. 9 November 1993.

McFarlane, Anthony. *Colombia before Independence: Economy, Society, and Politics under Bourbon Rule*. Cambridge: Cambridge University Press, 1993.

McGuinness, Aims. "In the Path of Empire: Race, Popular Politics, and U.S. Military Intervention in Panama during the California Gold Rush, 1848–1860." Paper presented at the annual meeting of the Conference on Latin American History, Chicago, Illinois, 8 January 2000.

——. "Searching for 'Latin America': Race and Sovereignty in the Americas in the 1850s." In *Race and Nation in Modern Latin America*, ed. Nancy P. Appelbaum, Anne S. Macpherson, and Karin Alejandra Rosemblatt. Chapel Hill: University of North Carolina Press, 2003.

McNamara, Patrick J. "Sons of the Sierra: Memory, Patriarchy, and Rural Political Culture in Mexico, 1855–1911." Ph.D. diss., University of Wisconsin, 1999.

Mejía Arango, Juan Luis. "Las minas de oro y los extranjeros en Riosucio." In *V Encuentro de la Palabra*. Manizales: Imprenta Departmental, 1989.

Melo, Jorge Orlando. "La economía neogranadina en la cuarta década del siglo XIX." In *Sobre Historia y Política*. Medellín: Editorial Lealon, 1979.

——. "Vicitudes del modelo liberal (1850–1899)." In *Historia económica de Colombia*, ed. José Antonio Ocampo. Bogotá: FEDESARROLLO and Siglo XXI, 1987.

——. "Etnia, región y nación: El fluctuante discurso de la identidad (notas para un debate)." In *Identidad: Memorias del Simposio Identidad Etnica, Identidad Regional, Identidad Nacional*, ed. Myriam Jimeno et al. Bogotá and Medellín: Instituto Colombiano de Antropología, COLCIENCIAS, and Fundación Antioqueña de Estudios Sociales, 1989.

——, ed. *La historia de Antioquia*. Medellín: Suramericana de Seguros, 1988.

Mignolo, Walter. *Local Histories/Global Designs: Coloniality, Subaltern Knowledges, and Border Thinking*. Princeton, N.J.: Princeton University Press, 2000.

Molina, Gerardo. *Las ideas liberales en Colombia, 1849–1914*. Bogotá: Tercer Mundo, 1971.

Morales Benítez, Otto. *Testimonio de un pueblo*. Bogotá: Banco de la República, 1962.

——. *Revolución y caudillos: Aparición del mestizo en América y la revolución económica de 1850*. Mérida, Venezuela: Universidad de los Andes, 1974.

——. *Cátedra caldense*. Manizales: Banco Central Hipotecario, 1984.

——. *Memorias del mestizaje*. Bogotá: Plaza and Janes, 1984.

——. "La colonización antioqueña: Un aspecto de la revolución económica de 1.850." In *La colonización antioqueña*, ed. FICDUCAL. Manizales: Imprenta Departmental, 1989.

——. "Importancia de la provincia en la historia regional." *Supía Histórico* 2 (November 1990): 319–55.

——. "Alcance de las historias regionales." *Boletín de historia y antigüedades* 78, no. 775 (September 1992): 937–75.

Múnera, Alfonso. *El Fracaso de la Nación: Región, clase y raza en el Caribe colombiano (1717–1810)*. Bogotá: Banco de la República and El Ancora, 1998.

Nader, Laura. *Harmony Ideology: Justice and Control in a Zapotec Mountain Village*. Stanford, Calif.: Stanford University Press, 1990.

Nieto Arteta, Luis. *Economía y cultura en la historia de Colombia*. Bogotá: Tiempo Presente, 1942.

O'Brien, Michael. "On Observing the Quicksand." *American Historical Review* 104, no. 4 (October 1999): 1204–7.

Ocampo, José Fernando. "Historia y dominio de clases en Manizales." Manizales, 1970. Manuscript.

Ocampo López, Javier. *Otto Morales Benítez: Sus ideals y la crisis nacional*. Bogotá: Grijalbo, 1993.

Oquist, Paul. *Violence, Conflict, and Politics in Colombia*. New York: Academic Press, 1980.

Orlove, Benjamin. "Putting Race in its Place: Order in Colonial and Postcolonial Peruvian Geography." *Social Research* 60, no. 2 (summer 1993): 301–36.

Ortega Ricaurte, Carmen. *Diccionario de artistas en Colombia*. Bogotá: Tercer Mundo, 1965.

Ortiz Mesa, Luis Javier. *El federalismo en Antioquia, 1850–1880: Aspectos políticos*. Medellín: Universidad Nacional, 1985.

Ortiz Sarmiento, Carlos Miguel. *Estado y subversión en Colombia*. Bogotá: CEREC, 1985.

Osborne, Peter D. "Milton Friedman's Smile: Travel Culture and the Poetics of a City." In *Space and Place: Theories of Identity and Location*, ed. Erica Carter, James Donald, and Judith Squires. London: Lawrence and Wischart, 1993.

Ospina, Tulio. "Disertación sobre los antecedentes y consecuencias de la independencia en Antioquia." *Repertorio Histórico* 15 (January 1942): 305–24.

Ospina de Navarro, Sofía. "La casa antioqueña." In *El pueblo antioqueño: 6 estudios de 6 autores de renombre*. Medellín: Editorial Granamérica, 1972.

Ospina Vásquez, Luis. *Industria y protección en Colombia*. 2d ed. Medellín: Oveja Negra.

Pacheco, Margarita. *La fiesta liberal en Cali, 1848–1854*. Cali: Centro Editorial Universidad de Valle, 1992.

Palacios, Marco. *Coffee in Colombia, 1850–1970: An Economic, Social, and Political History.* London: Cambridge University Press, 1980.

——. "La fragmentación regional de las clases dominantes en Colombia: Una perspectiva histórica." *Revista Mexicana de Sociología* 42, no. 4 (October–December 1980): 1663–89.

——. "El espejo de los enigmas." Introduction to vol. 1 of *Arquitectura de la Colonización Antioqueña,* by Néstor Tobón Botero. Bogotá: Fondo Cultural Cafetero, 1985.

——. *Entre la legitimidad y la violencia: Colombia, 1875–1994.* Bogotá: Editorial Norma, 1995.

Park, James William. *Rafael Nuñez and the Politics of Colombian Regionalism, 1863–1886.* Baton Rouge: Louisiana State University, 1985.

Parsons, James J. *Antioqueño Colonization in Western Colombia.* 2d ed. Berkeley: University of California Press, 1968.

Patiño Millan, Beatriz. "Riqueza, pobreza y diferenciación social en la Antioquia del siglo XVIII." Medellín, 1985. Photocopy.

——. "Factores de unidad en el Nuevo Reino de Granada y la posterior formación del Estado Nacional." *Estudios Sociales,* no. 3 (Medellín) (September 1988): 97–128.

——. "La provincia en el siglo XVIII." In *Historia de Antioquia,* ed. Jorge Orlando Melo. Medellín: Suramericana de Seguros, 1988.

Patiño Noreña, Bonel. *Contribución para un enfoque socio-económico de la tenencia de la tierra en Caldas.* Manizales: Universidad Cooperativa, 1979.

Patiño Pavas, Uriel. "Estudio socioeconómico del resguardo indígena de Cañamomo y Lomaprieta." INCORA, Regional Antiguo Caldas, Riosucio, 1993. Photocopy.

——. "Estudio socioeconómico del resguardo indígena de San Lorenzo en Riosucio, Caldas." INCORA, Regional Antiguo Caldas, Riosucio, 1993. Photocopy.

Pérez, Felipe. *Jeografía física i política de los Estados Unidos de Colombia.* 2 vols. Bogotá, Imprenta de la Nación, 1862–63.

Piedrahita, Diógenes. *Apuntes para la historia de Toro.* Cali: n.p., 1939.

——. "Riosucio." *Boletín de la Academia de Historia del Valle del Cauca* (Cali) 29 (July 1961): 864–83.

Pombo, Manuel. *De Medellín a Bogotá.* Bogotá: Colcultura, 1992.

Poole, Deborah. "Racial Diversity and Racial Unity in Oaxaca: Rethinking Hybridity and the State in Post-Revolutionary Mexico." Paper presented at the New York City Latin American History Workshop, January 2001.

Posada-Carbó, Eduardo. *The Colombian Caribbean: A Regional History, 1870–1950.* Oxford: Clarendon Press, 1996.

——. "Limits of Power: Elections under the Conservative Hegemony in Colombia, 1886–1930." *Hispanic American Historical Review* 77, no. 2 (1997): 245–79.

Poveda Ramos, Gabriel. "Breve historia de la minería." In *Historia de Antioquia,* ed. Jorge Orlando Melo. Medellín: Suramericana de Seguros, 1988.

Prakash, Gyan, ed. *After Colonialism: Imperial Histories and Postcolonial Displacements.* Princeton, N.J.: Princeton University Press, 1995.

El pueblo antioqueño: 6 estudios diferentes de 6 autores de renombre. Medellín: Editorial Granamérica, 1972.

Radcliffe, Sarah, and Sallie Westwood, *Remaking the Nation: Place, Identity, and Politics in Latin America.* London: Routledge, 1996.

Ramírez, Agudelo. *El Gran Caldas: Portento del despertar de Antioquia*. Medellín: Ediciones Autores Antioqueños, 1989.

Rappaport, Joanne. *The Politics of Memory: Native Historical Interpretation in the Colombian Andes*. Cambridge: Cambridge University Press, 1990.

——. *Cumbe Reborn: An Andean Ethnography of History*. Chicago: University of Chicago Press, 1994.

Rausch, Jane. *The Llanos Frontier in Colombian History, 1830–1930*. Albuquerque: University of New Mexico Press, 1993.

Reeves, René. "Liberals, Conservatives, Indigenous Peoples: Subaltern Roots of National Politics in Nineteenth-Century Guatemala." Ph.D. diss., University of Wisconsin, 1999.

Reichel-Dolmatoff, Gerardo, and Alicia Reichel-Dolmatoff. *The People of Aritama: The Cultural Personality of a Colombian Mestizo Village*. Chicago: University of Chicago Press, 1961.

Rénique, Gerardo. "Race, Region, and Nation: Sonora's Anti-Chinese Racism and Mexico's Post-Revolutionary Nationalism, 1920s–1930s." In *Race and Nation in Modern Latin America*, ed. Nancy P. Appelbaum, Anne S. Macpherson, and Karin Alejandra Rosemblatt. Chapel Hill: University of North Carolina Press, 2003.

Restrepo, Vicente. *Estudio sobre las minas de oro y plata en Colombia*. Bogotá: Silvestre y Compañía, 1888.

Robledo, Emilio. "Orígenes de Riosucio." *Archivo Historial* 2 (August 1919): 42–49.

Rodríguez J., Pablo. "Las estructuras agrarias en el Cauca, 1800–1880." In *III Congreso de Historia Colombiana*, by Universidad de Antioquia, Departamento de Historia. Medellín: Universidad de Antioquia, 1983.

Roediger, David R. *The Wages of Whiteness: Race and the Making of the American Working Class*. London: Verso, 1991.

Rojas de Ferro, Cristina. "Identity Formation, Violence, and the Nation-State in Nineteenth-Century Colombia." *Alternatives* 20, no. 2 (April–June 1995): 195–224.

Roldán, Mary. "Genesis and Evolution of La Violencia in Antioquia, Colombia (1900–1953)." Ph.D. diss., Harvard University, 1992.

——. "Violence, Colonization, and the Geography of Cultural Difference in Colombia." Paper presented at the annual meeting of the Latin American Studies Association, Washington, D.C., September 1995.

——. "Violencia, colonización y la geografía de la diferencia cultural en Colombia." *Análisis Político*, no. 35 (September–December 1998): 3–26.

——. *Blood and Fire: La Violencia in Antioquia, Colombia, 1946–1953*. Durham, N.C.: Duke University Press, 2002.

Röthlisberger, Ernst. *El Dorado: Estampas de viaje y cultura de la Colombia suramericana*. 2d Spanish ed. Bogotá: República de Colombia, Instituto Colombiano de Cultura-Colcultura, Biblioteca Nacional de Colombia, 1993.

Röthlisberger, Walter. "El Occidente de Colombia." In *El Dorado: Estampas de viaje y cultura de la Colombia suramericana*, by Ernst Röthlisberger, 2d Spanish ed. Bogotá: República de Colombia, Instituto Colombiano de Cultura-Colcultura, Biblioteca Nacional de Colombia, 1993.

Safford, Frank. *Aspectos del siglo XIX en Colombia*. Medellín: Ediciones Hombre Nuevo, 1977.

——. "Significación de los antioqueños en el desarrollo económico colombiano: Un examen crítico de la tésis de Everett Hagen." In *Aspectos del siglo XIX en Colombia.* Medellín: Hombre Nuevo, 1977.

——. "Race, Integration, and Progress: Elite Attitudes and the Indian in Colombia, 1750–1870." *Hispanic American Historical Review* 71 (February 1991): 1–33.

Safford, Frank, and Marco Palacios. *Colombia: Fragmented Land, Divided Society.* New York: Oxford University Press, 2002.

Saffray, Charles. *Viaje a Nueva Granada.* Bogotá: Ministerio de Educación, 1945.

Samper, José María. *Ensayo sobre las revoluciones políticas y la condición social de las repúblicas colombianas.* Bogotá: Biblioteca Popular de Cultura Colombiano, Ministerio de Educación, and Editorial Centro, 1983.

Samper Kutschbach, Mario. "Labores agrícolas y fuerza de trabajo en el suroeste de Antioquia. 1850–1912." *Estudios Sociales,* no. 2 (Medellín) (May 1988): 7–43.

Sánchez, Efraín. *Gobierno y geografía: Augustín Codazzi y la Comisión Corográfica de la Nueva Granada.* Bogotá: Banco de la República and El Ancora Editores, 1999.

Sánchez, Gonzalo, and Donny Meertens. *Bandoleros, gamonales y campesinos: El caso de la Violencia en Colombia.* Bogotá: El Ancora, 1983.

Sanders, James. "Contentious Republicans: Popular Politics, Race, and Class in Nineteenth-Century Southwestern Colombia." Ph.D. diss., University of Pittsburgh, 2000.

——. "Belonging to the Great Granadian Family: Partisan Struggle and the Construction of Indigenous Identity and Politics in Southwestern Colombia, 1849–1890." In *Race and Nation in Modern Latin America,* ed. Nancy P. Appelbaum, Anne S. Macpherson, and Karin Alejandra Rosemblatt. Chapel Hill: University of North Carolina Press, 2003.

Santa, Eduardo. *La colonización antioqueña: Una empresa de caminos.* Bogotá: Tercer Mundo, 1993.

Santos Vecino, Gustavo. "Las sociedades prehispánicas de Jardín y Riosucio." *Revista colombiana de antropología* 32 (1995): 245–87.

Scarano, Francisco. "The Jíbaro Masquerade and the Subaltern Politics of Creole Identity Formation in Puerto Rico, 1745–1823." *American Historical Review* 101, no. 5 (December 1996): 1398–1431.

Scott, James C. *Weapons of the Weak: Everyday Forms of Peasant Resistance.* New Haven, Conn.: Yale University Press, 1985.

Scott, Joan Wallach. *Gender and the Politics of History.* New York: Columbia University Press, 1988.

Sepúlveda Sepúlveda, Jaime. "Intereses sociales en la creación del Departamento del Quindío." Thesis, Universidad del Quindío, 1981.

Serje, Margarita. "The Reverse of the Nation: The Wild Territories in Colombia." Paper presented at the symposium on New Approaches to the Study of Social Conflict in Colombia, Madison, Wisconsin, 23 March 2001.

Silva, Renán, ed. *Territorios, regiones, sociedades.* Cali: Universidad del Valle and CEREC, 1994.

Skidmore, Thomas. *Black into White: Race and Nationality in Brazilian Thought.* 2d ed. Durham, N.C.: Duke University Press, 1993.

Soja, Edward. *Postmodern Geographies: The Reassertion of Space in Critical Social Theory.* London: Verso, 1989.

Sommer, Doris. *Foundational Fictions: The National Romances of Latin America.* Berkeley: University of California Press, 1991.

Sowell, David. *The Early Colombian Labor Movement: Artisans and Politics in Bogotá, 1832–1919.* Philadelphia: Temple University Press, 1992.

Spalding, Karen. *Huarochirí: An Andean Society under Inca and Spanish Rule.* Stanford, Calif.: Stanford University Press, 1984.

Stein, Stanley J., and Barbara H. Stein. *The Colonial Heritage of Latin America.* New York: Oxford University Press, 1970.

Steiner, Claudia. *Imaginación y poder: El encuentro del interior con la costa en Urabá, 1900–1960.* Medellín: Editorial Universidad de Antioquia, 2000.

Stepan, Nancy Leyes. *"The Hour of Eugenics": Race, Gender, and Nation in Latin America.* Ithaca, N.Y.: Cornell University Press, 1991.

Stern, Alexandra Minna. "From Mestizophilia to Biotypology: Racialization and Science in Mexico, 1920–1960." In *Race and Nation in Modern Latin America,* ed. Nancy P. Appelbaum, Anne S. Macpherson, and Karin Alejandra Rosemblatt. Chapel Hill: University of North Carolina Press, 2003.

Stern, Steve J. "New Approaches to the Study of Peasant Rebellion and Consciousness: Implications of the Andean Experience." In *Resistance, Rebellion, and Consciousness in the Andean Peasant World, Eighteenth to Twentieth Centuries,* ed. Steve J. Stern. Madison: University of Wisconsin Press, 1987.

——. *Peru's Indian Peoples and the Challenge of Spanish Conquest: Huamanga to 1640.* Madison: University of Wisconsin Press, 1993.

——. *The Secret History of Gender: Women, Men, and Power in Late Colonial Mexico.* Chapel Hill: University of North Carolina Press, 1995.

——, ed. *Resistance, Rebellion, and Consciousness in the Andean Peasant World, Eighteenth to Twentieth Centuries.* Madison: University of Wisconsin Press, 1987.

Stoler, Ann. "Carnal Knowledge and Imperial Power: Gender, Race, and Morality in Colonial Asia." In *Gender at the Crossroads of Feminist Knowledge,* ed. Micaela di Leonardo. Berkeley and Los Angeles: University of California Press, 1991.

Stoller, Richard. "Liberalism and Conflict in Socorro, Colombia, 1830–1870." Ph.D. diss., Duke University, 1991.

Stutzman, Ronald. "El Mestizaje: An All-Inclusive Ideology of Exclusion." In *Cultural Transformations and Ethnicity in Modern Ecuador,* ed. Norman Whitten. Urbana: University of Illinois Press, 1981.

Suárez de Alvarez, Ivonne. "El papel del oro en la formación regional de Antioquia." In *V Congreso de Historia de Colombia: Memorias (Armenia 1985),* by Congreso de Historia. Bogotá: Guadalupe, 1985.

Taussig, Michael. *The Devil and Commodity Fetishism.* Chapel Hill: University of North Carolina Press, 1980.

——. *Shamanism, Colonialism, and the Wild Man: A Study in Terror and Healing.* Chicago: University of Chicago Press, 1987.

Thongchai Winichakul. *Siam Mapped: A History of the Geo-body of a Nation.* Honolulu: University of Hawaii Press, 1994.

Thurner, Mark. *From Two Republics to One Divided: Contradictions of Postcolonial Nationmaking in Andean Peru*. Durham, N.C.: Duke University Press, 1997.

Tirado Mejía, Alvaro. *Descentralización y centralismo en Colombia*. Bogotá: Oveja Negra, 1983.

Tobón Botero, Nestor. *Arquitectura de la Colonización Antioqueña*. 4 vols. Bogotá: Fondo Cultural Cafetero, 1985.

Triana Antorveza, Adolfo. *Legislación indígena nacional*. Bogotá: Editora Guadalupe, 1980.

Troyan, Brett. "State Formation and Ethnic Identity in Southwestern Colombia, 1930–1991," Ph.D. diss., Cornell University, 2002.

Twinam, Ann. *Miners, Merchants, and Farmers in Colonial Colombia*. Austin: University of Texas Press, 1982.

United Nations. Economic and Social Council. Commission on Human Rights. "Report by Dr. Maurice Glèlè-Ahanhanzo, Special Rapporteur on Contemporary Forms of Racism, Racial Discrimination, Xenophobia and Related Intolerance. Addendum: Mission to Colombia." E/CN.4/1997/71/Add.1. 13 January 1997.

Universidad de Antioquia. *El pueblo antioqueño*. 2d ed. Medellín: Universidad de Antioquia, 1960.

Urban, Greg, and Joel Sherzer, eds. *Nation-States and Indians in Latin America*. Austin: University of Texas Press, 1991.

Uribe Angel, Miguel. *Geografía general del Estado de Antioquia en Colombia*. Medellín: Secretaría de Educación y Cultura de Antioquia, 1985.

Uribe de Hincapié, María Teresa, and Jesús María Alvarez G. "Algunos elementos para el análisis de la configuración del poder regional: El caso antioqueño." In *III Congreso de Historia Colombiana: Memorias (Medellín 1981)*, by Universidad de Antioquia, Departamento de Historia. Medellín: Universidad de Antioquia, 1983.

——. "Regiones, economía y espacio nacional en Colombia, 1820–1850." *Revista Lecturas de Economía* (Medellín) (January–April 1984): 161–62.

——. "El parentesco y la formación de las élites en la Provincia de Antioquia." *Estudios Sociales*, no. 3 (September 1988): 49–93.

——. *Raíces del poder regional: El caso antioqueño*. Medellín: Editorial Universidad de Antioquia, 1998.

Uribe de Hincapié, María Teresa, and Clara Inés García. "La espada de las fronteras." Insert in *El Colombiano* (Medellín), 23 May 1993, 32–45.

Uribe-Uran, Victor M. *Honorable Lives: Lawyers, Family, and Politics in Colombia, 1780–1850*. Pittsburgh: University of Pittsburgh Press, 2000.

Uribe Vargas, Diego, ed. *Las Constituciones de Colombia*. 3 vols. Madrid: Ediciones Cultura Hispánica, 1977.

Urrego, Miguel Angel. "Control social, matrimonio y resistencia popular en Bogotá: La parroquia de Las Aguas, 1900–1930." In *Los imaginarios y la cultura popular*, ed. José Eduardo Rueda Enciso. Bogotá: CEREC, 1993.

——. *Sexualidad, matrimonio y familia en Bogotá, 1880–1930*. Bogotá: Ariel Fundación Universidad Central, 1997.

Valencia Llano, Albeiro. "Evolución socioeconómica de las comunidades indígenas de Caldas (siglos XVI-XIX)." *Revista de la Universidad de Caldas* 4 (May–August 1983): 104–221.

———. "Papel del colonizador antioqueño en la descomposición de los resguardos indígenas de Caldas (siglo XIX)." In *III Congreso de Historia Colombiana: Memorias*, by Universidad de Antioquia, Departamento de Historia. Medellín: Universidad de Antioquia, 1983.

———. *Manizales en la dinámica colonizadora, 1846–1930*. Manizales: Universidad de Caldas, 1990.

———. *Colonización, fundaciones y conflictos agrarios*. Manizales: Imprenta Departamental, 1994.

———. *Vida cotidiana y desarrollo regional en la colonización antioqueña*. Manizales: Universidad de Caldas, 1996.

Valencia Llano, Alonso. *Estado soberano del Cauca: Federalismo y Regeneración*. Bogotá: Banco de la República, 1988.

———. *Empresarios y políticos en el Estado Soberano del Cauca, 1860–1895*. Cali: Facultad de Humanidades, 1993.

Vallecilla Gordillo, Jaime. *Café y crecimiento económico: El Antiguo Caldas, 1870–1970*. Manizales: Universidad de Caldas, 2001.

Van Cott, Donna Lee. *The Friendly Liquidation of the Past: The Politics of Diversity in Latin America*. Pittsburgh: University of Pittsburgh Press, 2000.

Van Young, Eric, ed. *Mexico's Regions: Comparative History and Development*. San Diego: University of California Center for U.S.–Mexican Studies, 1992.

Vélez, Humberto. "El Gran Cauca, de la autonomía relativa a la disintegración territorial, 1810–1910: Un caso de cambio histórico en la región política." In *Estado y economía en la Constitución de 1886*, ed. Oscar Rodríguez Salazar. Bogotá: Controlaría General de la República, 1986.

———. "La Regeneración: Algo más que un proyecto político." In *Estudios sobre la Regeneración*, ed. Lénin Flórez and A. Atehortúa. Cali: Imprenta Departmental del Valle, 1987.

Vélez L., Antonio, ed. *Alfredo Vásquez Cobo, "El Candidato Reo."* Bogotá: Editorial Aguila Negra, 1921.

Verlinden, Charles. *The Beginnings of Modern Colonization: Eleven Essays with an Introduction*. Ithaca, N.Y.: Cornell University Press, 1970.

Vidal Perdomo, Jaime. *¿Decentralización, regionalización, federalismo?* Bogotá: Universidad Externado, 1981.

Vilegas Vilegas, Lucily, and Clara Inés Aramburo Siegert. "Paisas: Más . . . más allá." Insert in *El Colombiano* (Medellín), 9 May 1993, 1–18.

Vinasco Calvo, Arnulfo. *Frente a la huella del tiempo*. Bogotá: Nuevas Ediciones, 1989.

Von Schenck, Friedrich. *Viajes por Antioquia en el año de 1880*. Bogotá: Banco de la República, 1953.

Wade, Peter. "The Language of Race, Place, and Nation in Colombia." *América Negra*, no. 2 (December 1991): 41–65.

———. *Blackness and Race Mixture: The Dynamics of Racial Identity in Colombia*. Baltimore: Johns Hopkins University Press, 1993.

———. *Music, Race, and Nation: Música Tropical in Colombia*. Chicago: University of Chicago Press, 2000.

Weinstein, Barbara. "Racializing Regional Difference: São Paulo vs. Brazil, 1932." In *Race and Nation in Modern Latin America*, ed. Nancy P. Appelbaum, Karin Alejandra

Rosemblatt, and Anne S. Macpherson. Chapel Hill: University of North Carolina Press, 2003.

Whitten, Norman, ed. *Cultural Transformations and Ethnicity in Modern Ecuador.* Urbana: University of Illinois Press, 1981.

Williams, Derek. "Negotiating the State: National Utopias and Local Politics in Andean Ecuador, 1845–75." Ph.D. diss., State University of New York at Stony Brook, 2001.

Williams, Raymond. *Keywords: A Vocabulary of Culture and Society.* Rev. ed. New York: Oxford University Press, 1983.

Williams, Raymond L. *The Colombian Novel, 1844–1987.* Austin: University of Texas Press, 1991.

Zambrano, Fabio. "Región, Nación e Identidad Cultural." In *Imágenes y reflexiones de la cultura colombiana: Regiones, ciudades y violencia,* ed. COLCULTURA. Bogotá: COLCULTURA, 1991.

Zapata Bonilla, Jorge Eliecer. *Historia de Supía.* Manizales: Imprenta Departmental, 1980.

——. "Introducción a la historia minera del alto occidente de Caldas." *Registros de Historia* 1, no. 1 (January–March 1987): 25–34.

——. "Existencia Jurídica de San Lorenzo de Riosucio desde 1627." *Registros de Historia* 5, no. 6 (July 1990): 25–29.

——. "La minería en el occidente de Caldas: Grupos étnicos comprometidos en esta industria." *Supía Histórico* 2 (October 1993): 601–12.

Zuluaga Gómez, Víctor. *Documentos inéditos para la historia de Caldas, Choco y Risaralda.* Pereira: Universidad Tecnológica, 1988.

——. *Historia de la comunidad indígena chamí.* Bogotá: El Greco Impresores, 1988.

——. "Resguardo indígena de Cañamomo y Lomaprieta." *Supía Histórico* 2 (October 1993): 594–600.

——. *Vida, pasión y muerte de los indígenas de Caldas y Risaralda.* Pereira, Risaralda: Universidad Tecnológica de Pereira, 1994.

Zuluaga Vélez, Horacio. "Causas de la desaparición del resguardo de los Tabuyos en Anserma (Caldas)." *Supía Histórica* 2 (April 1994): 693–720.

INDEX

Aburra Valley, 18, 54
Amancebamiento escandaloso, 188
Ancízar, Manuel, 17, 210
Anderson, Benedict, 20, 21
Andes, 54
Anserma, 53, 57, 63, 82, 154
Antioqueño colonization, 13, 53, 59, 75,
76; in Caldas, 12, 53–54, 157; in Cauca,
55–56, 63, 127, 157, 212; and Cauca
elite, 13–14, 52–56, 78–79, 120, 128; and
coffee, 114, 124; Conservative party in,
59; controversy surrounding, 77; dismemberment of resguardos, 13, 71, 78,
120–21, 128; in El Rosario, 125–26; and
family connections, 75; and indígenas,
80–103; and indigenous identity, 203;
and indigenous lands, 25, 54–58, 62, 63,
64, 120; and intermarriage, 86; in La
Montaña, 59, 64, 80, 86, 125; and land
disputes, 54–55, 74, 130–32; and Law 89
of 1890, 130–32; in Oraida, 59; and partisan political networks, 103; and progress, 77, 120, 203; in Pueblo Nuevo, 118;
regional chauvinism, 143; regional formation, 13; in Riosucio, 4, 6, 24–25,
118–20, 160; in San Lorenzo, 186, 196; in
Supía-Cañamomo, 66, 68; and vagrancy,
46. *See also* Antioqueños; Antioquia

Antioqueños: and Catholicism, 35–36,
116, 151; Conservative party in, 116; as
deserving settlers, 58, 120; in European
travel descriptions, 34–38; as homogeneous, 34–35; Jewish heritage of, 35, 40;
and La Violencia, 180; in opposition to
other, 18, 151; and patriarchy, 35; racial
descriptions of, 36–38, 228 n.14; stereotypes of, 10, 14, 34–35, 52, 58, 118, 120,
161, 203; and whiteness, 14, 35, 39, 56,
118, 151, 217; as Yankees, 34, 37. *See
also* Antioqueño colonization;
Antioquia

Antioquia, 31–51; as beauty, 25, 33; class
conflict in, 49; colonial social structures in, 41; Conservative party in, 45–
46; elites in, 41, 45–50, 148; exceptionalism of, 41; and family metaphors,
46, 50, 150–51; geography of, 31; identity in, 33, 38, 48, 145, 151; as imagined
community, 33; as internal other, 50;
and La Violencia, 179; Liberal party in,
45, 46; mining in, 40–42, 71; patriarchy
in, 50; political coherence in, 49; popular protest in, 43; racial and sexual
stereotypes of, 25, 41, 151; racial composition of, 41–42; regional identity,
49–50; resguardo lands in, 60; slavery

Cattle ranching, 125

Cauca, 31–51; Antioqueño settlements in, 11, 13, 25, 38, 48, 52–56, 79, 212; as the beast, 25, 33; blacks of, 47–48; class conflict in, 42–43; during colonial period, 41; colonization of indígenas in, 78–103; Conservative party in, 117; and creation of Caldas, 145–46; elites, 13, 42–43, 49, 53, 59; elites and colonization, 53–78; geography of, 31; incorporation into greater Antioquia, 78, 127; internal other, 50; Law 44 of 17 October 1873, 62, 63; Law 90 of 1859, 61, 63, 83–84, 139, 189; Liberal party in, 45, 47; mining in, 42, 71–72; natural resources of, 40; northern districts of, 53, 56–61; as other, 33; partisan conflict, 42; Popayán as capital of, 42, 175; popular protest in, 43; and race, 25, 42, 48, 161, 163; rebellion of 1860 in, 59; slavery in, 42–43; sovereignty of, 44, 58; as virgin territory, 12; War of 1876–77 in, 47; War of the Supremes in, 43; whitening and, 53, 56, 212

Cauca Law 90 of 1859, 61, 63, 83–84, 139, 189

Cauca River, 1, 6, 40, 42

Caudillos, 44

Census taking, 84–86

Chamí indígenas, 57, 121, 125, 234 n.10; and Catholic Regeneration, 126–27; and land disputes, 126; in Pueblo Rico, 145

Chávez, Bartolomé, 72, 73, 117, 239 n.47

Chocó, 38

Chocoano, 222 n.8

Chorographic Commission, 16–17, 32–35, 37

Church of La Candelaria, 9

Church of San Sebastián, 8

Civil War of 1876–77, 97–98, 169, 179

Civil War of 1885, 108

Civil War of 1899–1902. See Thousand Days War

Cock family, 137

Cock, Nestor Bueno, 159–60

Codazzi, Agustín, 37

Coffee Growers' Federation, 151, 200, 254 n.19

Coffee, 26, 78; and Antioqueño colonization, 103, 124; in Caldas, 12, 142, 145, 152–53, 155; contested history of, 211; Golden Era of, 155; and La Violencia, 25; in Manizales, 209; production and exportation of, 114, 152–55, 209, 212; and race, 27; in Riosucio, 26, 119, 125; statistics for, 255 n.26

Coffee Region, 142–56; administrative departments of, 12; as agricultural heartland, 212; Antioqueño colonization of, 124; contested history of, 211; emergence of, 26, 78; indígenas in, 103, 184; unification of, 209; La Violencia in, 25; and whiteness, 2–3, 209. See also Caldas

Colombia: and agrarian conflict, 199; constitutions of, 43–44, 108–13, 120–21, 140, 200, 214–15; contemporary political violence, 210; contemporary regionalism in, 211; as country of regions, 27, 31, 207; economic development of, 40; ethno-linguistic minorities in, 210; federalism in, 16, 25, 32, 44; human rights reports about, 221 n.5; immigration to, 53; independence wars in, 16; indígenas of, 113, 199, 201, 214–15; map of, 2; as mestizo nation, 27, 180, 214; pluriculturalism in, 214; racial distinctions in, 210; resguardos in, 61; slavery in, 44; Spanish conquest, 82; and Thousand Days War, 115–16; topography of, 40; United States of, 32, 45. See also Nation; New Granada

Coloniality, 14

Colonization/Colonizacíon, 3, 8, 11–15, 26, 81, 222 n.12

Columbus, Christopher, 140

Community/Comunidad, 20–23, 183

Conquest, 170

Conservative party: in Antioquia, 45–49, 59; in Caldas, 142; and Catholic Church, 44, 46; in Cauca, 59; and Civil War of 1876–77, 97; and clergy, 44; elec-

Gould, Jeffrey L., 63, 120

Green, W. John, 180

Guamal, 159; as Antioqueño, 218–19; black community of, 66, 133, 159, 217; and gender, 243 n.10; gold mining in, 57; land disputes in, 217–18; racial identities, 216; whiteness, 217

Guática, 53, 57, 62

Guerrillas, 2, 7, 50, 115–16, 167–68, 182, 200–201, 210. *See also* ELN; EPL; FARC

Gulf of Urabá, 19

Gutiérrez, Benigno, 121

Gutiérrez de Pineda, Virginia, 17–18, 224 n.24

Helg, Aline, 147

Hernández, José, 62, 236 n.22

Hettner, Alfred, 38

Hijos de la Montaña, 146, 150

Hispania, 159

Historical Conservatives, 115, 193–94

Historical narratives, 4–8, 175–82, 218

Hoyos, José Joaquín, 90

Hoyos, Manuel María, 64–65

Iberia, 159

Identity, 185–87, 201, 206

Imagined community: Caldas as, 145; contested, 21, 220; nation as, 188, 207, 220; peasant villages as, 204; political parties as, 101; and power, 181–82; and race, 181; racial communities as, 220; region as, 33, 161, 188, 208, 211, 220; Riosucio as, 21, 101, 163, 181; theory of, 20–21; and violence, 178

Independence War of 1810–21, 16, 57

Independents/Independientes, 97, 107

Indians. *See* Indígenas

Indígenas, 10, 80–103, 124–41, 167–75, 184–205; and Antioqueño settlers, 61, 74, 79, 130, 203; and Cauca Law of 1859, 83, 84; as civilized, 236 n.22; and coffee, 213; colonial institutions, 81, 212; and colonization, 22, 25, 66, 78, 80–103; and conflict over Río Sucio, 172; and Constitution of 1991, 214–15;

and defense of cabildos and resguardos, 22, 82, 87–93, 94–95, 101, 129–32, 212, 215; and economic growth, 119; in 1880 uprising, 99–100; factionalism among, 91; identity of, 102, 144, 186, 203, 212, 217; and land disputes, 22, 80, 90, 130–32; and land privatization, 53, 60–71, 80–81, 127–28, 130–32, 139, 196, 198, 237 n.30, 249 n.5, 250 nn.6, 12; land rights of, 52, 61, 70, 85, 111–13, 120–21, 124, 130–32; Law 44 of 17 October 1873, 62–70; Law 89 of 1890, 110–13, 120–21, 124, 127, 130–32, 200, 212; Law 90 of 1859, 87–88; legal rights of, 21–22, 61, 84, 91, 102, 110–14, 120–21, 124, 132, 138, 212; loss of landholdings of, 60, 62, 117, 128, 173; as mestizos, 24; and Mosquera, 61; and natural resources, 22, 52, 65, 130–38; as other, 4, 19; and partisan politics, 59, 82, 87–99, 97, 103, 148; patron-client relationships, 25, 93; and progress, 120–21, 213; during Regeneration, 111–13, 124–41; and regionalism, 11; and religious institutions, 87, 90; and resistant adaptation, 81; in rights movement, 199, 214; in Riosucio, 1, 11, 21–22, 52, 82, 144, 170; as savages, 110–13, 120–21, 127, 170; and Spanish conquest, 82, 174; stereotypes of, 10, 35, 39, 52, 58, 127, 174, 191. *See also* Cañamomo-Lomaprieta; Chamí indígenas; La Montaña; Quinchía; Resguardos indígenas; San Lorenzo; Supía-Cañamomo; Tabuyo; Tachiguí

Ingrumá, 56, 176

Jardín, 54, 126

Jimeno, Myriam, 140

Juntas de empadronamiento, 84

Lame, Manuel Quintín, 139

La Montaña, 57, 80–92, 96–103, 150, 185; Antioqueños in, 59, 80, 125; census of, 84, 242 n.7, 243 n.12; Conservative party in, 97; factionalism in, 91; and

Progresistas, 43

Progress: and Antioqueños, 214; and black communities, 213; elite visions of, 37; meanings of, 213, 216; and indigenous communities, 213; and mestizo communities, 213, 220; and race, 13, 27, 220; redefinition of, 214; and whiteness, 14, 27, 212, 220

Province of Marmato, 118

Pueblos indios, 57

Pueblo Nuevo, 118

Pueblo Rico, 145

Quiebralomo, 57, 155, 170–73, 177

Quincentenary, 214

Quinchía, 53, 57, 60, 62, 127–28, 132, 159, 170, 180, 182

Quindío Valley, 143, 145, 148–49

Quintero, Ulpiano, 99, 100

Race/Raza, 9–11; antioqueña, 9, 142; as binary opposition, 7; classifications of, 10, 208; contemporary distinctions of, 210; cosmic, 210; and democracy, 210; and gendered metaphors, 146–47; and geography, 10–11, 25, 37, 40–43, 208, 220; granadina, 210; and hierarchical categories, 3, 11, 24, 144; in historical narratives, 7, 168–83; historical usage of, 10; and identity and space, 10, 23, 133, 149, 178, 217, 219–20; indígena, 9; and intermarriage, 179; and La Violencia, 180; meanings of, 10, 216, 222 n.7; and memory, 176–77; and nation, 10, 180; and national policy, 211; and opposition to Caldas, 157–60; and progress, 208, 210–11, 216, 220; quiebralomeña, 9; during Regeneration, 107, 110, 208; and region, 11, 144, 148–49, 207–10, 219–20; and resource transferals, 10; riosuceña, 182; scientific discourse of, 146, 208, 252 n.7; social construction of, 10; whitening of, 24, 211. *See also* Racial geography; Racialization

Racial geography: and agricultural communities, 38–39; of Argentina, 211–12; of Brazil, 211–12; and Chorographic Commission, 17; and climate, 34, 37; and colonization, 3–4, 23; contestation of, 219–20; and costumbrista fiction, 17; of Cuba, 211–12; in European travel accounts, 37, 40, 48; and hierarchies, 208; of Mexico, 212; and mining communities, 38; moral qualities of, 37; and partisan politics, 23, 26, 98–99, 179–80, 194–95; of Peru, 208, 212; and racial difference, 35–37; and Regeneration, 118; and regional differentiation, 20, 25, 207. *See also* Race/Raza; Racialization

Racialization: in Caldas, 158–60, 209; and identity, 23, 26, 207, 209; meaning of, 11; and progress, 211; and regional differentiation, 3–4, 20, 23, 33–40, 58, 78, 144, 146, 149, 162, 207–9. *See also* Race/Raza; Racial geography

Radical Liberals, 45, 59, 69, 230 n.27

Rappaport, Joanne, 140, 169, 203, 257 n.3

Regeneration, 26, 97, 107–23; and Catholicism, 107, 109–10, 126–27, 208, 246 n.7; causes of, 108; as celebration of Spanish heritage, 208; and Decree 74, 110–14; economic policies of, 109; effects of, 108; goals of, 122–24; and harmony, 176; indígenas as savages, 110; indigenous policy in, 110–14, 120–24, 129, 132, 138, 140–41, 189, 208; institutionalization of racial hierarchy in, 107, 110; and Law 89 of 1890, 110–14; partisan rivalries in, 107, 121–24; redistricting during, 117–18, 158; regional divisions in, 107; resguardos and economic growth in, 119; as transition from federal era, 107, 176; and Vatican, 109; as White Republic, 107, 110, 114, 118, 178, 208

Region/Región, 15–20; consolidation of, 207; as constituted by space and time, 219; construction of, 20; and cultural practices, 39, 148; discursive notion of, 19, 148–49; economic implications, 149; and federalism, 208; and gender, 37, 147, 151; hegemony of, 219; as iden-

Nancy Appelbaum is an Assistant Professor of History
and Latin American and Caribbean Studies at the State
University of New York at Binghamton. She is the editor,
with Anne S. Macpherson and Karin Alejandra Rosemblatt,
of *Race and Nation in Modern Latin America*.

Library of Congress Cataloging-in-Publication Data
Appelbaum, Nancy P.
Muddied waters : race, region, and local history in Colombia,
1846–1948 / Nancy P. Appelbaum.
p. cm. — (Latin America otherwise : languages, empires,
nations)
Includes bibliographical references and index.
ISBN 0-8223-3080-6 (cloth : alk. paper)
ISBN 0-8223-3092-X (pbk. : alk. paper)
1. Colombia—History, Local. 2. Riosucio (Caldas,
Colombia)—History. 3. Regionalism—Colombia—History. 4. Land
settlement—Colombia—History. 5. Patron and client—Colombia—History.
6. Colombia—Race relations. I. Title. II. Series: Latin America
otherwise.
F2271.9.A66 2003   986.1′05—dc21   2002151088